Flip the System

Many educationalists believe that education is threatened on a global scale by forces of neoliberalism, through high-stakes accountability, privatization and a destructive language of learning. In all respects, a GERM (Global Education Reform Movement) has erupted from international benchmark rankings such as PISA, TIMMS and PIRL, causing inequity, narrowing of the curriculum and teacher deprofessionalization on a truly global scale.

In this book, teachers from around the world and other educational experts such as Andy Hargreaves, Ann Lieberman, Stephen Ball, Gert Biesta, Tom Bennett, Pasi Sahlberg and many more, make the case to move away from this uneducational economic approach, to instead embrace a more humane, more democratic approach to education. This approach is called 'flipping the system', a move that places teachers exactly where they need to be – at the steering wheel of educational systems worldwide.

This book will appeal to teachers and other education professionals around the world.

Jelmer Evers is a history teacher in a secondary school and is involved in classroom innovation. Jelmer gives advice, workshops and guest lectures on new forms of pedagogy and is involved in designing a new innovative teacher training college. He writes columns and articles for educational magazines and has edited *Het Alternatief*. He was nominated for Teacher of the Year 2012 and named one of the Netherlands' 23 'New Radicals' by national magazine *Vrij Nederland* in 2013. He was nominated for the Global Teacher Prize in 2014.

René Kneyber is a mathematics teacher in a secondary school. He has written popular books on classroom authority and discipline and has edited multiple high-profile books, including the Dutch book *Het Alternatief* and the Dutch translation of *Embedding Formative Assessment* by Dylan Wiliam. In 2015 he became a member of the Dutch Education Council on royal commendation.

Flip the System

Changing Education from the Ground Up

Edited by
Jelmer Evers and René Kneyber

Routledge
Taylor & Francis Group
LONDON AND NEW YORK

First published 2016
by Routledge
2 Park Square, Milton Park, Abingdon, Oxon OX14 4RN

and by Routledge
711 Third Avenue, New York, NY 10017

Routledge is an imprint of the Taylor & Francis Group, an informa business

British Library Cataloguing-in-Publication Data
A catalogue record for this book is available from the British Library

Library of Congress Cataloging in Publication Data
Evers, Jelmer.
Flip the system : changing education from the ground up / Jelmer Evers and René Kneyber.
pages cm
Includes bibliographical references and index.
1. Education--Philosophy. 2. Educational change. 3. Critical pedagogy. I. Kneyber, René. II. Title.
LA134.E94 2016
370.1--dc23
2015009254

ISBN: 978-1-138-92996-8 (hbk)
ISBN: 978-1-138-92998-2 (pbk)
ISBN: 978-1-315-67857-3 (ebk)

Typeset in Bembo by
Servis Filmsetting Ltd, Stockport, Cheshire

MIX
Paper from responsible sources
FSC® C013056

Printed and bound in Great Britain by
TJ International Ltd, Padstow, Cornwall

Contents

Illustrations

Preface

The Dutch education system has had a noteworthy history of top-down reforms, either motivated through ideology or inspired by an attempt to cut budgets. Ten years ago things turned for the worse when policy makers attempted to implement even more, now neoliberal, reforms. Yet, there was little resistance: after years of reforms, our colleagues had become tired and docile. So, in December 2012, because we felt the issues of neoliberalism weren't addressed convincingly enough by the education field itself, we as two individual teachers, Jelmer Evers and René Kneyber, joined forces to reclaim our beloved teaching profession ourselves.

Of course, we are kind of an odd duo. René, being more of a traditionalist, who seats his students in rows in lessons that are quite teacher focused, is almost a direct opposite to Jelmer, a progressive history teacher, who uses computers to deliver personalized and blended learning to his students, in a very student-centred way. At the time, René had just finished work on a book on professional authority in the Professional Pride series with Thijs Jansen – chief editor, researcher at the Tilburg University, and co-founder of the Professional Honour Foundation in Holland. This landmark series opened with the book *Professional Pain* in 2005, which became famous for its harsh management bashing, and received a sequel in *Professional Pride* in 2009, which aimed to provide means to counter the issues addressed in *Professional Pain* and received an English translation in 2010.

After finishing work on their book on professional authority, Thijs suggested that René should work with Jelmer on a Professional Pride book aimed at the domain of education. And so, nearing the end of 2012 the two of us met up in a Dutch café to outline a new book in the series, quickly dubbed *The Alternative*, with an impressive 'wanted' list of contributors. We aimed to have international experts such as Andy Hargreaves, Dennis Shirley, Michael Fullan, Howard Gardner, Paul Kirschner and Gert Biesta on board, but we also wanted a full range of teachers who would, in one way or the other, contribute to the book. To our pleasant surprise nearly everyone we aimed for agreed, and was even *eager*, to be involved, and delivered their contribution in time – in retrospect, the unlikeliest of things – so that we could, around World Teachers' Day in 2013, release the book.

The success of the book has since been phenomenal, not just in terms of sales, being one of the most popular education books in recent years. Not just in terms of the amount of buzz in social media, the attention in the media or the fruitful debate that it has generated. But more than anything, in terms of the political impact this book has had. The system has since moved away from its ambition for high-stakes accountability and changed its perspective on the profession, and we're seeing a slow introduction of teachers into all levels of policy decision making.

In the same stretch of time, a couple of months after the Dutch book was released, we got in touch with Fred van Leeuwen from Education International to talk about an international version of the book. We had become familiar with EI when our country hosted the International Teacher Summit in Amsterdam. Fred van Leeuwen, being a Dutchman as well, had noticed the buzz surrounding the book in Holland, and when we proposed to work together on an international book in order to empower teachers around the world, he was immediately enthusiastic. The discussion quickly turned from if to how and when.

In a sense, working on this book has been a lot easier than working on its Dutch predecessor. With the Dutch book we only knew what issues we wanted to address, but not how we intended to solve them. Much of our conclusions fell into place while working on the book. With this book, it seemed entirely the other way around. Now we knew exactly what to aim for, a crystal-clear focus on what the 'new' teaching profession should look like, but we felt uncomfortable in regard to the issues we were addressing. As intimately familiar as we were with the Dutch situation, so unfamiliar were we with the global situation, and its at best completely incomparable education systems.

We feel we have Education International to thank for getting past this initial anxiety. Not only have they done marvellous work in identifying global issues, but they have financed many reports that cover these issues and we were able to make great use of their contents. They also let us pitch our 'international' version of *The Alternative* to live international crowds, which helped to assure us that although the local situation of every education system was different, our message of the emancipation of the teacher profession, of *flipping the education system*, resonated warmly across the globe.

It also showed us that the need for our message is urgent indeed, as from our many conversations and the contributions we received it became clear that teachers feel lost in terms of what they are working for. Yet we need teachers to safeguard that which makes education *educational*. So, there much is at stake. Therefore we'd like to recall the wisdom of Hillel the Elder, who asked:

> If I am not for myself, who will be for me?
> But if I am only for myself, who am I?
> If not now, when?

Acknowledgements

This is an unlikely book. Two teachers from the Netherlands editing and writing a book with the aim to formulate a framework for educational change, worldwide. It is easier for teachers and researchers from the English-speaking world to gain traction with their ideas. From the moment we started on the Dutch book we already recognized the need for an international version. But how do you go from a relatively obscure language area to a global English-speaking audience? And yet here it is. Just like *Het Alternatief* the book itself symbolizes the message: a collaborative effort by teachers, researchers and other stakeholders to reflect on educational change and to put those ideas into practice. A book like this doesn't write itself and we have a lot of people to thank for making this happen.

First of all we'd like to profoundly thank all the authors for their wonderful ideas and their precious time. Some of whom, like Andy Hargreaves, Alderik Visser and Dick van der Wateren, Gert Biesta, Kim Farris-Berg and Edward Dirkswager agreed to write new articles after they already graciously contributed to *Het Alternatief*. Because of this Dutch book this international follow-up came to be, therefore we would like to thank all those authors as well for the important groundwork they have done. In this respect, an even bigger thank you goes out to Thijs Jansen and everyone at the Professional Honor Foundation who have worked for over a decade to fight for professional honor and support professionals in their struggle against neoliberalism, including the publication of a series of books that we consider this book to be a part of. Surely, we stand on the shoulders of giants.

Flip the System wouldn't have been possible without the financial and logistical support of Education International. We'd like to thank general secretary Fred van Leeuwen for giving us this opportunity. When Jelmer sent Fred an email to discuss the possibility of a new book we were immediately invited to Brussels and found that EI was already working on a broader scope for teacher unions and professional bodies. Education International is doing amazing work to give teachers a voice on an international level, and it is in that spirit that *Flip the System* was supported. David Edwards and John Bangs especially have given us tremendous support. They've given us invaluable feedback on the book, introduced us to different international crowds and have been working tirelessly to promote the book. Besides that they've become good friends. Thanks David and John!

To gain a global audience you need a global publisher and it was Anna Clarkson from Routledge who took the chance to publish the book. Right from the start she was an enthusiastic supporter of the ideas and the book. She was crucial in structuring the content and ideas. We'd also like to thank Katharine Atherton, Christopher Byrne and Sarah Steele for giving critical editorial support and Gert Biesta, Howard Stevenson, Wouter Sanderse and Karen Seashore for writing a recommendation for our book proposal to Routledge.

From the Netherlands, the Dutch professional body the Onderwijscooperatie also supported us financially and logistically right from the start with *Het Alternatief* and again with *Flip the System*. Both Annet Kil and Bert Groenewoud are doing wonderful work for the profession and they've supported us personally on so many levels for which they have our profound gratitude. Hugh McLean is doing invaluable work with Open Societies Foundation, and David Frost, besides supporting the book, arranged for us to attend the Leadership and Learning seminar in Cambridge where we met leading thinkers on global education issues. That seminar gave us invaluable insights and contacts for the book.

Most importantly we'd like to thank our students for letting us experience the joys and frustrations of teaching. Teaching is about experience and this book wouldn't have been written without all the profound experiences, high and low, we had in teaching. Jelmer's final push to engage in policy and start writing came from numerous conversations with a student. Thanks Tycho.

Finally we'd like to thank our families. Writing, editing and networking on top of the actual teaching job is extremely time consuming. Ilja and Audrey have supported and encouraged us all the way through. There's nothing like having the unconditional support from those you love. As Ilja insists on reminding us: "*Nihil Volentibus Arduum*/Nothing is too difficult for those who try." All children deserve to be in a school that instills that mindset, all children deserve the best education we can provide.

In the end it is for them that this book is written.

Introduction

Jelmer Evers and René Kneyber

> It is said that Mithridates trained himself to drink poison.
> Like him we learn to swallow, and not to find bitter,
> the venom of servitude.
>
> Étienne de la Boétie, *Discourse on Voluntary Servitude*, 1548[1]

There was a time, perhaps not even forty or fifty years ago, when education was not the subject of furious political debate. Education and the people who made it happen, the teachers, were regarded with trust. There was hardly any external accountability, no teaching decision or learning outcome that needed to be justified, there was nobody telling teachers what to do. As we might call it now: old professionalism.

But under the influence of political and social changes, the teaching profession has been transformed. During the last couple of decades many countries have engaged in educational reform. Clearly most of these reforms started through the identification of a crisis: the high trust placed in education and teachers had suddenly become unfounded. For instance, in the USA we can see this identification in the shape of the influential report from 1983, 'A Nation at Risk' (Gardner, 1983), which opened with the ominous words: 'Our nation is at risk. Our once unchallenged preeminence in commerce, industry, science, and technological innovation is being overtaken by competitors throughout the world.' Education, it was claimed, was failing: 'We have, in effect, been committing an act of unthinking, unilateral educational disarmament.'

A similar pattern can be seen in the publication of *The Black Papers* (Cox & Dyson, 1971) in the UK in the '70s, which sought to address that country's educational failings, and in the '80s in New Zealand in the influential reports 'Administering for Excellence' (New Zealand Government, 1988) and 'Tomorrow's Schools'.[2] However, the sense of crisis turned global when OECD began publishing its PISA survey in 2000 (OECD, 2001). Although the PISA results are intended to be used for comparing systems in order to provide countries with system information, they have led, especially among politicians, to a feeling of pressure and fear of 'falling behind'. Indeed, the international rat race that has ensued has even caused top performers such as Holland to address the growing concern, with its 2008 report 'Time for Education' (Dijsselbloem, 2008), and Finland's fall in 2013 on the international ranking has led to heated discussion there.[3] A key feature of this crisis mindset is that egalitarian or other motives are being replaced with economic, even economistic, ones, probably due to the explicit PISA focus on linkage between learning outcomes and labour market needs.

The perceived crisis is then used to push an agenda of 'raising the bar', of improving the 'quality' of education through raising the performance of tests on certain subjects, and similar to the areas PISA tests: language, mathematics and science. Sometimes this narrowing of aims emerges because of political opportunism, but also because raising the bar in subjects such as history proves complicated: a redesign of the curriculum around these subjects can lead to heated debate and be politically fraught (see for example Ravitch, 2010).

Neoliberal Reforms

If we ignore the debate on the relevance of international benchmarks such as the PISA results – including whether the raising of this bar is a desirable one, and whether it is being raised in the proper direction for its intended purposes – at least for now, we can start to see a highly similar approach in the means in which countries intend to improve the performance of their systems. In many countries, governments turn to neoliberal-looking reforms, under the assumption that an education system that resembles a market will, through the checks and balances inherent in such a 'market constellation', push schools to achieve higher results. That through the spirit of competition, where schools contend for students, these schools become driven to perform better, become more innovative and more focused on student learning. Of course this is never more than a semi-market, as it is still state funded. However, not content with just the introduction of parent choice, and voice, and pitting schools against each other as competitors, governments nudge schools further into privatization through the use of high-stakes accountability, looking for ways to calculate a teacher's 'added value'. Those schools or teachers that are not found to add enough value, are deemed to be 'failing', and a government may shut them down or lay them off, or may publicly shame schools or individual teachers, whilst rewarding those that are seen to be 'succeeding', so as to 'improve' education. Some countries even go the extra mile and turn parts of their education systems into actual markets, attempting to dismantle public education altogether, something we can see clearly in the highly privatized education system of Chile.

Whenever these 'markets' of education fail, or reveal their inherent shortcomings, the neoliberal 'solution' to this is a further attempt to increase the privatization of education. For example, a recurring problem within privatized systems is that these systems widen the achievement gap because parents who are higher educated make better decisions in terms of school choice and can make better use of the transparency provided by league tables than lower-educated parents. Furthermore, schools tend to become more opportunistic in terms of which students they select in order to uphold their market position. A neoliberal reaction to this 'issue' could be to form strong brands of schools, in the spirit of the McDonald's copy–paste approach to fast food, using brand reliability to provide market information to poor choosers (Ball, 2013). Another reaction could be to further regulate the market to restrict parental choice to some extent, and to restrict the selection of students by schools.

In any event, it is clear that this neoliberal approach to reform makes education less accessible to all, and benefits some more than most. More troubling perhaps is that it views education as a commodity rather than a public service; not as something *of* the public, but something that is delivered *to* the public. This economistic focus ignores the democratic and educational dimensions of education.

The Death (and Life) of the Teacher

In summary, it is clear that the neoliberal shift in reform has led, in a more postmodern sense, to the death of the teacher (Biesta, 2013): the death of the very idea that a teacher has something to contribute, the very idea that the teacher has a meaningful voice in regard to his work, to what he wants to achieve through his work and by which means he achieves it. Although it is a common and oft-cited belief that the quality of a system is determined by the quality of its teachers, that particular belief is of no benefit to teachers. In the neoliberal perspective, the teacher is viewed as a trained monkey, and it is simply a question of finding the right stick to beat him with, or the right brand of peanuts, to make him do the desired dance in front of the audience. The teacher is no longer viewed as a professional, but as a labourer who simply has to follow evidence-based methods in order to secure externally determined goals. In some countries he is even perceived as disposable: give someone a crash course in education, teach him a number of evidence-based methods and let him grind in the machine until he is either burned out or eager to work in a different field of work after two or three years. Worryingly, to some this is even a desirable perspective on the teaching profession.

So clearly, the old days, where teachers decided on matters of curriculum and delivery without any kind of accountability, are over. By and large, through neoliberal reform, teachers' professional identities have been monopolized in many countries by aspects of managerial professionalism. As Judyth Sachs wrote in her book *The Activist Teaching Profession* (2003, p. 26):

> Where devolution and decentralization have been at the core of reform agendas teachers are placed in a long line of authority in terms of their accountability for reaching measurable outcomes through the principal, to the district/regional office, to the central office.

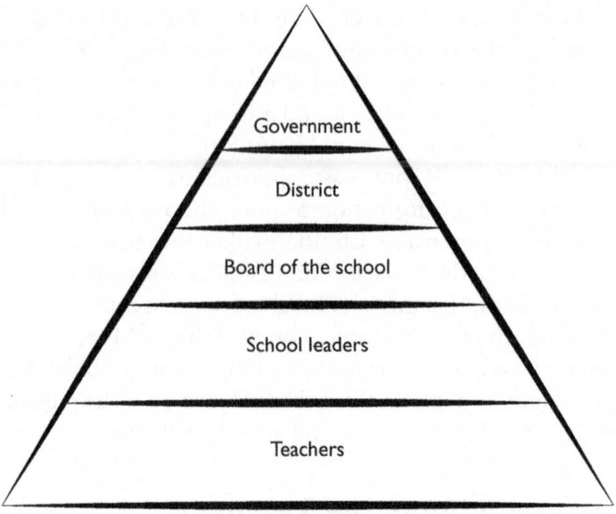

Figure 0.1 'Teachers are placed in a long line of authority in terms of their accountability for reaching measurable outcomes through the principal, to the district/regional office, to the central office' (Sachs, 2003, p. 26).

So under neoliberal reform the professional identity becomes populated with aspects of corporate professionalism, working efficiently and effectively to meet standardized criteria for success for both students and teachers.

There are many issues with this view of teacher professionalism. Most importantly, with its sheer focus on measurable results that once produced will – somehow, in some way – benefit the nation in a global economy, one might argue that teaching is no longer upheld as being a profession. Rather, the term 'voluntary slavery' – a term first coined by the 17-year-old Étienne de la Boétie – comes to mind, with teachers losing their moral agency. The question as to whether teachers perceive that the outcome of their work – or the methods through which to acquire those results – is desirable has no part in the equation. When we take this point even further, we can see that is exactly why this take on teaching, as a managed profession, won't work and isn't working. Good education requires professionals who reflect and make judgments and act upon what is educationally desirable. Ultimately education is not about preparing individuals for their place in the global economy, but rather for every child in every other circumstance something else, *something more*, could be at stake. Consequently, high-quality education does not necessarily equate with high performance on (standardized) tests, or – on a system level – equate with high performance on international benchmarks. But if that is not the definition of high-quality education, or 'good' education, then what is?

We view the failure of the teaching profession (as a global entity) to answer this question as one of the major reasons for the rapid expenditure of neoliberalism across the globe. As the saying goes: 'If you stand for nothing, you will fall for anything.'

The Educational Professional

Interestingly, some are opting for a more democratic take on teacher professionalism (for instance, see Apple, 1996). Apple suggests that the alternative for state control is a democratic professionalism that seeks to demystify its work and build alliances between teachers and other 'stakeholders'. The major benefit of this particular view is first of all that it allows for actual moral agency, and secondly that it allows for a broader kind of accountability that values internal accountability – between teachers or schools – as well as external accountability – to external stakeholders, but certainly not exclusively to the state – within which all groups come to understand the nature and the limitations of each other's work and perspectives. This is in stark contrast to the 'free for all' professionalism of old, but without the arbitrary restraints of the neoliberal paradigm: now its limits are continuously defined through democratic conversation and negotiation.

Yet, a similar 'democratic' case could be made for any other profession. So even if democratic professionalism is the contemporary answer to the issues of neoliberal reform, there is still the question as to what dimension of the teaching profession actually makes the teacher educational. So, as an antidote to neoliberalism, there is a strong need for teachers to connect and to reflect on the purposes of education, and to think and act coherently in terms of their teaching methods. That is: we believe teachers as a profession should generate a new 'language of education', to strengthen education against external forces that threaten a good education for every child. Democratic professionalism as an answer therefore calls also for *educational coherence*, a thorough alignment with the purposes of education.

'Flip the System' and the Issue of Power

So if high-quality education cannot, by definition, be produced through a managed version of the teaching profession, how should the system position itself towards the profession, and how should the profession position itself towards the rest of the system?

Our answer to this is that the educational system requires to be *flipped*. Replacing top-down accountability with bottom-up support for teachers.

Whereas in the left pyramid of Figure 0.2, teachers answer to every layer above them – where the question 'What can the teacher do for me?' resonates throughout the system – the pyramid on the right details the complete opposite situation. Here teachers answer to themselves as a collective profession and to the rest of society on an equal level. The questions that resonate throughout this flipped system are: 'How are teachers doing? What do they want? And what can I do to support them?'

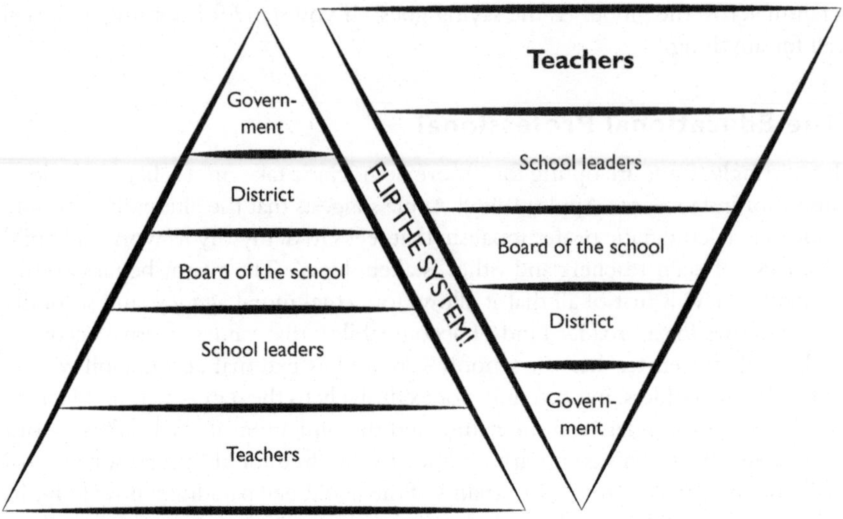

Figure 0.2 Flip the System!

It also means that because they are supported, the teachers in a *flipped system* are obligated to take the lead. Teachers do not wait to be told what to achieve and how to achieve it; instead they show leadership in regard to the how and the what. And this is where teacher leadership fits into our flipped model of education. In educational terms, *teacher leadership* is a relatively new concept. It is, however, a slightly confused concept, with differing definitions, and expectations abound (York-Barr and Duke, 2004). Even if we take a thoughtful definition from the book *Awakening the Sleeping Giant* by Katzenmeyer and Moller (2009), it stills leaves plenty to be desired: 'teacher leaders lead within and beyond the classroom; identify with and contribute to a community of teacher learners and leaders; influence others toward improved educational practice; and accept responsibility for achieving the outcomes of their leadership.' The biggest question of all is who decides when the teacher leader has 'achieved' his 'outcome' and who decides whether someone is a teacher leader or not. Although the teacher leadership concept shows promise, within this definition it can as easily become another tool for domestication: not an instrument for deregulation and professionalization, but an instrument for reregulation and deprofessionalization.

Therefore we'd like to extend this definition. First of all, we believe teacher leadership should not be locked into formal positions. To 'awake the sleeping giant', so to say, *every* teacher should attempt to impact in and outside of their classroom, to identify with and contribute to the community of teacher leaders, to influence improved educational practice and to accept responsibility for achieving the outcome of their leadership. It should not become, to put it more bluntly, a new aristocracy in which some teachers are leaders and some teachers are followers. Secondly, teacher leaders should have the capacity to reflect on the purpose of their work, so that they can judge individually and as a profession whether what is required of them and their students is desirable *or not*. Third of all, *all* teacher leaders should strive towards a collective professional autonomy. In order to acquire the trust that is essential for a collective autonomy to function, teacher leaders should actively strive for professional honour, not only through the development of high professional standards, but also through building active trust with other stakeholders, such as students, parents, the municipality and the state.

The major issue when we view a flipped system as a desirable outcome of system intervention, is that we have to consider how we would move there. Moreover, particularly problematic is that in some countries teachers have deprofessionalized to such an extent that they act as if they were 'dead', using government pressures and regulations as a sort of 'safety blanket' to justify their lack of professional–ethical behaviour.

Therefore, *flipping the system* should more resemble a process of emancipation than a 'system intervention', a process where the 'voice' of teachers is given a meaningful place, whereas before it was considered to be just 'noise' (Rancière, 1999). However, the process cannot originate from a starting point of inequality, with teachers attempting to overcome this inequality. Teachers should instead act on an assumption of being equal, refusing and interrupting the working of powers in the educational system and laying claim to positions and discretional space that they have not previously been entitled to. To initiate this process, it is not simply a question of the government telling teachers to emancipate. It is rather a question of teachers initiating this process themselves.

About this Book

It is from this standpoint that we want to view our book: a book initiated and coordinated by two teachers, in which we have invited researchers and teachers alike to discuss the neoliberal issues that plague education on a global scale. We didn't ask anyone for permission to write this book: we just started; we don't care whether some might view it as marginal 'noise', because we perceive it as a meaningful voice. On the one hand, we've chosen to include some in-depth articles on the subjects we have touched in this introduction – from the problems with neoliberal policy to how to organize collective autonomy – but we have also made room for small vignettes and interviews from around the world, to show that teachers not only share the same struggles on a truly global scale, but that they share a common thing: a universal pride and passion for that thing called education, an inspiring potential that needs fostering in order to unfold, but that cannot be squeezed by government demands.

Notes

1 http://www.constitution.org/la_boetie/serv_vol.htm.
2 http://en.wikipedia.org/wiki/Charter_schools_in_New_Zealand#Tomorrow.27s_Schools.
3 http://news.xinhuanet.com/english/culture/2013-12/04/c_132938962.htm.

References

Apple, M. (1996). *Cultural Politics and Education.* New York: Teachers College Press.

Ball, S. (2013). *Global Education Inc.: New Policy Networks and the Neoliberal Imaginary.* Oxford: Routledge.

Biesta, G. (2013). *The Beautiful Risk of Education.* Boulder: Paradigm Publishers.

Cox, C. B. and Dyson, A. E. (1971). *The Black Papers on Education.* London: Davis-Poynter Ltd.

Dijsselbloem, J. (2008). *Tijd voor onderwijs.* Den Haag: SDU uitgevers.

Gardner, D. P. (1983). A Nation at Risk. Washington, DC: The National Commission on Excellence in Education, US Department of Education.

Katzenmeyer, M. and Moller, G. (2009). *Awakening the Sleeping Giant: Helping Teachers Develop as Leaders.* Thousand Oaks, CA: Corwin Press.

New Zealand Government (1988). Administering for excellence. Effective administration in education. Report of the Taskforce to Review Education [The Picot Report]. Wellington: Government Printer.

OECD (2001). *PISA: Knowledge and Skills For Life.* Paris: Organisation for Economic Co-operation and Development.

Rancière, J. (1999). *Dis-agreement: Politics and Philosophy.* Minneapolis: University of Minnesota Press.

Ravitch, D. (2010). *The Death and Life of the Great American School System: How Testing and Choice Are Undermining Education.* New York: Basic Books.

Sachs, J. (2003). *The Activist Teaching Profession.* Berkshire/New York: Open University Press.

York-Barr, J. and Duke, K. (2004) What do we know about teacher leadership? Findings from two decades of scholarship. *Review of Educational Research*, 74(3), 255–316.

Part I

A Global Problem

Accountability, Privatization and Control

In recent decades, many educational systems around the globe have started to adopt neoliberal-looking reforms; reforms that aim to model their educational system to a market and to implement businesslike techniques such as benchmarking to improve education. The spread of neoliberalism happens at an alarming rate, so that the famous Finnish education expert Pasi Sahlberg likens it to a virus, calling it GERM: the Global Education Reform Movement. Yet, only the most naïve commentator would perceive this spread as an accidental infection of one country to the other. No, this 'infection' is by all means deliberate. An active group, whom Dezalay and Garth (2002) call neoliberal *technopols*, navigate a complex and dense network of thinktanks, ministries, treasuries and policy agencies in order to spread neoliberalism across the globe.

It's easy to view the actions of these individuals and groups (well documented in Stephen Ball's *Global Education Inc.* (2012)) as being purely inspired by the capital that they generate from selling key policy ideas. But one can easily overlook the fact that it's also a strong ideological push; that they truly believe that education will actually benefit from being organized as a market. That improving the scores on (narrow) tests will actually benefit a nation at large.

But as teachers, we know nothing in education is ever easy.

In the first part of this book, 'A Global Problem: Accountability, Privatization and Control', we take a deeper look at the problems associated with this neoliberalism rollout. Dutch teacher **Alderik Visser** carefully dissects the hidden motives and beliefs that underpin neoliberal reforms, why education cannot but 'fail' and why democratic and educational professionalism will prove an important, yet arduous step forward.

Dick van der Wateren, a Dutch teacher, and **Audrey Amrein-Beardsley**, a US researcher, reveal why measuring education quality is less objective and more troublesome than some would have you think, and propose a more democratic take on teacher evaluation that incorporates self-reflection.

In the interview that follows, UK-based researcher **Stephen Ball** explains the effects of neoliberalism on national education systems, how relationships and identities are altered and how neoliberalism 'travels' from one nation to the other as the result of an organized push of ideology.

William C. Brehm interviews a Cambodian teacher who struggles with her care for *all* of her students and a partly privatized educational system with a lack of resources for public education. Her point of view illustrates the universal value that drives teachers: good education for all children.

Dutch teacher **Art Broekman** provides a chilling case study from Cambodia of neoliberal reforms in effect. He not only demonstrates how neoliberalism is fundamentally changing the Indonesian education system, he also shows how these reforms are actively advocated – in this case by the World Bank.

Sophia Gorgodze interviews a teacher in Georgia who comments on the positive and negative aspects of reforms in her country. It is only at the end of the interview that she suddenly realizes what she has lost as a teacher. A telling example of how neoliberal reforms subtly change the outlook on our profession.

And in the final interview of Part I, senior researcher **Thijs Jansen** criticizes the voluntary slavery of many professionals and makes a case for the return of professional honour, proposing a neorepublican alternative to neoliberal reforms.

References

Ball, S. J. (2012). *Global Education Inc.: New Policy Networks and the Neo-Liberal Imaginary*. London: Routledge.

Dezalay, Y. and Garth, B. G. (2002). *The Internationalization of Palace Wars: Lawyers, Economists and the Contest to Transform Latin American States*. Chicago: University of Chicago Press.

Chapter 1

Testing towards Utopia

Performativity, Pedagogy and the Teaching Profession

Alderik Visser

Performance

Education is costly. On average, the richest countries in the world spend 5.6% of their GDP on initial and post-initial education and another 4.1% on tertiary education. That's considerably less than the money spent on public health (9.2%), but in most countries of the OECD, education still ranks among the top three expenses burdening the public household. Yearly, the largest economies of the world 'invest' between $8000 and $9000 (US) per student enrolled in mandatory education, about a third of which ($2500 to $3400) is paid as salaries for teachers (OECD, 2014a, 2014b).

Taxpayers and governments are willing to provide for all that funding, if the schools employing all these teachers 'deliver' what they are expected. Parents want 'good' schools in their vicinity, i.e. such that endorse a similar worldview to their own and acknowledge their child's existence (Ball & Vincent, 1998; Plank & Sykes, 1999). Industry and tertiary education demand knowledgeable, skilled, 'learnable' youngsters, quick to learn the trade in their new environment. Governments provide schools with the infrastructure and the means to achieve all this, hoping that the ensemble of arrangements will help a stable, more or less integrated society further to prosper.

By and large, education systems live up to these expectations. Without massive, high-level schooling of boys and girls – the enormous growth of secondary and tertiary education helping those especially in welfare states to climb the social ladder – the present wealth of many nations seems simply non-feasible (OECD, 2014a; Piketty, 2014). At the same time, schools and educational systems always fail, *structurally*, when it comes for instance to the emancipation or 'integration' of underprivileged groups, smooth 'matches' with labour markets or easy access to higher education, not to mention the 'production' of a just, more equal society (Ainscow, 2013). But most of all, perhaps, many *individual* institutions seem suboptimal in countless *individual* cases where children somehow do not live up to expectations or embrace their potential.

Given these real or perceived flaws, governments have all the reason in the world to scrutinize and possibly reconsider their expenditure on education. Is all this money spent on teachers 'invested' properly if so many individuals and whole groups seem not to benefit from it? It's not so much the answer that is important here – depending on the focus and the method of inquiry, it could be manifold – but the way in which this question was and is put: *do individual taxpayers get enough value for their money?* Series of similar policies and measures have been unleashed in all developed countries to both measure and maximize educational output using managerial tactics and techniques in order to address this question. The actual form these 'incentives' has taken may vary per region or country, but the overall trend has been towards more responsivity and vertical responsibility (Hargreaves, 2013; Hargreaves & Shirley, 2012; Meyer et al., 2014; Waslander, Pater & Van Der Weide, 2010).

Responsive schools were created by relabelling parents and – in higher education – students as *customers*, their choices to 'buy' educational services presumably giving direct feedback on their quality. To help these 'customers' make choices, data about these services were gathered so as to visualize their relative quality. The output figures also served to show the outside world – taxpayers, government officials – that money was well spent and could be used internally as indicators for possible improvements (Biesta, 2010; Earl, 2013; OECD, 2014a; Schleicher, 2013).

In order to make this vertical responsibility feasible, harmonization of curricula and standardization of tests and test practices have become a rather dominant means of making systems 'transparent' and, hence, comparable. Although not the case everywhere, test-based accountability has become particularly ubiquitous and thorough in the United States, and not every school inspectorate has been as rigorous as the English Ofsted system (Ravitch, 2010). Given differing national or regional contexts, parents have either been given few, rather symbolic rights (Switzerland), or their 'consumer power' remains considerable (the Netherlands). Likewise, full 'harmonization' of national curricula to enable nationwide comparisons – planned for Australia and the USA – is not feasible in other countries (McGaw, 2013; Zhao, 2013). Yet everywhere that the Global Education Reform Movement, or GERM (Sahlberg, 2011), has infected, educational practices have been reframed in the same 'neoliberal' way.

The most problematic aspect of this GERM might not be the fetish of numbers as such – even though all this measuring, as we will see, does affect the measured. Neither is it the common form these measurements take: lists, rankings, national, even international comparisons of educational 'productivity'. Nefarious especially seems the assumption that 'quality' (of education) is a set of given variables, the outcome of a clearly circumscribed and controllable process that can be optimized infinitely (Biesta, 2004; Nida-Rümelin, 2011). Once thought to enhance efficiency by breaking down state-driven bureaucracy, this cult of performativity has itself materialized in additional institutional layers to administer, manage, test and control educational processes. Managers and politicians now steering their schools and systems long distance, manipulating and monitoring Key Performance Indicators (KPIs), have, quite comically, started to mimic Stalinist social-planning engineers. But the tragedy is, of course, that where everything and everyone can theoretically become 'better', teachers and their children may very well work as hard as Stakhanov and yet still fail to outperform their average.

Principles

> How did this change come about? I do know. What can make it legitimate? That question I think I can't answer.[1]

This shift in educational policies is part and parcel of the same paradigm, within which (semi-) public services, ever since the 1980s, have been reformed by means of deregulation and privatization. The general idea behind such 'Reaganomics' was, and still is, that 'markets' can produce more and better goods and services more cost effectively than government bureaucracies will ever do. We do not want to embark on a general, ideological, discussion about the pros and cons of this so-called 'neoliberalism'. It is worth noticing, however, that some of the concepts used casually by advocates of market policies seem not as easy to apply in more complex contexts such as education, health care and the like.

First of all, it is good to bear in mind that in Adam Smith's original vision of a 'free' market, neither an atomistic individual, nor a completely abstemious state is presupposed. Driven by an innate 'moral sense', both consumers and producers are not merely optimizing their gains, but share an active interest in the wellbeing of their own community and that of the Commonwealth at large (Achterhuis, 2010). Possible non-optimal outcomes of trade being too free can and need, likewise, to be corrected by an active government driven by the very same ideals and priorities. In the contemporary, more libertarian version of 'market thinking', governments are – at best – however, seen as instrumental for such 'markets' freely to thrive. In the same fashion, morality, a set of shared values, is often seen not as a *prerequisite for*, but merely as *the result of* 'markets'; that is, of free individuals interacting economically. Numerous scandals in the (semi-) public sphere, both before and after the 'credit crunch', may by now have dampened this overt optimism, but that is not at stake here. The question is: to what extent *can* market economics *on principle* be made to apply to the field of education?

Only partially, even a 'market fundamentalist' like Milton Friedman would argue. Education is not a collective good like oxygen or sunlight, but all developed countries make sure that their children benefit from it. If we want this to continue, in order for individuals to mature, citizens to integrate and workers to qualify, the state cannot but take up an active role. Apart from providing for the basic infrastructure, guaranteeing some coherence and controlling the levels of mandatory education, governments need to make up for 'market failure' lurking in scarcely populated areas and on specialist vocational domains (Friedman, 1955).

Across the board, conservative, liberal and social democratic governments have nonetheless tried to 'liberalize' the realms of initial and post-initial education. Given that education still largely is a public or semi-public service – no country but Chile going as far as to 'privatize' general education – national or regional educational systems are now thought to function as quasi-markets, with at best an oligarchy of suppliers competing with one another from the grassroots level up to the supranational sphere. What that has led to, or might possibly lead to, will be scrutinized in more depth in the following paragraphs.

The last general remarks to be made here concern the language with which we 'think' education. It is not so strange or unexpected that in capitalist, individualized societies, we have come to conceive of education primarily in terms of private choices, utility, benefits, costs. At the same time, people do feel some unease about defining 'good' schools as being those that add maximum value to raw materials called 'children'. Along with Michael Sandel, we may ask ourselves whether indeed every aspect of society can or ought to be framed in a utilitarian, 'capitalist' way, and which deeply held convictions might be endangered when we do so (Sandel, 2012). In the case of education it seems obvious that other such values *are* indeed at stake, as a consequence of which 'schools' might never become fully 'optimized' the way 'markets' and companies supposedly can.

Paradox

> Schools are thought to make children free, but everywhere they're in chains.[2]

In a sense, schools have always been 'failing'. School-critique – mostly cast in phrases like the one above – has been a persistent feature in modern discourse at least since Rousseau (2010/1762; see Oelkers, 1989, 1995). We do not need to endorse his political or pedagogical views to understand that the immanent tension he alludes to is possibly an antinomy. How can we possibly educate children to become 'free' individuals within the confines of a rule-governed system? Learn 'for life' in a simulated, stiff environment? Become 'themselves' in the hands of others?

Educationalists, teachers and parents have tried incessantly to bridge this unbridgeable gap, founding 'new' schools that were intended to be more free, friendly or child centred. But systems are persistent. The state – that is, national, regional and/or local governments – has long had other ideas about what compulsory education should achieve, as have Churches, big industry, unions, political groups and parties, the scientific community, et cetera.

During the 19th century, wars were fought – quite literally so – about the ideological foundation of mandatory education, the different outcomes of which have largely shaped the contours and the *couleur locale* of national and regional, of public and private educational structures in modern nations.

Waves of reform have stirred the educational landscapes of the 20th century, a panacea of pedagogical and political movements trying to make schools instrumental to their own idea of utopia or the good life. As much as these may have had longer, larger impact, none of these movements has *essentially* changed the structure and outlook of organized education (Oelkers, 1995; Tyack & Cuban, 1995). Systems being what they are – systemic – the ideals and interests of children, of parents, of individual teachers have been, and perhaps need to be, evened out by other forces holding stakes in state-sponsored education.

Over the past twenty years, however, positions in the field have changed. Fundamentally. With the introduction of modes of New Public Management, governments all across the developed world have been seen to defect to the side of the critics. Whether their 'permanent revolution' to make education 'better' really works out the ways it is envisaged, or whether education is 'sold' to the public at large is open for debate. But paradoxically, the quest for 'excellence' seems to have taken the vein of old-fashioned school critique – about *individual* children living up to the maximum of their potentials. With governments (and the ICT lobby) taking on the position of Rousseau himself – promoting 'free' development of schools and children in and through a thoroughly controlled environment – it is no longer 'the system' as such, 'big money' or any other real or imaginary oppositional force, but individual *schools* and, most fiercely, failing *teachers* who seem to bar the road to utopia.

Positivism

As much as politicians of any sorts pay lip service to 'market-oriented' policies and pretend these were 'post-ideological', they are not. In the case of education, the ideology of 'the market' is partly sustained, partly blurred by outright utopian expectations about what schools can or ought to accomplish. The vocabulary may have changed, the means to effectuate it may be envisaged differently, but some idea of social engineering or *social physics* is deeply engrained in educational discourse. This is neither good nor bad and makes perfect historical sense, but it's one of the reasons why schools and especially teachers are persistently perceived to fail.

Having been a teacher of history and philosophy in Dutch secondary education for more than fifteen years, I have been held to foster both multiculturalism and more nationally defined citizenship, to battle racism, promote environmentalism, prevent bullying, fight terrorism, obesity, drugs and sexual violence, raise awareness about the social position of women, homosexuals, transgenders, et cetera, et cetera. Partly, this moral activism refers back to the enlightened optimism from which our schools originally sprouted. And no matter how small, big or real a perceived social problem is, it is instinctively gratifying, politically easy to justify and, yes, rather cheap to make teachers responsible for solving them. With social bonds further eroding, due for instance to technology, migration and individualization, schools, for their part, are simply the last stronghold of civil society with enough coverage to uplift the underprivileged. It's precisely here that the boundaries between educational endeavours and therapeutic approaches tend to get blurred, general education having (or regaining) the sociological function of 'normalizing' behaviour (Furedi, 2011).

The mechanisms at work here are as old as they are contestable. Often mediated by outbursts of *moral panic*, 'unwanted' behaviour, as shown typically by *social groups*, is turned into *individual* problems, a matter of values and the 'right' attitude, to be fostered by schools (Hunt, 1999; Visser, 2006). Never asked, seldom trained, teachers are 'simply' expected to perform such social work as an add-on to the regular curriculum. Archetypically cast in a highly moralistic vein, interventions like these rarely show the immediate effects hoped for, contributing to the general dismay with schools and the teaching profession: why can't they just do what they are paid for?

I believe sincerely that most teachers do, or at least try, but teaching *is* indeed – too often the analogy has been made – different from the medical profession: it's more difficult! The amount of possibly relevant variables in any given educational situation being close to infinite, every act can be meaningful, but no single effect predictable. The 'culture of measurement' may try to repel this unpredictability, prioritizing some variables over others, but its effect on teachers and teaching seems rather the opposite: expectancy, responsibility, workload and the opportunity to fail have all been augmented, as has the rift between 'good' schools and 'bad' ones (Biesta, 2010, 2014). Itself part and parcel of a positivist – that is, thoroughly utopian – paradigm, the myth of measurability does in fact 'eat itself', in the sense that numerous players in the field are busy beating or literally cheating the system. Inflation of grades, test scores and diplomas, concealed and outright fraud, are not incidental, but rather endemic in a system that seems to force administrators to focus on the quantity of the output rather than on the quality of the processes (Koretz, 2008). And the stricter the selection criteria are made in order to manipulate the 'input' of any high-quality school, and the harder children are taught a narrowed-down curriculum to become expert takers of high-stakes tests, the more devastating the combined impact of chance, contingency, contextuality – the human factor – will be perceived to be (Ravitch, 2010; Wateren, 2013).

A very popular means of exorcizing this uncomforting uncertainty is *transparency*. On the surface level, transparency is a buzzword that alludes to rationalization of complex processes, and is as such a form of social engineering. In a transparent company or school, roles and responsibilities are regulated and clear. Transparency legitimizes hierarchies but also fosters individual responsibility, even 'democracy', in the sense that everyone is made directly accountable for his or her successes and failures. That's also the reason why transparent systems are so prone to pedantry and bureaucracy: in many a school in the USA, Sweden and the Netherlands, teachers spend so much time administering their education, that they lack sufficient time to actually educate.

On a deeper, mythical, psychological level, transparency is also the dream – or the nightmare – to create Momo's 'window to the soul', so as to read and possibly control people's deepest thoughts and emotions (Schneider, 2013). As this 'black box' has thus far not been opened, systems of evaluation and self-evaluation have been widely introduced, to make workers not only, but certainly also, in education, 'work on themselves' to become even 'better'. So benevolent are the languages of reflection, of peer, self- and student assessment, and regardless of how my Personal Development Plan will indeed contribute to my *lifelong learning*, that transparency *is* used as a means of governance – or indeed as 'political psychopharmacy' (Olssen, 2008; Schneider, 2013). Assigned before the Permanent Quality Tribunal (Maschelein & Simons, 2008; Simons & Maschelein, 2006), in which managers, colleagues, students and parents are all represented, teachers may very well promise to become 'better', in the sense that they will more meticulously abide with the rules, the protocols. Possibly, they will even succeed at helping students, school districts or nations attain better rankings and grades. But will this actually make them 'better' as teachers and enhance the quality of their teaching?

Professionalism

Popular imagery knows of teachers in two forms only. In the more romantic, heroic version, they are heart-warming, selfless idealists who succeed in making children jump over their shadows, defying the limits seemingly set by nature, nurture and the (evil) system. It's Robin Williams in *Dead Poets Society* (1989) mixed with the real-life French teacher in the *Être et Avoir* (*To Be and to Have*, 2002). Dianegative to this positive image (T+) is the dreary, cynical *frontocrat* who hates 'the system' as much as she identifies with it, for which she chastises herself perhaps even more than the children she has to drag along (T−). She's known from children's fiction (Roald Dahl!) and regularly shows up in ego-documents, especially, but not only from older reminiscences/youth memories (see for example Zweig, 1948).

Everyone knows that these are stereotypes, but still everyone recognizes, and yes, uses them to categorize his or her own memories. *Topoi* of romantic school critique themselves, they surely antedate the present neoliberal revolution in education. What makes them interesting here, is that both images are actively used (micro-)politically – at different levels and for different reasons.

Publicly, education policies endorse, and indeed embrace T+ as living specimens of teacher excellence. More or less openly, they are contrasted with teachers of the type T−, who fail to develop practices that fit the needs of individual learners in the 21st century. It's here that, as noted before, the 'permanent revolution' to enhance quality education seems to converge with romantic school critique: desperate to catch up with Finland, Singapore and other 'high-performing' nations, 'big government' actively promotes non-systemic approaches and (ICT) solutions to solve perceived 'crises' in education. Within the given paradigm, however, the effects of these and other measures need to be monitored, tested, ranked, published, et cetera. Thus, controlled from a distance by perverse and perverting systems of 'institutionalized suspicion', critical teachers admonish that test-based accountability hinders them from developing into T+ teachers, and in fact forces them into the role of T−.

A rather old, neo-Marxist theory might help us get to the kernel of this apparent conflict. In his influential *Theory of Communicative Action*, the German sociologist Jürgen Habermas divides the world in two archetypal spheres, which he calls the 'lifeworld' and the 'system' (Habermas, 1981). In the lifeworld, which encompasses both private life and the public sphere, people engage with one another in terms of equality and humanity, led by the Kantian adage that 'every man is treated as an end in itself'. The (capitalist) system – which structures not only the economical sphere, but also technology, science and the media – contrarily sees things, animals and humans primarily as means to external ends such as productivity, gain or control. Societies becoming ever more complex, functions formerly belonging to the lifeworld have been – and still are – taken over by this expanding system, and indeed need to be. However, in the face of this 'colonization' of our lifeworld – that is, of both the private and the public sphere – Habermas warned and still warns of 'systemic rationality' threatening our democratic way of life (Murphy & Skillen, 2013).

One of the many things one could bring up against this rigid theory of Habermas's is that he does not apply it to education: schools, classes, lessons are always by their very nature both 'lifeworld' and 'system'. On a micro-level, they are mini worlds where teachers and their students interact, engage, practise their roles as democratic citizens, reflective adults, et cetera. At the macro-level, schools are instrumental in selecting and qualifying human resources so as to reproduce and further sustain a productive society. At the same time, Habermas does shed light on the immanent conflict sketched above.

From the perspective of teachers, recent reform policies can easily be dramatized as an onslaught of the system on 'their' lifeworld and on those of their children: more and younger than ever before, students are subjected to a competitive system geared towards extrinsic goals and needs. Governments and policy makers could counter that that's only half the story: if schools 'simply' meet basic requirements, they have more freedom than ever to arrange primary processes the way they want to. In fact, schools are actively supported to develop their own 'profiles', and more 'professionalism' in and through thriving 'school cultures'.

What it all boils down to is how 'quality' is conceived of, and how, consequently, 'professionalism' can be enacted. In the 'systemic' version, quality is quite tightly defined as the measurable output on certain KPI, and professionals are primarily recruited to organize or cause 'learning' to meet these objectives. One could be inclined to identify these as the typical 'T−' teachers just described, but that would be too simplistic. If the Dutch Minister of Education publicly incites teachers to become 'competent rebels' (Bussemaker, 2014), she quite literally invokes the image of 'T+' in a context of 'systemic', vertical accountability.

From the point of view of teacher professionalism, however, quality might be somehow preconceived, but is never really given. Like craftsmen, professional teachers ideally shape quality in interaction with the material; that is, while educating their students within their individual potential as moral subjects, citizens, human resources, and much else (Sennett, 2008; Biesta, 2014). In real school life, too, aspects of 'T+' and 'T−' coexist, even fuse within any teaching professional, as tests and some teaching towards them might be somehow 'part of the job'. But the point is that the prudence or practical rationality, the professional judgement that transcends the logic of mere measurement, has become so irrelevant to schools' 'quality-control cycle' that important values and aims – growth, becoming, patience, relationship, et cetera – are indeed driven by the school's lifeworld. The tension between these two types of quality/rationality, provoking different ideas about professionalism, may not be resolved very easily. But beyond other clearcut dichotomies – old school versus new school, 'T+' versus 'T−' – it seems to me that a new, or rather a reinvigorated idea of *pedagogical* professionalism, combined with schemes to organize accountability horizontally, that is, community based rather than competitively, seems to hold the most promise as a place to move forward from.

Pedagogy

Whether education reform policies of the past twenty years have 'succeeded' or 'failed' is impossible to judge: in some places they may have, at other they might not, and anyhow, it's all a matter of perspective. What seems obvious, however, is that attempts to 'marketize' education have had perverse side effects, such that clash with our deepest convictions about what education ought to 'produce' or be about. Especially, the introduction of quality-control systems and feedback mechanisms, as developed in the private sector, and the persistent 'culture of measurement' that has come along with it, has caused education – or 'learning' – to become essentially 'worth-less': it serves no other purpose than itself. That, we need to change.

The first, and probably the most difficult thing is to try and develop a new common language to 'think' education anew, beyond the now dominant discourse of input and output, comparison and competition, excellence and performance, and back to what is at stake: maturation of children and adolescents. Hopefully – but even more problematically – such a new discourse would bring us also beyond the age-old dichotomies of new schools versus old schools, individuals versus the community, and everyone against the system. *Pedagogy* – conceived of here in the *continental* sense as a distinctive field of theories and practices concerning all educational endeavours and institutions – seems to offer more and more useful critical, analytical discourse than the languages of 'mere' educational science and technology, developmental psychology, neurobiology, and the like (Biesta 2010, 2014; Visser, 2013; Ziehe, 2004). As important as these fields may be in their own right, they each seem to largely sustain the 'myth of measurability' (as well as other myths) at the expense of the broader, more inclusive view of the education we are in need of now – one that takes the moral, the political, the relational, yes, the more subjective, subjectivating side of education into full account.

Secondly, and more feasibly, teachers would do well to reclaim or take more 'professional space', i.e. confidently take up their roles as professionals and actively participate in discourse on education policies, not only within the confines of their schools, but on all other levels, too: in districts, on the national, the supranational level. Such a renewed or reinvigorated *pedagogical* professionalism doesn't come for free: it entails the responsibility to give shape, actively, both individually and commonly, to a professional identity based on extended levels of reflection and skills in a number of relevant fields.

A good way to start working towards this pedagogical professionalism would be, thirdly, to reclaim schools. Schools might not only become more efficient and effective by focusing on the outside world – with achievements, products, profiles, or whatever – but also, or even more so, by turning the focus inwards (Sangiovanni, 1998; Bruggencate, 2012). By twisting the general question 'what do students need to achieve?' into a more specific, school-based 'what can and do we want our children to achieve?', school managers and/or professional teachers-as-leaders can give input and direction to a *pedagogical* reorientation of school-based education. We're not talking about new epithets or profiles, but about the wilful creation of commonly held goals and values, about giving *meaning* to learning and to school life by managers, teachers, parents *and* students alike.

Critics might moan that this is exactly what the 'neoliberal' revolution in education has tried to bring about: a more diversified supply of educational 'goods', the quality of which is guaranteed by the state. But that's not exactly what I envisage. Within a system of 'centralized decentralization', known in countries like Singapore or the Netherlands (see for example Tan & Ng, 2007), it's not very difficult so see national or regional governments develop rather crude, general benchmarks for different types of education, ideally in close cooperation with other stakeholders such as parents, teachers, other educational institutions, private parties and the scientific community. With teachers and school communities taking up their professional responsibility in the way I have sketched above, vertical accountability may be supplanted, or indeed 'flipped' by systems of horizontal accountability, schools explaining and justifying their idea of 'quality' and the means to achieve them to those directly involved (Hooge, Burns & Wilkoszewski, 2012). With governments taking up an active role in helping schools that show difficulty establishing such a professional culture – possibly in alignment with teacher training institutions – and catching up on the unresolved and now often neglected problems of equity and equal access to educational resources (Earl, 2013), pluralist educational landscapes might sprout, delivering high-quality education not for extrinsic, but for intrinsic goals.

In this ideal world, inspired teams of professional teachers need no standardized criteria or nationalized curricula to deliver good education – they'll take care of it themselves. In order to get such professional teams going, we need more than the mere 'active participation' of teachers and possibly students, but genuine deliberative practices engaging all stakeholders, and commonly developing a new language to think and talk education at their own schools. Such democratic processes will prove difficult, frustrating and time consuming, but eventually they will also deliver 'good' schools, with a more realistic view on what they can and cannot achieve and particularly with a stronger 'lifeworld' for both teachers and students.

Notes

1 A slightly twisted quote from the famous opening lines of Rousseau's *Du Contrat Social* (1762), published in the same year as his *Émile*. In a modern translation: *'Man is born free, and everywhere he is in chains. Here's one who thinks he is the master of others, yet he is more enslaved than they are. How did this change come about? I don't know. What can make it legitimate? That's a question that I think I can answer.'* http://www.earlymoderntexts.com/pdfs/rousseau1762.pdf.

2 See note 1.

References

Achterhuis, H. (2010). *De Utopie van de Vrije Markt.* [The Utopia of the Free Market.] Rotterdam: Lemniscaat.

Ainscow, M. (2013). Equity: The big challenge for education systems. In Janc Malone (2013).

Ball, S. and Vincent, C. (1998). 'I heard it on the grapevine': 'Hot' knowledge and school choice. *British Journal of Sociology of Education*, 19(3), 377–400.

Biesta, G. J. J. (2004). Education, accountability, and the ethical demand: Can the democratic potential of accountability be regained? *Educational Theory*, 54(3), 233–252.

Biesta, G. J. J. (2010). *Good Education in an Age of Measurement, Ethics, Politics, Democracy.* Boulder, CO: Paradigm.

Biesta, G. J. J. (2014). *The Beautiful Risk of Education.* Boulder CO: Paradigm [Education, Philosophy and Culture].

Bruggencate, G. ten (2012). Modeling the influence of school leaders on student achievement: How can school leaders make a difference? *Education Administration Quarterly*, 48(4), 699–732.

Bussemaker, J. (2014). Vaardigheden voor de toekomst: Lezing conferentie KNAW. [Skills for the future: Lecture at the Royal Dutch Academy for Sciences.] http://www.rijksoverheid.nl/regering/bewindspersonen/jet-bussemaker/toespraken/2014/03/17/lezing-minister-bussemaker-bij-symposium-knaw-vaardigheden-voor-de-toekomst.html.

Earl, L. (2013). Accountability as a collective professional responsibility. In Janc Malone (2013).

Friedman, M. (1955). The role of government in education. http://www.edchoice.org.

Furedi, F. (2011). *Wasted: Why Education Isn't Educating*. New York: Continuum.

Habermas, J. (1981). *Theorie des kommunikativen Handelns*. [Theory of Communicative Action.] Frankfurt aM: Suhrkamp.

Hargreaves, A. (2013). Teleporting change: The dynamics and distortions of international benchmarking. In Janc Malone (2013).

Hargreaves, A. and Shirley, D. L. (2012). *The Global Fourth Way: The Quest for Educational Excellence*. Thousand Oaks, CA: Corwin Press.

Hooge, E. H., Burns, T. and Wilkoszewski, H. (2012). Looking beyond the numbers: Stakeholders and multiple school accountability. OECD Working Papers, No. 85, OECD Publishing. http://dx.doi.org/10.1787/5k91dl7ct6q6-en.

Hunt, A. (1999). *Governing Morals: A Social History of Moral Regulation*. Cambridge: Cambridge University Press.

Janc Malone, H. (2013). *Leading Educational Change: Global Issues, Challenges, and Lessons on Whole-System Reform*. New York: Teachers College Press.

Kneyber, R. and Evers, J. (2013). *Het Alternatief: Weg met de afrekencultuur in het onderwijs*. [The Alternative – Down with the Culture of Accountability.] Amsterdam: Boom.

Koretz, D. (2008). *Measuring Up: What Educational Testing Really Tells Us*. Cambridge, MA: Harvard University Press.

Maschelein, J. and Simons, M. (2008). De wil tot kwaliteit. In *De schaduwzijde van onze welwillendheid: Kritische studies van de pedagogische actualiteit*. [The will to quality. In The other side of our benevolence: Critical studies of pedagogical actuality.] Leuven: Acco.

McGaw, B. (2013) Australian school improvement with transparent, fair comparisons. In Janc Malone (2013).

Meyer, H.-D., Tröhler, D., Labaree, D. F. and Hutt, E. L. (2014). Accountability: antecedents, power, and process. *Teacher College Record*, 116 090301 (2014).

Murphy, M. and Skillen, P. (2013). The politics of school regulation: Using Habermas to research educational accountability. In M. Murphy (ed.), *Social Theory and Education Research. Understanding Foucault, Habermas, Bourdieu and Derrida*. Abingdon: Routledge.

Nida-Rümelin, J. (2011). *Die Optimierungsfalle: Philosophie einer humanen Ökonomie*. [The Optimization Trap: Philosophy of a Humane Economy.] München: Irisiana.

OECD (2014a). Education at a Glance 2014: OECD Indicators. OECD Publishing. http://dx.doi.org/10.1787/eag-2014-en.

OECD (2014b). http://www.oecd.org/newsroom/health-spending-starts-to-rise-but-remains-weak-in-europe.htm.

Oelkers, J. (1989). *Reformpädagogik: Eine kritische Dogmengeschichte*. Weinheim/Basel: Juventa.

Oelkers, J. (1995). *Schulreform und Schulkritik*. [School Reform and School Critique.] Würzburg: Ergon (Reihe: Erziehung, Schule, Gesellschaft).

Olssen, M. (2008). Understanding the mechanisms of neoliberal control: Lifelong learning, flexibility and knowledge capitalism. In A. Fejes and K. Nicoll (eds), *Foucault and Lifelong Learning: Governing the Subject*. Abingdon: Routledge.

Piketty, T. (2014). *Capital in the 21st Century*. Harvard: Harvard University Press.

Plank, D. N. and Sykes, G. (1999). How choice changes the education system: A Michigan case study. *International Review of Education*, 45(5/6), 385–416.

Ravitch, D. (2010). *The Death and Life of the Great American School System: How Testing and Choice Are Undermining Education*. New York: Basic Books.

Rousseau, J.-J. (2010/1762). *Profession de Foi du Vicaire Savoyard*. Édition de Bruno Bernardi. Dossier de Gabriella Radica. Paris: Flammarion.

Sahlberg, P. (2011). *Finnish Lessons: What Can the World Learn from Educational Change in Finland?* New York: Teachers College Press.

Sandel, M. (2012). *What Money Can't Buy: The Moral Limit of Markets*. New York: Farrar, Strauss, & Giroux.

Sangiovanni, T. J. (1998). Leadership as pedagogy, capital development and school effectiveness. *International Journal of Leadership in Education: Theory and Practice*, 1(1), 37–46.

Schleicher, A. (2013). International comparisons as a lever for policy reform. In Janc Malone (2013).

Schneider, M. (2013). *Transparenztraum: Literatur, Politik, Medien und das Unmögliche*. [The Dream of Transparency: Literature, Politics, Media and the Impossible.] Berlin: Matthes & Seitz.

Sennett, R. (2008). *The Craftsman*. New Haven, CT: Yale University Press.

Simons, M. and Maschelein, J. (2006). The permanent quality tribunal in education and the limits of education policy. *Policy Futures*, 4, 294–307.

Tan, C. and Ng, P. T. (2007). Dynamics of change: Decentralised centralism of education in Singapore. *Journal of Educational Change*, 8(2), 155–168.

Tyack, D. and Cuban, L. (1995). *Tinkering towards Utopia: A Century of Public School Reform*. Cambridge, MA: Harvard University Press.

Visser, A. (2006). Opvoeding, media en geweld: Over de grenzen van het jongste beschavingsoffensief. [Education, media, violence: On the limits of the latest civilization offensive.] *Ethiek en Maatschappij*, 9(3), 76–93.

Visser, A. (2013). Marktfilosofie, Onderwijsutopie: Leraren tussen 'leefwereld' en 'systeem'. [Market philosophy and educational utopia: Teachers between 'lifeworld' and 'system'.] In Kneyber and Evers (2013).

Waslander, S., Pater, C. and Van der Weide, M. (2010). Markets in education: An analytical review of empirical research on market mechanisms in education. OECD Education Working Papers, No. 52, OECD Publishing.

Wateren, D. van der (2013). Zin en onzin van testen, vergelijken en afrekenen. In Kneyber and Evers (2013).

Zhao, Y. (2013). Directions of change: Why the USA and China are moving in opposite directions. In Janc Malone (2013).

Ziehe, T. (2004). Pädagogische Professionalität und zeittypische Mentalitätsrisiken.

[Pedagogical professionality and timetypical mentality risks.] Paper presented at the CSP Conference, June 2004. Oslo: Hogskolen i Oslo.

Zweig, S. (1948). *De Wereld van Gisteren: Herinneringen van een Europeaan.* [Yesterday's World: Memories of a European.] Amsterdam: Allert de Lange.

Chapter 2

Measuring What Doesn't Matter

The Nonsense and Sense of Testing and Accountability

Dick van der Wateren and Audrey Amrein-Beardsley

Introduction

Fair enough. Any government likes to know if their education budget is well spent. It then makes sense to look at education outcomes, and the ones that supposedly are easiest to interpret are test scores, report card grades and graduation rates. If these numbers are lower than expected, appropriate measures can be taken, bad teachers fired and bad schools closed. Simple.

Yet, it has been known for a long time that these raw numbers do not give a reliable picture of the quality of a school or a teacher, as there are other factors influencing student achievement. Socio-economic status of the students' families is one of the most important of these. A more reliable method (or, so it's thought) to assess a teacher's quality is the students' progress (or lack thereof) in a given period of time. This so-called 'value added' can then be used as an objective measure to hold the teacher accountable. Can't be difficult. Or, can it?

Given the high stakes that are involved, it makes sense to ask how reliable the various value-added models (VAMs) are, whether they are fair and what the alternatives are for evaluating teachers and schools.

In this chapter we will argue that it is far from simple to use value-added models to control the quality of education, which a number of countries (with the US in the lead) have opted for and others have their eyes on. Moreover, the illusion of control does more damage than good. It could, of course, be argued that the numbers speak for themselves, but numbers never do. Few people really ask how reliable these numbers are, if they are realistic measures of a school's education outcome and what are the alternatives to warrant the quality of education.

We will answer questions about the usefulness of test scores, whether grades and test scores are reliable indicators of the quality of teaching, whether teachers' VAMs are reliable, valid and fair and whether high-stakes decisions based on them are a good idea at all.

Some of these questions have been answered by Harvard professor Daniel Koretz. His book *Measuring Up: What Educational Testing Really Tells Us*

(Koretz, 2008a) discusses a number of misunderstandings about standardized tests. He explains – in a language that is understandable even for laypersons who are not mathematical or statistical experts – what they are, how they are made, how the end scores are calculated and how these are interpreted.

There are many misunderstandings about standardized tests. It starts even with the word 'standard'. There is nothing special about standardization. We use it all the time in our daily lives. There is a standard for length, the metre (or the yard, if you like). Without such a standard we cannot know if London is further from Amsterdam than Paris. Standards are also common in schools when we measure the progress of our students. Students are regularly tested at the same time, under similar conditions and with the same test questions. This helps us and our students to determine whether they move forward, or need a little more help (formative assessment). In principle, large-scale standardized tests, such as school leaving examinations, school or college admission exams, are no different. So far so good. The problem is not so much *how* students are tested – that is usually well founded. Testing is a science in itself, based on careful research of test items and statistical methods. The question is *what* is being tested, or rather, should be tested, and for what purpose.

At the end of this chapter we will propose an alternative assessment system that we believe is more reliable and fair than assessment based solely on students' test scores. Contrary to a VAM-based accountability, our proposal actually helps teachers and schools to improve.

Pros and Cons of Testing

When we ask our teacher colleagues about their definition of 'good education', their eyes often glaze over. Or, we hear that 'we don't have time for that', we 'must increase our output', or 'improve our achievement'. It is not uncommon for improvement to start even before there is a good vision about education.

This is exactly the problem with the testing, measuring and ranking – and the culture of 'Measure and Punish' (Amrein-Beardsley, 2014) – that policy makers worldwide have become addicted to. What exactly is being measured? Strictly speaking, it is no more than just what is being measured, namely students' grades, standardized test scores, or number of graduates. Whether these data realistically measure education quality remains largely unanswered, unless we unthinkingly define good education as: high scores in mathematics and reading/language arts, since these are the subjects that are commonly assessed by large-scale standardized tests. Even then we may ask if those numbers reflect what we want to assess.

Testing is an essential element of all education. It is hard to imagine education that does not in some way or another assess if a child has mastered something that has been taught. This does not necessarily involve formal tests. Testing occurs even outside school. Humans learn by trial and error, always and under all circumstances, from the day they are born. See how children learn to walk, ride a bike, skate, play a game. This is a continuous learning process, whereby they correct themselves and others, without grades or exams.

Likewise, learning without assessment is impossible in the classroom, whether students test themselves, or the teacher tests the students. At any time during the learning process we, as well as our students, need to know if they have mastered what we have taught. This can take two forms. The first, formative assessment, diagnostic testing, or assessment *for* learning, is a method whereby teachers collect information to make better-informed decisions about their teaching and to provide feedback to their students (Wiliam, 2011). The second, summative assessment, or assessment *of* learning (like grades), on the other hand, judges the educational outcome and is the basis for decisions about students, such as promotion, or school or university admission. Teachers can also be summatively assessed, even to the point that high-stakes decisions, e.g. salary raise, bonus, job termination, or school closure, are based on students' outcomes.

One of the consequences of teachers' summative assessments, which promoters of high-stakes testing happily ignore, is score inflation, test scores that turn out higher than the actual level of the students (Koretz, 2008a). The more there is at stake, the more likely it is that test results are unreliable and do not reflect what students really know, or how well they have been educated. Test score inflation occurs when students are instructed only in those parts of the curriculum that will be the subject of the upcoming standardized tests: i.e. *teaching to the test*. Other causes of test inflation are the teaching of tricks to answer test items (test training) and sometimes even downright fraud.

Standardized tests usually are very small samples of the large domains of knowledge and skill that students have mastered (Koretz, 2008a). Most standardized tests only assess mathematics and reading/language arts, subjects that – in the economic view of education – are thought of the highest value. Even in those subjects, they do not effectively assess students' depth of knowledge and understanding, their ability to think critically, analytically or creatively, their ability to solve contextual problems, or even accomplish authentic, performance-based tasks (Amrein-Beardsley, 2014).

Moreover, children's learning is not a linear process. Rather, they learn in spurts, quite unpredictably, and differently from child to child. This is particularly true for children, say, up to the age of seven, but even older children and teenagers develop in relatively unpredictable ways. Therefore, what students should achieve at a certain stage of their development, and thus what their teachers should be accounted for, can only be described in broad terms.

Test results also appear to depend strongly on factors that are outside the influence of teachers and schools, so-called out-of-school factors. We will come back to this below.

Finally, test scores are indicators of what students know or do not know, can or cannot do. That is all. They do not tell us anything about the causes of high or low test scores (Koretz, 2008a). This means that we will need to investigate those causes independently from the tests, supported by good scientific evidence.

The point here is that all the sophisticated VAM statistics in the world do not help us when the underlying data are inaccurate and unreliable. The analysis will never tell more or be more accurate than the data.

'The Beautiful Risk of Education'

Before we start evaluating teachers on the basis of the test results of their students – before we even start testing those children and teenagers – we should ask ourselves *what* it is we should test. And even before that comes the question of *what* education is *for* – in other words: how do we define good education? There is little point in trying to measure the effect of teachers if we cannot answer the questions, 'Effective for what? Effective for whom?' (Bogotch, Mirón & Biesta, 2007). These questions go largely ignored in discussions about evidence-based education, international comparisons and accountability. Doing so reduces good education to the production of high test scores in just a few subjects. The implicit assumption, that the few subjects that are tested are the only, or even best, indicators of good education, is not supported by research evidence.

Gert Biesta (Professor of Educational Theory and Policy, Luxemburg University) argues in several of his papers and books that the culture of measuring and accountability entirely misses the point of what education is about. In his contribution to this book he explains his view on what the purpose of education should be. In summary, good education has three dimensions: qualification, socialization and subjectification (Biesta, 2009, 2014). Qualification is teaching students knowledge, skills, values and dispositions, so they become qualified to do things. Socialization is educating students to become part of existing social, political, cultural and professional traditions, and to become part of a democratic society. Subjectification refers to the process of becoming autonomous, responsible and critical adults. In this way, subjectification is opposed to socialization, as it allows an individual to be independent of social structures and traditions. This makes education an instrument of enlightenment *('Bildung')* and emancipation.

Qualification is the primary focus of those education systems where measurement and accountability – by VAMs and the like – are used to control the quality of learning. There is a simple reason for that. Progress in the area of knowledge and skills can be relatively easily tested, particularly for reading/language arts and mathematics. If we look more critically, however, we will see that even in those subjects, only a very small subset of the entire domain can be assessed with the most common standardized test tools and, arguably, not the essential subsets of those subjects. If we agree that education is about more than just the few things that can be measured with standardized tests, then the testing and accountability movement has drifted far from what we believe good education is.

Good education is about finding the right balance between the three dimensions of qualification, socialization and subjectification. The purpose of education is to help children and young people find their way into the world, and therefore goes far beyond the mere knowledge and skills that are the objects of bubble tests.

The title of this section is the title of Biesta's book published in 2014. It is called *The Beautiful Risk of Education* for a reason. Education is a risky business indeed, since there is no predictable cause-and-effect relationship between input (teaching) and output (learning). We have to abandon the illusion of total control of the education process.

The phrase 'learning outcomes' reflects the notion that education is a production process. However, we do not produce students, nor do we produce our children. Just as our children are born to us and we show them the way in the world, students come to our classes and we help them to develop their talents and grow as people (Biesta, 2014).

If we want to improve education and make it more effective, we need to ask: effective for what? (Bogotch, Mirón & Biesta, 2007). 'Effective teaching' is a meaningless concept if we do not specify what this teaching aims to achieve, taking the three dimensions of good education into account. We also need to ask: effective for whom?, since what may be effective for one student or group of students may not be effective for others. The solution is not more or better testing, but a curriculum that leaves plenty of room for individual schools and teachers to develop their own standards and programmes in response to local needs. We will return to this at the end of this chapter.

The reader can test these ideas for themselves. Just remember your old teachers. Who do you remember best? Who made the greatest impact on your life? Are they the ones who helped you score high on standard achievement tests, or are they the role models, the ones who believed in you, supported you, helped you to 'become who you are'?

This vision of education as a risky process that we cannot absolutely control, radically opposes the economically driven vision that is dominant around the globe and that is manifest most clearly in the measure-and-punish policy of which VAMs are the main instrument.

What are VAMs?

The various value-added models (VAMs) that now operate in education measure student growth on large-scale standardized achievement tests in certain subject areas, mainly mathematics and reading/language arts. They supposedly correct for all sorts of variables related to student background characteristics and demographics, and classroom- and school-level characteristics. A statistical analysis of these variables produces a single number for each teacher that is

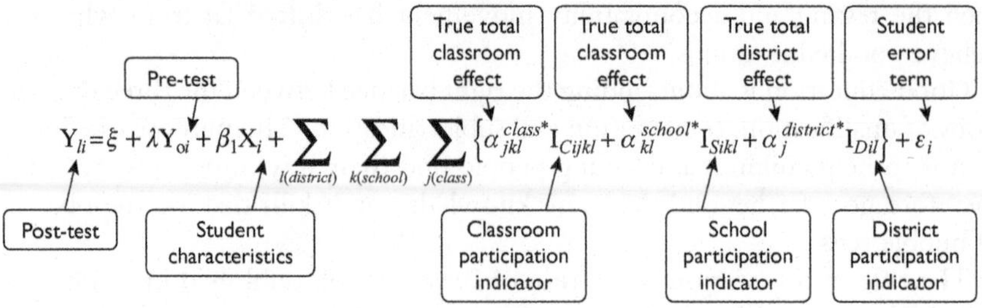

Figure 2.1 Calculation of a teacher's value-added score.

assumed to reliably measure his/her contribution to the growth of his/her students, the 'value added'. These numbers are used to rank teachers and schools and determine who 'excels' and who 'fails'.

Value added is a concept originating from economics and econometrics. Prominent economists (e.g. Hanushek, 2009; Hanushek & Rivkin, 2010) strongly advocate value-added models as a means to enhance education. This immediately raises the first problem when the concept is applied to education. The underlying assumption – false, as we will argue later – is that there is a causal relationship between instruction by a teacher and growth of student achievement, i.e. the difference between 'input' and 'output'.

The calculation of a teacher's value-added score is mathematically complex and only comprehensible for those who are familiar with all the statistical details (see Figure 2.1).

This is a second problem with VAMs: they are completely non-transparent for those who are evaluated by this system, i.e. the teachers, the schools and the school districts. They have no way of knowing whether their value-added scores have been calculated correctly, which makes it hard for them to understand the decisions based on those scores, particularly if they are unfavourable. They will have to blindly accept that the termination of their jobs, or the closure of their schools, is a fair decision based on solid analyses.

How Good Are VAMs?

If teachers are to be held accountable for the progress of their students, it must be decided how much progress is enough for a given time interval. Since the targets set by policy makers are hardly backed by research evidence, they come down to little more than pure guesswork. Expectations about the rate and degree of improvement in some American states are very unrealistic (Koretz, 2008a). Unfortunately, policy makers, awed by the apparent 'objectivity' of value-added models, either do not bother, or are unable to critically evaluate the science behind these models. They naïvely trust the validity and reliability of VAMs and expect their voters to do the same. John Ewing (2011), in a critical analysis of the statistics behind VAMs, calls this 'mathematical intimidation'.

Reducing very complex processes to just a few simple numbers makes a politician look like a powerful decision maker.

Since VAMs are based on standardized tests that only sample a few subject areas (usually mathematics and reading/language arts, which account for no more than 20% of all subjects), teachers of other subjects – science, humanities, arts and physical education – are unfairly accounted for results they have no part in.

VAMs are based on a number of assumptions that we will discuss here.

The first and most important assumption that underlies all VAMs is that teachers are the most important factors influencing students' learning and achievement. Yet, abundant research evidence (ASA, 2014) indicates that only about 1–14% of the educational outcome can be attributed to schools. Within schools, the contribution by teachers – the teacher effect – may be strong, but there are still other factors, such as class size, teaching resources, school budgets and the like, that operate alongside. The remaining 86–99% out-of-school factors are outside the control of teachers and schools. According to the Coleman Study 'Equality of Educational Opportunity' (Coleman et al., 1966), they are, first of all, those correlated to socio-economic background, including things like parents' attitudes towards education; domestic stability and support; access to books, resources and technologies in the household; quality of healthcare and food; exposure to arts, culture and travel, etc. Other out-of-school factors are student motivation, emotional or learning disabilities, second-language proficiency and cultural backgrounds.

Washington Post's Zachary A. Goldfarb (2014) had a good look at the 2014 SAT scores. The SAT is a standardized test widely used for college admissions in the United States. Goldfarb found a strong correlation between family income and student SAT scores. Students from educated families also tend to do better, as do students from white or Asian backgrounds compared to other ethnic groups. Socio-economic background is the one dominating factor determining a child's success in education in all standardized tests, not just SAT. So, the good news is, standardized tests do a good job at mapping socio-economic status, but there are easier, and cheaper, ways to do that.

Every teacher knows that it is far easier to teach homogeneous classes with students from wealthy families and parents with an academic background, in a school with the latest high-tech teaching materials, than to teach classes with students from many cultural backgrounds, from poor migrant families, with sometimes illiterate parents who only speak their mother language, in a school that is lacking even the most basic teaching resources. It is reasonable to assume that the teachers in both cases are, on average, equally effective – although we secretly believe that any teacher who survives many years under the most unfavourable conditions probably is a better teacher than those who can do their job in almost leisurely circumstances.

Therefore, if VAMs truly and completely corrected for socio-economic background and other out-of-school factors (which they do not), we would only see marginal differences between schools and teachers. But then, the whole rationale for the VAM exercise, for identifying 'good' and 'bad' teachers and schools, and removing the 'bad apples', would disappear.

The second assumption underlying the application of VAMs is that good teachers will be good regardless of the context. Research evidence (ASA, 2014) indicates that the teacher effect (1–14%) is not strong enough to overcome the influence of out-of-school factors, which account for 86–99% of the variance in test scores. Teachers are only a small influence on student achievement, especially when student achievement is defined and measured by large-scale standardized achievement tests that measure a very small sample of the curriculum (which is almost always the case).

Teachers do matter, however. Just remember again our old teachers. Yet their influence on our academic lives amounted to only 1–14%, if defined by student achievement on standardized tests. Their most important impact, in fact, was the unmeasurable influence on our lives that helped us become who we are today. Still, even that influence is dwarfed by out-of-school influences like the ones we discussed before and including interactions with parents, siblings, other relatives and friends.

For purposes of accountability, teacher effects are grossly exaggerated. Because it is believed that teachers matter so much, it makes sense to hold them accountable for everything that is wrong in education, such as low PISA ranking or the achievement gap. Without VAMs it would be impossible to objectively identify effective and ineffective teachers and to make appropriate policy decisions.

The third assumption exposes an interesting paradox. While on the one hand teachers are identified as the most important influence on students' achievement, on the other hand, teachers are often (and not just in America) depicted as lazy, unqualified and spoiled (*viz.* long summer holidays), and as hindering educational progress. This is the case when many newspapers publish value-added scores of schools and teachers, publicly naming, blaming and shaming the supposedly bad teachers. The rationale behind this is that if we remove the bottom 5–10%, the worst teachers, the quality of our education systems will improve dramatically and will bring them to the very top of the worldwide PISA race (Hanushek, 2009). First of all, this raises the question, how long do we need to continue removing these 5–10%? Until there is only one 'Superman' (or Superwoman) teacher left? But the main issue is that the bottom 5–10% is neither easily identified, nor consistent from one year to the next.

Gary Rubinstein (2012) tested the assumption of reliability and consistency using VAM data on 18,000 New York City teachers. He started from three simple assumptions with which most people will agree:

1. A teacher's quality does not change by a huge amount in one year.
2. Teachers generally improve each year.
3. A teacher in her second year is way better than that teacher was in her first year.

Even if we doubt the first two, nobody in their right mind will disagree about the last. As Rubinstein puts it:

> Anyone who taught will admit that they managed to teach way more and way better in their second year. Without expending so much time and energy on classroom management, and also by not having to make all lesson plans from scratch, second year teachers are significantly better than they were in their first year.

This is not what the VAMs show us. Gary Rubinstein selected data on 707 teachers who were first-year teachers in 2008–2009 and who stayed for a second year in 2009–2010. It appeared that many teachers who scored high in their first year, scored low in their second year. The reverse also holds. Many teachers who scored low in their first year appeared to have improved in their second year. In fact, Rubinstein demonstrated that, contrary to our everyday experience that the vast majority of starting teachers do improve, just 52% of the teachers were better in their second year. In other words, here and elsewhere VAM data show that there is a 50–50 chance of improvement.

It does not get better in any of Rubinstein's other analyses of the data. Teachers' scores jump up and down from year to year across all of the VAM statistics. The whole expensive VAM operation, including high-stakes decisions impacting the lives of dedicated teachers, simply is no better than flipping a coin.

The problem with the assumption of causality is that there is no simple cause-and-effect relationship between what a teacher does and the achievement of his or her students. One reason is the out-of-school factors, accounting for 86–99% of the test results. The other reason is that VAMs are designed to only measure changes in student achievement over time but *not* to attribute this growth to some cause (i.e. teacher, administrator, school, district, state, or programme quality). Therefore, VAMs are unfit for formative assessment, i.e. to help improve education, despite all the claims by their proponents.

As we have seen, there is a growing amount of good empirical evidence that puts all current VAMs into serious question. (For details and references, see Amrein-Beardsley, 2014). In summary, VAMs are:

1. **Unreliable**, e.g. a teacher classified as adding value in one year has 25–50% chance of being classified as subtracting value the next year
2. **Invalid**, e.g. there is limited evidence that teachers who post high value-added scores are effective using at least one other correlated criterion
3. **Biased**, e.g. teachers of certain students who are not randomly assigned to classrooms have more difficulties demonstrating growth
4. **Unfair**, e.g. only teachers of mathematics and language arts with pre- and post-test data in certain grade levels are being held accountable

5. **Fraught with measurement errors** negating their summative uses, e.g. inordinate amounts of missing data, variables that cannot be controlled, measurement errors caused by non-traditional, non-isolated, non-insular and 'non-egg-crate' classrooms
6. **Inappropriate for formative use** given their non-transparency, e.g. teachers and administrators do not understand the models being used to evaluate them, and of limited instructional value, e.g. data estimates are difficult to understand or use for instructional decision making. Accordingly, they are being
7. **Used inappropriately to make consequential decisions**, e.g. teacher termination, merit pay, while their
8. **Unintended consequences are going unrecognized**, e.g. teachers leaving/refusing assignment to grades in which value-added estimates matter most, teachers leaving teaching altogether out of discontent or to protest, teachers choosing not to teach students who are most likely to hinder growth, principals 'stacking' classes to make sure certain teachers can demonstrate 'value added' or growth or vice versa, etc.

It is ironic that the very economists and econometricians who have not been able to foresee the worldwide economic crisis, now try to convince us of the validity of their models of accountability. The weakness of economical models is their failure to take into account notoriously unpredictable and statistically unaccountable human factors as irrational behaviour, market disorder, fashion trends, greed, white collar crime, etc. (Kopcke, Little & Tootell, 2004). Similarly, many factors that determine the quality of education – and are, many would agree, crucial – cannot be forced into rigorous statistical models. Econometric models such as VAMs are, therefore, least likely to produce reliable assessments of teacher quality.

What Are the Alternatives?

> Any intelligent fool can make things bigger and more complex . . . It takes a touch of genius – and a lot of courage – to move in the opposite direction.
>
> Albert Einstein

Although we are neither geniuses nor overly courageous ourselves, we want to propose an alternative evaluation system that is both simpler and more reliable than the present VAMs. It has the added advantage that it is based on trust, is transparent and fair, combines quantitative data with human judgement, involves the teachers and schools to be evaluated, evaluates all aspects of education and produces data to support improvement.

All of the above does not imply that there are no bad teachers, or bad schools, and that we should not do anything about that. On the contrary, although the number of really bad teachers and schools probably is very small (which no one actually knows, as there is hardly any research providing such numbers), appropriate measures should be taken in those cases. The problem is not so much with what needs to be done, but on the basis of what criteria. Our alternative comprises two elements. One is a comprehensive curriculum that leaves plenty of freedom for schools and teachers to adapt to local needs and circumstances. The other is a teacher assessment system that is supported by research and has proven itself in other professions. One cannot exist without the other. Without a clear vision of the content and purpose of education, assessing its outcomes is rather pointless. On the other hand, once there is general (and democratic) agreement about a curriculum, it will be necessary to regularly verify whether the goals have been met.

Curriculum

A complete discussion of school curricula is beyond the scope of this chapter, so we will confine ourselves to a brief outline. For a more comprehensive discussion, we refer to the collection of papers 'Reinventing the Curriculum: New Trends in Curriculum Policy and Practice', edited by Mark Priestley and Gert Biesta (2013).

As we argued at the beginning of this chapter, before starting to test students and evaluate teachers, there must be agreement about what is good education. On the basis of the three dimensions, qualification, socialization and subjectification (Biesta, 2014), we may develop a 'New Curriculum' (Priestley & Biesta, 2013) that involves and interconnects all subjects and has great relevance for the students.

When thinking about a curriculum, we need to ask: should education be driven by economic considerations, or should it be driven by human concerns, such as democracy, social and ecological justice and peaceful human coexistence (Biesta & Priestley, 2013)? Another point is to what extent a new curriculum should be detailed by the national government, or left to schools and teachers in response to local needs. We need to convince policy makers that it is also in their interest to move away from the current trend of 'narrow aims, central control and measurable outcomes' and give teachers the freedom to develop their own 'New Curriculum'. Such a curriculum stands a better chance than many of the present test-driven national curricula to help children and young people to grow as responsible, autonomous, creative and critical human beings and participants in a democratic society.

Assessment

We propose that evaluation of teachers, schools and school districts occurs at the local level, as this is where out-of-school factors can be best evaluated. Our proposal follows practices that are common in other professions and at most universities.

It is supported by good scientific evidence (see Chapter 8 in Amrein-Beardsley, 2014), and is based on the use of multiple measures, such as supervisor and peer observations and feedback, student and parent feedback and teacher portfolios, in addition to test-based data. Colleagues can be elected to serve as professional members of educators' representative juries.

Teachers should be allowed to self-report and reflect on their work, so as to clarify the outcome of the other evaluation methods (interpretation of test results, supervisor and peer observations, student and parent evaluations, teacher portfolios). Each school and school district should have the right to use the resulting data in context, with the survey's strengths and weaknesses interpreted in context.

The Scottish education system offers a good example, combining a comprehensive curriculum, the 'Curriculum for Excellence' (the national curriculum for learners from age 3 to 18, which was implemented in 2010–2011), with strong and fair evaluation procedures. Scottish schools not only have freedom to develop their own curriculum, but also to evaluate their teachers according to their homegrown vision and set of education values and standards. Evaluation first and foremost serves as formative assessment, i.e. to improve the performance of teachers and their schools, as is clearly stated in the instructions by HM Inspectorate of Education 'How Good Is Our School? The Journey to Excellence: Part 3' (HMIE, 2007).

Policy makers may feel that they will lose control of quality of education. However, our proposal has several advantages for them as well. First, the bureaucratic load, and therefore cost, will be greatly reduced if teacher and school accountability is moved to the local level. Second, VAMs give an illusion of measurability and objectivity that leads to a false sense of control and a great risk of losing exactly those people who are most needed: the most expert, most caring and most responsible teachers, who give their students more than just high test scores. Third, our proposal gives teachers and their schools a strong impetus for improvement, as there is continuous feedback from the evaluation process.

It is our hope that policy makers will find the courage and a touch of genius to take the 'beautiful risk of education' and dare to have faith in the dedication, responsibility and professionalism of those who teach the next generation.

References and Further Reading

American Educational Research Association (AERA), American Psychological Association (APA) and National Council on Measurement in Education (NCME) (2014). *The Standards for Educational and Psychological Testing*. Washington, DC: American Educational Research Association.

Amrein-Beardsley, A. (2014). *Rethinking Value-Added Models in Education: Critical Perspectives on Tests and Assessment-Based Accountability*. New York: Routledge.

ASA (2014). ASA Statement on Using Value-Added Models for Educational Assessment. Alexandria, VA: American Statistical Association, p. 7.

Baker B. D., Oluwole J. O. and Green P. C. (2013). The legal consequences of mandating high stakes decisions based on low quality information: Teacher evaluation in the race-to-the-top era. *Education Policy Analysis Archives*, 21(5), 1–71. http://epaa.asu.edu/ojs/article/view/1298.

Baker, E., Barton, P. E., Haertel, E., Ladd, H. F., Linn, R. L., Ravitch, D., Rothstein, R., Shavelson, R. J. and Lorrie, S. A. (2010). Problems with the use of student test scores to evaluate teachers. *EPI Brief*, 278, 1–27.

Biesta, G. (2009). Good education in an age of measurement: On the need to reconnect with the question of purpose in education. *Educational Assessment, Evaluation and Accountability*, 21, 33–46.

Biesta, G. (2014). *The Beautiful Risk of Education*. Boulder, CO: Paradigm.

Biesta, G. J. J. (in press). Improving education through research? From effectiveness, causality and technology, to purpose, complexity and culture. *Policy Futures in Education*.

Biesta, G. J. J. and Priestley, M. (2013). A curriculum for the twenty-first century? In M. Priestley and G. J. J. Biesta (eds), *Reinventing the Curriculum: New Trends in Curriculum Policy and Practice*. London: Bloomsbury.

Bogotch, I., Mirón, L. and Biesta, G. (2007). 'Effective for what; effective for whom?' Two questions SESI should not ignore. In T. Townsend (ed.), *International Handbook of School Effectiveness and School Improvement*. Dordrecht/Boston: Springer, pp. 93–110.

Coleman, J. S., Campbell, E. Q., Hobson, C. J., McPartland, F., Mood, A. M., Weinfeld, F. D. et al. (1966). *Equality of Educational Opportunity (COLEMAN) Study (EEOS)*. Washington, DC: US Government Printing Office.

Croxford, L. and Cowie, M. (2008). How do schools in Scotland measure their own progress? *AERS Feedback to Schools*, 4, 1–4.

Ewing, J. (2011). Mathematical intimidation: Driven by the data. *Notices of the AMS*, 667–673.

Goldfarb, Z. A. (2014). These four charts show how the SAT favors rich, educated families. http://www.washingtonpost.com/blogs/wonkblog/wp/2014/03/05/these-four-charts-show-how-the-sat-favors-the-rich-educated-families/.

Goldstein, H. and Leckie, G. (2008). School league tables: What can they really tell us? *Significance*, 5, 67–69.

Goldstein, H., Rath, T., and Hill, N. (2000). The use of value added information in judging school performance. *Perspectives on Education Policy*. London: Institute of Education, p. 40.

Grossman, P., Cohen, J., Ronfeldt, M. and Brown, L. (2014). The test matters: The relationship between classroom observation scores and teacher value-added on multiple types of assessment. *Educational Researcher*, 43, 293–303.

Hanushek, E. A. (2009). Teacher deselection. *Creating a New Teaching Profession*, 168, 172–173.

Hanushek, E. A. and Rivkin, S. G. (2010). Using value-added measures of teacher quality. doi: 10.1037/e722242011-001.

HMIE (2007). *How Good Is Our School? The Journey to Excellence: Part 3*. Livingston, UK: HMIE.

Kopcke, R. W., Little, J. S. and Tootell, G. M. B. (2004). How humans behave: Implications for economics and economic policy. *New England Economic Review*, pp. 3–35

Koretz, D. (2008a). *Measuring Up: What Educational Testing Really Tells Us*. Cambridge, MA: Harvard University Press, p. 353.

Koretz, D. (2008b). A measured approach: Value-added models are a promising improvement, but no one measure can evaluate teacher performance. *American Educator*, Fall, 19–39. Retrieved from http://www.aft.org/newspubs/periodicals/ae/fall2008/.

Leckie, G. and Goldstein, H. (2011). A note on 'The Limitations of School League Tables to Inform School Choice'. *Journal of the Royal Statistical Society: Series A (Statistics in Society)*, 174, 833–836.

Leckie, G. and Goldstein, H. (2014). The limitations of using school league tables to inform school choice. *Journal of the Royal Statistical Society: Series A (Statistics in Society)*, 172, 835–851.

McCaffrey, D. F., Lockwood, J. R., Koretz, D., Louis, T. A. and Hamilton, L. (2004). Models for value-added modeling of teacher effects. *Journal of Educational and Behavioral Statistics*, 29(1), 67–101.

Pivovarova, M., Broatch, J. and Amrein-Beardsley, A. (2014) Chetty et al. on the American Statistical Association's recent position statement on value-added models (VAMs): Five points of contention. Teachers College Record, 1 August. http://www.tcrecord.org. ID Number: 17633.

Polikoff, M. S. (2014). Does the test matter? Evaluating teachers when tests differ in their sensitivity to instruction. In T. J. Kane, K. A. Kerr and R. C. Pianta (eds), *Designing Teacher Evaluation Systems: New Guidance from the Measures of Effective Teaching Project*. San Francisco, CA: Jossey-Bass, pp. 278–302.

Priestley, M. and Biesta, G. (eds) (2013). *Reinventing the Curriculum: New Trends in Curriculum Policy and Practice*. London: Bloomsbury.

Reeves, J. (2013). The successful learner: A progressive or an oppressive concept? In M. Priestley and G. Biesta (eds), *Reinventing the Curriculum: New Trends in Curriculum Policy and Practice*. London: Bloomsbury.

Rubinstein, G. (2012). Analyzing Released NYC Value-Added Data Parts 1–6. http://teachforus.org/. Retrieved from http://garyrubinstein.teachforus.org/2012/02/26/analyzing-released-nyc-value-added-data-part-1/.

Ryan, R. M. and Weinstein, N. (2009). Undermining quality teaching and learning: A self-determination theory perspective on high-stakes testing. *Theory and Research in Education*, 7, 224–233. doi:10.1177/1477878509104327.

Wiliam, D. (2011). *Embedded Formative Assessment*. Bloomington, IN: Solution Tree Press, p. 200.

Chapter 3

On Neoliberalism and How It Travels

Interview with Stephen Ball

René Kneyber

What is neoliberalism?

I want to make clear from the outset that I use the term neoliberalism with some trepidation. It is one of those terms that is used so widely and so loosely that it is in danger of becoming meaningless. What I mean by neoliberalism is expressed very nicely by sociologist and anthropologist Ronen Shamir. Neoliberalism, he says, 'is treated neither as a concrete economic doctrine nor as a definite set of political projects. Rather, I treat neoliberalism as a complex, often incoherent, unstable and even contradictory set of practices that are organized around a certain imagination of the "market" as a basis for the universalization of market-based social relations, with the corresponding penetration in almost every single aspect of our lives of the discourse and/or practice of commodification, capital-accumulation and profit-making.' I like this quote, because it recognizes both the material and the social relations involved.

In my mind, we can distinguish between two types of neoliberalism: neoliberalism with a big 'N', that focuses on the economization of social life and the creation of new opportunities for profit, and neoliberalism with a small 'n', through the reconfiguring of relationships between the governing and the governed, power and knowledge and sovereignty and territoriality. Neoliberalism is about both money and minds, and, as I usually argue, is a nexus of common interest between various forms of contemporary capital and the contemporary state.

Finally, we can also divide neoliberalism into three interrelated and uneven phases: these are 'proto' neoliberalism, 'roll-back' neoliberalism and 'roll-out' neoliberalism. 'Proto' neoliberalism is the intellectual project, shaped by Hayek and Friedman and other economic and libertarian theorists. It was meant as an 'alternative' to the Keynesian welfare state. 'Roll-back' neoliberalism refers to the discreditation, or, even active destruction, of Keynesian–welfarist and social–collectivist institutions. The third neoliberal wave, 'roll-out' neoliberalism, refers to the construction and consolidation of neoliberalized state forms, modes of governance, and regulatory relations in order to stabilize neoliberalism.

What is the impact of neoliberalism?

I think neoliberalism has had a profound impact on the relationships between people in the public domain. The 'policy technologies' of education reform work on individual practitioners, work groups and whole organizations to reconstitute social relations and forms of esteem and value. But it also reshapes sense of purpose and notions of excellence and good practice. They provide a new language, a new set of incentives and disciplines. Targets, accountability, competition and choice, leadership, entrepreneurism, performance-related pay and privatization articulate new ways of thinking about what we do, what we value and what our purposes are. They work together to render education a 'commodity' rather than a public good.

But also, in regard to your question, they provide a new set of roles, positions and identities within which what it means to be a teacher, what it means to be a student or learner, or a parent are all changed. They bring into play new roles and relationships, those of client/consumer and competitor, manager/managed, contractor, appraiser/inspector/monitor, and they exclude or marginalize previous roles, loyalties and subjectivities. They change what is important and valuable and necessary.

The language we've started to use under this new paradigm is important. New public management organizations are now 'peopled' by human resources that need to be managed. Learning is re-rendered as a 'cost-effective policy outcome'. Achievement is now a set of 'productivity targets', and I could go on. The scope and complexity of these reforms are breathtaking, extending from the ways in which teaching and learning is organized in classrooms, to new state modalities.

However, and I'd say *crucially*, it is a mis-recognition to see these reform processes as simply a strategy of devolution and deregulation. In the end they are processes of re-regulation. So they are not the abandonment by the state of its controls over public services, but the establishment of a new form of control, what we can call 'controlled decontrol', the use of devolution and autonomy as 'freedoms' set within the constraints and requirements of 'performance' and 'profitability'.

The manager is therefore a relatively new actor on the stage of public sector organizations. The term 'educational management' began to be used in the 1970s, and brought with it a set of methods, ideals and concepts from the private sector. The manager became an agent of change and a cipher for policy. From the 1980s we've seen a significant shift in education policy to devolve powers to managers to control their budgets, their workforce and internal decision making, in order to allow for innovative and creative ways to achieve new goals and purposes, and ultimately to explore alternatives to direct public provision and make service provision 'contestable and competitive'.

To return to your question on impact, together, management, the market and performativity have effects of various sorts on interpersonal and role relationships – both vertical and horizontal – within schools, colleges and universities. We can see increased emotional pressures and stress related to work; an increased pace and intensification of work; and changed social relationships. There is evidence of increased, sometimes even intentional, competition between teachers and departments. There is a concomitant decline in the sociability of school life. Professional relationships become increasingly individualized as opportunities for communities and professional discourse diminish and relationships are made amenable to and redefined as a 'contract' form or ones of 'contractual implication' within and between institutions. There is an increase in paperwork, systems maintenance and report production and the use of these to generate performative and comparative information systems; an increase in surveillance of teachers' work and outputs; a developing gap, in values, purpose and perspective, between senior staff, with their primary concern for balancing the budget, recruitment, public relations and impression management, and teaching staff, whose primary concern is with curriculum coverage, classroom control, students' needs and record keeping.

So what are the effects of this on the student level?

The flow and the reach of education policy is extensive and expanding. More and more of the life of students is affected by policy. What this flood of policies articulates is the production of a new kind of worker, citizen, learner, with dispositions and qualities. It doesn't stop at developing a sense of how to be, but also requisite feelings and morals. We can see this in the rise of the phrase 'lifelong learning', where every adult seems to have a personal learning plan, and every organization attempts to become a learning organization. In Bernstein's terms one might call this the outlines of a 'totally pedagogized society', wherein learning takes place infinitely. We are expected to make the most of ourselves – to be creative, innovative and entrepreneurial. Fact of the matter is that all of this is driven by the subordination of social policy to the demands of labour-market flexibility and/or employability and the perceived imperatives of international competitiveness through which and in the name of which 'the individual and "its" society become ever more interwoven'.

So what do you think of 'personalization'?

Personalization is relatively new on the education policy landscape. The extent to which the rhetoric of personalization is translated into actual practice remains to be seen, but I'm worried that it provides new opportunities for forms of differentiation and social advantage – which parents will without question pursue.

Yet it is also an instance where social and education policy are becoming focused on individualism. You could see it as a manifestation of a dissolving of traditional parameters, social and political institutions and their protective frameworks. Ultimately it leads to a situation, as Beck says, 'where people have been removed from class commitments and have to refer to themselves in planning their individual market biographies'. This tale of self-determination is of course an engine for particular inequalities. Those deemed unfit for these conditions of freedom are subject to interventions for remediation, and enforced activation. Within welfare social policies those interventions will be aimed at cultivating appropriate personal attributes – such as self-esteem, self-confidence, self-motivation, ambition and efficacy.

Despite its many problems, we've seen a huge rise in the uptake of neoliberal-looking reform on a global scale. How do these policies travel from one country to the other so rapidly?

The neoliberal discourse is continuously being adjusted, learning from other policies and reflexive on an institutional level. We need to take this into consideration. As soon as we take neoliberalism seriously it becomes clear that education policy analysis cannot be limited to the boundaries of a nation state. One could even argue that more and more states are losing the ability to control their education systems – something we can refer to as *denationalization*.

For instance, take the Clinton Global Initiative's annual meeting, which brings together heads of state, government and business leaders, scholars and NGO directors. They analyse pressing global issues, discuss solutions and create partnerships that enable them to create positive social change. Business philanthropy and business relationships such as these provide conduits for the international mobility of generic policy ideas, and means for the insinuation of particular forms of knowledge and types of relationship inside the state for representatives of business. These business philanthropies can act as national and international policy brokers.

Let me give you an example of this export of reform ideas. The Partnerships for Learning – Deutschland (PfL) was developed from a London pilot in 1996 initiated by the accountancy and consultancy firm KPMG, working with the Business in the Community (BitC) charity. Since its UK launch, 5,000 head teachers have been matched with a business partner. Over 1,200 companies throughout the United Kingdom have been involved. KPMG also participated in the extension of this programme in Germany, together with companies like Herlitz, Deutsche Bank and Siemens. It provides mentoring support to head teachers in Berlin, Brandenburg and Frankfurt. Since 2005, altogether 86 schools have registered for the German scheme.

Another example of the mobility of policy ideas via networks of business philanthropy is the Teach First programme. This originated in the USA as Teach for America and was imported into England as Teach First (TF); it is a teacher training and recruitment programme aimed at placing graduates from elite universities in socially disadvantaged schools for two years (although in England around 60% of participants now stay on beyond their initial two-year commitment). TF (which is supported by a mix of corporate and government funding) is now the largest single graduate recruiter from Oxford and Cambridge and it is being exported globally through Teach for All [see its website for funders] to countries including Germany, Estonia, Latvia, India,

Australia, Lebanon and Chile. TF brings new concepts and language into teacher education programmes and has received high-level political support in the US, UK and the importing countries.

Another example of international links and movements comes from a business philanthropy network established by the Private Equity Foundation (PEF), a UK-based private equity and venture-capital-funded charity, which now also operates in Germany through the Forum for Active Philanthropy and recently made its first 'investment' in the Hamburger Hauptschulmodell (HHM). This is a charity helping young people in the transition from school to work. PEF is looking to expand further and in France is currently working with the KPMG France Foundation 'to learn more about the charity landscape and identify organizations that we may be able to work with' [PEF website].

But one even more telling example is Cambridge Education, which works in partnership with universities, NGOs and other private companies and is involved in a range of projects with the Gates Foundation, and offers among its policy 'products' versions of the English school inspection model to other countries. Cambridge did hold a national contract for school inspection work in England. New York City, Thailand and Beijing have all 'bought' this model.

In my work, I've mapped out many of these examples. They go a long way to show that neoliberalism is neither natural nor inevitable; it is being done and planned and enacted. They also show that money and ideas join up in an organized way for advocacy activities to propose policies and to programme reform. This is part of what Peck and Tickell refer to as the 'deep process' of neoliberalization, and they argue that 'one of the more far-reaching effects of this deep process of neoliberalization has been the attempt to sequester key economic policy issues beyond the reach of explicit politicization'. So, for example, capital, through philanthropic foundations, invests in the work of think tanks and advocacy networks and policy entrepreneurs, with the intention and hope of exacting extensions to the commodification of the social, the creation of new markets and the deregulation of existing ones. As Connell put it: 'Neoliberals continue to attack public enterprise, bureaucrats, red tape, regulatory agencies, unions, cooperatives, welfare dependency, and other hangovers from what they see as a discredited past.' In relation to this, neoliberalism is well organized and very practical.

How can teachers resist this neoliberalism running rampant in so many education systems?

The resistance against flows of neoliberalism is quite different from our previous struggles, because it entails also resisting our own practices. It is about confronting ourselves. If we follow the logic of critique, we find out that we are precisely the ones to be blamed. Resisting the dominant discourses implies that we must change our understanding of what it means to be a teacher. All of this involves constant and organized work on the self; that is, as Foucault said, the 'establishment of a certain objectivity, the development of a politics and a government of the self, and an elaboration of an ethics and practice in regard to oneself'.

Over the years I've received many emails from teachers, email exchanges about the effects of neoliberalism on their work that were initiated by teachers. The emails are, as I'd like to see it, a part of the process of struggle against, of critique, of making things intolerable, of 'unsettling' and the struggle to be different. In line with Foucault I would say that we can think about resistance and freedom without having to rely on the mobilization of grand narratives, or simple normativities. We simply have to have the courage to refuse the mundane, in turning away from excellence, in unsettling truths. It is clear that a possibility for such lies in relations with others who share the same discomforts. These others might not be available in the school or in the staffroom, but they may be within everyday social relations, union meetings, on Twitter, Facebook or on blogs. The point is that these commonalities are not established from a priori political positions, but through work on and over and against practices and on what it means to be a teacher, what it means to be educated, and what it means to be revocable.

Stephen Ball is Karl Mannheim Professor of Sociology of Education, Institute of Education, University of London. His areas of interest are education policy analysis and social theory, such as the Global Education Reform Movement. He brings to bear on these issues the tools and concepts of 'policy sociology' and in particular the methods of Michel Foucault and Pierre Bourdieu. He has published a number of books, including The Education Debate *and the noteworthy* Global Education Inc.: New Policy Networks and the Neoliberal Imagery.

Vignette I

Changing Education in Action

Cambodia: The Embattled Teacher

William C. Brehm

Botum Chenda is a lower secondary school science teacher in Preah Go, a semi-rural town in northwestern Cambodia.[1] She has been teaching grades seven, eight, and nine since 2007. During my time shadowing and interviewing Chenda in 2014, I discovered the complex reality of teachers as they navigate an education system marked by hidden privatization. This is what I learned.

Privatization of public education in Cambodia manifests primarily in the form of private supplementary tutoring (called *rien kuo thoeumda*), which augments mainstream schooling in terms of curricular content and teacher salary. Chenda is a mainstream schoolteacher who provides fee-based private tutoring to her own students after school hours inside public school classrooms. Although the spaces appear similar on the surface – the teacher, students, and classrooms are the same – Chenda uses different pedagogies in the two spaces. Whereas she uses teacher-centered pedagogies mainly in the form of lectures in mainstream school, she uses student-centered pedagogies by focusing on example problems (called *Lomhat*) in private tutoring.

Private tutoring gives Chenda additional time to cover the national curriculum by focusing on *Lomhat*. Chenda explained to me that chemistry is only taught two hours each week, which is not enough time to teach quality lessons. Oftentimes she has to rush through the *Lomhat* in government textbooks during mainstream school in order to complete the curriculum on time. Other times she creates her own *Lomhat* as a supplement to the textbooks, but is not allowed to use them in mainstream school.

In addition to extra teaching time, private tutoring provides Chenda supplemental income from students who pay fees. Chenda earns 528,000 Riel (US$132) per month as a mainstream schoolteacher and approximately 800,000 Riel (US$200) per month from private tutoring fees. Without the extra income from private tutoring, Chenda would have to find a second job, most likely unrelated to teaching, in order to earn a living wage.

Private tutoring is considered hidden because educational actors do not 'officially' recognize it as a (different) system. Government officials do not regulate private tutoring, because they see it as a teacher's business and therefore outside of mainstream school policy. In this view, privatization is 'hidden' because it is not considered part of the mainstream school system. Students, parents, and teachers, meanwhile, do not recognize private tutoring as different from, or separate to mainstream schooling, because they believe it is a necessary part of the education system. Privatization in this view is 'hidden' because it is considered a normal part of the schooling system. These opposite ways of understanding private tutoring create an educational system that is partly based on free-market principles: students can choose to attend private tutoring or not and teachers decide what and how to teach during the extra classes.

As a hidden system operating in a free market, private tutoring contributes to social inequality, and teachers are often blamed for the consequences. Students who cannot pay the private tutoring fees are necessarily excluded from a space of education deemed necessary by parents and teachers for quality education. The excluded students receive less educational instruction than those students who can pay. In some cases, government officials and parents blame teachers for giving out examination answers during private tutoring as a way to financially profit from the system. These teachers are believed to be corrupting the education system by selling examination answers and scores.

In Chenda's opinion, the social inequalities from private tutoring arise because of the structural defects of the public education system, not because of unethical teachers. Private tutoring is only necessary, she believes, because mainstream schooling is too short, the curriculum too long, and the salaries too low. Private tutoring, in turn, remedies these system-wide deficiencies by providing more time for student learning and additional money for underpaid teachers. Overall, Chenda understands the social dangers posed by private tutoring, but believes, for the most part, the positives outweigh the negatives.

In response to the negative consequences, Chenda has implemented a de facto system of redistribution. She allows students to pay what they can for tutoring classes, offering children from poor families the chance to attend extra classes for free. In effect, she has created a system of equitable community financing whereby families with disposable income pay for the tutoring of other students. This payment system allows Chenda to increase her salary while also providing most students additional instruction time. Although this system does not reach all students, it does reduce some of the inequality arising from a system of hidden privatization.

In addition, Chenda recognizes that some teachers provide examination answers during private tutoring in order to manufacture student demand. Nevertheless, she believes this is the exception, not the rule. Most teachers do not participate in educational corruption. When I directly asked her about providing examination answers in private tutoring, she responded by saying, 'Teachers will always help their students because if lots of students fail the exam, it's the teacher's fault. But the teachers don't usually tell everything on the exam; they just tell some points for students to learn.'

Chenda highlights the complexity of private tutoring as a hidden but necessary space of mainstream schooling. Arising from an under-funded educational system, private tutoring is an area where students and teachers work together to overcome the restraints of mainstream schooling. The additional learning time provided by private tutoring increases the quality of education for students and gives a living wage to teachers. Like most teachers, Chenda hopes the public education system will develop so that private tutoring is not needed. Until that time comes, however, Chenda will do whatever it takes to ensure her students receive a quality education.

William C. Brehm is a doctoral candidate in the faculty of education at the University of Hong Kong. His dissertation research uses network spatial theory to understand educational privatization in Cambodia. Previously, he worked with This Life Cambodia, Digital Divide Data, Open Society Foundations, Paññāsāstra University of Cambodia, *European Education: Issues and Studies*, and Lehigh University. In September 2015, he will commence a Japan Society for the Promotion of Science post-doctoral fellowship at the University of Tokyo. He can be reached at will.brehm@gmail.com.

Note

1 In order to protect Chenda's identity, I have used pseudonyms for her name and for the town where she works.

Chapter 4

The Effects of Accountability

A Case Study from Indonesia

Art Broekman

This chapter was originally published as Broekman, A. (2013). "The rationale and effects of accountability policies on the work and motivation of teachers: Evidence from Indonesia." In A. Verger, H.K. Altinyelken & M. de Koning (eds), *Global Managerial Education Reforms and Teachers: Emerging Policies, Controversies and Issues in Developing Contexts* (pp. 19–36). Brussels: Education International.

Introduction

In the last decades, countries across the world feel the need to expand and improve their education system in order to become more economically competitive. In this context, teachers are placed in the 'policy spotlight', because most governments believe that improving the quality of teachers is essential for competitiveness (Tatto, 2006). This has led to numerous policies that mainly consist of developing a quality assurance framework, in which the obligations of teachers and other education standards are detailed to ensure that schools and teachers meet certain goals (Vongalis-Macrow, 2007). Recent developments in Indonesia demonstrate that policy makers in this country have joined this global tendency where setting standards, monitoring and appraising teachers, and forging closer links between performance and reward are considered as effective ways to increase the quality, motivation and accountability of teachers. Unsurprisingly, this has several implications for the work of teachers.

This chapter focuses on the global trend to enhance teacher accountability and explores the consequences of some new 'accountability policies' on teachers' work in Indonesia. The chapter is mainly based on empirical data, collected during fieldwork in Java (Indonesia) in spring 2010. Semi-structured interviews with 16 teachers, 12 head teachers and 19 other educational stakeholders (e.g. policy makers, consultants) were held to explore the views and opinions about teacher motivation and accountability. Additionally, a questionnaire was distributed among approximately 335 teachers in urban schools in Jakarta and rural schools in the district of Yogyakarta.

In the first section, the global 'accountability movement' will be explained.

Subsequently, in the second section, the Indonesian situation concerning accountability will be addressed. Special attention will be given to some recent policy initiatives developed under the *Better Education through Reformed Management and Universal Teacher Upgrading* (BERMUTU) project. In the third section, the policy process for the adoption and development of these policies will be explained. Finally, in the fourth section, initial reactions and reflections concerning the implementation of these policies will be given. In the conclusion, some critical comments and questions will be raised to illustrate the potential shortcomings and risks of the policy choices made by Indonesian policy makers concerning accountability. It is argued that the policies might not reflect an appropriate understanding of the factors that motivate and demotivate Indonesian teachers.

Making Teachers More Accountable: A Global Trend

The desire to hold schools and teachers more accountable is not new, as this aspiration surfaced in most developed countries in the 1960s. However, the 'New Right', during the mid- to late 1980s, gave new energy to this aspiration in some core developed countries (including Australia, New Zealand and the United Kingdom). From this ideological perspective, it was assumed that greater accountability would lead to a better correspondence between public goals and the objectives of schools. It was also believed that it would improve the performance of schools, typically defined and measured by traditional achievement criteria (Leithwood & Earl, 2000). Securing compliance with globally determined standards of quality in teacher learning and practice became another argument to create or reinforce accountability measures (Tatto, 2007).

A main feature of this *'new accountability'* (Tatto, 2007, p. 8) is the introduction of market principles in school systems. West et al. (2011) illustrate how these market principles have gained significant influence on accountability structures within the education system in England. They identify seven types of accountability, which are present in school-based education, and argue that hierarchical and market accountability have become the dominant accountability regimes in English schools. This, in turn, has led to a focus on performance data and examination results. As a consequence, other types of accountability that involve debating and questioning, such as 'participative accountability', are pushed into the background.

The new accountability is part of what some call the 'Global Education Reform Movement', because the values and assumptions of the accountability movement of the 1980s have spread out all over the world through more intensive dynamics of global educational borrowing and lending (Sahlberg, 2006, p. 264). In such dynamics, governments emulate the educational policies and practices of the more successful countries or adopt reforms legitimated by international organisations including the World Bank and the Organisation for Economic Co-operation and Development (OECD) in order to minimise the uncertainties that exist about the outcomes of education reforms (Tatto, 2006). A recent publication of the World Bank, called *Making Schools Work: New Evidence on Accountability Reforms*, is illustrative in this respect. The report includes a review of recent global experiences with two types of policies that are thought to make teachers more accountable for results: contract tenure reforms and pay-for-performance reforms. The authors synthesise the experiences with these reforms in various countries and conclude that these reform experiences "permit a preliminary typology of examples that merit consideration by any education policy maker concerned with raising student learning" (Bruns et al., 2011, p. 200). Both the World Bank and OECD are very influential on the way countries think about their education systems and the policies they design in order to improve them. However, this does not necessarily mean these are the best policies to adopt in all type of contexts.

Leithwood and Earl (2000) provide a useful framework to discuss policy initiatives that try to make the teaching profession more accountable. They distinguish four different approaches to accountability. Each approach has certain assumptions about the amount of change required in schools, the nature of the change and how this change can be achieved. *Market competition* approaches are based on the assumption that increased competition for students among schools, for example by introducing a school voucher system, will lead to more accountability. The *decentralisation approach* focuses on failing teacher accountability to (higher) levels within the government. It is assumed that teachers are more responsive to local values and preferences of parents and the local community when the power to make decisions about curriculum, budget, and personnel is in the hands of the parents or the community. *The management approach* consists of the introduction of more rational administrative procedures to create more goal-oriented, efficient, and effective schools. A main consequence of this approach to accountability is that monitoring progress and financial incentives and rewards become more common in schools. Accountability strategies with a *professionalisation approach* assume that the contribution of professional practice in schools is essential to their outcomes. Solutions and improvements are sought in standardised professional practices (e.g. teachers' classroom instructional practices) and school-level decision-making in key decision areas such as budget and curriculum (Leithwood & Earl, 2000).

The implications of accountability measures on teachers' work are manifold. Teachers around the world are confronted with predetermined learning targets, intensive monitoring through standardised assessment and testing mechanisms, tightened external inspection to control the performance of teachers and schools and more performance-related compensation and other reward-sanction structures (Sahlberg, 2004). Other related consequences are the development of standards for recruiting and selecting new teachers and new systems of accreditation and certification (Tatto, 2007).

As will be seen, these developments have influenced teachers' labour in Indonesia as well.

The Case of Indonesia

For decades, the Indonesian education system was firmly centralised. This came to an end when Indonesia was severely hit by the Asian crisis at the end of the 1990s, forcing the government to initiate a series of large-scale reforms. In 1999, two decentralisation laws with an enormous impact on education made it possible for the central government to reduce its expenditure and give more responsibility to local governments and at household level. At that time, the country was also subjected to the policy prescriptions of the Washington Consensus. The World Bank advocated the devolution of responsibilities and the International Monetary Fund (IMF) conditioned the 'post-crisis rescue package' to the implementation of market deregulation and privatisation (Kristiansen & Pratikno, 2006).

The most recent legal framework in Indonesia for the development of education is Law N° 20, which was issued in 2003. On the basis of this law, the Indonesian government has implemented several reforms to change education practices at school level and to provide quality education. The reforms include, among other things, the implementation of school-based management, a school-level curriculum, school-based teacher professional development, teacher certification, international benchmarking, and national examinations (Firman & Tola, 2008).

In the last few years, Indonesian teachers have been the focus of policy reform. With more than three million teachers, Indonesia manages one of the largest teacher workforces in the world and it has to deal with a number of problems and challenges. High absence rates among primary-school teachers seem to be common (Chaudhury et al., 2006) and many teachers do not have the minimum qualifications required by the Ministry of National Education (Arze del Granado et al., 2007). Overall, the Indonesian government attributes the poor performance of Indonesian students in international student assessment tests to the poor quality of Indonesian teachers (Jalal et al., 2009). Therefore, massive reforms have been undertaken in recent years to try to improve the 'quality, welfare and performance' of Indonesian teachers. In particular, the 'Law on Teachers and Lecturers' (Law N° 14 in 2005, hereafter called Teachers' Law) and the 'Better Education through Reformed Management and Universal Teacher Upgrading' (BERMUTU) project have had a major impact on teachers.

The Teachers' Law

The Teachers' Law is designed "to provide a much-needed incentive for teachers to improve their qualifications and professional skills" (Jalal et al.,

2009, p. 17). The law determines minimum qualifications for teachers and outlines a new teacher certification process. Teachers need to have a minimum academic qualification of at least four years of post-secondary education and to obtain practical experience as a classroom teacher. Teachers also have to pass a certification examination that will test their skills in four competency domains (pedagogical, professional, personal and social) before becoming a certified teacher. Once teachers are certified, they will receive a professional allowance (equal to their base civil service salary), a smaller functional allowance, and a special allowance when working in areas where teachers are much needed (also equal to the base civil service salary). Overall, this means that teachers can see their salary doubled or tripled (Jalal et al., 2009). In return for this salary improvement, certified teachers are obligated to undertake professional development activities and they will need to be monitored more regularly.

The BERMUTU Project

The implementation of the Teachers' Law is assisted by the BERMUTU project. This central government project is partly funded by the World Bank with a loan (US$86 million) and a grant of the Dutch government (US$52 million). Three Directorates of the Ministry of National Education (MONE) are responsible for its implementation. The objective of BERMUTU is "to contribute to the improvement of the overall quality and performance of teachers through enhancing teachers' knowledge of subject matter and pedagogical skills in the classroom" (World Bank, 2007, p. 3). The project runs from 2007 to 2013 and consists of four components: 1) reforming university-based teacher education; 2) strengthening structures for teacher improvement at the local level; 3) reforming teacher accountability and incentives systems for performance appraisal and career advancement; and 4) improving programme coordination, monitoring and evaluation.

Both the Teachers' Law and BERMUTU fit perfectly with the global accountability movement. Typical elements of this movement are picked up by policy makers and find their way into the Indonesian education system. In particular, the third component of BERMUTU can be considered as a typical 'new accountability' policy. It aims at improving teacher performance and accountability by developing a new incentive system and a new instrument for performance appraisal. Or, in other words, the state wants to motivate teachers to perform better by altering their career and salary progression and the way teachers are assessed. A closer look to this policy initiative will be given in the next section.

The New System of Performance Appraisal

BERMUTU's third component on accountability and incentives tries to activate more directly what is legislated by the Teachers' Law. Its main objective is "to develop an integrated framework designed to sustain and continually enhance the quality and accountability of teachers after they are certified" (World Bank, 2007, p. 48). All the activities within the third component are coordinated and overseen by a taskforce of the Directorate General of Quality Improvement of Teachers and Education Personnel (PMPTK). In the process of designing policies, procedures and instruments, special attention is given to the career structure and career progression of Indonesian teachers. The career structure of teachers used to be the same as the civil service structure, but this will change because of the Teachers' Law. Another important element is that policy makers try to forge closer links between performance and reward.

In the new structure, there are four professional levels for teachers: *Guru Pertama* (Novice Teacher), *Guru Muda* (Junior Teacher), *Guru Madya* (Senior Teacher), and *Guru Utama* (Master Teacher). Each of these professional levels consists of several grades. In order to progress to the next grade, teachers are obligated to accumulate a certain amount of 'credit points' each year by participating in professional development activities. These credit points can be earned by attending seminars, writing an assignment that will be evaluated, participating in a workshop and so on. In addition, for each teacher profile there are standards that have to be met in order to progress to a certain level and thus to a higher salary scale. The achievement of such standards will be controlled through the assessment of individual teachers. The development of a system of performance appraisal is therefore an essential element of the third component. In addition, setting up a structure for *continuing professional development* (CPD) and dealing with underperforming teachers are important policy areas.

Performance Appraisal and Continuing Professional Development

In 2007, MONE defined 24 competency areas for public and private school teachers. The National Education Standards Agency (BSNP) did some further work on these competencies. In 2008, the agency published the sixth version of the 24 competencies, which were eventually reduced to 14 groups covering four areas: pedagogical, professional, social, and personal. In the second half of 2010, MONE piloted a new performance appraisal system, developed under BERMUTU, whereby teachers are assessed annually according to these competencies. In order to do this, the competencies are described as performance indicators that can be observed and monitored, and teachers are ranked on a five-point scale for each competency group.

This performance appraisal process consists of two different assessments: classroom observations and audits. The classroom-based activities are assessed by three annual observations. Teachers are observed twice at the beginning of the year to identify their strengths and weaknesses. Then there is a continuing professional development system in place, which will help teachers to improve in those areas where they are considered to be below standard. Each school should have a CPD coordinator who will help teachers to shape their CPD programme. The CPD coordinator can approach several sources, mainly the district's educational officer, to find out what can be made available. What is available within the school in terms of mentoring? What is available through the professional teacher working groups? What is available outside the school using additional funds? The coordinator and the teacher will then decide which activities the teacher will undertake. The third and final observation takes place at the end of the year, which will be the actual assessment. For those activities that cannot be observed in the classroom, teachers will be audited three times during the year and the score is averaged over the year.

The outcome of this performance appraisal will influence the amount of credit points that teachers earn during the year, and thus the speed of their career progression. This, in turn, will affect their salary. The 'best' performing teachers can multiply their earned credit points by 125 per cent, while 'under-performing' teachers see their credit points reduced by 75 per cent. Teachers are expected to spend a minimum of four years at each of the four professional levels, but if a teacher is appraised with 125 per cent each year, he/she can progress rather quickly. But if a teacher loses 75 per cent of the earned credit points, he/she can spend more than 10 years in the same grade. Therefore, the career progression and income of teachers is directly related to their performance appraisal.

Managing 'Underperforming' Teachers

At the moment, Indonesian teachers are considered to have 'a job for life', because they can only be dismissed for inappropriate behaviour. Teachers cannot be sanctioned for any professional deficiency. Underperforming teachers, mostly those who do not fulfil disciplinary conditions mandated by the government, can be transferred to another district. This, however, rarely happens. PMPTK is now proposing, through BERMUTU, a new system for managing underperforming teachers. This system is closely related to performance appraisal and CPD, as it should work together. The performance appraisal system will identify the proficiency level of teachers according to the legislated pedagogical, professional, personal and social competencies. If teachers are consistently underperforming on these domains, and do not take advantage of opportunities to develop, a disciplinary sanction should follow. If teachers are unable to improve or unwilling to improve, given a fair chance, then they should be taken out of the profession. At the time of research, the policies and instruments for managing underperforming teachers were not very well developed. The main reason for this is that the necessary legislation is lacking. A consultant, who is closely involved in the reform, presumes that this process will take a long time, because it is considered to be very contentious and in the vanguard of a very substantial social change. Besides, this approach to underperforming teachers requires adequate facilities and opportunities for teachers to improve their competencies. At this moment, these facilities and opportunities are often lacking.

Global Ideas in a Local Context?

It is not difficult to recognise the elements of the 'new accountability' global trend in the new policies developed under BERMUTU. To start with, increasing global economic competition seems to be the driving force behind the policy efforts. The higher-level objective, to which BERMUTU aims for, is "to increase Indonesia's productivity and its competitiveness in the global economy" (World Bank, 2007, p. 3). Moreover, international tests, like the Trends in International Mathematics and Science Study (TIMSS), are considered as important elements that motivate the Indonesian government to implement large-scale reforms such as the Teachers' Law and BERMUTU. The comments of an international consultant at the World Bank are illustrative:

> On the ranks of TIMSS, Indonesia is right down. And the worst thing of all is that Singapore is up ahead and so is Malaysia and they get a bit upset about that. They compare themselves very much with Malaysia, because Malaysia is like a sister or brother Muslim nation. So they are looking forward to the next TIMSS to see whether there have been improvements.

Furthermore, the designed instruments and their objectives show agreement with global tendencies. Indonesian policy makers appear to have a 'management-approach' to accountability. With the development of the new performance appraisal system, it seems that Indonesia is moving towards a situation where setting performance standards, monitoring progress and financial incentives and rewards are becoming more common in schools. Indonesian policy makers seem to believe that "if you measure teachers, using indicators that are not directly related to their classroom performance, then everything else will fall into place and teachers will perform as you want them to perform if you keep measuring them" (former international consultant at MONE). It seems that another perception among policy makers is that increasing teacher salaries will be a main motivator and that teachers can be motivated by creating hurdles that they need to jump before they can earn a higher salary. These developments and perceptions follow market rhetoric logic and can be linked to the new accountability movement as well.

Policy makers at MONE emphasised that BERMUTU is an Indonesian project, but the influence of international actors became visible during the research. There are, for instance, several international consultants who are hired by MONE and support the taskforce of PMPTK. They bring their experience and knowledge of 'international best practices' into the ministry.

Other policy borrowing mechanisms have been involved as well, such as study visits to Sri Lanka, England, Scotland, Australia, Malaysia and Singapore. These visits, attended by policy makers at MONE, were organised by the World Bank and one of the international consultants working for MONE. The purpose of the visits was to learn about in-service development of teachers in the visited countries. In this way, international organisations and consultants were able to steer the process of agenda setting and policy design, by introducing policy makers to certain ideas, concepts and strategies.

The World Bank is of particular interest in these terms, because it supports BERMUTU, not only at the ideational level, but also materially, through a loan. Clearly, the main ideas behind the third component reflect an approach that is in line with the current education agenda of this organisation. Economical and managerial rationales are central to the World Bank and accountability, management, promotion and career progression fit within such rationales. An international education development specialist explained the focus on these topics as follows:

> Many projects tend to neglect the teachers in terms of teaching and learning. Why? Well, part of the answer lies in the background of the people who design these projects. Quite often, they are economists or development specialists, particularly in finance and planning, but not teachers. So, in many cases, you don't have someone with a strong background in education or teaching. As a result, things are conceptualised as a problem in planning, finance, accountability or management.

Eventually, these themes find their way into the ministry, and policy makers pick up the views and ideas propagated by donor and lending agencies. For example, a former international consultant at the World Bank commented that:

> In the past, the World Bank did this basic education project and they often leveraged its loans. They said for example: "We lend you money to repair schools or to build primary schools, but the money has got to be managed by the local community in a transparent manner". This was an attempt by the Bank to introduce better and more transparent management procedures.

The same mechanisms are at work in the case of BERMUTU. In addition to providing funds, the World Bank officially has a supervising role: it makes sure that the activities and the process are on track to achieve the development objectives. The World Bank also makes recommendations and gives technical input when necessary. Several informants, however, give more weight and influence to the Bank. Recommendations are taken seriously, because the Indonesian government relies (at least partly) on the World Bank's funds and expertise of international best practices in the process of policymaking. An example shows that the World Bank is pushing its own ideas and visions. A former international consultant at MONE, for instance, stated that:

> More recently, I began to feel that the World Bank was beginning to have an impact again. They feel that we have neglected one aspect, which is promotion of teachers. Their view is when teachers become head teachers or a head of department. it is a form of promotion. Therefore it needs to be looked at in a way which will encourage these appointments to be merit-based. But I don't think that Indonesia is ready for that. I think that there are many other things that need to be sorted out first. The Bank has got this idea that schools will advertise posts and the school committee will interview candidates and make an appointment based on the results of the interviews, as they do in Australia. But, in Indonesia, it does not work like that. I know that they are not happy with the fact that we did not address this. I know that there is going to be an extension of the project and I guess this is something the Bank is going to address.

Finally, the World Bank is also considered as a 'complicating factor', because it is pushing for its financial timeframe. As a result, the project is characterised as a process of rushing to meet immediate deadlines and spending money. According to an international consultant at MONE, it often happens that this rush to spend money takes over and becomes the predominant factor in decision-making. This is a disadvantage because, without this pressure, things would have been developed in a more thoughtful way.

Some Initial Reactions and Reflections

In several countries, efforts to introduce performance-based systems have not been very successful. The main reason for this is that appraisal instruments are too complicated and that major changes in pay structures are absent. As a consequence, new appraisal systems are seen with scepticism by most teachers (Bennell & Akyeampong, 2007).

Therefore, it is interesting to look at the reactions of Indonesian teachers on the new policies developed under BERMUTU. Unfortunately, at the time of this research, the policies were not yet piloted or communicated to the teachers. This is in itself already an interesting fact, as BERMUTU started in 2007. However, it is possible to give some initial reactions and reflections on the policy efforts. In order to do this, Fullan (2001) provides a useful framework. Fullan argues that the implementation process is influenced by several factors divided in three categories: the characteristics of the policy itself (characteristics of change), the local context of the policy (local characteristics), and the context of the broader society (external factors).

The factors included in the characteristics of change are need, clarity, complexity and quality/practicality. This means that, in order to achieve a successful implementation, the policy (a) has to correspond with the priority needs of schools and teachers, (b) has goals and outcomes which are clear for teachers, (c) does not require a difficult and *complex* change of teachers and individuals responsible for implementation, and (d) should be considered by teachers to be of good *quality* and *practical* issues need to be covered. The four factors included in local characteristics are district, community, principal and teacher. Fullan argues that the implementation process will be more difficult if school districts and communities have had negative experiences with implementation processes in the past. Next to this, the attitude and role of principals is essential for a successful implementation as they manage the changes at the school level. Finally, the psychological state of teachers can make "him or her more or less predisposed toward considering and acting on improvements" (Fullan, 2001, p. 98). If teachers are open to changes in life, for example, they will be more likely to accept the new policy. External factors refer to the opinions of actors in the broader society, like the government and other stakeholders such as teacher unions. When the ideas of policy makers and teachers vary too much, the implementation process will be difficult (Fullan, 2001).

With Fullan's implementation theory in mind, there are several pitfalls to discern that may impede a successful implementation of the policies developed under BERMUTU. If these pitfalls are not addressed successfully, paradoxically, the implementation of the new performance appraisal system could act as a huge de-motivator for teachers, rather than a motivator.

Needs

In this study, teachers were asked about factors that will influence their motivation positively (see Figure 4.1). The results show that teachers consider their salary, their skills and competencies, and the opportunities to improve themselves as important determinants of their motivation. However, higher priority is given to the availability of teaching and learning resources, which are often lacking or inadequate in Indonesian schools. Indeed, 49 per cent of the respondents strongly agree with the statement: "I will work harder if the school conditions will be improved". The percentages are much lower for the statements, "I will work harder if the head teacher visits my classes more often" (14 per cent) and "I will work harder if I would be evaluated more often" (13 percent). Promotion opportunities are considered to be of less importance as well (20 per cent). The same conclusions can be drawn from the in-depth interviews. These findings indicate that the priority needs of teachers and the priorities of the policy makers do not match. While teachers especially need better school conditions and more teaching and learning facilities, the policies focus mainly on evaluation and promotion. The improvement of school facilities and learning materials are not foreseen in the reform, while they are considered by many teachers as crucial elements in improving education quality.

Teachers were asked to respond to the following statements:

S1. I will work harder if I get a higher salary.
S2. I will work harder if the head teacher visits my classes more often.
S3. I will work harder if I have more opportunities to upgrade my teaching skills.
S4. I will work harder if I will be evaluated more often.
S5. I will work harder if the school conditions (good study materials, adequate classroom conditions, etc.) will be improved.
S6. I will work harder if I have a better chance of promotion.

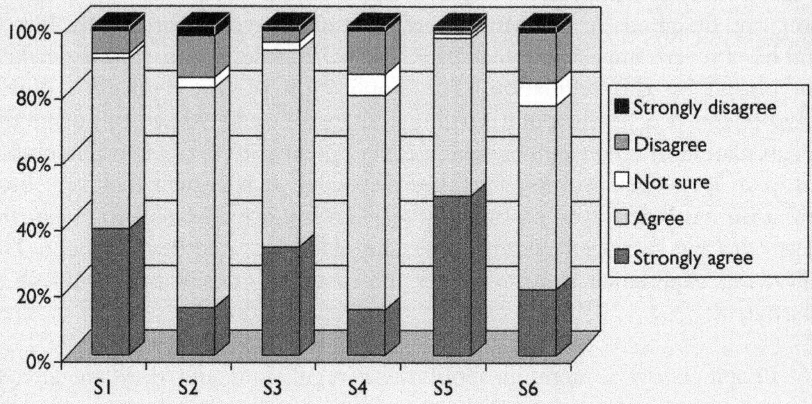

Figure 4.1 Teacher responses to statements concerning several motivational factors

Complexity

If we look at the complexity of the policies, some critical comments can be made as well. First of all, the danger exists that performance appraisal becomes proceduralised and bureaucratised. Within the Ministry and the schools, there is much resistance against an appraisal system where actual decisions concerning teachers are made by an individual who assesses whether a teacher is performing well or not. An international consultant from MONE commented that:

> Nobody wants to make a decision about things. They asked: "Can we just count indicators?" And we said: "Ok, we will try to make the system more procedural, but somewhere along the line you have to observe performance and assess it against a standard." But it is very strongly resisted. Teachers don't value a process whereby they have to think about something. They want it to be proceduralised. And I think that's the major risk with this whole system. That it just becomes a meaningless checklist.

Bureaucratisation is lurking, because the new procedures demand a lot of paperwork. The whole process starts with a self-evaluation, then teachers should make CPD plans and, finally, there is a formative appraisal. There has to be an audit trail, because an evaluation team within the district has to decide on the credit points and any promotion opportunities. On paper, it might seem feasible, but the success of this whole system depends upon whether the procedures and actual activities can be made realistic, practical, useful and acceptable enough to the users. Teachers might experience the additional paperwork and CPD activities, next to their teaching job, as a burden.

Even more pressing, however, is the credit point regulation. This regulation was designed by the Ministry of Administrative Reform (MENPAN) and has a severe impact on what BERMUTU can do, because policy makers are bound by this regulation. The implication of this regulation is that CPD becomes a 'credit point earning activity'. Teachers have to pursue the accumulation of credit points, which is very quantitative, rigid and hierarchical in order to get promoted to the next level. It is argued that very little attention has been given to the way teachers are actually performing in the classroom and that it effectively blocks any self-motivated development. The following experience from a former international consultant at MONE is illustrative:

> People know something about these regulations and they are already collecting credit points. To a certain extent, this also happened in the past, but it becomes more extreme now. If you attend an international seminar, for instance, you get more credit points than a national seminar. Last weekend, I was invited to be a speaker at an international seminar in a small town in West Java, organised by the teachers there. And they could say it was 'international' because I was there. I was the international element. And 250 teachers spent their Sunday listening to talks so that they get a certificate. Who knows whether they heard anything that has been said, or whether they were changed in any way by what was said? Only two people got an opportunity to ask questions, so it was completely unidirectional. This is happening all over the place. And BERMUTU made it worse.

Another concern related to the credit point system is the amount of credit points that can be earned with a certain activity. A national consultant working for MONE argued that the credit point system should be more proportional. The CPD activities, which are major tasks, yield relatively few points. This can de-motivate teachers, especially when these CPD activities are pushed by the government and not undertaken because of an intrinsic desire to develop.

The teaching working groups, which managed themselves quite successfully in the past, are now also bureaucratised from the top down. The modules, which teachers have to use whether they need them or not, will be designed in the centre. And each teaching working group has to have a constitution and a bank account that has to be audited every year. It is too early to tell if this will influence the success of these working groups, but there are concerns that, if teachers are not allowed to decide for themselves what the working groups will do, they will lose their spontaneity and their ability to respond to local needs. Because of this quantitative and top-down character of the policies, some people even perceive BERMUTU as "a wonderful opportunity that has been lost" (a former international consultant, MONE).

In Indonesia, most teachers consider a motivated teacher as someone who is disciplined and comes to school on time. Professional indicators, such as good class management, and creative and effective teaching were mentioned less by the teachers to indicate motivated teachers. This is understandable since Indonesian teachers have never been assessed on and adequately trained in their qualities and competencies before. Therefore, the new system will mean a major shift for teachers in their thinking about performance and motivation, or even about their profession. This shift, however, can only be achieved if there is a shift in thinking about the process of teaching and learning and the profession as a whole among all involved stakeholders (policy makers, government officials, head teachers, etc.). In this light, it is essential that the government values teachers primarily for their commitment to be excellent and involved educators, instead of for their willingness to serve the government. It is important that, during this complex change, teachers get the support and encouragement they need through CPD and adequate teacher training. Policy makers should not underestimate this. At this moment, the CPD structures and training opportunities for teachers are not well developed and definitely need more attention.

Quality and Practicality

Some main assumptions behind the policies are that teachers can be motivated by evaluating them more often, by rewarding better-performing teachers (by paying them a higher salary), and by punishing poor performing teachers (by postponing promotion opportunities). Based on the questionnaire, it seems that Indonesian teachers support these assumptions in some way. Of all teachers, 89 per cent indicated that regular teacher evaluation will motivate them to perform better and 94 per cent indicated that paying a higher salary to better-performing teachers is a good policy to motivate teachers. The opinions are more divided when it comes to punishing poor performing teacher (by postponing promotion opportunities): 67 per cent of the respondents think this is a good policy to motivate teachers.

However, the current study also shows that regular classroom observation by the principal is not considered by many teachers as a good method to motivate them and provide feedback. Therefore, it is important to know how teachers perceive classroom observations, because these observations can only be effective if teachers consider them as a helpful instrument to develop their skills and achieve personal growth. In order to develop any commitment among teachers to the objectives of the new appraisal system, it is important that teachers have the confidence that these observations and assessments are subject to accurate and objective measurement, and they will be supported and not punished on the basis thereof. Otherwise, it can become a source of stress instead of a moment of reflection. In this respect, it is also important that principals are committed and enabled to constructively observe classroom practice and to fulfil a supportive function. More and better training for principals in this respect is essential.

Related to this issue is the hierarchical character of Indonesian society. The Javanese political elite can be considered as "the most status conscious and hierarchically minded in the world" (Liddle, 1989, cited in Boyle, 1998, p. 99). This is reflected in the orderly structure of power and authority within the government and the civil service. In daily practice, this means that each government official or civil servant is either the superior or the inferior of another (Boyle, 1998). Therefore, it should be taken into account that only a superior would have the authority to conduct the performance appraisal. At the time of research, policy makers believed that teachers should be trained as evaluators because it is unmanageable for supervisors and head teachers to do all the observations and assessments themselves. However, there are doubts about whether a teacher, trained as an evaluator, will have enough authority to do the assessments. Of all questioned teachers, a majority (92 per cent) indicated that the evaluation should be done by the head teacher. An Indonesian educational specialist even argued that assessments can only be successful and fair if teachers are assessed by someone who is external and impartial. A former international consultant at the World Bank suggested that "otherwise it will be corrupted, because that is the culture here".

Another important matter is the availability of resources to offer teachers enough support in their professional development process. Improving the performance of teachers by assessing *what they need to become better teachers* will only be effective if teachers have access to several sources and facilities once their weaknesses are identified. If not, the performance appraisal will be an isolated element and it will lose its value. As a consequence, teachers might not take the annual appraisal seriously. This issue is extremely relevant in rural and remote areas, where resources and facilities are limited or even lacking. Good CPD structures should be in place, before the performance appraisal becomes an obligated activity within the teaching profession.

External Factors

External factors might affect the implementation process as well, because resistance to the policies and reforms are to be expected. MONE is aware about the potential opposition from the teacher unions, because the management of underperforming teachers is very controversial and requires some substantial changes. An international consultant at MONE argued that:

> My understanding of what happened in the past is that the teachers' union is large, very knowledgeable and therefore politically very powerful. And it won't like this for its members, the fact that teachers are going to be held accountable for their professional behaviour. Besides, this will be the first group of people, who for the first time will be told, "You don't have a job for life, your job depends on your ability to do the job and if you don't do it, you are not going to stay". The other parts of the civil service will probably see that if it applies to 70 per cent of the civil service, then the other 30 per cent will follow sooner or later. They won't like it either.

The reason why the teacher unions might resist the new performance appraisal system is probably more nuanced than this quote implicates. It is not that they necessarily oppose any attempt to hold teachers more accountable for their professional behaviour: the unions and their members are just as concerned with the quality of teachers as the government. Gunter Ismail, the president of the Indonesian Teachers Associations Federation (FSGI), argues that, "Promotions for teachers should be based on their teaching, personality, social behaviour and professional competency" (*Jakarta Post*, 6 October, 2011).

The resistance of teachers and their unions comes mainly from concerns about workload, poor CPD structures and the fairness of the process. In October 2011, the FSGI called on the government to review its teacher policies. The union argues that the current policies are not oriented on quality improvement, but reflect a fixation on quantity (*Kompas*, 5 October, 2011). Recently, the FSGI has also rejected a ministerial decree requiring publication or scientific work from teachers to qualify for promotion and argued instead that promotion should be based on the skills and competencies of teachers. In their view, the policy is also unrealistic and discriminatory against teachers. FSGI general secretary Retno Listyarti explains:

> We understand that the policy aims to improve teachers' quality. But how can we be required to publish papers or scientific work while we must also handle up to 14 classes?
>
> (*Jakarta Post*, 6 October, 2011)

According to the Indonesian Teachers Association (PGRI) chairman Sulistyo, the government has not given its best in improving teachers' working conditions or providing protection, appreciation, education and sustainable training for teachers (*Kompas*, 5 October, 2011). The position of the unions is understandable: holding teachers accountable for their professional behaviour is risky, particularly when the measurement of their 'performance' is not always under their control, linked to financial reward and when the mechanisms for such evaluations are based on questionable methods.

Concluding Remarks

Indonesian policy makers have joined a global tendency through which setting standards, monitoring and appraising teachers, and forging closer links between performance and reward are considered as effective ways to increase the quality, motivation and accountability of teachers. It can be questioned, however, if these policies reflect an appropriate understanding of the motivators and de-motivators among Indonesian teachers. Some critical comments can be made to illustrate the shortcomings and potential risks of the path chosen by Indonesian policy makers in this respect.

First of all, policy makers tend to neglect the importance of adequate facilities for the motivation of teachers. Indonesian teachers are convinced that better classroom conditions and the availability of more and better teaching and learning materials will have a big influence on their job satisfaction and motivation. Many teachers in Indonesia do not have the necessary tools and materials to do the job well. This impedes the quality of education and can give teachers a feeling of being incompetent. This in turn can be demoralising and de-motivating. Therefore, the facilities should be in place, before teachers can be motivated by actively using motivators like 'growth' and 'job advancement'. It is useless to create committed and competent teachers, without giving them the right tools. The same applies to good CPD structures. If these are not in place, the performance appraisal will lose its value. This issue is extremely relevant in rural and remote areas, where resources and facilities are limited or even lacking.

Second, policy makers need to bear in mind that money does not work as a motivator in a straight-forward way. If teachers are not paid enough, they might not be sufficiently motivated. But once teachers are satisfied with their salary, money might lose its value as a main motivator. Indonesian policy makers give the impression that they mostly believe in the idea of 'carrots and sticks'. Teachers are obligated to undertake activities to earn credit points in order to get promoted to a higher salary scale. This top-down and quantitative character of the performance appraisal has a potential risk, as other important motivational factors are neglected. Research shows that autonomy, mastery and purpose lead to better performance and personal satisfaction instead (Fisher, 1978; Lock, Cartledge & Knerr, 1970; Rainey, 2001; Ryan, 1982). Indonesian policy makers must recognise that the profit motive (earning a higher salary) gets unmoored from the autonomy, mastery and purpose motive when teachers undertake continuous professional development activities reluctantly. In this situation, there is no question of self-motivated development and, consequently, it will not be very effective or it will even demoralise teachers. Therefore, policy makers should take the sense of ownership and professional autonomy among Indonesian teachers as a starting point when designing new policies to increase the motivation and accountability of teachers. Listening to their advice, using their expertise and giving them freedom and scope to take initiative would be a good start to engage and motivate teachers.

Third, it appears that Indonesian teachers and policy makers have a different understanding of the concept of 'motivation'. This difference arises from two different paradigms that are dominant within both groups. It can be argued that Indonesian teachers perceive motivation and performance from a 'discipline' paradigm, due to the institutional cultures within the education system. Policy makers are starting to approach motivation and performance from a 'professionalism' paradigm. If teachers continue to approach their job from the discipline paradigm, the danger exists that there will not be much understanding for the ideas and objectives of the new policies. This, in turn, means the policies might not achieve the desired results or will have even a demoralising and de-motivating effect on teachers. Teachers, for instance, might experience the new appraisal system and observations by the head teacher as a source of stress instead of a tool to develop their own professionalism. Hence, it is desirable that a paradigm-shift will take place among teachers and that teachers consider themselves above all as professional educators. As argued in this chapter, this change requires much support for teachers and a shift in thinking of all other involved stakeholders as well.

Another important issue is that this kind of policy can worsen the daily work of teachers, as increased bureaucratisation and a related increase in workload for teachers is lurking. The designed policies and instruments seem feasible on paper, but in reality, things work out differently. In order to design instruments which are valid, reliable, practical and acceptable, it is important that policy makers have a good understanding of the reality within schools. Most teachers spend the bulk of their time in the classroom or doing classroom related activities. What will happen if these teachers, all of a sudden, need to spend several hours a week on activities that are not directly related to classroom activities? Besides, where can a teacher in a remote area get access to support and advice? Where are the in-service opportunities going to come from? Who is actually going to do the performance appraisal? These questions are especially important when the career of teachers is going to depend on this, because a lack of clear answers can be very de-motivating for teachers.

Finally, policy makers should get away from the traditional understanding that in-service training for teachers involves taking them away from the school and putting them in a training centre a long way from the reality of schools and lecturing them. The new continuous development process for teachers consists mainly of activities for which teachers have to leave the classroom. This is unfortunate, because teachers are probably much more involved when their professional development takes place in their own school or classroom. Moreover, it will be more effective and useful as well. When there is, for instance, a strong mentoring system in place within the school, teachers can be assisted with their own professional development in a more direct and personal way. Teachers will be encouraged to look at themselves, to look at their classrooms, to work with and support colleagues, and to think about what they can contribute to the development of their school.

Indonesian policy makers need to be well aware of the (possible) consequences of their policies. It can even be questioned if the new performance appraisal system is the most desirable form of reform that the Indonesian system needs to increase the quality of education. Developing opportunities for teachers to upgrade their qualifications and setting up a structure for continuing professional development is desirable, but sanctioning teachers, especially if the CPD structures are not well developed, is not an ideal policy. Besides, one of the most dangerous consequences of education policy based on 'market rhetoric logic' is that teachers are treated like 'education units' and, as a result, they are performing as such and not as involved and committed professionals (Vongalis-Macrow, 2007). Furthermore, these policies can stimulate competition and can lead to a lack of co operation among teachers. This is not desirable, because teaching is a team task and teachers have a shared responsibility. Therefore, when importing market and hierarchical models of accountability uncritically, Indonesian policy makers have to be careful that they do not demoralise the Indonesian teachers rather than empowering them to teach better.

References

Arze del Granado, F.J., Fengler, W., Ragatz, A. and Yavuz, E. (2007). *Investing in Indonesia's Education: Allocation, Equity, and Efficiency of Public Expenditures*. Washington, DC: The World Bank.

Bennell, P. and Akyeampong, K. (2007). *Teacher Motivation in Sub-Saharan Africa and South Asia* (Educational Paper no. 71). London: DFID.

Bjork, C. (2005). *Indonesian Education: Teachers, Schools, and Central Bureaucracy*. New York and London: Routledge.

Boyle, J. (1998). "Cultural influences on implementing environmental impact assessment: insights from Thailand, Indonesia and Malaysia." *Environmental Impact Assessment Review*, 18(2), 95–116.

Bruns, B., Filmer, D. and Patrinos, H.A. (2011). *Making Schools Work: New Evidence on Accountability Reforms*. Washington, DC: The World Bank.

Chaudhury, N., Hammer, J., Kremer, M., Muralidharan, K. and Rogers, F.H. (2006). "Missing in action: Teacher and health worker absence in developing countries." *Journal of Economic Perspectives*, 20(1), 91–116.

Firman, H. and Tola, B. (2008). "The future of schooling in Indonesia." *Journal of International Cooperation in Education*, 11(1), 71–84.

Fisher, C.D. (1978). "The effects of personal control, competence, and extrinsic reward systems on intrinsic motivation." *Organizational Behavior and Human Performance*, 21, 273–288.

Fullan, M. (2001). *The New Meaning of Educational Change.* New York and London: Teachers College/Columbia University.

Jalal, F., Samani, M., Chang, M.C., Stevenson, R., Ragatz, A. and Negara, S.D. (2009). *Teacher Certification in Indonesia: A Strategy for Teacher Quality Improvement.* Jakarta: Ministry of National Education Indonesia/The World Bank.

Kristiansen, S. and Pratikno, Y. (2006). "Decentralizing education in Indonesia." *International Journal of Educational Development*, 26, 513–531.

Leithwood, K. and Earl L. (2000). "Educational accountability effects: an international perspective." *Peabody Journal of Education*, 75(4), 1–18.

Lock, E.A., Cartledge, N. and Knerr, C.S. (1970). "Studies of the relationship between satisfaction, goal-setting, and performance." *Organizational Behavior and Human Performance*, 5, 135–158.

Rainey, H.G. (2001). "Work motivation." In R.T. Golembiewski (ed.), *Handbook of Organizational Behaviour; Second Edition, Revised and Expanded* (pp. 19–42). New York: Marcel Dekker, Inc.

Ryan, R.M. (1982)."Control and information in the intrapersonal sphere: an extension of cognitive evaluation theory." *Journal of Personality and Social Psychology*, 43, 450–461.

Sahlberg, P. (2004). "Teaching and globalization." *Managing Global Transitions,* 2(1), 63–83.

Sahlberg, P. (2006). "Education reform for raising economic competitiveness." *Journal of Educational Change,* 7, 259–287.

Tatto, M.T. (2006). "Education reform and the global regulation of teachers' education, development and work: A cross-cultural analysis." *International Journal of Educational Research,* 45, 231–241.

Tatto, M.T. (2007). "International comparisons and the global reform of teaching." In M.T. Tatto (ed.), *Reforming Teaching Globally.* UK: Symposium Books.

"Teachers protest publication, scientific work requirements." (6 October, 2011). *The Jakarta Post.* Retrieved from http://www.thejakartapost.com/news/2011/10/06/teachers-protest publication-scientific-work-requirements.html [Date accessed: 1 March, 2012].

"Teacher workload needs evaluation." (5 October, 2011). *Kompas*, p.12. Retrieved from http://bectrustfund.wordpress.com/2011/10/05/teacher-workload-needs-evaluation [Date accessed: 1 March, 2012].

Vongalis-Macrow, A. (2007). "I, Teacher: re-territorialization of teachers' multifaceted agency in globalized education." *British Journal of Sociology of Education*, 28(4), 425–439.

West, A., Mattei, P. and Roberts, J. (2011). "Accountability and sanctions in English schools." *British Journal of Educational Studies*, 59(1), 41–62.

World Bank. (2007). *Indonesia–Better Education through Reformed Management and Universal Teacher Upgrading (BERMUTU)* Washington, DC: World Bank. Retrieved from http://documents.worldbank.org/curated/en/2007/04/7564815/indonesia-better-education-through-reformed-management-universal-teacher-upgrading-bermutu.

Vignette 2

Changing Education in Action

Georgia: The Conflicted Teacher

Sophia Gorgodze

Interview with private school teacher in Tbilisi
Subject of Teaching: History
Teacher's Age: 46
Experience: 15 years

'I remember one of my groups about seven years ago, most of the students were refugees from Abkhazia, quite a difficult class to manage. If I had started with our curriculum and tests and writing assignments we use today, nothing would have come out of it. I chose a totally different way of teaching. Students chose the topics they liked and developed projects around those topics, we did nothing else during the whole semester! And can you imagine, we had wonderful results, I achieved the desired outcomes. We even invited guests for project presentations at the end. Today I will not be able to do this and obviously would not achieve such results if I happen to have a difficult group like that.'

This was the end of an hour-long interview with the history teacher in a private school, who had seemed quite positive about the controlled teaching and learning. But then when the recorder was off and we were done, she remembered her success years back and we both realized how new regulations and control have impacted teaching and learning processes, particularly for vulnerable groups.

To better achieve what markets require and what parents strive for, school quality-assurance services insist that teachers do multiple tests in class, which takes most of their teaching time and leaves less space for creativity and critical thinking.

'We have slain critical thinking of our children by these tests. Tests do not enable us to analyze something or to be creative; this only allows for more pre-defined thinking. This is what has changed lately; we have more tests to complete now. My students find it difficult to write a historical essay, and you might ask why should it be difficult? Because of the way we assess them is through a test, and the test does not require them to write such types of essay. True, at university entrance examinations we have an essay included, but that has little significance: the argumentative essay is only a tiny part of that test, and the emphasis is elsewhere. And we, teachers, try to adjust our teaching to this principle because this is exactly what the market requires of us. And the market requires it because this is exactly the indicator of success, whether the candidate passed university entrance tests and became a student or not.'

Despite the fact that she is not happy with the overall trend towards more testing and less creativity in a country, as well as less autonomy given to the teachers, she thinks that school-level control and accountability system keeps teachers in shape.

'Our school has the ISO certificate – can you imagine a type of control system we have? Everything is controlled, but this is not necessarily bad. When you know what is controlled, then it helps you work. The state gives you a national curriculum, textbooks and the direction in which to go, and the ISO helps you to arrange the study process effectively. We have electronic journals, and ISO has multiple forms to fill out to make sure we have done what we were expected to do. This is good in a way, because if you have a failure in a certain area, this is well documented and you can work on its improvement.'

In this private school, like in many others, cameras are everywhere, and as we were recording I was told a camera was watching us as well. Teachers think this is more for student security reasons than for teachers, and parents like this extra service. Teachers have become used to it, and it does not bother them much.

'In a private school we still have this *free air*, some autonomy to better teach our students, which means you think less about the kind of pressure and control that we have in other aspects. But when we had Mandatories[1] in school there was an impression that they were for controlling the teachers. They are no longer in school and we only have a guard now.'

The concept of the 'best' teacher is the one who is creative, but it seems that uncreative teachers are also necessary in the current educational system.

'Probably the best teacher is the creative one. But nobody is against standard teachers: they also do their work and it is not absolutely necessary that all of us be very creative. We comfortably coexist in our school. For higher grades, for example, when the time approaches to pass university entrance exams, the administration allocates those teachers who have a reputation for preparing students for tests in the best way. Everyone expects them to do this job well, and they really do it well!'

A few years ago, a school ranking system was introduced. The so-called school branding envisaged assigning stars to each school according to different criteria, including conditions within the school and the number of certified teachers.[2] Even though this positioned this particular private school quite well among other schools, the teacher still questions such ranking of schools.

'Maybe school ranking and assessment is not a bad idea, but when you think of it, you also differentiate between the students. Some live in a place where they cannot go, or afford to go, to a good school, so if someone studies in a dismal school and consequently school ranking is low, why should these children be discriminated against, compared to children studying in a brand new school conforming to European standards? On the other hand, it is good that all schools are in a nice condition, but if it is not possible, what can children do?'

Teacher assessment by the state is a positive thing; however, she thinks the format could be changed, as it seems that this imposed activity is more about the government's interest in teacher failures, and not in their success, which she finds disappointing.[3]

'Some kind of assessment of teachers is necessary, of course. I went through certification, it kind of summed up what I knew. True, it involved much anxiety as I was very tired when I had to take the test, but it is still necessary. I have been a teacher for 15 years, and I would be lying if I said I do not need to refresh my knowledge and review where I am at, to assess myself. But this assessment should not be a priority only for me: it should be important for the government as well. They should see and respect our efforts. What we have now is a one-sided interest, as if assessment is only for us, the teachers. If you as a government are also interested in what I do, show me, prove to me that you are interested and have an adequate reaction to my success.'

In a private school there is this sense of competition with other schools, but currently, as the school is established as a respectable one, they do not worry about this competition. Teachers also compete, but this is not an unhealthy competition, this teacher believes.

'There is a benefit to this competition. You see better what your strengths and weaknesses are, and try to improve.'

On the other hand, all this demands a lot of effort from teachers: providing what the state requires of them, along with additional service that they think parents want too.

'We work so hard here to meet the expectations from the state and offer services beyond that. We are like in a prison here [laughs], from morning to the evening.'

The teacher shared with me that she thought it would be beneficial for government to seek advice from those who really know about teaching and learning. If competent teachers were in charge of policymaking, it would only have positive results. Another problem, however, is that we have fewer and fewer competent teachers.

'Maybe the government should ask a question: why is it that we do not have competent teachers? Why is it that they cannot contribute much, either to teaching in school or to policymaking? The answer is simple: because you were not listening to the teachers for so long . . . You cannot approach education only from the point of view of good management, you should know about teaching and learning, you should know the teacher's life. We cannot make the government do anything: but at some point the government will realize that they really need well-educated people, and once they realize that, then they will listen to the teachers.'

Interviews were conducted by **Sophia Gorgodze**. Sophia is a lecturer at Ilia State University, Tbilisi, Georgia. She teaches future teachers and school administrators education-related courses. Sophia had previously worked for the

Ministry of Education and Science in Georgia and had been the Director of the National Center for Teacher Professional Development. She earned her MA in International Education Policy from Harvard Graduate School of Education in 2007.

Notes

1 Mandatories are resource officers at schools that come under the Ministry of Education and Science, and are responsible for keeping order in schools. A few years ago, even private schools were obliged to have Mandatory, even if they already had their own guard. Now it is not obligatory for private schools to have such personnel, and many private schools dismissed them.

2 This practice of school branding is currently suspended following the changes in the Ministry's top management.

3 Teacher Certification was introduced in 2010 and envisaged all teachers passing two exams, one in a subject matter and one in professional skills. Certified teachers got a monthly supplement of GEL75, which is roughly US$37.

Chapter 5

On Quality and Professionalism

Interview with Thijs Jansen

René Kneyber

> Striving for professional honour is the foundation for achieving good education for all.

Professional Pain

In 2005 we published a book called *Professional Pain: Why Holland isn't working.* I had a gut feeling, at the time, that there was a theme there, of Dutch professionals who had become the victim of eager governments imposing market forces on their professions, making drastic changes without consulting with the professionals and consistently driving to improve efficiency and effectiveness.

It turned out I was spot on: the book became a huge success. People were bringing their book to work, making photocopies of articles and hanging them on the wall in their workplace. They seemed to especially enjoy the harsh management-bashing of some articles, and the quote from the philosopher Ad Verbrugge: 'The process thinking of managers has bereft the world of its soul' was one of those lines that kept coming back.

In these last ten years I have changed my position on this subject somewhat. I still believe professionals are at times the victim of too eager a government or too eager a management. But I do think that professionals in part have called this victimhood upon themselves. A horrible case in point are the doctors employed by insurance companies, who saw their right to discretion stripped away from them and could no longer exercise professional confidentiality. Yet they only started protesting when they were in danger of losing their company car.

There is a danger that if unions work only to keep the professional happy, focusing on the 'bread and circuses', there will never be a real discussion about whether their work is of good quality or is making any sense. In many professions we have reached a situation where one could arguably speak of voluntary slavery: professionals have become inured to their own bad habits, are satisfied with poor-quality work as long as they receive adequate benefits, and are represented by paladins who sustain this status quo by keeping the powers-that-be in place.

The Quality of Work

I feel the book was in large part a success because we had addressed a topic that nobody was talking about, at least in the political domain: the quality of work. There has of course always been a strong lobby for more money and bigger salaries, but professional organizations that focused on the quality of their work had become increasingly marginalized.

The essential point here is that it is always easier to talk about money than quality. It is not without reason that Robert Pirsig wrote in *Zen and the Art of Motorcycle Maintenance* that:

> Any philosophic explanation of Quality is going to be both false and true precisely because it is a philosophic explanation. The process of philosophic explanation is an analytic process, a process of breaking something down into subjects and predicates. What I mean (and everybody else means) by the word 'quality' cannot be broken down into subjects and predicates. This is not because Quality is so mysterious but because Quality is so simple, immediate and direct.

Within a profession, a discussion on quality of work, or what makes work 'good', is therefore difficult. It's very hard to find agreement among professionals on what is good. Neoliberal reform is in part an attempt to overcome this issue and to make quality of work tangible or measurable, or even objective, and is also an attempt to enforce this perspective of quality on teachers. A glaring issue is of course that for instance the OECD with PISA are defining educational quality outside of national curricula and outside of what teachers have taught. The philosopher John Dewey has said on this issue that it is a wrong thing to judge a profession based on norms and measures that are not part of the work itself. I believe that is a deep truth. For any outside organization to have such a profound impact on the teaching profession is entirely worrisome.

It's hard for me to understand this harassment of professionalism. Any country will benefit from good-quality work, and professionals are surely the ones to define what that quality is. Yet it is too often the case that governments, and even the professionals themselves, believe that he who pays the piper calls the tune. Sometimes governments will shift some control over to the profession by separating the 'how' and the 'what': governments decide 'what' teachers should achieve, and they are then 'free' to decide how to achieve it. But even that is, to me, extremely contentious. Governments should support a profession, but should leave the 'how' and the 'what' to them.

Professional Honour

There is a serious lack of these political–philosophical arguments in the current education debate. In our follow-up to *Professional Pain, Professional Pride – A*

Powerful Force, we therefore described a neorepublican approach to professionalism. Republican freedom is of course the opposite of slavery, and a republican civilian will avoid getting into a position where he or she can be humiliated by someone else. By governing themselves, professionals can be free from random exercises of power. However, I'm not talking about a negative freedom, where one is free to do whatever one likes with total disregard to others. To become free is an arduous process at best, one that has to be taken up with others, if only because one's individual freedom implies the restriction of the freedom of others. In this model for high-quality work, professional honour is of the greatest importance: professionals must hold each other to the highest standards in order to (re)gain the trust of society.

We have proposed a three-step approach to this professional honour. First of all, there should be a basic professionalism: teachers spend a long time developing skills and should, not unimportantly, enjoy their work. They should also foster a curiosity for improving their practice and follow this through in collaboration with others. Within this basic professionalism, doing a good job is a reward in itself.

Secondly, a teacher should have a sense of professional pride in his or her achievements, and will seek ways to gain the acknowledgement from others. This 'coming out', of being proud of one's work, is not without its problems, however. As the outside world might have a different set of standards to those of the teacher, for instance when the outside world is very 'market oriented', there is a danger of corruption, where the love of a job well done is replaced by a desire for the acknowledgement of outsiders. Professional pride should therefore always strive to reach a middle ground between humility and cockiness.

Finally, the third step is professional honour itself. Professional pride you can have, but honour and recognition you have to earn. Professionals must expect high standards of themselves and each other in order to be trusted by the rest of society.

A good example of this is the General Teacher Council in Scotland. The Teacher Council is not an instrument of the government, but is a tool of the profession, which makes sure all teachers are involved in high-quality professionalization. The board of the council consists of union members, teachers, parents and a few random elections. It is not an instrument of the government at all. In fact, it is a perfect case in point: the government should support the council, but should have no say in it, because it is in government's interest to have a strong profession.

So, according to this view, there are a few things that as a profession you should never allow. First of all, you should not allow anyone to be a teacher if they have no interest in improving their practice. Secondly, you should also be extremely wary of professional corruption through outside forces, and thirdly, you cannot allow teachers to say, 'Just leave me to my teaching,' because striving for professional honour is the foundation of a good education for all.

Thijs Jansen is a former researcher at the Tilburg University and co-founder of the Professional Honour Foundation. This organization strives to enhance 'good work' in the public domain. Over the years he has published, and is working on, several books on professionalism and professional honour.

Part II

A New Paradigm

Flip the System

The right question, in the face of neoliberal reform, is probably 'what is good education?' To answer it, one could engage in an intensely philosophical debate on the purposes of education. But that would hide the true worth of this question, as it is not just a question of content or purpose, but sooner or later, a question of power: 'who decides what is good education?' It is a question of who decides, of who has the power, who lays claim to the purposes and aims, who decides when education has been a 'success' or when education is 'failing'. And it is clear that in systems that have adopted neoliberal-looking reforms, for all its smoke and mirrors of devolved control, it is the state that decides what the purpose of education is. In the end it is education that has to solve society's ills, and it is schools that need to deliver.

Some might shrug their shoulders and say, 'Is not the responsibility of the state to provide quality education?' Since the government pays enormous amounts of money to provide for an education system, doesn't it make sense to have ownership over its purposes? Is it not simply a matter of 'common sense'? Not so, if we look at the first couple of contributions to this book. There is nothing wrong with the state wanting high-quality education, of course, but providing high-quality education through market mechanics and devolved control is troublesome at best, and counterproductive at worst, as it in no way unlocks the potential that resides in teachers.

The answer to what good education is, and who decides, it seems, is therefore strongly linked to what a good professional is and who decides. In the 'flip the system' model that we discussed in the introduction of this book (Figure 0.2, p. 6), we make a definitive stand on who should decide: teachers should be the ones who are in the lead when it comes to education. Of course, we are not advocating a 'free for all'. Instead, we're advocating a situation where teachers have collective autonomy, have democratic conversations with other stakeholders on what they should achieve, and most importantly should actively strive for more professional honour.

However, after the first part of this book, which details many of the issues with neoliberal reforms, a lot remains unsaid about the theoretical foundations of our proposed solution of flipping the system. In this second part we want to look into these foundations in more detail. To begin with, Dutch educationalist **Gert Biesta** warns us of the 'learnification' of education, and presents a broader, multidimensional perspective on the purposes of education. His perspective has consequences for what teacher professionalism should – and should not – entail.

In the second chapter, UK researchers **John Bangs** and **David Frost** note that nonpositional teacher leadership 'is an essential dimension of teacher professionalism' and make the case for a policy climate and union action that enhance teacher leadership.

UK researcher **Howard Stevenson** and **Alison Gilliland** from Ireland map out the road towards a new democratic professionalism that is both collective and active, and debate the need for a positive goal for the profession. They view unions as pivotal in this transformation, stating that teachers must come to understand that they *are* the union.

Andy Hargreaves warns of two ideas gone bad, autonomy and transparency, and shows how the concept of collective autonomy can restore their integrity, and finally, research from Scotland by **Mark Priestley**, **Gert Biesta** and **Sarah Robinson** examines the oft-overlooked concept of teacher agency. They argue that (collective) autonomy does not necessarily lead to agency, and they show an additional need for looking at the context wherein teachers act.

Chapter 6

Good Education and the Teacher

Reclaiming Educational Professionalism

Gert Biesta

Introduction: In Praise of the Teacher?

A lot of what is currently happening in educational policy and educational research is having a significant impact on educational practice, and most explicitly on the position of the teacher. While nowadays many voices claim that the teacher is the most important 'factor' in the educational process, such claims are not only problematic in that they are based upon narrow views about what education is supposed to achieve – often taking their cues from large-scale measurement systems such as PISA – but also because they tend to mean what they say. That is, they see the teacher as a 'factor' and believe that, in order to increase the 'output' of the educational system (which is the rather shallow definition of educational improvement used in the discussion), it is important to make sure that this 'factor' works in the most effective and efficient way possible. That this 'factor' is a human being and, even more so, that this 'factor' is an educational professional who should have scope for judgement and discretion, is all too often forgotten in the excitement about the repositioning of the teacher.

In this chapter I offer a number of reflections on this situation. Firstly I seek to give an indication of why I think that teacher judgement is essential in education, and what kind of judgements teachers need to make. I do this in the context of a discussion about the problematic impact of the language of learning on the theory and practice of education, and argue for the need to refocus the discussion on the normative question of *good* education, rather than technical questions about effective education or competitive questions about excellent education. This requires, amongst other things, that we have an informed understanding of the particular nature of the purposes of education and make judgement about educational process and practice in light of what we seek to achieve. Secondly, I discuss recent changes in the context in which teachers are supposed to enact their professionalism and act professionally. I argue that three tendencies that are often presented as developments in the ongoing professionalisation of teaching – treating students as customers; being accountable; and replacing subjective judgement with scientific evidence – are actually undermining opportunities for teacher professionalism, rather than enhancing them. Taken together, the two lines of the chapter provide indications for how teacher professionalism might be regained and reclaimed.

The Learnification of Education

Over the past decade I have written about a phenomenon to which I have referred as the 'learnification' of educational discourse and practice (for the term see Biesta, 2010; for the wider analysis see Biesta, 2004, 2006, 2013). 'Learnification' has to do with the impact of the rise of a 'new language of learning' on education. This rise is evident in a number of discursive shifts, such as the tendency to refer to pupils, students, children and even adults as 'learners'; to redefine teaching as 'facilitating learning', 'creating learning opportunities', of 'delivering learning experiences'; or to talk about the school as a 'learning environment' or 'place for learning'. It is also visible in the transformation of the field of adult education into that of lifelong learning.

The rise of the language of learning is the outcome of a range of loosely connected developments in the theory, policy and practice of education. These include the critique of authoritarian forms of education that focus solely on the activities of the teacher; the rise of new theories of learning, particularly constructivist theories; and also – and this is particularly pertinent in the shift towards lifelong learning – the influence of neoliberal policies that seek to burden individuals with tasks that in the past used to be the responsibility of governments and the state. The language of learning has not only impacted on research and policy, but has also become part of the everyday vocabulary of teachers in many countries and settings (see, for example, Biesta, Priestley & Robinson, in press).

What is the problem? Perhaps the briefest way to put it, is to say that the point of education is *not* that students learn. The point of education rather is that students learn *something*, that they learn it for a *reason*, and that they learn it *from someone*. Whereas the language of learning is a process language that, at least in English, is individual and individualising – you can only learn for yourself and cannot 'learn' for someone else – education always needs to engage with questions of content, purpose and relationships. We also have to bear in mind that the word 'learning' can actually refer to a very wide range of different phenomena. Think, for example, of the difference between what it means to learn to ride a bike, to learn the second law of thermodynamics, to learn to be patient, to learn that you are not good at something, and so on. This is another reason why the suggestion that education is about making students learn is at least unhelpful and potentially misleading, for both students and teachers.

The problem with the language of learning, therefore, is that it easily keeps us away from the key education questions of content, purpose and relationships. This means that the language of learning is an *insufficient* language for articulating matters in education. Similarly *theories* of learning are insufficient for capturing what education is about. At most they provide us with insight into the dynamics of the learning that takes place in educational contexts and settings, but they cannot give us access to and insight into (the construction and justification of) these contexts and settings themselves. For this we need theories of education and educating.

Theorising Education Educationally: The Threefold Question of Purpose

Of the three questions that are at stake when we try to capture what education is about, the question of purpose is the central and most fundamental one. This is for the simple reason that if we do not know what it is we seek to achieve with our educational arrangements and endeavours, we can make no decisions about which content is most appropriate and what kind of relationships are most conducive. Some authors have therefore even gone as far as to say that the purpose is *constitutive* of education, which means that education *necessarily* needs a (sense of) purpose. In more technical terms this means that education is a teleological practice; that is, a practice constituted by a 'telos' – the Greek word for the 'point' and purpose of a practice.

There is, however, something special about education, which, if I see it correctly, distinguishes it from many other human practices. This is the fact that in education the question of purpose is a *multi-dimensional* question. The reason for this stems from the fact that education tends to function in relation to a number of different domains, and in my work I have suggested that three domains can be distinguished, to which I refer as qualification, socialisation and subjectification. Qualification has to do with the transmission and acquisition of knowledge, skills and dispositions. This is important because acquiring knowledge, skills and dispositions allows children and young people to 'do' something – it qualifies them. This 'doing' can be very specific, such as in the field of vocational and professional education, or it can be more wide, such as in general education that seeks to qualify children and young people for their lives in complex modern societies.

But education is not just about knowledge, skills and dispositions. Through education we always also represent and initiate children and young people into traditions, and ways of being and doing, such as cultural traditions, professional traditions, political traditions, religious traditions, and so on. This is the socialisation function of education. Socialisation is partly an explicit aim of education, but, as research in the sociology of education has shown, it also works behind the backs of students and teachers by reproducing existing social structures and inequalities. In addition to qualification and socialisation, education always also impacts on the student as person, positively or negatively. This is the domain of subjectification, which has to do with the way in which children and young people can come to exist as subject of initiative and responsibility (rather than as object of the actions of others).

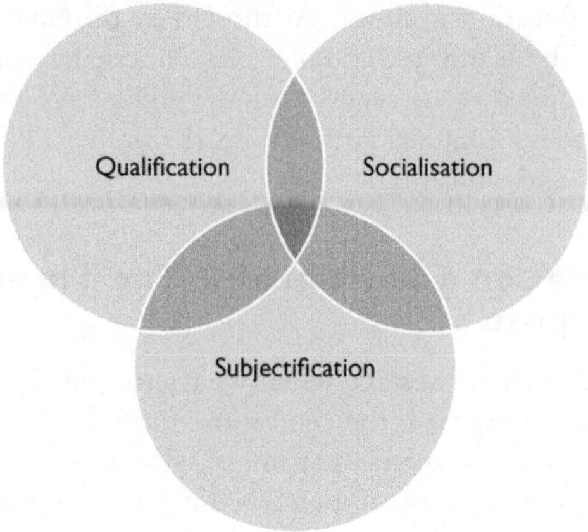

Figure 6.1 The three domains of educational purpose.

If it is the case that education always functions within these three domains – we could also say: if it is the case that education always *impacts* in these three domains – then it means that as educators we need to take responsibility for what it is we seek to achieve in each of these domains. Hence they not only appear as three *functions* of education, but also as three *domains of educational purpose*. I prefer to refer to them as domains of educational purpose rather than three educational purposes, in order to highlight that in each domain there can be widely different views about what, for example, knowledge is and how it can be acquired, or about what it means to exist as a human subject. Although the three domains of purpose can be distinguished from each other, they cannot really be separated. Even if we are 'just' trying to give our students some knowledge, we are at the same time impacting on them as persons – to have knowledge will, after all, potentially empower them – and in doing so we are always also representing particular traditions, for example by communicating that this particular knowledge is more useful or valuable or true than other knowledge.

Looking at education in this way gives us a broad conception of what education is for, one that acknowledges that in education we always need to engage with content, tradition *and* the person. This way of looking at education also makes it possible to see what the problem is with one-sided conceptions of education that only focus on one of the three dimensions. The issue here is not only that such conceptions are out of balance, so to speak, but also that a one-sided emphasis on one of the domains can often do damage in one or more of the other domains. This is what we are particularly seeing with the current emphasis on achievement in the domain of qualification, where excessive pressure on our students (and teachers, for that matter) to perform in that domain (and within that domain on a very small number of subjects) is beginning to have a significantly negative impact in the domain of subjectification; that is, on the personhood of the student. To put it bluntly: excessive emphasis on academic achievement causes severe psychosocial problems amongst young people, particularly in cultures where failure is not really an option.

The Centrality of Judgement

If we look at education in this way, that is through the angle of purpose and through an acknowledgement that in education the question of purpose poses itself as a three-dimensional question, then this has a number of important implications for the design, enactment and justification of education – implications that, so I wish to suggest, are first of all relevant for the work of the teacher. And what this way of looking makes visible is the essential role that judgement plays in education.

There is first of all a need for judgement about what it is that we seek to achieve in each of the three domains and about how we can keep the three domains of purpose in an educationally meaningful balance. This is not just an abstract question that we need to resolve at the highest level of policy or curriculum development. It is a concrete question that returns again and again in the educational situation, not only in a general sense but also in relation to each individual student. To speak about a possible balance between the three domains should not blind us to the fact that although there are possibilities for synergy between qualification, socialisation and subjectification, the three domains do stand in tension to each other. This means that a second judgement that needs to be made – again not only at a general level but always also in relation to each individual student at each point in time – is how we deal with the 'trade-offs' between the three domains; that is, what we are willing to temporarily give way in in one or two of the domains in order to focus on one of the domains. It is, after all, quite legitimate to focus our educational endeavours and the educational efforts of our students for a limited period of time on one particular dimension of the educational spectrum. Sometimes we do want our students to focus on mastering particular knowledge or skills and pay less attention to socialisation and subjectification. In other cases we know as teachers that what matters most at this point in time for this student is the student's formation as subject – and there are good reasons why, with this in mind, we can and should put the other dimensions between brackets. But one-sidedness ultimately comes at a price, so the question is what price we are willing to pay for a temporary emphasis on one of the dimensions. And I wish to highlight once more that the current emphasis in many countries and settings on just driving up academic achievement comes at a very high price.

In addition to judgements about the domains, their balance and the trade-offs, teachers also need to make judgements about the appropriate educational 'forms' – the pedagogy, the curriculum, the organisation of the classroom, and so on. The reason for this – and this is another peculiarity of the practice of education – is that the means of education are not indifferent in relation to the ends, but are actually constitutive of them. Which means, in more plain language, that students not only learn from what we say, but also from how we do – and that they often focus more on how we do than on what we say, particularly if there is a (performative) contradiction between the two. Teachers therefore also need to make a judgement about the educational appropriateness of the ways in which they teach and organise their education. This also shows an important limit to the whole idea of educational effectiveness, as the most effective ways to bring about a particular 'outcome' may not necessarily be the most educational ones. After all, it may well be that we can drive up our students' performance by threatening them with punishment, or by offering them money if they manage to perform in the way we want. But many would see this as an educational way to proceed.

This not only reveals the absolutely crucial role of judgement in teaching – and these judgements are crucially 'of the teacher' because these judgements have to be made in always new, unique and concrete situations (I will return to this point below). I also wish to highlight that judgement about balance, trade-offs and educational forms are entirely pragmatic in the technical sense of the word – that is, that we can only come to a judgement with reference to what it is we seek to achieve or bring about. This insight is an important antidote against educational fashions and categorical statements, such as the idea that education should be flexible, or that students should always have transparent knowledge about what it is that is expected from them. Whether this is desirable always depends on what it is that we seek to achieve. Hence sometimes education needs to be flexible and personalised; in other cases it needs to be strict, structured and general. In some cases education needs to be centred on the student; in other cases it needs to be centred on the teacher. In some cases everything that we expect from the students should be visible and clear to them; in other cases we need to work with a sense of mystery and openness.

Pragmatism, Normativity and the Question of Good Education

The need to think of all these judgements as pragmatic – that is, as necessarily connected to what it is we seek to achieve – shows the problem with claims coming from research that try to tell teachers what they should do, what is meaningful and useful and 'works', and what doesn't work, what is effective and what is not. The issue here – and I keep being surprised how often this is forgotten – is that something never 'works' in the abstract but always works in relation to a particular purpose or set of purposes. To say, for example, that homework is of no use – a claim apparently supported by research reported by Hattie (2008) – is a meaningless statement if we do not specify what it is not useful *for*. And while there may be no positive evidence that homework impacts significantly on academic achievement (which by the way could also be because there's simply no proper research about this available), this does not mean that we should abolish homework, as it may well be of significant use for, say, the domain of subjectification. After all, to make a student responsible for a task outside of the controlling 'gaze' of the teacher, is important if we want to help students to become responsible for themselves – to be subjects – rather than that they are entirely driven and controlled from the outside – and thus remain objects. In this sense I strongly disagree with Hattie when, in reference to my work, he comes to the conclusion that although there is more to education than academic achievement, in the end that is what matters most (see Hattie, 2008, pp. 254–255), thus reinforcing the one-dimensional view of education in which only qualification seems to count.

All this also shows – and this is perhaps the most important point – that in the design, enactment and justification of education we have to engage with normative questions. This is why I have emphasised in my own work that it is of crucial importance that we engage with the question of good education, and do not make the mistake of thinking that it suffices to talk about, for example, effective education. Although effectiveness is a value, it is a process value, in that it only refers to the degree in which a particular course of action is able to bring about a desired result. But making education more effective does not automatically mean that it makes education good. To put it bluntly: there is ineffective and effective torturing, but that doesn't make effective torturing good. The discourse of effectiveness is therefore only relevant within the confines of a large discourse about what is educationally desirable – a discourse, in other words, about what makes education *good*. To speak about good education also provides an alternative for another trend in contemporary education 'speak', which is the idea of excellent education. The problem with excellence is that it very quickly brings about a competitive mind-set, where some schools or some educational systems are supposed to be more excellent than others. In my view the educational duty is simply to ensure that there is good education for everyone everywhere.

Judgement and the Democratisation of the Professions

So far I have suggested that (1) education is a teleological practice; that (2) the telos of education is three dimensional; and that because of this there is (3) a need for judgement with regard to the three domains of purpose of education, their balance, the 'trade-offs' and the educational forms. I have also stated that these judgements are first and foremost 'of the teacher', because the teacher is confronted with unique situations that in some respect are always new and hence call for judgement rather than the application of protocols or the enactment of alleged evidence about 'what works'. If education requires judgement, and if this judgement is 'of the teacher', then it would follow that teachers have ample space and opportunity to exercise their professional judgement. Yet it is here that we encounter a set of problems that have to do with the way in which the professional space for teachers is currently being constructed and 'policed', namely in such a way in which the scope for judgement is being significantly curtailed and in some cases even completely undermined. How has this happened, how might this space be reclaimed, and what are some of the pitfalls that teachers may face in trying to reclaim this space?[1]

To understand how the context for teacher professionalism has changed over time, it is useful to start with the classical definition of professions (see, for example, Freidson, 1994), in which it is argued that professions denote special domains of work because they (1) have an orientation towards the promotion of human wellbeing; for which (2) they need highly specialised knowledge and skills; and (3) work in relationships of authority and trust. These three aspects not only provide a *definition* of the professions – particularly the 'traditional' professions (doctors, lawyers, priests) – but are also given as a justification for why professions need to regulate themselves, rather than that they are ruled from the 'outside'. While this particular account of the professions is not without reason, it can easily be abused, not only with regard to the internal regulation of the professions but also, and more importantly, in relation to the clients professions are supposed to serve. Here it is all too easy for authority to turn into authoritarian ways of operating, where 'doctor knows best' and where clients become positioned as objects of the power exercised by professionals rather than as partners in the relationship.

Authoritarian forms of professionalism and even more abuse of professional power were the main target of the client emancipation movements that emerged in the 1960s and 1970s, first of all in the domain of psychiatry but also in the domain of mainstream health, and this within the context of wider emancipation movements such as the student revolts of 1968. This was one way in which the professions were 'broken up' from the outside and were challenged to develop more equitable and democratic ways of working. A similar impetus came also from the incorporation of the professions in the project of the welfare state in many Western countries after the Second World War, where the services offered by the professions were seen as central to welfare state provision. This not only opened up the professions to wider questions about public health and the common good, but also – because the professions were to a large extent funded by the public purse – involved the professions in the process of public and democratic accountability. Although these developments did not resolve all problems at once, they did help to make professions more democratic and more accountable and in this regard did help to steer professions away from authoritarian modes of operation. In this way they also set a standard for developments in other fields of work (that often sought to claim professional status themselves as well), including the field of education.

Post-Democratic Distortions: The Erosion of Professionality

If these developments have helped to push the professions towards less authoritarian and more democratic and accountable ways of working, then it seems reasonable to expect that further developments along these lines will strengthen the democratisation of the professions. From this angle, then, it appears that we should welcome and embrace recent developments that emphasise the importance of seeing clients as customers who need to be served and satisfied; of making the operation of the professions entirely transparent so that they can be even more accountable; and of basing the professions on scientific evidence about 'what works', rather than subjective judgements from individual professionals. While at first sight this may sound plausible – and demands for a focus on the customer, for transparency and for evidence-based ways of working are often 'sold' in this way – I wish to suggest that these developments actually do the opposite of what they claim to do, and hence entail an erosion of responsible, accountable and democratic professionalism. Why is this so? Let me briefly say something about each of these developments with reference to the field of education (although similar arguments can and should be made for other domains of professional work).

Is it indeed a good idea to treat students as customers and give them what they want? Does this indeed give them a much-needed 'voice' in the educational process and thus enhance the overall quality of the educational endeavour? I do not think that this is the case, and the reason for this has to do with the fundamental difference between economic transactions and professional transactions such as education.[2] Whereas in economic transactions we start from the assumption that customers know what they want, so that the main task of providers is to give them what they want, either for the lowest price or, more realistically, for the best price–quality ratio, the whole point of professional practices such as education is that they do not just service the needs of their clients, but also play a crucial role in the definition of those needs.

We go to the doctor because we do not feel well, but trust that the doctor will be able to indicate what the reason for this is, and will be able to suggest a treatment based on this. Similarly, we go to school not to get what we already know that we want. Rather we go to school – or we send our children to school – because we want to receive an education, and here we would expect that teachers will move students *beyond* what they already know that they want; that is, that teachers open up new vistas, new opportunities, and that they will help children and young people to interrogate whether what they say they want or desire, is actually what they should desire.[3] To turn the student into a customer, and just to work on the assumption that education should do what the customer wants – probably on the assumption that the customer is always right – is therefore a distortion of what education is about, a distortion that significantly undermines the ability of teachers to be teachers, and of schools, colleges and universities to be educational institutions (rather than shops). This is, of course, not to suggest that students should have no voice in what goes on – as this would turn education back into authoritarian modes of operation – but it is crucial to see that the voice of the student and the voice of the teacher are very different voices that come with different responsibilities and expectations.

I do not want to spend too many words on the second development that has been going on in education for quite some time now: that is, the demand for accountability. While accountability in itself is a good and important idea – professionals need to be accountable both to the immediate clientele they serve and to the wider public – there is a crucial difference between democratic forms of accountability that engage in substantive exchanges between professionals and their 'stakeholders' about what, in the case of teaching, good education looks like, what its parameters are, and how we might come to a judgement about how good education is, and the bureaucratic forms of accountability that trouble contemporary education. If democratic accountability has an orientation on what makes education good, bureaucratic accountability has become an aim in itself – a monster that constantly needs to be fed with more data in order to show how education meets certain standards, without being able to raise any questions about whether the standards so defined are an accurate and meaningful expression of what should matter in education. Onara O'Neill's Reith lectures from 2002 (O'Neill, 2002) still provide a highly accurate account of what is wrong with the contemporary culture of accountability.

One problem she highlights is that while in theory 'the new culture of accountability and audit makes professionals and institutions more accountable to the public', in practice 'the real requirements are for accountability to regulators, to departments of government, to funders, to legal standards' (O'Neill, 2002). A second problem she highlights is that while again in theory 'the new culture of accountability and audit makes professionals and institutions more accountable *for good performance*', in practice 'the real focus is on performance indicators chosen for ease of measurement and control rather than because they measure accurately what the quality of performance is' (O'Neill, 2002). As I have put it elsewhere, the predicament is whether in all this we are measuring and assessing what we value, or whether we have ended up in a situation where we are valuing what is being measured; that is, a situation where measurement has turned into an end in itself, rather than a means that should help to get a discussion going about what good practice – and in our case: good education – is.

The slightly more recent demand that professional practices should be based upon scientific evidence about 'what works' rather than that they should crucially rely on professional judgement, entails a similar distortion of professional practices such as education. There are two reasons for this. One is that, as I have tried to show in the first part of this chapter, the question as to 'what works' is a meaningless question if we do not add the question of *for what* something is supposed to work. Without an engagement with the question of purpose, the idea that there can be evidence about 'what works' in education remains an empty idea – or, and this is more likely to be the case, with the push for 'what works' comes already an idea of what education is supposed to work for, and more often than not this boils down to some narrow interpretation of academic achievement.

That education needs to 'work' with reference to a number of different domains, that what may 'work' in relation to one domain may not necessarily also 'work' with reference to the other domains and may actually create an adverse impact, and that even strategies that are proven to 'work' need to be judged on their educational value – punishments or bribes may work pretty well, but nonetheless we should not be using them in education – is all hardly ever considered in the suggestion that education should become 'evidence based'. In addition, and this is the second reason, the logic of 'working' is a logic of production and control, whereas education is not a process whereby teaching is a cause and learning the effect. Education is a process of communication, encounter and interpretation. It is not a process of causes and effects but of actions and possible consequences, and also in this regard the logic of 'what works' is not only inappropriate for education, but amounts to a distortion of it. The greatest problem for teachers is the suggestion that evidence about 'what works' can replace the need for judgement – and I hope to have provided sufficient arguments for seeing that this is simply not possible.

Conclusion: Reclaiming Teacher Professionalism

If we wish to reclaim a space for teacher professionalism and educational professionalism more generally, it is first of all important to see current developments in the field of education for what they are and not for what they pretend to be. It is important to see – and make visible to the profession and the wider public – that these developments do not enhance teacher professionalism or good education but actively contribute to undermining and eroding the striving towards good education and meaningful professional conduct. While part of the strategy for reclaiming professionalism means going against these developments and treating them as distortions of democratic and accountable professional action, it is at the very same time important that teachers and other educational actors have a clear sense of what their profession actually is about. That is why we also need a robust account of education. This is an account that does not fall for the fashionable idea that education is nothing but the facilitation of learning, but that engages openly and straightforwardly with the teleological character of education, and with the complexities of the fact that education always has to concern itself with three domains of purpose, and that the ongoing challenge is to maintain an educationally meaningful balance between the three. This challenge lies at the heart of accountable teacher professionalism.

Notes

1 Within the confines of this chapter I can only give the nub of the argument; for more detail see Biesta (in press).

2 Feinberg's 2001 essay on choice, need-definition and educational reform provides an extremely clear analysis of what the problem here is.

3 On the educational importance of the transformation of what is desired into what is desirable see Biesta (2014).

References

Biesta, G. J. J. (2004). Against learning: Reclaiming a language for education in an age of learning. *Nordisk Pedagogik*, 23, 70–82.

Biesta, G. J. J. (2006). *Beyond Learning: Democratic Education for a Human Future*. Boulder, CO: Paradigm Publishers.

Biesta, G. J. J. (2010). *Good Education in an Age of Measurement: Ethics, Politics, Democracy*. Boulder, CO: Paradigm Publishers.

Biesta, G. J. J. (2013). Interrupting the politics of learning. *Power and Education*, 5(1), 4–15.

Biesta, G. J. J. (2014). *The Beautiful Risk of Education*. Boulder, CO: Paradigm Publishers.

Biesta, G. J. J. (in press). Education, measurement and the professions: Reclaiming a space for democratic professionality in education. *Educational Philosophy and Theory*.

Biesta, G. J. J., Priestley, M. and Robinson, S. (in press). The role of beliefs in teacher agency. *Teachers and Teaching: Theory and Practice*.

Feinberg, W. (2001). Choice, autonomy, need-definition and educational reform. *Studies in Philosophy and Education*, 20(5), 402–409.

Freidson, E. (1994). *Professionalism Reborn: Theory, Prophecy, and Policy*. Chicago, IL: University of Chicago Press.

Hattie, J. (2008). *Visible Learning*. London/New York: Routledge.

O'Neill, O. (2002). *BBC Reith Lectures 2002: A Question of Trust*. Retrieved from http://www.bbc.co.uk/radio4/reith2002.

Chapter 7

Non-Positional Teacher Leadership

Distributed Leadership and Self-Efficacy

John Bangs and David Frost

The EFA Global Monitoring Report, published by UNESCO in early 2014, is a shocking reminder of the enormity of the educational challenge facing humanity as a whole. In relation to the quality of education, the report says that there are 250 million children who are unable to read, write or do basic mathematics even though some of these are actually in school. This 'global learning crisis' is nothing less than an international catastrophe and, in spite of initiatives such as Global Education First, it is ongoing. In calling upon governments to take action, the Global Monitoring Report highlights the pivotal role of teachers:

> An education system is only as good as its teachers. Unlocking their potential is essential to enhancing the quality of learning. Evidence shows that education quality improves when teachers are supported . . .
>
> (UNESCO, 2014, p. i)

Important as the UNESCO report is, there is a significant omission. The strategies proposed seem on the face of it to be laudable: they include recruiting more teachers and better teachers; providing better training for teacher educators so they can improve teacher training; deploying good teachers to the locations where they are most needed; incentivising teachers with better career opportunities linked to differentiated pay scales; collecting better data about teachers so as to regulate and hold them to account; improving curriculum design; training teachers especially in assessment for learning. This is problematic, however. While the UNESCO report is right in saying that unlocking the potential of teachers is essential, it appears to leave the teaching profession as the passive recipient of education reforms. It is perhaps less surprising that in other recent reports, such as 'The Learning Curve' published by Pearson (Economist Intelligence Unit, 2014), the teaching profession's role is wholly absent.

The debate on whether reforms are effective when they are imposed on the teaching profession is now up and running, most notably in the recent International Summits on the Teaching Profession (Asia Society, 2011, 2012,

2013, 2014), which have addressed this fundamental question. Indeed as long ago as the 1980s, Susan Rosenholtz (1987), for example, posed this question in the context of attempts to reform the USA education system: 'Education reform strategies; will they increase teacher commitment?' The question is still of the utmost relevance today. It is clear from the evidence mentioned above and from other sources (e.g. Fullan, 2011) that for education systems to develop successfully, the teaching profession has to be the main partner in education reform. We argue here that high-quality education for all young people and the developments of education systems are dependent on the potential within the teaching profession being successfully unlocked. We believe that, crucially, issues concerning teachers' self-efficacy, voice and leadership have to be at the centre of educational development at all levels.

In this chapter we draw from a number of sources: first, a study for Education International (Bangs and Frost, 2012) under the title of 'Teacher Self-efficacy, Voice and Leadership: Towards a Policy Framework'; second, our experience of the series of international summits on the teaching profession; third, the discussions in the Cambridge seminars hosted by LfL, OECD, EI and OSF (Frost, MacBeath & Swaffield, 2013), and fourth, the research and development that has taken place within the International Teacher Leadership initiative (Frost, 2011). We draw upon all of these to make the case for a fundamental shift in the role of teacher voice and leadership in relation to educational transformation. In particular we argue for non-positional teacher leadership whereby teachers can become energised and inspired to become agents of change with an enhanced sense of moral purpose.

We begin with a brief exploration of the concept of self-efficacy and its relationship to teacher leadership.

Self-Efficacy and Teacher Leadership

The OECD's Teaching and Learning International Survey (TALIS) explored teachers' reported self-efficacy (OECD, 2005). A secondary analysis that followed focused on this, highlighting the link between teachers' efficacy beliefs and students' learning outcomes (Scheerens, 2010). Teachers who believe in their own efficacy will be resilient, able to solve problems and, most importantly, learn from their experience. Self-efficacy is linked to the concept of agency, which is a fundamental human capacity that can either be enhanced or diminished by experience (Frost, 2006). Self-efficacy is a key dimension of well-being of course, but our interest here is in something more fundamental than simply having comfortable working conditions. Bascia (2008) argues that the link between teacher satisfaction and their effectiveness is more interesting than feelings and motivation. The organisational context and the nature of the professional culture are pivotal in enabling teachers to develop positive self-efficacy beliefs (Leithwood, 2006). The kinds of working environment associated with teacher self-efficacy beliefs include 'participation by teachers in decisions affecting their work' and 'collaboration among teachers' (Tschannen-Moran & Barr, 2004). These are most likely to flourish within environments characterised by distributed leadership and operationalised through teacher leadership.

A distributed leadership perspective recognises that leadership involves collaborative and interactive behaviour through which organisations are maintained, problems are solved and practice is developed (Gronn, 2000, 2002; MacBeath, Oduro & Waterhouse, 2004; Spillane, Halverson & Diamond, 2004; Spillane, 2006). The OECD's 'Improving School Leadership' report (Pont, Nusche & Moorman, 2008) advised schools to adopt distributed leadership, but regrettably it emphasises managerialist strategies such as organisational structures and incentivisation through career structures and more rigorous accountability mechanisms. We have seen this sort of approach in the UK and OECD countries, but the problem is that this denies the entitlement of *all* teachers to exercise leadership and to develop leadership capacity.

Distributed leadership fosters collaborative professional cultures within schools, which can unlock untapped potential in teachers and increases the capacity of schools to meet the needs of pupils and enhance educational achievement. Researchers are also beginning to produce hard evidence of the benefits of distributed leadership; studies such as Hallinger and Heck's (2010) are finding positive links between collaborative forms of leadership and improved student outcomes. Distributed leadership also has the potential to shift principals and their senior teams away from micromanagement of staff and towards providing developmental support for teachers. In this environment, a climate of trust between the formal school leadership and classroom teachers can flourish. So the idea of distributed leadership is appealing, but it carries with it the hazard of being interpreted as a strategy whereby principals simply distribute management responsibilities within schools rather than engineer changes in culture that expand the capacity of teachers to lead.

In contrast, a key characteristic of the International Teacher Leadership (ITL) project's view of distributed leadership is that all teachers are entitled, as professionals, to initiate and lead change, contribute to knowledge building and to have influence, both locally within their own schools, and more widely through collective action (Frost, 2011, 2014). It is essentially about voice, but not merely with teachers as the subject of consultation from above, rather it implies the right to set the agenda and to both create and validate solutions to educational problems. The ITL project's approach to teacher leadership invites teachers, regardless of rank, position or delegated responsibility, to join a programme which provides support in the form of tools for reflection and planning, together with a forum where teachers can discuss and share their experience of leading innovation.

The secondary analysis of the TALIS[1] data talks of professional development that is integrated in everyday school practice and encompasses teachers' roles in 'secondary processes' through which they make their contributions as members of 'modern professional organisations'.

> This additional emphasis on secondary roles is also promoted as part of the modernisation of the teaching profession. They include teachers as researchers, as receivers of feedback from colleagues, as innovators, as active colleagues, as collaborators of principals, and as manifesting what is sometimes called 'teacher leadership'.
>
> (Scheerens, 2010, p. 191)

This is where we see the joining up of an agential approach to teacher and school development with a view of distributed leadership that is not only more democratic in nature but also carries with it the potential to build teachers' self-efficacy and so enhance their effectiveness. It may be supposed that teachers are happy to concentrate on the daily reality of their classroom practice, leaving the responsibility for decision-making and institutional improvement to others. We put this to the test in a recent study for Education International (EI), the global federation of teacher unions.

Gathering Views of Teachers and Unions

In 2011, EI commissioned an investigation into the extent to which teachers across the world have opportunities to influence the context and circumstances of their professional work, and the value they put on this. The research generated data about the current environment and existing opportunities for teachers to exercise leadership, influence policy, shape professional practice, and build professional knowledge. It also explored teachers' links with colleagues in other schools and with the wider professional community. The purpose of this study was to provide an analysis that could assist teacher unions in putting forward policies that could lead to the enhancement of the confidence, professional knowledge, self-efficacy and professional development of teachers.

Our method was essentially qualitative, with two dimensions: one involved teachers being invited to participate in 'survey workshops' in a range of countries, and the other was a series of interviews with officials in a number of teacher organisations. Data collection was guided by a common set of themes:

- teachers' leadership of innovation and development
- teachers' influence in policy and practice
- choice and judgement in matters of pedagogy
- leadership of continuing professional development
- teachers' roles in curriculum development
- responsibility for relationships and communication with parents
- school evaluation/inspection

- teachers' roles in assessment of pupils' learning
- teacher performance assessment/appraisal
- the creation of professional knowledge
- teachers' voice and influence
- strategies and policies that would enhance self-confidence and self-efficacy.

(Bangs & Frost, 2012)

The questioning and discussion around these themes explored both current experience and teachers' aspirations regarding the scope of their professional roles. Focus group facilitators were provided with detailed guidance and the tools to support activities that would enable the participating teachers to reflect on their experience and articulate their views regarding their present circumstances and their hopes for the future.

The overall purpose of this survey was to enable groups of teachers to express their views about the extent to which teachers are currently able to take responsibility, have influence and contribute to the leadership of the development of practice in their schools. The activity enabled teachers to give opinions about the conditions that nurture teacher voice and influence, the extent to which teachers are consulted, and the strategies and policies that would enhance self-confidence and self-efficacy. In addition to indicating the extent to which they currently have influence, exercise judgement and take responsibility in relation to the above, the workshop enabled teachers to indicate the extent to which they believe that they *should* do so. That is to say, respondents were asked to indicate both actual practice and the importance to them of these practices.

The survey was supplemented by interviews with teachers in England who were recipients of Steve Sinnott Fellowships (Bubb, 2010) and alumni of the national teacher training programme, Teach First.

Outcomes of the EI Study

Our survey confirmed that, when it comes to policy making at both national and international levels, teachers themselves remain the ghosts at the feast. However, the data indicated overwhelmingly that teachers, whether they are in the UK, Macedonia or Hong Kong, regard it as of the utmost importance to have influence on the direction of policy at both school and system levels. A comment by a teacher working in the Bulgarian state school system reflected the views of many when she said this:

> We want the inclusion of us, the ordinary teachers, in the development of documentation, criteria, state educational standards, curricula and textbooks; actually listening to teachers' opinions.

It might be assumed that if given the opportunity to be more influential, teachers would merely clamour for higher salaries and better working conditions, but even where these are shamefully inadequate, teachers nevertheless express their moral concern for the needs of their students.

In our survey, teachers judged the provision of professional development opportunities according to the extent to which they enabled them to make a difference to their classroom practice. Most agreed that professional development should be 'teacher led', although to some this was simply a matter of choice about which programmes they could participate in; for those who had experience of teacher leadership, it usually meant that teachers should actually lead professional learning. This involves not only setting the direction and goals of their own learning, but taking the initiative to support the professional learning of their colleagues as well.

The curriculum is also a significant site of struggle, even though in many countries a government-mandated curriculum is now the norm. The major sticking point seems to be the role of teachers in the processes through which the official curriculum is designed. In Greece, for example, it was reported like this:

> Teachers that have a long experience in classrooms do not have a role in developing curriculum. Teachers should participate or at least give feedback on the curriculum.
>
> (Record of group discussion in Greece)

Teachers in the main are happy to accept that other members of society have a right to influence the content of the school curriculum and that it is ultimately a political matter to some extent, but they clearly express two aspirations: first, to be part of the process of curriculum review and planning, and second, to be free to use their professional expertise to decide how to operationalise the curriculum in their particular school contexts and classrooms.

The link between teachers and parents was also an important talking point in our survey workshops. There is an extensive literature to support the belief that parents have a key role to play in their children's education and that good liaison between home and school is essential (Desforges & Abouchar, 2003; Goodall, 2013). In our survey for EI, most teachers agreed that liaising with parents is an important dimension of their work; however, many teachers reported that only the principal could communicate directly with parents. Teachers reported this as being demeaning, indicating a lack of trust, which is a word that crops up again when teachers are asked about the process of school evaluation. Most teachers readily agree that external agencies have a part to play, but when judgements about the effectiveness of a school have no teacher input at all, the result can be demoralising. The evaluation of teachers was also an interesting point of discussion in our survey, with many teachers feeling very negative about their experience of this, although it is significant that the teachers who had participated in teacher leadership programmes were heavily in favour of mutual evaluation, which goes hand in hand with peer coaching.

One of the themes in the study for EI was concerned with 'knowledge building', a term which failed to strike a chord with many of the teacher participants. It was clearly not something they were accustomed to talking about. Perhaps this is unsurprising in the light of the OECD's findings on the question of knowledge management in education. This is the business of 'capturing, creating, distilling, sharing and using know-how' (Collison & Parcell, 2004) and it is something that education systems do not do well (CERI, 2008). Again, it was significant that those survey participants who were connected with teacher leadership programmes said that they see themselves as having key roles in the creation and dissemination of professional knowledge.

When asked for written responses to a question about what enhances their self-efficacy, teachers tended to focus on the need for respect and trust on the part of society and government. For many, the message to policy makers was 'leave me alone!' This message was heard loud and clear in Denmark and in the USA, where one US teacher said:

> Ninety-nine per cent of my interactions with administrators deals with the paperwork they need to justify or defend their actions. This slows me down and isn't constructive.

Most of the teachers consulted in our study expressed frustration at what they saw as meddling by politicians, and in some countries, for example Turkey, teachers called for the de-politicisation of schooling.

Not all responses were protestations. This statement by a teacher in the HertsCam Network in the UK seemed to suggest that there is a room for optimism.

> My self-confidence and belief in making a positive difference is enhanced by feeling that my opinion is valued. Teachers are in close contact with pupils in everyday practice and thus have an immediate understanding of issues affecting the learning and well-being of pupils. Acknowledgement of this and consultation with teaching staff will empower a workforce with the confidence needed to drive development.

A common point made by teachers everywhere was that school principals have a key role in creating the conditions for enabling teachers to have a voice and to contribute to the development of policy and practice.

The Teacher Unions' Perspective

The teacher workshops were supplemented by interviews with senior officials and lay leaders of four teacher unions/federations in the United

States, Canada, Norway and Australia. Union representatives were asked whether they believe that their core business is to raise the levels of teachers' self-efficacy, voice and leadership. Their response was an emphatic 'yes' and best summarised by the interviewee from the National Education Association in the US who said, 'teacher leadership is a concept whose time has come'.

Indeed Bascia's (2008) description of 'what teachers want from their unions' – e.g. professional development and learning, establishing the right to participate in decision making, articulating and promoting a positive professional identity – matches the approach of the unions represented in this study. Although not all unions currently choose to adopt this role, the evidence from our study is that they have the capacity to do so. The ideas that teachers put forward about enhancing their roles indicates the enormous potential available to unions, in both developing practical strategies which would enhance the professional capacity of teachers and in enhancing the force of unions' representations with employers and governments.

The teacher unions consulted in this study take a number of approaches to enhancing the professional capacity of their members. One focuses on enhancing the collective voice of teachers through, for example, providing professional development and networks for teachers where the state is clearly unable or unwilling to do so. The AEU's relationship with the Australian Federal Government is an example of this. It targets areas of provision such as professional development for beginning teachers in remote areas with the aim of making a difference to teachers' lives. Indeed for a number of unions, including the four unions in our study, this approach has a wider policy purpose: that of enhancing the professional community and professional self-confidence of teachers. Indeed it has been argued that continuing professional development should be seen as a dimension of educational reform and innovation rather than as discrete training or personal development programmes (Frost, 2013).

Another approach was to evaluate teachers' working conditions. Some unions such as the Elementary Teachers' Federation of Ontario have started to question whether teachers' conditions of service need to reflect teachers' professional leadership. Its commissioned study argued that teachers' working conditions needed redefining so that factors that enhanced teachers' self-efficacy could be included (Leithwood, 2006). Such a move raises the question of whether teachers' conditions-of-service agreements, which are purely protective, are adequate enough to secure, for example, the right of teachers in schools to be able to offer and expect reasonable responses to their professional views. The evidence from our study and the wider ITL study (Frost, 2011) is that teachers not only expect to engage in discussion about their own areas of professional practice, but expect to be involved as professionals in strategic discussions about school policies. Teachers' conditions of service should therefore enhance the capacity of teachers to lead professionally.

The Future of the Teaching Profession

The argument that teachers should shape their own professional lives in schools, and that their professional voice should be heard both individually and collectively, is now taking centre stage. The publication of the OECD's Programme for International Student Assessment 2012 has added to the evidence base. While PISA says that schools in higher-performing systems have more autonomy, it also says that such autonomy will 'not, of itself, result in better outcomes':

> Schools with more autonomy tend to perform better than schools with less autonomy when the school system, as a whole, uses such accountability arrangements as setting clear objectives of what students are expected to learn and sharing information about outcomes, and/or when principals and teachers work together to manage schools.
>
> (OECD, 2013, p. 192)

OECD's recent Teaching and Learning International Survey 2013 (OECD, 2014) goes even further. It found correlations between high levels of teacher self-efficacy, job satisfaction and professional collaboration. These findings led the OECD to give its clearest statement yet on the importance of teacher leadership:

> Teacher leadership is important for many reasons . . . teachers who report that they are provided with opportunities to participate in decision making at a school level have higher reported levels of job satisfaction in all TALIS countries and higher feelings of self-efficacy in most countries.

The report concluded that school principals should share decision making and policy makers should provide guidance on how to cultivate distributed leadership in schools. The significance of OECD's findings and recommendations cannot be underestimated. They can be used to challenge governments to support policies that enhance teacher self-efficacy, voice and leadership. They also make EI's decision to commission its study look positively prescient. While we recognised the limitations of the survey on which this report (Bangs & Frost, 2012) is based, we believed that our evidence provided sufficient grounds to be able to identify a number of recommendations for policy makers to consider. Within our study we put these seven points forward as dimensions of an enabling policy environment.

1. Policy should lead to the provision of opportunities and support for teachers to exercise leadership in the development and improvement of professional practice.

2. Policy should seek to establish the right to be heard and to be influential at all levels of policy making, including the content and structure of the curriculum.
3. Policy should protect and enhance teachers' right to determine how to teach within the context of collegial accountability.
4. Policy should support teachers in setting the direction of their own professional development and in contributing to the professional learning of their colleagues.
5. Policy should recognise the key role that teachers have to play in building collaborative relationships with parents and the wider community.
6. Policy should promote the role of teachers in pupil assessment, teacher appraisal and school evaluation.
7. Policy should enable teachers to participate in activities that lead to the creation and transfer of professional knowledge.

We believe these seven points could certainly provide the basis for teacher union policy initiatives to create system-level guidance on teacher leadership and distributed leadership. However, on reflection there is perhaps one overarching policy dimension that should be added: all policies should be evaluated to see whether they enhance teacher self-efficacy and job satisfaction.

Other surveys confirm the importance of these recommendations. For example, evidence from a recent mass survey of teacher attitudes in the United States confirms the arguments that system-wide improvement depends on enhancing teachers' voice. The benefits that teachers themselves say accrue from being involved integrally in determining practice and policies include: 'increased teamwork and collaboration among teachers', '[getting] policy in sync with best practices' and '[putting] students first, creating more benefits to the students' (MetLife, 2010). This indicates a deep-felt desire to influence proactively the discourse about what works in teaching.

Some policy makers will take a lot of convincing that teachers have the appetite or the capability to enact their professional lives in the ways referred to above. However, persuasive evidence is provided by a recent study on 'non-positional teacher leadership' in 15 countries. The evidence presented there supports the view that:

> teachers really can lead innovation; teachers really can build professional knowledge; teachers really can develop the capacity for leadership, and teachers really can influence their colleagues and the nature of professional practice in their schools. However, what is abundantly clear is that teachers are only likely to do these things if they are provided with appropriate support.
> (Frost, 2011, p. 57)

The concept of *teacher leadership* carries the potential for focusing on a range of activities and conditions that enhance the professional capacity of teachers.

Teacher Leadership and Professional Capacity

Teacher leadership has been promoted as a key lever in educational reform for many years, particularly in the USA (York-Barr & Duke, 2004). Notable milestones in the literature include: 'Assessing the Prospects for Teacher Leadership' (Little, 1988), 'Teacher Leadership: What Are We Learning?' (Lieberman, 1992), *Awakening the Sleeping Giant: Helping Teachers Develop as Leaders* (Katzenmeyer & Moller, 2001), *Developing Teacher Leaders: How Teacher Leadership Enhances School Success* (Crowther et al., 2002) and *Teacher Leadership* (Lieberman & Miller, 2004). In the American literature it is a common assumption that in order to exercise leadership, teachers need to occupy the position of 'teacher leader'. An alternative approach was adopted in the International Teacher Leadership initiative, in which it is assumed that leadership does not have to be related to a position but is an essential dimension of teacher professionality:

> [Teacher leadership] . . . whereby teachers can clarify their values, develop personal visions of improved practice and then act strategically to set in motion processes where colleagues are drawn into activities such as self-evaluation and innovation. This approach rests on the assumption that the enhancement of human agency within a culture of shared responsibility for reform and the outcomes for all students is essential for learning for all members of learning communities.
>
> (Frost, 2011, p. 10)

This approach could be referred to as non-positional teacher leadership.

Non-Positional Teacher Leadership

The book published in October 2014 – *Transforming Education Through Teacher Leadership* (Frost, 2014) – contains accounts of teacher leadership which, collectively, explicate a theory about teacher professionality and educational transformation. This theory has been enacted and operationalised by teachers and those who facilitate teacher leadership in the HertsCam Network and sister networks linked by the ITL initiative in a total of 15 countries. It could be summarised with the aid of Figure 7.1.

The vision is for a strategy that provides expert facilitation that would enable the majority of teachers, not just the talented or ambitious few and not just those designated as teacher leaders or those who occupy a formal position in the organisation, to become the new professionals that Fullan called for in the early 1990s (Fullan, 1993).

The vision portrayed in the book is operationalised through the idea of the development project whereby individual teachers are invited to identify a professional concern and then act strategically to address it. Leadership in this

Figure 7.1 Non-positional teacher leadership: a vision developed in context.

context is conceptualised as influence (Yukl, 2010; Fairman & Mackenzie, 2014). The facilitation that supports this is school based and it is self-sustaining because it is provided by experienced teachers rather than by experts from local government, universities or private providers. There is good evidence from the work of HertsCam and the sister networks within the ITL initiative that teachers can develop the capacity to organise and create the infrastructure for professional development and support for teacher leadership (Frost, 2011). Essential features of the approach include:

- individualised, time-bounded project work that mobilises teachers' moral purpose and taps into their capacity for agency
- school-based workshops led by experienced teachers who have the skills to facilitate
- a well-designed set of tools that support reflection, planning, consultation and discussion
- networking arrangements that enable teachers not only to build professional knowledge together but also to inspire each other to act strategically to bring about change.

The outcomes of such development projects is school improvement, which is commonly understood in terms of increased levels of student attainment, but what is important is the practice development that contributes to improvement. The development of practice includes that which builds capacity for learning and organisational capacity. Teacher leadership as construed here changes the professional culture of the school. Arguably such practice development creates 'knowledge in situ', but through teachers' networks it can be subject to a dialogic process that adds to professional knowledge in the system.

This is not codified and turned into professional standards but can be discerned in the exchange of accounts and ideas between teachers at network meetings and in their published stories. A key dimension of such stories is their power to inspire others and mobilise moral purpose.

There is evidence that this can work both in contexts such as the UK and in more challenging scenarios such as Bosnia and Herzegovina (Frost, 2011). New programmes based on the non-positional teacher leadership were launched in Palestine and Egypt in October 2014. It is envisaged that further adaptations of the tools and techniques used will show that the model has potential for universal application that can address the global learning crisis identified by the UNESCO report (2014).

There are two reasons for suggesting that this model of non-positional teacher leadership is the way forward. First, this approach goes to the heart of the matter by focusing on the question of teachers' moral purpose or commitment. This seems to be universal in that, with the right kind of support, teachers everywhere can experience a reigniting of their professionality and enhancement of their sense of moral purpose. Second, this approach is a low-cost option because the creativity, drive and expertise come from the teachers themselves. This is not just a matter of cultivating teachers' capacity to improve their own and their colleagues' practice, but it is also about enabling teachers themselves to become the main source of support for teacher leadership. Teachers who facilitate programmes of support for teacher leadership and organise network opportunities do so for the professional satisfaction it brings, rather than because of financial incentives, which means that relatively low levels of funding can enable this to happen.

Whether the emphasis is on the work of teacher leaders or on the exercise of leadership on the part of all teachers, there is nevertheless a degree of consensus that educational reform demands that teachers need to be empowered and enabled to be influential.

The OECD's own policy has developed since 2011. Its Background Report for the International Summit on the Teaching Profession (ISTP) (OECD, 2011) provided strong implicit backing for the concept of teacher leadership when it quoted the International Labour Organization and UNESCO call for 'professional freedom and the active participation of individual teachers in deciding a range of professional issues – curricula, pedagogy, student assessment and issues relating to the organization of education' (ILO/UNESCO, 2006, p. vi). More directly, the Background Report emphasised the importance of institutional arrangements that enabled professional-led standard setting and quality assurance in teacher education, induction, performance and career development (OECD, 2011). Indeed the OECD followed these comments up by providing a summary of our report for EI in its background document for the 2014 international summit (Schleicher, 2014). The Teaching and Learning International Study 2013 emphasised the importance of teacher leadership and highlighted the fact that teachers who participated in decision making at school level experienced higher levels of job satisfaction and self-efficacy. It went on to recommend that:

> it is not only worth school principals devolving some of the responsibility for school-level decision making to teachers, but policy makers should consider providing guidance on distributed leadership and distributed decision making at a system level.
>
> (OECD, 2014, p. 7)

Individual and Collective Voices

All the evidence points to the opportunities now available to the teaching profession and its unions to promote and define teacher leadership and, using the accumulating practice and evidence, to argue for teacher self-efficacy, voice and leadership to be at the centre of systemic teacher policies. The role of teacher unions in enhancing the capacity of teachers to show professional leadership is essential. Teacher unions can exercise leadership on behalf of teachers but can also empower their members as individuals to act strategically on initiatives that may be driven by values and principles not necessarily in line with current policy. Indeed as Bangs and MacBeath argue, this form of leadership could be described as collective teacher leadership (Bangs & MacBeath, 2012).

The international summits and the dialogue they create provide powerful support to teacher unions that seek partnership with governments and employers in creating teacher policies. The evidence from our study is that a number of teacher unions already encourage teachers' professional autonomy and leadership. They provide high-quality professional development and promote evidence-based policies on the curriculum, assessment, standards, pedagogy and evaluation. Crucially they provide the sites for their members to discuss and contribute to those policies. Despite the turbulence facing public education, we believe there are significant new opportunities for all teacher unions to enhance teachers' efficacy, voice and leadership and ensure that teachers' voices are heard in the processes of educational reform.

In conclusion, we hope we have made the case for enabling teachers to exercise leadership independently of management roles and organisational structures. There is now abundant evidence that teachers are able to embrace an extended mode of professionality in which they are influential in matters of policy and practice. They can direct their own professional learning and support that of their colleagues. They can contribute to the development of policies on improving their own schools and the wider system. It is crucial to note, however, that this is not a matter merely of allowing this to happen, but one of positively enabling it. In such enablement, while school principals have the prime responsibility to create the conditions that favour teacher leadership, teacher unions can also have a significant role. What is urgently needed is a policy climate that makes it easy for these enabling conditions to be developed.

Note

1 Teaching and Learning International Survey TALIS by the OECD is an international survey programme which focuses on the learning environment and the working conditions of teachers in schools.

References

Asia Society (2011). *Improving Teaching Quality: Report on the International Summit on the Teaching Profession*. New York: Asia Society.

Asia Society (2012). *Teaching and Leadership for the 21st Century: Report on the International Summit on the Teaching Profession*. New York: Asia Society.

Asia Society (2013). *Teacher Quality: Report on the International Summit on the Teaching Profession*. New York: Asia Society.

Asia Society (2014). *Excellence, Equity and Inclusiveness: Report on the International Summit on the Teaching Profession*. New York: Asia Society.

Bangs, J. and Frost, D. (2012). *Teacher Self-efficacy, Voice and Leadership: Towards a Policy Framework for Education International*. Brussels: Education International.

Bangs, J. and MacBeath, J. (2012). Collective leadership: The role of teacher unions in encouraging teachers to take the lead in their own learning and in teacher policy. *Professional Development in Education*, 38(2), 331–343.

Bascia, N. (2008). What teachers want from their unions: What we know from research. In M. Compton and L. Weiner (eds), *The Global Assault on Teaching, Teachers and their Unions*. New York: Palgrave MacMillan.

Bubb, S. (2010). Advancing teaching and learning: Capitalising on professional development. *Curriculum Management Update*, November, 3–10.

CERI (Centre for Educational Research and Innovation) (2008). *21st Century Learning: Research, Innovation and Policy Directions from Recent OECD Analyses*. Paris: OECD.

Collison, C. and Parcell. G. (2004). *Learning to Fly*. Sussex: Capstone.

Crowther, F., Kaagan, S. S., Ferguson, M. and Hann, L. L. (2002). *Developing Teacher Leaders: How Teacher Leadership Enhances School Success*. Thousand Oaks, CA: Corwin Press.

Desforges, C. and Abouchar, A. (2003). *Involvement, Parental Support and Family Education on Pupil Achievements and Adjustment: A Literature Review*. London: Department for Education and Skills.

Economist Intelligence Unit (2014). *The Learning Curve: Education and Skills for Life, a Report*. London: Pearson.

Fairman, J. C. and Mackenzie, S. V. (2014). How teacher leaders influence others and understand their leadership. *International Journal of Leadership in Education: Theory and Practice*. doi: 10.1080/13603124.2014.904002.

Frost, D. (2006). The concept of 'agency' in Leadership for Learning. *Leading and Managing*, 12(2), 19–28.

Frost, D. (2011). *Supporting Teacher Leadership in 15 Countries: The International Teacher Leadership Project, Phase 1 – A Report*. Cambridge: Leadership for Learning, University of Cambridge Faculty of Education.

Frost, D. (2013). Teacher-led development work: A methodology for building professional knowledge. HertsCam Occasional Papers, April. HertsCam Publications, http://www.teacherleadership.org.uk/about-teacher-leadership.html.

Frost, D. (ed.) (2014). *Transforming Education Through Teacher Leadership.* Cambridge: LfL.

Frost, D., MacBeath, J. and Swaffield, S. (2013). Sustaining teachers' professional growth. *Inform No. 1.* Cambridge: LfL.

Fullan, M. (1993). Why teachers must become change agents. *Educational Leadership*, 50(6), 12–17.

Fullan, M. (2011). Choosing the wrong drivers for whole system reform. Centre for Strategic Education Seminar Series 204, www.cse.edu.au.

Goodall, J. (2013). Parental engagement to support children's learning: A six point model. *School Leadership and Management*, 33(2), 133–150.

Gronn, P. (2000). Distributed properties: A new architecture for leadership. *Educational Management and Administration*, 28(3), 317–338.

Gronn, P. (2002). Distributed leadership as a unit of analysis. *The Leadership Quarterly*, 13, 423–451.

Hallinger, P. and Heck, R. (2010). Collaborative leadership and school improvement: Understanding the impact on school capacity and student learning. *School Leadership and Management*, 30(2), 95–110.

ILO/UNESCO (2006). Joint ILO/UNESCO Committee of Experts on the Application of the Recommendations concerning Teaching Personnel Report, Ninth Session, Geneva, 30 October–3 November.

Katzenmeyer, A. and Moller, G. (2001). *Awakening the Sleeping Giant: Helping Teachers Develop as Leaders (2nd edn).* Thousand Oaks, CA: Corwin Press.

Leithwood, K. (2006). *Teacher Working Conditions that Matter: Evidence for Change.* Toronto: Elementary Teachers' Federation of Ontario.

Lieberman, A. (1992). Teacher leadership: What are we learning? In C. Livingston (ed.), *Teachers as Leaders: Evolving Roles.* Washington, DC: National Education Association.

Lieberman, A. and Miller, L. (2004). *Teacher Leadership.* San Francisco, CA: Jossey-Bass.

Little, J. W. (1988). Assessing the prospects for teacher leadership. In A. Lieberman (ed.), *Building a Professional Culture in Schools* (pp. 78–106). New York: Teachers College Press.

MacBeath, J., Oduro, G. and Waterhouse, J. (2004). *The Distributed Leadership Toolkit.* Nottingham: National College for School Leadership.

MetLife (2010). *The MetLife Survey of the American Teacher: Collaborating for Student Success. ED509650.* www.metlife.com.

OECD (2005). *Teachers Matter: Attracting, Developing and Retaining Effective Teachers.* Paris: OECD.

OECD (2011). *Building a High Quality Teaching Profession – Lessons from Around the World. Background Report for the International Summit on the Teaching Profession.* Paris: OECD.

OECD (2013). *PISA 2012 Results: What Makes Schools Successful? Resources, Policies and Practices* – Volume iv, Paris: OECD.

OECD (2014). *Talis 2013 Results: An International Perspective on Teaching and Learning.* Paris: OECD Publishing. http://dx.doi.org/10.1787/978926419626-en.

Pont, B., Nusche, D. and Moorman, H. (2008). *Improving School Leadership, Volume 1: Policy and Practice.* Paris: OECD.

Rosenholtz, S. (1987). Education reform strategies: Will they increase teacher commitment? *American Journal of Education*, 95(4), 534–562.

Scheerens, J. (2010). *Teachers' Professional Development: Europe in International Comparison. An Analysis of Teachers' Professional Development Based on the OECD's Teaching and Learning International Survey (TALIS)*. Luxembourg: Office for Official Publications of the European Union.

Schleicher, A. (2014). *Equity, Excellence and Inclusiveness in Education: Policy Lessons from Around the World. Background Report for the International Summit on the Teaching Profession.* Paris: OECD.

Spillane, J. (2006). *Distributed Leadership*. San Francisco: Jossey-Bass.

Spillane, J., Halverson, R. and Diamond, J. (2004). Towards a theory of leadership practice: A distributed practice. *Journal of Curriculum Studies*, 36(1), 3–34.

Tschannen-Moran, M. and Barr, M. (2004). Fostering student achievement: The relationship between collective teacher efficacy and student achievement. *Leadership and Policy in Schools*, 3, 187–207.

UNESCO (2014). *Teaching and Learning: Achieving Quality for All.* Paris: UNESCO.

York-Barr, J. and Duke, K. (2004). What do we know about teacher leadership? Findings from two decades of scholarship. *Review of Educational Research*, 74(3), 255–316.

Yukl, G. (2010). *Leadership in Organizations (6th edn).* Upper Saddle River, NJ: Pearson Education.

Chapter 8

The Teachers' Voice

Teacher Unions at the Heart of a New Democratic Professionalism

Howard Stevenson and Alison Gilliland

Introduction

Teachers across the world are under pressure. It seems that everywhere, the demands on teachers are increasing whilst at best the growth of resources fails to keep pace. In very many parts of the world, and especially following the global economic crisis, resources devoted to education are diminishing. The pressure is on to get 'more for less' from public education systems, and those who work in them.

Teachers experience these developments in many forms, but perhaps most sharply in the form of labour intensification – put simply, the relentless drive to work teachers harder and harder, sometimes until they simply burn out. Many school systems now operate on a high-turnover–low-cost model of teaching which cycles through an endless process of 'bring in–burn out–replace'. However, a parallel but arguably more significant development is the drive to assert ever greater control over the content of teachers' work – what teachers do, how they do it and teachers' ability to decide for themselves what is the most appropriate way to perform their job. Hence the trend to scrutinise teachers' work forensically, and to convert key elements of the educational process to a number that can be easily measured, compared and ranked. Where this is happening, teachers experience their work as being stripped of its pedagogical richness and complexity, to be replaced by a process of management by numbers.

In this chapter we set out to show how teachers can reclaim their teaching. We do so by making the case for a new democratic professionalism based on the fundamental values of social justice and democracy and with teachers' professional agency at its core. In the chapter we identify three domains of professional agency as areas of teachers' work where it is vital that teachers are able to make and shape decisions. However, our view is that teachers must understand their agency as both individual and collective, and we argue that if teachers are to genuinely 'flip the system', then this can only be achieved if teachers organise collectively. Teacher unions, therefore, as the independent and democratic organisations that represent teachers' collective voice, are not only at the heart of a new democratic professionalism, but must be central to both making the case for it and mobilising teachers to achieve it. We conclude the chapter by setting out the steps that unions must consider in order to mobilise teachers around a much more optimistic and hopeful vision of teaching.

Teacher Professionalism and Teachers' Voice

The concept of professionalism has always been problematic when applied to teachers as an occupational group. Traditional notions of professionalism were grounded in identifying the traits associated with 'classic professions', such as law and medicine. They emphasised a professional knowledge base and associated levels of expertise, professional autonomy, a commitment to public service and professional self-regulation. In most jurisdictions these are not characteristics that can be readily applied to teachers. There is little evidence of consensus about the role and status of pedagogical knowledge as it applies to the practices of teachers, whilst notions of professional autonomy have always been complex. Finally, professional self-regulation has seldom existed in the ways in which it is evident in many other professions. For these reasons, teaching has often been identified as a 'semi-profession' (Etzioni, 1969).

Given these debates, some have suggested the concept of professionalism when applied to teachers is 'beset with conceptual difficulties and ambiguities' (McCulloch, Helsby & Knight, 2000, p. 14) to the point that they question whether it has any meaningful intellectual value. Whilst we have sympathy with such an approach, we also argue that notions of teacher professionalism cannot be ignored, because conceptions of 'professionalism' cannot be disconnected from much wider questions about how society perceives teaching, and what it means to be a 'good teacher'. Notions of the 'good teacher' are not fixed (Connell, 2009) and are in turn bound up with the on-going discourse and disputes about the nature and purposes of education. This approach was recognised by Ozga and Lawn (1981) when they argued that the concept of professionalism, and the struggles over its meaning, are best understood as a construct mobilised by competing groups in society to legitimate different, and oftentimes quite contradictory, approaches to teaching as work. Hence the state might refer to teacher professionalism in terms of responsibility and respect (the teacher as 'model citizen'), whilst teachers might emphasise a professionalism based on expertise and pedagogical knowledge in order to make the case for greater autonomy.

This struggle over the meaning of professionalism is at the heart of many of the current debates about teaching and the role of teachers. Neoliberal education reformers have always been deeply sceptical of the concept of professionalism, seeing it as a device used by 'producers' to protect their vested interests at the expense of 'consumers'. Such an analysis is grounded in the concept of 'producer capture' articulated by many New Right theorists (Demaine, 1993). Within education the New Right are particularly cautious, as they see producer interest groups (such as teacher unions and educational researchers) asserting a dangerous ideological influence on schooling, and hence young people. Here the concept of teacher professionalism is seen as reinforcing the interests of what is often presented as the 'education establishment'. Hence the argument that such producer interests must be curbed, in particular when organised in the form of unions, and that this is most effectively achieved by introducing the 'discipline' of market forces into public services. Many have argued that it is these pressures that have driven a form of 'managerial professionalism' whereby teachers' professionalism is recast in terms of an ability to achieve specified performance targets in a competitive (quasi-) market environment (Stevenson, Carter & Passy, 2007).

For many years these ideas have been challenged by those who have made a case for a more optimistic and hopeful vision of professionalism and in this chapter we draw on two of these sources in particular. Firstly we are indebted to Judyth Sachs (2003) and her work relating to *The Activist Teaching Profession*. Sachs' book made a major contribution to thinking about teacher professionalism in new and more optimistic ways, but in particular it emphasised that professionalism must be both collective and active. Professionalism is more than passive membership of a club, but teachers must be active in creating and re-creating their collective professional identities. We also draw on Geoff Whitty's (2008) case for 'democratic professionalism', in which he emphasises the need for teachers to work 'beyond the profession' in order to draw broader constituencies into the educational process. According to Whitty, such a democratic professionalism

> seeks to demystify professional work and forge alliances between teachers and excluded constituencies of students, parents and members of the wider community with a view to building a more democratic education system and ultimately a more open society.
>
> (p. 44)

Teachers' Voice and Teacher Unions

Ambiguities relating to the nature of teacher professionalism as a concept are also evident in relation to the role and purpose of teachers' unions as the organisations that articulate teachers' collective and professional voice. The use of the term 'union' clearly associates such organisations with the labour movement, and the notion of the teacher as a worker. This is an important statement of an objective position. The vast majority of teachers are employees, in an employment relationship in which their labour power (the ability to work) is traded in an exchange relationship with an employer (whether that is in the public or the private sector). Teaching is work and teacher unions therefore might rightly be expected to have a clear role in relation to defending and extending the pay and working conditions of their members. However, within the teaching profession, the role of teacher unions has always been much more complex, with unions often claiming to be both labour union *and* professional association. Teacher unions therefore represent teachers' collective voice across a very broad range of issues.

Our argument is that the 'industrial vs professional' debate within teacher unionism will always be an underlying tension that can never be completely resolved, but that to frame discourses about teacher unions solely in these terms is unhelpful and unproductive. The issues facing teachers, and the contexts in which teachers teach will always be determined by a mix of so-called professional, industrial and policy issues. For example, a *policy* to reduce class sizes has both a pedagogical dimension *(professional)* and a workload implication *(industrial)*. Similarly, we believe it is not possible to challenge the spread of the managerialism that blights many teachers' lives without having a wider political analysis of the global education reform movement (GERM) that has spawned it and drives it. Questions of politics and professionalism can never be artificially separated from more fundamental questions about the role of teacher unions in protecting basic pay and conditions.

Our view is these diverse issues need to be fused together to define a new vision of a democratic professionalism and that teacher unions have a central role in both articulating what this might look like, and, crucially, mobilising teacher support to campaign for it. At one level teacher unions are at the heart of teacher professionalism because of their ability to represent the collective voice of teachers. However, teacher unions also represent the *means* by which a new democratic professionalism can be achieved. A new democratic professionalism will always need to be argued for, (re-)defined and fought for. Mobilising teachers around these aims will be a key challenge for teacher unions as they resist the spread of the GERM.

In the following section we develop our ideas about what a new democratic professionalism might look like, and subsequent to this we set out the role of teachers' unions in mobilising teachers in pursuit of these aims.

Re-asserting Teachers' Voice: Making the Case for a New Democratic Professionalism

Underpinning our argument in this chapter, and the analysis in this book, is that there is currently a global struggle for the heart of education as a publicly provided democratic service. Inevitably this looks different around the world, but the threat has assumed the form of a global movement, and hence the response must be similarly global in form. Our conviction is that teachers must challenge the managerial view of professionalism that underscores the global education reform movement, and in its place articulate a much more optimistic vision of what education can look like, and what it can mean to be a teacher. Here we outline a framework that might underpin a new democratic professionalism, and in the final section we set out the organising strategies that teachers, working through their unions, will need to adopt in order to make the prospect of a democratic professionalism a genuine possibility.

Our vision of a new democratic professionalism is based on three core principles:

- that teaching is a process of social transformation and that it should be underpinned, above all else, by values of social justice and democracy
- that teaching is a technically complex process in which teachers need to draw on professional knowledge, pedagogical theory and personal experience in order to exercise professional judgement. Professional judgement requires agency by which teachers are able to make meaningful decisions based on assessments of context. The concept of teachers' professional agency must be at the heart of a democratic professionalism
- that teachers' professional agency must be considered as both individual and collective. At times teachers will be able to assert their agency as individuals, quite appropriately. However, in order to secure meaningful influence in relation to the fundamental elements of teachers' working lives, teachers will need to assert their influence collectively.

We are clear that any vision of a new democratic professionalism must be grounded in values that recognise the role and responsibility of public education, and hence the role and responsibilities of those who work as educators. Clearly there will be a wide range of views about what those values should be, and how these might be expressed. However, our view is that education is a public good and therefore the core values informing the service should reflect a commitment to social justice and democracy. If education is a citizenship entitlement, then it must be underpinned by a commitment to equality. Similarly a commitment to democracy recognises the central role education plays in creating an active, participatory citizenship. It also recognises that if schools have a role in preparing young people to be active citizens in a democracy, then schools themselves must be models of democratic practice.

In addition to this, we argue that democratic professionalism is underpinned by a strong sense of teacher agency whereby teachers can exercise meaningful levels of control and influence in relation to three key areas of their work – we identify these as three domains of professional agency.

The first domain of professional agency is in relation to teachers' ability to shape learning and working conditions. Learning and working conditions can be considered to include all those factors that frame the environment within which teachers work, and in which students learn. Such a list of factors is inevitably very broad. It would include issues such as the size of the class, the way classes are formed, the use of technology to support learning, the amount of preparation time a teacher receives, and pay and reward determination. These are all aspects of teachers' working lives in which a democratic professionalism would ensure that teachers were involved in meaningful decision making.

The precise form of this will inevitably vary but could include a range of possibilities, from the freedom of teachers to make individual decisions about their own classroom through to national collective bargaining processes. The list of issues presented here also highlights the unhelpful divisiveness that flows from distinguishing between so-called 'industrial' and 'professional' issues and instead recognises that all these factors have the ability to shape the learning experience.

The second domain of professional agency pertains to the development and enactment of policy. In this context we identify policy as the operational statements of values that frame the contexts within which teachers work. Policy is often perceived as the preserve of upper-case-P politicians, and is 'what governments do'. This is clearly a decisive factor in framing the contexts of teachers' work; however, our notion of democratic professionalism sees teacher agency in relation to policy operating at many different levels, with institutional policy making having a very significant impact on teachers and their work. Meaningful teacher agency in relation to the development and enactment of policy would ensure that teachers' voices were heard not only in relation to national issues, such as the development of national curricula, but also, crucially, at school level.

The third domain of professional agency we identify relates to teachers' ability to develop their professional knowledge and professional learning, and teachers' agency in this regard emphasises the ability of teachers to assert control over their own professional development. One feature of a managerial professionalism relates to the ways in which teachers' professional knowledge has often been ignored as particular pedagogical practices have been imposed on teachers, whilst in other cases professional development has been used crudely to promote national initiatives or organisational objectives. These initiatives are often geared to meeting externally imposed targets, rather than being driven by the professional needs of the teacher. In a democratic professionalism, teachers could expect to assert much more control over their own professional development, with correspondingly lower levels of imposition.

We argue here therefore that a democratic professionalism, based on fundamental values of social justice and democracy, emphasises teacher control and influence in relation to three domains of professional agency – shaping learning and teaching conditions, developing and enacting policy and enhancing pedagogical knowledge and professional learning. In making this case we also assert the need to consider agency as working at many different levels – from the individual classroom, through intermediate tiers (the school, local or regional government) to national government, and indeed to supra-national institutions. However, we also wish to highlight the need to see agency as both individual and collective.

Many aspects of teacher agency that we have referred to should quite appropriately be a matter for individual teachers. A feature of any form of professionalism should be the scope for individual autonomy, and for those with high levels of skill and expertise to be able to exercise professional judgement without the need for micro-management from above. However, in relation to many of the issues raised in this chapter, agency cannot be exercised at the level of the individual. This may reasonably be applied to the level of government, where the capacity of individuals to make a difference is understandably limited. However, such an argument can be applied elsewhere in the system, when we recognise that there are many occasions when teachers must organise collectively if they are to be able to assert their influence. This is why teachers' unions are at the heart of a democratic professionalism, partly, and most obviously, because they promote collective agency by combining together and asserting the amplified voice of organised teachers. Teacher unions also have a central role to play in challenging managerialism more generally and thereby creating the spaces in which teachers can exercise their individual agency.

In this analysis teacher unions are central to the development of a new democratic professionalism. However, if teacher unions are to be successful in setting this agenda they will need to work differently in order to draw a broader range of members into participation in the union. As such, mobilising for a new democratic professionalism requires unions to renew themselves, but also offers the possibility of creating the conditions for renewal itself.

Renewing Teacher Unionism: The Importance of Organising for a New Democratic Professionalism

We have argued thus far that public education systems globally face a major threat, and that teacher unions represent a powerful bulwark against the attacks of the global education reform movement. However, teacher unions cannot afford to only be defensive in the face of this threat, but rather they need to assert a much more hopeful and optimistic vision of what it means to be a teacher. In this chapter we have sought to map out the broad features of what a new democratic professionalism might look like. Our argument is that this cannot be a vision that unions articulate *for* teachers, or on behalf of teachers – but that teachers must see themselves as integral to the union. This is the essence of collective agency and the notion of an activist professionalism.

Our argument is that if teacher unions are to successfully articulate a new democratic professionalism, then this must form part of a wider process of renewal, in which the unions themselves develop as active, vibrant and engaging organisations. In summary, teacher unions as organisations must become models of the new democratic professionalism they seek to promote. In practical terms this involves the development of an organising culture in teacher unionism. We believe such an organising culture is predicated on three different elements:

Organising Around Ideas

We have already argued that the 'industrial vs professional' debate within teacher unionism has been unhelpful. So-called industrial and professional issues cannot be readily separated, and the bifurcation serves to divide. Our view is that teacher unions must develop a much more holistic analysis of the teacher's role, in which working conditions, professional issues and policy are all linked. This necessarily requires teacher unions to make explicit the political dimensions of policy that are often only implicit. The global education reform movement is a politically driven movement grounded in a globalised neoliberalism. A pedagogical issue such as assessment and testing cannot be separated from the wider questions of the purposes of assessment and testing. Who is driving the demand for more testing? For what purpose? Who gains as a result? These are ideological arguments and they need to be challenged ideologically. This is why teacher unions must not retreat from engaging in 'professional' issues, but they must also locate these issues in a much wider political context. Organising around ideas requires teacher unions to engage in the battle of ideas that must be won if the neoliberal dismantling of public education is to be successfully challenged. This is not a battle to be waged amongst the policy elites and disconnected intellectuals, but one in which teachers are actively engaged as 'organisers of ideas' (Stevenson, 2008).

Organising From the Base

A common feature of labour unionism is a desire to centralise, as this is perceived as an effective means of securing equity. National collective bargaining for example has been seen as pivotal to securing national pay scales, and therefore equal pay within particular national contexts. One consequence of this has been the centralisation of union structures as union organisation mimics the bargaining structures within which unions function. Such structures can have many merits, especially in contexts where national bargaining has been maintained. However, there is always a danger that over time the grassroots membership becomes disconnected and passive. Collective agency is asserted, but in a largely transactional manner. Members pay their subscription and then expect the union to represent them. Teachers are part of the union, but they do not expect, and often are not expected, to be active participants. The danger is that within a union a dependency culture on local 'hero leaders' can develop, and in the longer term grassroots organisation atrophies. Organising from the bottom up directly challenges this approach by ensuring that teachers recognise they *are* the union. This then requires the active development of the union at its base by engaging members in union activity. This may be quite traditional in form, such as organising around a local grievance, but our argument is that traditional notions of 'activism' are no longer sufficient and a much more inclusive approach to 'activism' needs to be considered. Participating in union-organised professional development for example is an important way in which teachers experience and connect with their union, and through which the battle of ideas discussed above is advanced.

In summary, we believe that teacher unions need to focus attention on building the base in their organisations. Teachers need to experience their union as a key part of their identity and 'live' the union whether it be through traditional workplace activity, union-organised professional development or union-sponsored social and cultural initiatives. None of this is easy – it can be costly in resources and requires a long-term perspective. It is, however, unavoidable if teacher unions are to build a strong organisation capable of halting, and then reversing, the forward march of neoliberalism in public education.

Organising for Unity

The term 'union' reminds us that the role of labour unions is to unite the disparate interests of individuals so that the fractured power of isolated employees is combined and magnified through collective organisation. Unity is perhaps the most basic principle of trade unionism. It is, however, a principle that has not always been replicated within teacher trade unionism. For reasons too complicated to elaborate on here, it is important to note that in many different jurisdictions teachers as an occupational group have failed to organise into a single union. As a consequence, so-called 'multi-unionism' in teaching is a common phenomenon. It can differ in form (different unions organising different groups of teachers, for example) but in several instances it includes different unions competing for the same teachers as members. It is difficult to see how this defiance of the basic principle of trade unionism can serve the best interests of teachers. Our argument is that such divisions are now dangerously complacent in the face of an unprecedented attack on public education systems and the teachers who work in them. A key feature of the market-driven GERM is its intent to break up and fragment, as a deliberate attempt to undermine the influence of producer interests within public education systems. Teacher unions cannot compound these divisions in the system by being further divided themselves. In order to facilitate renewal it will be important for unions to organise for greater co-operation, ideally in the form of union mergers.

Organising for unity cannot be seen as being purely about working for union amalgamations, which always carries the attendant risk of being a largely bureaucratic process. An activist professionalism must also develop unity in much more organic ways within and beyond the teaching profession. Within the teaching profession, in very many different contexts, there is a trend to greater diversity within the profession. Routes into teaching are becoming more diverse, and the teaching workforce can look correspondingly different. In many respects, although not in all, increasing diversity is to be welcomed.

There are, however, dangers that an increasingly heterogeneous profession becomes correspondingly more fragmented. The challenge for teacher unions will be to seek to unify the profession, when very many tendencies push in contrary directions. Organising for unity will require teacher unions to find the common interests between teachers, in a world where employer interests will be emphasising difference and division.

The search for unity cannot be confined to *within* the profession, but if it is to be successful as a movement for progressive change, it must extend *beyond* the profession. By this we mean that an activist democratic professionalism must involve an active engagement with students, parents and the wider community and that organising for unity must seek to develop common interests across diverse groups in the community. We see the forming of such alliances as central to building a broad movement capable of challenging the GERM, and turning the tide against it. Once again, we do not underestimate the difficulties of doing this. Indeed research we have been involved in has highlighted precisely how difficult this can be to achieve in practice. Teachers and parents are not always 'natural allies' and forging coalitions with community interests is complex and challenging. However, we see the development of popular alliances as not only central to developing the broad movement required for progressive change, but as fundamental to making any claim for democratic professionalism to be genuinely democratic.

Conclusion

Teachers are not simply at the heart of public education – they *are* its heart. The centrality of teachers, and teacher quality in education systems, is now widely acknowledged (OECD, 2005). However, very different visions of teaching are emerging (Hargreaves & Fullan, 2012). One approach uses the language of teacher quality whilst at the same time seeking to drive down the costs of teaching and de-skilling the work of teachers. It is based on a business model of education that seeks to maximise return on investment.

Teachers need to reclaim their teaching and assert a much more positive and optimistic vision of what teaching is, and what it means to be a teacher. It is not enough for teachers to be against managerialism and centralised imposition (although this can be an important springboard for activism). Teaching is intrinsically a hopeful endeavour and teachers need to be positive in their intent.

We believe this involves mobilising teachers, globally, around a much more positive vision of teaching that we set out in this chapter as a new democratic professionalism. This is not a model or a blueprint, but rather it offers a framework to think about teaching and the role of teachers. It is necessarily flexible and needs to be the subject of much more discussion and debate.

A new democratic professionalism recognises the complexity of teaching and the sophisticated skills involved in the teaching process. Crucially it highlights the need for teachers to be able to assert their professional voice in relation to all the fundamental elements that frame their work – learning and teaching conditions, pedagogical knowledge and professional development and education policy broadly defined from institutional to national and supra-national level. We identify these elements as the three domains of teacher professional agency. However, in making the case for professional agency we are also arguing that this needs to be located in a much deeper vision of democratic education.

Such a vision of a new democratic professionalism goes against the grain of current policy in many parts of the world. It therefore requires teachers to challenge current orthodoxy and 'flip the system'. Our argument is that this is simply not possible unless teachers recognise the need to act collectively, and organise accordingly. Individual teacher agency is important in a new democratic professionalism, but it is insufficient. Teachers must assert their agency collectively.

This is why teachers' unions are central to the new democratic professionalism, because they are the means by which collective agency can be asserted. They are by no means the only possibility for collective agency, and nor should they be. However, they are the organisations that provide teachers with a voice that is collective, independent and democratic. These three elements alone make teacher unions fundamental to a new democratic professionalism. Teachers cannot rely on a type of transactional collectivism ('what is the union doing about . . . ?'), however, but must recognise that they *are* the union. It is vital therefore that teachers understand that if they seek to change the system, it is their responsibility to be engaged in their union.

Teachers will not 'flip the system' unless, and until, they organise collectively. In this chapter we have attempted to trace out a vision of a new democratic professionalism that teachers can organise around. It is obviously incomplete and imperfect and we invite others to critique and develop the ideas presented here. As such, our vision of a new democratic professionalism is not an end in itself – but a means to an end. The ultimate end, which will always be just beyond our reach, is a much more inspiring and transformatory experience of education for young people in public schools. If that is a vision worth fighting for, then it is one for which teachers will need to organise collectively to achieve.

References

Connell, R. (2009). Good teachers on dangerous ground: Towards a new view of teacher quality and professionalism. *Critical Studies in Education*, 50(3), 213–229.

Demaine, J. (1993). The new right and the self-managing school. In J. Smyth (ed.), *A Socially Critical View of the Self-managing School*. London: Falmer.

Etzioni, A. (1969). *The Semi-professions and their Organization*. New York: Free Press.

Hargreaves, A. and Fullan, M. (2012). *Professional Capital: Transforming Teaching in Every School*. London: Routledge.

McCulloch, G., Helsby, G. and Knight, P. (2000). *The Politics of Professionalism: Teachers and the Curriculum*. London: Continuum.

OECD (2005). *Teachers Matter: Attracting, Developing and Retaining Effective Teachers*. Paris: OECD.

Ozga, J. and Lawn, M. (1981). *Teachers, Professionalism and Class: A Study of Organized Teachers*. London: Falmer Press.

Sachs, J. (2003). *The Activist Teaching Profession*. Buckingham: Open University Press.

Stevenson, H. (2008). Challenging the orthodoxy: Union learning representatives as organic intellectuals. *Journal of In-Service Education*, 35(4), 455–466.

Stevenson, H., Carter, B. and Passy, R. (2007). 'New professionalism', workforce remodelling and the restructuring of teachers' work. *International Journal of Leadership for Learning*, 11(15), available online at http://iejll.synergiesprairies.ca/iejll/index.php/iejll/issue/view/37.

Whitty, G. (2008). Changing modes of teacher professionalism: Traditional, managerial, collaborative and democratic. In B. Cunningham (ed.), *Exploring Professionalism, Bedford Way Papers*. London: Institute of Education.

Chapter 9

Autonomy and Transparency

Two Good Ideas Gone Bad

Andy Hargreaves

Autonomy and Autocracy

Educational reform has seen the rapid rise of two strategies to create higher standards in our schools: autonomy and transparency. Both of these strategies have honorable origins, but they have been co-opted and corrupted to achieve purposes that are the very opposite of their original intentions. This chapter sets out misuses and abuses of autonomy and transparency and proposes a more ethical and effective alternative: collective autonomy. Let's begin with autonomy.

One of the worst states of human existence is no autonomy. Zero autonomy is a state of totalitarianism that robs us of our ability to determine our own fate. A less obvious but also troubling state of human existence is complete autonomy in which anything and everything can be freely chosen, whatever the consequences.

When we have no autonomy, we have no freedom, choice or responsibility. We are not autonomous. We are automatons. We are like robots, with no free will. Totalitarian states oppose freedom, independence of thought and creativity of action. Dystopian novels depict people who are condemned to an existence of mechanized misery. German sociologist Max Weber (1992) described how the Chinese invention of bureaucracy that based the holding of office on objective merit rather than inheritance or patronage had, in modern times, turned into an 'iron cage' of inflexible procedures that constrained all discretion of action and judgment.

In excess, top-down reforms in public education have expressed and embodied these freedom-restricting characteristics of vast bureaucracies. Standardization and centralization of curriculum took away the capacities of teachers to create their own curriculum in ways that best met the needs and circumstances of their students. Scripted literacy programs, delivered at a prescribed pace, removed discretion of judgment from teachers and students. They undermined the essence of professionalism: to exercise discretionary judgment in the interests of diverse and individual clients. In line with Frederick W. Taylor's scientific management practices of the 1920s, tasks were broken down into minuscule, micromanaged parts to achieve maximum efficiency. Measured literacy and math outcomes drove more and more of the curriculum; arts and citizenship were pushed to the side (Robinson & Aronica, 2015; Westheimer, 2015).

One reaction to institutionalized autocracy has been greater autonomy. Autonomy promises liberation from oppression; a shedding of the shackles. Autonomy offers choice, discretion, and self-determination. In the New Hampshire motto: it is 'live free or die.'

But absolute or excess autonomy is in many ways as dangerous as no autonomy. Mao Zedong's purported (but not enacted) philosophy of letting a thousand flowers bloom is often referred to in derisory terms, and not only by the defenders of autocracy and bureaucracy. In *The Paradox of Choice*, Barry Schwartz (2004) argues that complete or infinite choice is as much of a tyranny as no choice at all, as people are overwhelmed by the plethora of alternatives and endure anxiety and suffering as they have to choose one option against endless others, including ones that might conceivably have been better. A restaurant menu that reads more like a book, a jeans shop with countless styles and cuts, and a selection of schools so wide that parents are terrified of making an inferior choice for their child – all these things characterize the tyranny of choice.

Although digital pioneers celebrate the coming of a borderless world, an existence without borders or boundaries is one where the ego has no limits, relationships are bereft of loyalty and attachment, and identities have no definition (Sennett, 2011). Our potential judgments and decisions are infinite. There is no moral compass to narrow down our choices and guide us. In a world of complete freedom, we are like children whose parents have abandoned us, living, in the classic words of Peter Marris (1974, p. 20), as adults with 'forged papers of maturity.'

Unbridled freedom leads to incoherence in systems, inconsistency in provision and inequality of educational opportunity as the privileged have more choices as well as greater capacity to act on them compared to the poor. This is the criticism of unlimited professional autonomy for teachers: that teachers will be free to exercise poor judgment as well as good judgment, to teach according to their idiosyncratic passions rather than in line with the best evidence, to create gaps and duplications in students' education as these students move up the grades or their parents move around the country, and to be oblivious to each other's work rather than deliberately building upon it. Unregulated professional autonomy, it has been argued, leads to inconsistency in innovation, imperviousness to scrutiny, and an educational world where enthusiasm doesn't always lead to excellence, and absence of enthusiasm and excellence is allowed to exist as well (Hargreaves & Shirley, 2009).

Two Flawed Alternatives

The answer to the excesses of free will and determinism in the teaching profession has been to pursue and promote particular kinds and combinations of autonomy and control – to create autonomy within certain kinds of limits. Two of these have become especially prevalent in recent years: school autonomy and professional transparency. Let's look at each of them.

The Seduction of School Autonomy

The increasingly influential literature on high-performing educational systems that has been produced by global policy organizations, corporate consultancies, and international publishing and technology giants, points to the proclaimed advantages of another kind of autonomy instead of professional autonomy: *school autonomy*. After years of standardization and prescription, school autonomy seems to promise a welcome new direction, a willingness to take curriculum and teaching decisions back from bureaucrats and return them to educators themselves (Caldwell & Spinks, 1992).

Despite what the policy discourse suggests, however, there is no movement here to give teachers back their professional autonomy. Instead, it is argued, schools and presumably their leaders perform best when they have school autonomy – when the school as a unit has autonomy and discretion over key areas of decision-making that are not prescribed by external authorities (OECD, 2011). Various high-performing educational systems are cited as exemplars of school autonomy. But the support for school autonomy also underlines and underwrites the policies and strategies of lower-performing systems that embrace the market forces that have led to charter schools in America, free schools in Sweden and academies in England.

In countries like Finland, school autonomy over issues like curriculum and pedagogy actually occurs within the context of strong, shared commitments to curriculum development and the common good of all students within each democratically elected school district or local authority (Sahlberg, 2015). In the US, England and Sweden, though, school autonomy has been about individual schools detaching themselves from local communities and control so they operate within national or state frameworks or regulations instead.

Two troubling trends are evident here.

- First, school autonomy is not about the autonomy of teachers to make decisions about important educational matters individually or together: it is about the autonomy of the school owner and/or school principal to operate without due regard for the community or for local democratic control.
- Second, school autonomy is not about the substantive core of teaching and learning – the opportunity for teachers to have individual and shared freedom and responsibility to design the curriculum and pedagogical strategies that exercise their own professional judgment in the interests of the students they know best. Instead, school autonomy is autonomy over

> hiring and firing of staff in an increasingly de-unionized system, as well as over budget decisions that tend to privilege hiring of younger, temporary and less expensive teachers, over experienced teachers who want to make teaching their chosen career (Hargreaves & Fullan, 2012).

School autonomy, in this regard, leads not to greater professional status and autonomy for teachers, but the exact opposite – a less professionalized workforce that has more limited preparation, stays in teaching for shorter periods, works quickly and compliantly, and then moves on to something else. This increases profits for school owners and lowers tax burdens among governments wanting to impose economic austerity by lowering the costs of human resources.

At the same time, schools within these systems remain largely constrained by the centralized curriculum requirements and national testing systems of their countries. They have autonomy over staffing and budgets provided they comply with the centralized requirements of curriculum and instruction. The job of principals and evaluation systems is to undertake more one-to-one evaluations of classroom teachers, using one of the standardized rubrics of teacher performance that is widely available, and, in time, to gain more control over their own staffing and budgeting strategies and decisions. Principals become agents of evaluation and of restructuring the teacher workforce in a younger, less costly and more thinly prepared direction in support of a financially disinvesting state. Not only do teachers then become de-professionalized by the seductive strategy of school autonomy: principals do too. Principals turn into de-professionalized performance managers and evaluators of teachers as individuals rather than builders of professional communities among all their staff within and across schools.

The result is that free schools, charter schools and academies become compartmentalized from each other. They operate as separate silos – and the only good silo is one that still has grain in it! As a consequence, schools are subject to intense curriculum and testing pressure from above and market isolation from their peers around them (Supovitz, 2014). If we did this to individuals rather than institutions, it would be regarded as a form of torture or abuse. School autonomy is not professional autonomy. It is divide and rule; not live free or die.

Combining top-down bureaucracy with individual school competitiveness in a system that is lowering the level of teachers' professional capital is reducing the opportunities for educators to interact and improve by working with each other. For this reason, systems and strategies are emerging to create more coherence between the top and the bottom and to create more opportunities and incentives for improvement of practice and results among teachers and their peers (Barber & Day, 2014). The ending of local control leads to other ways to establish coherence instead. One of them is transparency.

The Traps of Transparency

When something is transparent, you can see through it, like glass. Transparency consists of accuracy, clarity and openness or visibility. In the social rather than the physical world, transparency emerged as a way to make political and corporate power-holders more accountable. It was something used by the public and its democratic institutions to hold elites in check. Corporate transparency ensures that the accounts of powerful companies are open not only to shareholders, but also to public scrutiny. This guards against the creation of secret monopolies, the commission of financial fraud, the uncontrolled eruption of economic crises and the perpetration of political and financial corruption. Environmental transparency deters companies from discharging toxic pollutants that imperil public heath and safety.

Transparency International (2014) provides a global index of transparency and its opposite, corruption. The leading countries on transparency indicators are Scandinavian social democracies, the Netherlands, New Zealand and Singapore: societies that also have high-performing economies and educational systems. This kind of transparency that serves the public interest is, in this respect, closely associated with other desirable features of society such as economic and educational performance.

So does this mean that we can raise performance in public education by increasing transparency among teachers in and between schools? Dufour and colleagues (2006) argue that transparency leads to the de-privatization of teachers' professional practice, putting an end to the isolation, insularity and secrecy that are associated with mediocre or poor performance. It removes the right to hide incompetence and ineffectiveness behind the classroom door. It prevents teachers from being lone rangers or independent contractors within their profession. It promotes a teaching profession that supports the common good and student learning rather than the protection of teachers' individual self-interest.

In *The Six Secrets of Change*, Michael Fullan (2011) advocates combining transparency with a non-judgmental culture that refrains from being punitive. In other words inquiry, not inquisition, is the key to effective transparency. Fullan's idea of transparency is one where there is a continuous flow of data and results about performance, and about the processes and practices that produce these results. Good processes for inquiring into practice and how to improve it are combined with good data on a range of metrics that make practice mutually visible. The result is what Fullan calls *positive pressure* to raise the bar and narrow the gap of student achievement. This is also the essence of John Hattie's widely used ideas about visible learning, where part of the transparency that leads to improvement in practice is the use of open and clear information as well as feedback about whether teachers' practices conform to those that research indicates yield the highest positive effect sizes on student learning (Hattie, 2009).

In Fullan's work, the best uses of transparency occur not in hierarchical supervisory relationships where teachers' practices and results are open to increasing scrutiny by their supervisors and superiors but where teachers meet with their peers to identify and examine learning and achievement data together. This peer-to-peer interaction and inquiry, Fullan argues, gets the group to change the group, instead of using supervisors to conduct countless top-down evaluations on the teachers below them. This peer-to-peer process for improving practice is also being advocated as a way for schools to improve by banding together with statistical neighbors (schools serving similar kinds of students) to compare their practices and results and to make appropriate interventions as a consequence.

For Fullan, positive pressure is not punitive pressure. It does not involve using transparency of data to make hasty interventions that also incorporate punitive measures such as firing teachers and principals or closing their schools. Instead, transparency among peers makes practice and results visible, and instigates individual and shared responsibility for improved performance and better results in an evidence-based profession.

This advocacy for increased transparency as part of a new, improved professionalism seems an unassailable answer to top-down, punitive accountability. It promotes openness, inquiry, better communication, and shared responsibility for improvement.

Or does it?

In education and other organizations, one of our professional responsibilities is not only to embrace apparently impregnable good ideas that promise to have widespread benefits for practice, but also to inspect and critique them, to turn them on their heads, to examine the ways they might be misused or consider the undesirable consequences that might ensue. Collaboration, for example, can be a ruse to secure compliance. Growth mindsets can be employed as a tool to reduce the issue of inequality to the way teachers look at it. Transparency needs the same critical treatment. Transparency needs more transparency.

Transparency originated as a strategy to hold the powerful to account. In education, though, despite Fullan's emphases, it now often operates in the other direction. Data-driven transparency is being used as a bureaucratic tool to watch over the professional practice of teachers and to have teachers constantly watching over each other. This could explain a seemingly curious finding of a 2014 study by Boston Consulting on educators' perceptions of professional development. The study found that over 70% of administrators and professional development providers believed that one of their major priorities should be more time for professional learning communities, but 45% of teachers and other receivers of professional learning communities (which often amount to teachers examining and acting on performance data together) ranked them negatively (Boston Consulting Group, 2014). This shift in the direction and use of transparency as a strategy of improvement and accountability is making this originally good idea vulnerable to three major problems:

- the problem of mistrust
- the problem of hierarchy
- the problem of privacy.

The Problem of Mistrust

Transparency is not a substitute for trust or even a precondition for it. As we have seen, Northern European countries that have high scores on indicators of transparency also exhibit high performance economically and educationally. In *The Spirit Level*, Wilkinson and Pickett (2009) analyzed the relationship between countries and US states with different degrees of income inequality on the one hand and indicators of social and mental health on the other. Northern European countries have high rankings among nations where people feel that 'most people can be trusted.' Except for Singapore, which has a high transparency score but a low trust rating, democracies that score high on transparency also score high on social trust. These democracies are also characterized by low social inequality. In these cases, openness and transparency seem to be a consequence of high trust and low inequality rather than the opposite. More transparency, in other words, will not create more trust or less poverty.

In their research on school districts that make effective use of data for improvement, for example, Datnow and Park (2014) found that effective and transparent uses of data occur in districts where there is already high trust and stable leadership. Transparency builds on pre-existing relationships of high trust and leadership stability. It is not a substitute or even a springboard for these things.

In most cases, trust is therefore a prerequisite for effective transparency, not an outcome of it. Only in extreme cases when there have been egregious instances of fraud and corruption can transparency be a useful tool to start to restore trust by establishing openness of information. In most instances of professional practice, though, transparency is not an effective way to establish trust. Indeed, where there is already pervasive mistrust and unstable leadership, transparency will only create suspicion about the motives behind it (to remove unwanted teachers, perhaps) or about the unreliable nature of the indicators that underpin it (such as value-added measures of achievement, or particular measures of poverty or diversity) (Braun, 2015). Many teachers see right through these imposed efforts to increase transparency.

The Problem of Hierarchy

Downward transparency occurs when the occupants of power look down at those beneath them to see their performance from above. Downward transparency is the executive suite's glass floor. More data in the form of published test scores or regular evaluative observations of teachers' classrooms create constant surveillance and top-down control.

Lateral transparency occurs when it is peers who see each other's practices and results. Comparing publicized performance data from different schools, subjects or grade levels, as well as employing procedures for teachers to observe and provide feedback on each other's classrooms, make teaching less of a mutual mystery among teachers.

Upward transparency occurs when holders of power in political or corporate life are required to disclose information to those beneath them in relation to expenses, accounting, bonuses, contracts, expenditure, hiring decisions, environmental impact and so forth. Upward transparency is designed to protect the public and prevent misuses of power. It is an effort to hold leaders accountable, so their glass floor becomes everyone else's see-through ceiling.

When upward and downward transparency is in balance, we have what Richard Elmore (2000) calls reciprocal accountability. Within the education profession, downward and lateral forms of transparency are increasingly common in processes of data-driven improvement and accountability. But upward transparency, or what is called *sousveillance* (watching from below), is often lacking in the education profession (Mann, Nolan & Wellman, 2002). While teachers may find they are perpetually evaluated according to continuous streams of performance data from above, the practices and effectiveness of school principals and superintendents are less open to examination from below. There is even less transparency where the ownership of charter schools and charter school chains is concerned (Ravitch, 2014). While corporate executives are sometimes subject to 360-degree evaluations in order to assess their performance, this is rarely true of their educational counterparts who are school superintendents or principals of charter schools or public schools. Similarly, while teachers and principals are held accountable to a standard, employers are less often held accountable for providing the resources that would make it possible to meet that standard. Too often, transparency is about being able to see more clearly what is beneath and around us rather than also about looking up to examine and expose the actions of those above us.

The Problem of Privacy

Ever since Judith Warren Little wrote *The Persistence of Privacy* in 1990 (Little, 1990), the private nature of teaching as something that takes place behind closed doors has come to be viewed as a bad thing. Dan Lortie's 1975 book *Schoolteacher* bemoaned how individualism combined with presentism (a focus on immediate, short-term actions) led teachers to adopt conservative approaches to change. Susan Rosenholtz (1989) then initiated a quarter century of research studies that highlighted the advantages of collaborative professional cultures over individualistic ones for producing student success. DuFour, DuFour and Eaker (2008) went further and strategically advised that teachers' practice should be de-privatized so that what teachers did was more open and visible to their colleagues and administrators.

But just as *individualism* (a culture where everyone is constrained and expected to work by themselves) should not be confused with *individuality* (the ability and opportunity to express one's unique teaching talents), *privatism* (a defensive or even arrogant withdrawal from scrutiny) should not be confused with *privacy* (the sensitive sphere of personal thoughts and actions that usually have a right to be protected from intrusive inspection).

Professional privacy – keeping one's practice to oneself unless it is illegal or immoral – is therefore not always a bad thing. Do we need to know everything about everybody? A car rental service I have used for many years recently instituted the practice of asking customers, in one way or another, what they will be doing and where they will be going when they have their rental vehicle. After this had happened several times with myself and, I noticed, with other customers, I asked the company's employees why they did this. It was, they said, so they could make a judgment about which gas option would be best for the customer – returning with a full tank or pre-paying. But, I said, what if I was going to a funeral, or to see a lover, or to visit a psychiatrist? Should I tell them? Should I lie? What business is it of theirs? Wouldn't it be better, more honest, and, indeed, more upwardly transparent, if they simply asked me straight out which gas option I would prefer?

Transparency is not always good and privacy is not always bad – even in teaching. Unless I work in a culture characterized by very high trust, I may not want to share examples of all my students' work with my colleagues. The work may be of a poor standard but from a very troubled student. It may disclose embarrassing family secrets that are not yet the concern of my peers. I may be starting out in a new subject or grade level and want to find my feet before my new colleagues peer into my practice. I may have come to a new school with a background in a literacy strategy of which my new principal disapproves. I may be reluctant to innovate in a technology-enhanced innovation like instant polling or using Twitter as a feedback device if I know my principal or my peers will be viewing the results of my efforts in real time. I may be older, expensive and in the way of an administrator looking to cut budgets by hiring younger replacements. The transparent data of today may turn into evidence that can be used against me when austerity-driven layoff decisions are being made in the future.

There are no easy answers to these concerns but the concerns are genuine. There are rights to personal and also professional privacy. Privacy is a human value and not just or always a weakness or a shortcoming. We have to think more deeply about how to balance transparency with privacy and avoid holding one of them hostage to the other.

Collective Autonomy

Transparency is not and should not be an end in itself. Its purpose, in education, should be as a tool to secure improvement as well as some degree of accountability.

There are other ways to secure improvement and accountability, though. They can be summarized in the idea of *collective autonomy*.

In *Professional Capital*, Michael Fullan and I describe how a system of collective autonomy occurs where 'the group at the local level acts with discretion and internal accountability while defining itself as part and parcel of the larger system' (Hargreaves & Fullan, 2012, p. 175). In a system and culture of collective autonomy, professionals have more autonomy from the mandates and regulations of external bureaucracies, but less autonomy from each other (Hargreaves & Shirley, 2009).

School autonomy offers only freedom from certain aspects of bureaucracy, but does not require that schools or professionals have any responsibility to one another or to the students they all serve together. Transparency erodes individual autonomy by opening people's practice to scrutiny, but transparency is also open to misuse by the hierarchy and to unwarranted intrusions upon privacy. To avoid these problems, transparency seems to require the pre-existence of trust and shared responsibility. These are integral aspects of the higher order imperative of collective autonomy.

There are four defining features of collective autonomy:

- commitment to a common vision
- collective responsibility for success
- circulation of insights and ideas
- incessant communication.

Common Vision

In their work on the establishment of system coherence in five prize-winning school districts, Susan Moore Johnson and her colleagues describe how the leaders of the districts they studied worked especially hard to create and maintain a sense of moral purpose and direction in their districts, especially in the face of multiple reform mandates that were imposed from the outside (Johnson et al., 2015).

Research with my colleagues on unusually high performing organizations in business, sport and education documents how each of these organizations defined an inspiring vision or dream that drew the members of their organization together in pursuit of common causes such as introducing energy-efficient cars to the US market, not allowing poverty to be an excuse for educational failure, becoming a leading knowledge economy, or simply elevating people's sense of taste in beer (Hargreaves, Boyle & Harris, 2014). These dreams may or may not have been articulated with charisma, but they quickly came to be commonly held rather than being artificially imposed.

Collective Responsibility

Collective autonomy entails not only believing in the same things but also in taking shared responsibility for results. Collective autonomy is also collective responsibility. In a study of special education inclusion practices in ten Ontario school districts, my colleagues and I found that special education resource teachers worked with classroom teachers in their own classrooms to take collective responsibility for the success of all students who struggled with their learning, not just those who had been formally identified (Hargreaves & Braun, 2012). In high performing Finland, teachers and other professionals meet regularly together to discuss and decide on interventions relating to any students who may be a concern (Sahlberg, 2015). Corrie Stone-Johnson documents the responsible leadership practices of the head-teachers of three schools in northern England who took responsibility with their staffs for helping other schools who were struggling, as well as for leading their own (Stone-Johnson, 2014).

School autonomy is about my teachers, my students and my school. Collective autonomy is about taking responsibility together for all our students and all the schools in our communities and networks that we affect.

Circulation

In economies, if capital is going to grow, to produce a return on investment, it must be able to circulate or move around relatively freely. Without circulation, economies become stagnant. The same is true of air supply in sealed buildings. And without vigorous circulatory systems in our bodies, our hearts begin to weaken and our systems start to shut down.

Professional capital – the wealth or poverty of the collective knowledge or expertise in a profession – is no different. Knowledge needs to circulate if professional capital is going to grow. If schools are isolated from each other, or teachers and their leaders cannot travel out of their country or even out of state for professional learning, this restricts the circulation of insights, ideas and evidence that might lead to improvement. Sometimes the arteries of professional learning atrophy because of neglect. Sometimes, they are willfully blocked by senior administration, so that teachers and principals cannot access disruptive knowledge and ideas that have not been sanctioned by the system.

One way to circulate ideas, evidence and insights freely throughout the profession is through professional networks. In the Pacific Northwest, for example, Dennis Shirley and I, in combination with Education Northwest, are working with the states of Oregon, Washington and Idaho to build networks of schools that are committed to increasing student engagement in rural communities (Hargreaves, Parsley & Cox, in press). With the evidence-based support we have provided related to factors that explain success and failure in other networks, the members of the network designed their own network architecture – including who would be its participants, what would be the focus, how its members would interact, what tasks and activities they would initiate, and how all this would intersect with the larger system.

The network is not a cluster: a group or team assembled by others to implement top-down initiatives. It moves knowledge and practices around by itself through units of work on writing, observational tools for looking at student engagement, and so on. The point of the network is for ideas and practices to circulate in ways that improve the practice of teachers who are otherwise isolated from each other by vast distances. Its purpose is not to filter initiatives down from the top.

Incessant Communication

How do you put the 'collective' into collective autonomy? One of the key strategies is to communicate constantly. In Finland, school and systems administrators are constantly in schools, approaching everything with a problem-solving mentality and listening for the 'weak signals' when something may be wrong (Hargreaves, Halász & Pont, 2008). Singapore's society and its schools are held together and animated by endless intensive interaction, at meetings, networks, and in a seemingly constant round of food-laden meetings (Hargreaves & Shirley, 2012). The new leaders at a school in England that was performing far beyond expectations took the time to communicate their vision to everyone – even the lowliest substitute teachers, and the learning mentors from the community (Hargreaves & Shirley, 2012). Some administrators try to get coherence in a system through structural alignment of budgets, staff development, assessment strategies, and so on (Johnson et al., 2015). But the key cultural characteristic of a coherent system of autonomous professionals whose work hangs together coherently is that of incessant communication about values, priorities, practice, problems and results.

Conclusion

School autonomy is not professional autonomy. The alternative is collective autonomy. Effective professional autonomy in today's schools is not individual, but collective. It is not just autonomy that protects us from unwanted interference, but autonomy to do important things together. Collective autonomy is about constant communication and circulation of ideas in a coherent system where there is collective responsibility to achieve a common vision of student learning, development and success. Transparency has become a glass through which we look at each other or through which others look down on us. Collective responsibility is a mirror in which we see ourselves. Autonomy and transparency are good ideas that have gone bad. Collective autonomy is a way we can take back their essence and re-establish their original integrity.

References

Barber, M. and Day, S. (2014). *The new opportunity to lead: A vision for education in Massachusetts in the next 20 years*. Retrieved from Massachusetts Business Alliance for Education website: http://www.mbae.org/wp-content/uploads/2014/03/New-Opportunity-to-Lead.pdf.

Boston Consulting Group (2014). Teachers know best: Teachers' views on professional development. Retrieved from http://collegeready.gatesfoundation.org/article/teachers-know-best-teachers-views-professional-development.

Braun, H. (2015). The value in value added depends on the ecology. *Educational Researcher*, 44(2), 127–131.

Caldwell, B. and Spinks, J. M. (1992). *Leading the Self-managing School*. Florence: Psychology Press.

Datnow, A. and Park, V. (2014). *Data-driven Leadership*. San Francisco: Jossey-Bass.

DuFour, R., DuFour, R. B. and Eaker, R. E. (2008). *Revisiting Professional Learning Communities at Work: New Insights for Improving Schools*. Bloomington: Solution Tree.

DuFour, R., DuFour, R. B., Eaker, R. E. and Many, T. (2006). *Learning by Doing*. Bloomington: Solution Tree.

Elmore, R. F. (2000). *Building a New Structure for School Leadership*. Washington, DC: Albert Shanker Institute.

Fullan, M. (2011). *The Six Secrets of Change: What the Best Leaders Do to Help their Organizations Survive and Thrive*. San Francisco: Jossey-Bass.

Hargreaves, A., Boyle, A. and Harris, A. (2014). *Uplifting Leadership: How Organizations, Teams, and Communities Raise Performance*. San Francisco: Jossey-Bass.

Hargreaves, A. and Braun, H. (2012). Leading for all: Final report of the review of the development of Essential for Some, Good for All – Ontario's strategy for special education reform devised by the Council of Directors of Education. Toronto: Council of Directors of Education.

Hargreaves, A. and Fullan, M. (2012). *Professional Capital*. New York: Teachers College Press.

Hargreaves, A., Halász, G. and Pont, B. (2008). The Finnish approach to system leadership. In B. Pont, D. Nusche and D. Hopkins (eds), *Improving School Leadership, Vol. 2: Case Studies on System Leadership* (pp. 69–109). Paris: OECD.

Hargreaves, A., Parsley, D. and Cox, E. (in press). Designing and launching rural school improvement networks: Aspirations and actualities. *Peabody Journal of Education*.

Hargreaves, A. and Shirley, D. (2009). *The Fourth Way: The Inspiring Future for Educational Change*. Thousand Oaks: Corwin Press.

Hargreaves, A. and Shirley, D. (2012). *The Global Fourth Way: The Quest for Educational Excellence*. Thousand Oaks: Corwin Press.

Hattie, J. (2009). *Visible Learning: A Synthesis of over 800 Meta-analyses Relating to Achievement*. London: Routledge.

Johnson, S. M., Marietta, G., Higgins, M. C., Mapp, K. L. and Grossman, A. (2015). *Achieving Coherence in District Improvement: Managing the Relationship between the Central Office and Schools*. Cambridge, MA: Harvard Education Press.

Little, J. (1990). The persistence of privacy: Autonomy and initiative in teachers' professional relations. *The Teachers College Record*, 91(4), 509–536.

Lortie, D. C. (1975). *Schoolteacher: A Sociological Inquiry.* Chicago: University of Chicago Press.

Mann, S., Nolan, J. and Wellman, B. (2002). Sousveillance: Inventing and using wearable computing devices for data collection in surveillance environments. *Surveillance & Society*, 1(3), 331–355.

Marris, P. (1974). *Loss and Change.* New York: Pantheon Books.

OECD (2011). *School autonomy and accountability: Are they related to student performance?* Retrieved from http://www.oecd.org/pisa/pisaproducts/pisainfocus/48910490.pdf.

Ravitch, D. (2014). *Reign of Error: The Hoax of the Privatization Movement and the Danger to America's Public Schools.* New York: Chronicle Books

Robinson, K. and Aronica, L. (2015). *Creative Schools: The Grassroots Revolution that's Transforming Education.* New York: Viking Press.

Rosenholtz, S. J. (1989). *Teachers' Workplace: The Social Organization of Schools.* Harlow: Addison-Wesley Longman Ltd.

Sahlberg, P. (2015). *Finnish Lessons 2.0.* New York: Teachers College Press.

Schwartz, B. (2004). *The Paradox of Choice: Why Less Is More.* New York: Ecco.

Sennett, R. (2011). *The Corrosion of Character: The Personal Consequences of Work in the New Capitalism.* New York: W.W. Norton & Company.

Stone-Johnson, C. (2014). Responsible leadership. *Educational Administration Quarterly*, 50(4), 645–674.

Supovitz, J. (2014). *Building a lattice for school leadership: The top to bottom rethinking of leadership development in England* (Research Report No. 83). Retrieved from Consortium for Policy Research in Education website: http://cpre.org/sites/default/files/researchreport/2027_leadershipengland.Pdf.

Transparency International (2014). *The 2012 corruption perceptions index measures the perceived levels of public sector corruption in 175 countries and territories.* Retrieved from https://www.transparency.org/cpi2014.

Weber, M. (1992). *The Protestant Ethic and the Spirit of Capitalism.* London: Routledge.

Westheimer, J. (2015). *What Kind of Citizen? Educating our Children for the Common Good.* New York: Teachers College Press.

Wilkinson, R. G. and Pickett, K. (2009). *The Spirit Level.* London: Penguin Allen Lane.

Chapter 10

Teacher Agency

What Is It and Why Does It Matter?

Mark Priestley, Gert Biesta and Sarah Robinson

The concept of teacher agency has emerged in recent literature as an alternative means of understanding how teachers might enact practice and engage with policy (e.g. Lasky, 2005; Leander & Osborne, 2008; Ketelaar et al., 2012; Priestley, Biesta & Robinson, 2013). But what is agency? Agency remains an inexact and poorly conceptualised construct in much of the literature, where it is often not clear whether the term refers to the individual capacity of teachers to act agentically, or to an emergent 'ecological' phenomenon dependent upon the quality of individuals' engagement with their environments (Biesta & Tedder, 2007). In this chapter, we outline the latter conception of agency, developing a conceptual model for teacher agency that emphasises the temporal and relational dimension of the achievement of agency. Why does this matter? Recent curriculum policy in many countries heralds a [re]turn to the centrality of the teacher in school-based curriculum development. In many cases, this renewed emphasis on teachers is explicitly tied to change agendas, with teachers described as agents of change. And yet such change agentry (Fullan, 2003) and teacher agency more broadly are often circumscribed by features of the contexts within which teachers work – for example accountability mechanisms and other forms of output regulation of teachers' work – leading to engagement with policy that is often instrumental and blighted by unintended consequences. In this chapter, we illustrate how a detailed understanding of teacher agency and the conditions under which it is achieved offer considerable potential in enabling teachers to engage with curricular policy in more meaningful ways.

Introduction

Powerful discourses recently driving global education policy have emphasised the important role of teachers as the most significant within-school influence on school improvement (OECD, 2005; McKinsey & Co., 2007). Such discourses have been accompanied by at least two key trends within education policies in many countries. First, there is an emerging tendency in curriculum policy to construct teachers explicitly as agents of change (e.g. Goodson, 2003;

Nieveen, 2011; Priestley, 2011a). Thus, the last ten years have witnessed the development of new forms of national curriculum in a range of countries, for example Scotland's Curriculum for Excellence and the New Zealand Curriculum Framework (see Sinnema & Aitken, 2013; Priestley & Sinnema, 2014). Intrinsic to these developments is a renewed vision of teachers as active developers of curriculum, a significant shift given several decades of policies that have actively deprofessionalised teachers through highly prescriptive curricula (Priestley & Biesta, 2013). Second, parallel education policies have strongly emphasised the need to improve the quality of teachers through programmes of continuous professional formation, through for instance the development of teacher professional learning communities (Stoll et al., 2006; Daly et al., 2010), the institution of new teacher standards and calls for teaching to become a master's-level profession. In Scotland, such discourses are strongly reflected in the report *Teaching Scotland's Future* (Donaldson, 2010).

The emerging trends outlined above are problematic for a number of reasons. At a rhetorical level at least, they suggest a [re]turn to bottom-up approaches that put the teacher at the centre of the educational process, following decades of prescriptive, top-down, teacher-proof curricula. However, it is debatable whether the rhetoric is matched by actual moves towards greater teacher autonomy and influence. While tight curricular prescription of content – input, 'front door' regulation of teachers' work – appears to have become less fashionable in many countries in recent years, there has been a noticeable increase in the frequency and extent of output, 'back door' regulation – for example through school inspections and the evaluative use of attainment data (Kuiper, Nieveen & Berkvens, 2013). This has arguably done more to erode teacher autonomy than was the case under former, ostensibly more prescriptive approaches (Biesta, 2004). This 'giving with one hand and taking away with the other' (Leat, 2014) has been associated with the development of performative cultures in school and instrumental decision-making by teachers (Sahlberg, 2010; Keddie, Mills & Pendergast, 2011; Wilkins, 2011). Put simply, policy demands that teachers exercise agency in their working practices, then simultaneously denies them the means to do so, effectively disabling them; such policy overtly focuses on the individual dimensions of what it means to be an effective teacher, while ignoring or subverting the cultural and structural conditions that play an important role in enabling this to happen. This raises important questions about the relative balance between input and output regulation (ibid.; Leat, Livingston & Priestley, 2013). We would argue that the either/or-isms and pendulum swings witnessed in recent years between each extreme of this continuum are problematic, and that while tight prescription is counter-productive, policy ceding complete autonomy to schools is similarly unhelpful. Instead, what is needed is a sensible framing of curricular purposes and processes within policy (Biesta, 2009), or in other words a framework of specification that enables rather than constrains the development of constructive practices by teachers (Kuiper, Nieveen & Berkvens, 2013).

It is in this context that the concept of teacher agency is helpful, and indeed it has emerged in recent literature as an alternative means of understanding how teachers might enact practice and engage with policy (e.g. Lasky, 2005; Leander & Osborne, 2008; Ketelaar et al., 2012; Pyhältö, Soini & Pietarinen, 2012; Priestley, Biesta & Robinson, 2013; Pyhältö, Pietarinen & Soini, 2014). Nevertheless, the concept of teacher agency itself is not unproblematic: agency remains an inexact and poorly conceptualised construct in much of the literature, where it is often not clear whether the term refers to an individual capacity of teachers to act agentically or to an emergent 'ecological' phenomenon dependent upon the quality of individuals' engagement with their environments (Biesta & Tedder, 2007); and teacher agency often remains linked to limited agendas of school improvement, where agency is construed more narrowly as 'change agentry' (Fullan, 2003), teachers positioned as implementers of someone else's policy, and schools represented as being in deficit and in need of reform. In this chapter, we offer an alternative view of teacher agency, developing an ecological conceptualisation of agency that emphasises the importance of both *agentic capacity* and *agentic spaces* in shaping agency, and moreover views the *achievement of agency* as a temporal process (Emirbayer & Mische, 1998). This is an important conceptual distinction, often overlooked in writing about agency, which is crucial to our analysis of teacher agency. In the sections that follow, we first provide an overview of this theorisation of agency, before returning to the question of why this increasingly matters in the current context of education.

What Is Teacher Agency?

Agency

Our interest here lies in understanding the phenomenon of agency itself, rather than in explaining its role in shaping and determining social action. Developing a strong conceptualisation of the notion of agency allows us to ask how agency is 'achieved' in concrete settings and under particular 'ecological' conditions and circumstances (Biesta & Tedder, 2006). Our perspective on agency therefore differs from the sociological concept of agency as a variable in social action (for example in the longstanding structure/agency debate). Rather than seeing agency as residing in individuals as a property or capacity, the ecological view of agency sees agency as an emergent phenomenon of the ecological conditions through which it is enacted.

> [T]his concept of agency highlights that actors always act *by means* of their environment rather than simply in their environment [so that] the achievement of agency will always result from *the interplay of individual efforts, available resources and contextual and structural factors as they come together in particular and, in a sense, always unique situations.*
>
> (Biesta & Tedder, 2007, p. 137; emphasis added)

Agency, in other words, is not something that people can have; it is something that people do, or, more precisely, something they achieve (Biesta & Tedder, 2006). It denotes a 'quality' of the engagement of actors with temporal–relational contexts-for-action, not a quality of the actors themselves. Viewing agency in such terms helps us to understand how humans are able to be reflexive and creative, acting counter to societal constraints, but also how individuals are enabled and constrained by their social and material environments.

Agency, in this view, is both temporal and relational. We draw here on Emirbayer and Mische (1998), who have theorised agency with the dual aim of robustly conceptualising agency and overcoming the theoretical one-sidedness of existing theories of agency, which, in their view, tend to focus either on routine, or on purpose, or on judgement. They make a case for a theory of agency which encompasses the dynamic interplay between these three dimensions and which takes into consideration 'how this interplay varies within different structural contexts of action' (ibid., p. 963). For this reason they suggest that the achievement of agency should be understood as a configuration of influences from the past, orientations towards the future and engagement with the present. They refer to these three dimensions as the *iterational*, the *projective* and the *practical-evaluative* dimension respectively. In concrete actions all three dimensions play a role, but the degree to which they contribute varies. This is why Emirbayer and Mische speak of a '*chordal triad* of agency within which all three dimensions resonate as separate but not always harmonious tones' (ibid., p. 972; emphasis in original). Thus, they define agency as '*the temporally constructed engagement by actors of different structural environments – the temporal–relational contexts of action – which, through the interplay of habit, imagination, and judgement, both reproduces and transforms those structures in interactive response to the problems posed by changing historical situations*' (ibid., p. 970; emphasis in original). Agency thus appears as a 'temporally embedded process of social engagement, informed by the past (in its habitual aspect), oriented toward the future (as a capacity to imagine alternative possibilities) and "acted out" in the present (as a capacity to contextualize past habits and future projects with the contingencies of the moment)' (ibid., p. 963).

Teacher Agency

While agency *per se* has been extensively theorised, teacher agency – in other words, agency that is theorised specifically in respect of the activities of teachers in schools – has not received the attention it deserves. There has been little explicit research or theory development (Vongalis-Macrow, 2007) about this 'vague' concept (Pyhältö, Pietarinen & Soini, 2012) and existing change models tend to both underplay and misconstrue the role of teacher agency in educational innovation (Leander & Osborne, 2008). In this section of the chapter, we briefly set out our ecological model for understanding teacher agency, drawing explicitly on the temporal/relational conception of agency

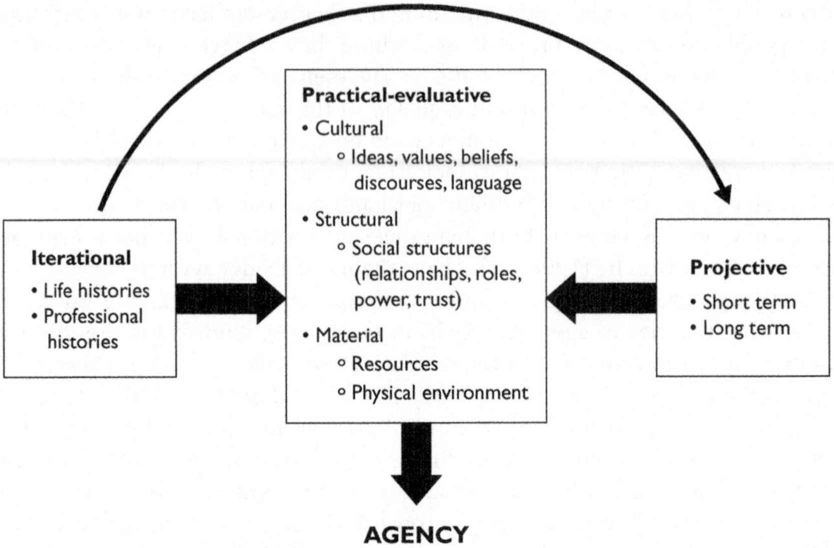

Figure 10.1 Teacher agency model.
(First published in Priestley, Biesta & Robinson, 2013)

outlined by Emirbayer and Mische (1998). The diagram above represents the key dimensions of the model, illustrating the ways in which we analytically separate out key elements of each dimension. With regard to the iterational dimension, we distinguish between the influence of the more general life histories of teachers and their more specific professional histories (which include both their own education as a teacher and the accumulated experience of being a teacher). With regard to the projective dimension, we distinguish between short-term and long[er]-term orientations of action. And with regard to the practical-evaluative dimension, we make a distinction between cultural, structural and material aspects.

The model highlights that the achievement of agency is always informed by past experience – and in the particular case of teacher agency this concerns both professional and personal experience. The model also emphasises that the achievement of agency is always orientated towards the future in some combination of short[er]-term and long[er]-term objectives and values. And it illustrates that agency is always enacted in a concrete situation, therefore both being constrained and supported by cultural, structural and material resources available to actors. The following sections outline these ideas in more detail.

The Iterational Dimension of Agency

Emirbayer and Mische's ideas are helpful because they first of all show that agency doesn't come from nowhere but builds upon past achievements, understandings and patterns of action. This is expressed in the iterational element of agency, which has to do with '*the selective reactivation by actors of past patterns of thought and action, routinely incorporated in practical activity, thereby giving stability and order to social universes and helping to sustain identities, interactions, and institutions over time*' (ibid., p. 971; emphasis in original). A key word here is 'selective'. Emirbayer and Mische note that while some writers suggest that 'the agentic reactivation of schemes inculcated through past experience tends to correspond to (and thus reproduce) societal patterns' (ibid., p. 981), this level of routinisation does not have to be the case. Actors do not always act from habit, following routinised patterns of behaviour, but are able to recognise, appropriate and refashion past patterns of behaviours and experience as they seek to *manoeuvre among repertoires* in dealing with present dilemmas and engage in *expectation maintenance* in their orientations to the future. A key implication here is that actors able to draw upon a rich repertoire of experience might be expected to be able to develop more expansive orientations to the future and draw upon a greater range of responses to the dilemmas and problems of the present context, than might be the case with their more experientially impoverished compatriots.

In respect of teachers, we would point to a number of iterational aspects that contribute to teacher agency. These include personal capacity (skills and knowledge), beliefs (professional and personal) and values. What these have in common is their rooting in past experiences. Clearly, for the teachers of tomorrow, it is important to attend now, in present contexts, to the nature of what will become those past experiences. This is where the importance of teacher education lies, not only in providing teachers with such resources, but also making them reflectively available, so that rather than a set of practical skills or competences, they can become resources for judgement and action (see also Biesta, in press). Such education (both initial education and continuing professional development) should thus focus on what we term resource building and reflective engagement – and if the focus is to be on developing agents of change and professional developers of the curriculum, then programmes of professional development should focus on interrupting habitual and socially reinforced ways of thinking about schooling and to encourage a reflective mind set. Arguably, this should include a thorough engagement with questions of educational purpose and with the principles of curriculum development and enactment.

Nevertheless, professional education forms only a small part of the formation of teachers' professional experience. Day-to-day experience in schools – dialogue with colleagues, exposure to school culture, and other professional engagement – would seem to be significant too. Restrictive contexts that deprofessionalise teachers must surely have long-term consequences on future teacher development. It might also be argued that teachers working in less innovative schools are less likely to experience a wider repertoire of responses to problematic situations than colleagues in schools where innovation is encouraged and supported – although it is important to bear in mind the distinction between innovation for innovation's sake and an orientation towards improvement, which sometimes also can mean resisting demands for change. Moreover, professional experience is perhaps less significant than personal experience in shaping teacher agency. Teachers' own schooling must be significant in the development of the capacity to question and innovate. Professional experience outwith education is another significant and interesting pointer to the sorts of agency achieved by teachers. For instance, recent research (Priestley et al., 2012) suggests that teachers with significant experience of working in other professions might have a wider repertoire for manoeuvre when faced with the challenges and ambiguities of the teacher's day-to-day work. It is interesting to reflect upon the sorts of experiences that might contribute to the future development of the sorts of qualities and capacities required by teachers if they are to become the sorts of active, professional agents of change envisaged in some policies. In turn there are significant implications here for those charged with configuring educational contexts.

The Projective Dimension of Agency

Emirbayer and Mische's approach also acknowledges that agency is in some way 'motivated'; that is, that it is linked to the intention to bring about a future that is different from the present and the past. This is encapsulated in the projective element of agency which encompasses '*the imaginative generation by actors of possible future trajectories of action, in which received structures of thought and action may be creatively reconfigured in relation to actors' hopes, fears, and desires for the future*' (Emirbayer & Mische, p. 971; emphasis in original). Such a process of continual imaginative reconstruction of the future involves 'draw[ing] upon past experiences in order to clarify motives, goals and intentions, to locate possible future constraints, and to identify morally and practically appropriate courses of action' (p. 989). An implication here is that people who are able to form expansive projections about their future trajectories might be expected to achieve greater levels of agency than those whose aspirations are more limited, at least to the extent that they have access to a wider repertoire of alternative futures. Whether such a repertoire is translated into action does, of course, not only depend on the repertoire itself but also on the contextual conditions under which teachers act (see below).

The projective dimension of teacher agency concerns teachers' aspirations in respect of their work – both long term and short term. Such aspirations may be entirely positive, relating to the development and welfare of students (Lasky, 2005), and lead to agency that is protective of students' interests (Osborn et al., 1997). Such agency may support policy intentions, or it may run counter to them (ibid.; Ladwig, 2010). In both cases, it can be driven by sincerely held, often long-term aspirations rooted strongly in teachers' values and beliefs (Belo et al., 2014). Or aspirations may be more narrowly instrumental, for example maintaining a 'normal desirable state' in the classroom (Brown & McIntyre, 1992) or 'playing the game' (Gleeson & Gunter, 2001). This game can take the form of fabrication of the school's image – careful impression management and discourses of excellence (Keddie, Mills & Pendergast, 2011) and the concealing of 'dirty laundry' (Cowie, Taylor & Croxford, 2007), as well as more serious corruption and cheating (Ball, 2003; Sahlberg, 2010). The forms of agency evident in these latter cases are clearly quite different from those in the former example, motivated by quite different aspirations, and often the result of systems of accountability and performativity that create perverse drivers and incentives.

Whatever the form these aspirations take, and whatever the motivation for them, we suggest that they are invariably largely rooted in teachers' prior experiences. Thus we must not under-estimate the importance of strongly held beliefs about subject identity, for example, or teachers' motivations to do their best for their students, as these are important in shaping the form aspirations will take. Teachers' prior professional experiences will help form such aspirations. Thus, for example, a previous experience of a negative school inspection may make teachers risk averse in their work, and hence aspirations are narrowed and agency circumscribed. It is our view that the types of teacher agency emerging in schools today has been significantly shaped by the past two decades of managerialism in education. Data emerging from our recent research in Scotland (Priestley, Biesta & Robinson, in press) suggest a link between past contexts and experiences and teachers' ability to frame expansive aspirations in their professional work. Our findings here are consistent with Salomon's (1992) argument that such approaches represent a derogation of teacher responsibility. He posited three types of teacher responsibility:

- a proper carrying out of role as teacher (necessary whether a teacher is transmitting content or orchestrating activity)
- responsibility for learning processes and outcomes
- serious consideration of method and content in the light of normative and moral criteria – i.e. consideration of long-term educational purposes and values. This responsibility is about 'giving serious consideration to the desirable and less desirable long-term effects of the constantly improvised learning environment'.

(p. 46)

Data from our own research suggest that the teachers in our project were highly efficient in getting the job done, despite inevitable difficulties encountered in terms of social, cultural and material constraints on their work. These teachers had a large repertoire of technical responses to enable their lessons to run smoothly. They were effective in achieving certain short-term goals, for example introducing new forms of pedagogy that were deemed suitable for Curriculum for Excellence. However, the data suggest a fairly narrow engagement with consideration of the longer-term 'effects' of education – 'desirable residues to be manifested later on' (ibid., p. 44).

The Practical-Evaluative Dimension of Agency

Although agency is involved with the past and the future, it can only ever be 'acted out' in the present, which is precisely what is expressed in the practical-evaluative dimension, which entails '*the capacity of actors to make practical and normative judgements among alternative possible trajectories of action, in response to the emerging demands, dilemmas, and ambiguities of presently evolving situations*' (Emirbayer & Mische, p. 971; emphasis in original). Judgements are both practical – shaped by the affordances and constraints of the context – and evaluative – for example judgements of risk in any given situation or judgement in relation to views about what is educationally desirable. Emirbayer and Mische's analysis emphasises the importance of context and structure, in that agency is seen as the 'temporally constructed engagement with different structural environments' (ibid., p. 970). The combination of context and time highlights that it is not only important to understand agency in terms of the individual's lifecourse: it is at the very same time important to understand transformations of contexts-for-action over time. According to Emirbayer and Mische, such contexts are primarily to be understood as social contexts, in that agency is 'always a dialogical process by and through which actors immersed in temporal passage engage with others within collectively organized contexts of action' (ibid., p. 974). However, we would argue that such contexts are also material, in that agency is partly shaped by the availability of physical resources and the nature of physical constraints.

Teaching has been characterised as a profession that is rife with ambiguity (e.g. Helsby, 1999), laden with emotional politics (Hargreaves, 1998), context dependent and contestable in terms of its aims. Teachers make daily decisions that are difficult, involving compromise and at times conflict with their aspirations, feeling coerced by what they might see as arbitrary and unnecessary intrusions into their work. Moreover they do so often on the basis of insufficient time to reflect and to engage in professional dialogue with colleagues. Thus, the practical-evaluative dimension forms a major influence on agency, powerfully shaping (and often distorting) decision making and action, both offering possibilities for agency (for example by making resources available) and inhibiting it (for example by creating perceptions of unacceptable risk). For the purposes of this chapter, we briefly offer the following two exemplar themes to illustrate the sorts of factors that act as part of the practical-evaluative dimension of teacher agency.

The first concerns conflicting pressures in teachers' work. In Scotland, for example, Reeves (2008) has documented tensions between a new curriculum that opens up possibilities for teacher agency, and quality-improvement initiatives (based around inspections, self-evaluation and attainment) that have been shown to corrode it (Helsby, 1999; Biesta, 2004; Perryman, 2012). Such tensions between input and output regulation can create impossible dilemmas for teachers, and as noted previously in the chapter can lead to instrumental decision making. The second theme relates to relationships in schools. In Scotland, for example, many secondary schools are organised hierarchically, with strong vertical structures, but more limited horizontal relationships. Research (e.g. Coburn & Russell, 2008) suggests that schools that develop effective structures to encourage such relationships cope more effectively with new policy, enabling teachers to engage dialogically with, and make sense of new policy. Coburn and Russell point to two aspects of such relationships: (1) tie strength (engendering trust); and (2) tie span – relationships that extend beyond the school, breaking cycles of inward-looking practice, and allowing access to external, expert knowledge. Our research in Scotland (Priestley, Biesta & Robinson, in press) strongly supports these conclusions, suggesting that, other factors being equal, teachers in schools affording strong relational resources achieve higher degrees of agency than their counterparts in schools where such resources are more limited.

Why Does Teacher Agency Matter?

Teacher agency can be therefore characterised as an emergent phenomenon, something that occurs or is achieved within continually shifting contexts over time, and with orientations towards past, future and present which differ within each and every instance of agency achieved. But why does this matter? Why is it important to understand how teacher agency occurs in educational settings? We offer, in this concluding section, a number of reasons why we believe that it is vital to understand teacher agency in the way outlined above, and the conditions that both make it possible and shape its manifestations.

A key implication is that if agency is achieved, rather than being solely about the capacity of actors, then the importance of context should be taken more seriously by public policy makers and leaders in public organisations, as such contexts may serve to disable individuals with otherwise high agentic capacity. A key point here is that while teachers may come to a situation equipped with substantial capacity (e.g. skills and knowledge) and strong educational aspirations, innovation may simply prove to be too difficult, or too risky to enact. This also shows why the language of 'capacity building' is misleading, as it seems to suggest that the key to teachers' agency lies with their capacity, rather than with the interplay of what teachers 'bring' to the situation and what the situation 'brings' to the teacher; that is, inhibits or promotes. A further corollary of this lies in the conclusion that if agency today is influenced by experiences from the past, then we can conclude that today's contexts will impact upon the future agency of teachers. Such conclusions have clear implications for those designing public policy today, particularly when the goal is to raise teacher capacity, for example their ability to develop a new national curriculum. As we noted earlier, public policy in respect of teacher development tends to focus on raising the capacity of teachers as individual actors; our view is that it needs to attend more explicitly to the cultural and structural domains that frame teachers' work.

A second implication lies in an observation by Emirbayer and Mische that what might pass for agency is not necessarily so. For example, agency may be involved in the reproduction of social patterns through active resistance to change, when to the casual observer what seems to be occurring is habitual behaviour by the actors concerned, or a lack of agency in the face of insurmountable problems. Priestley (2011b) documents the case of a teacher in just such a situation – someone swimming against the tide in a difficult environment, who nevertheless managed to hold true to deeply held principles. By contrast, 'actors who feel creative and deliberative while in the flow of unproblematic trajectories' (Emirbayer & Mische, 1998, p. 1008) may not be achieving high levels of agency, as they simply go with the flow.

This is an important implication when one considers the difference between autonomy and agency. As we noted in the opening part of the chapter, many critics of current policy advocate autonomy as a means of freeing up schools and enabling change. However, autonomy (understood here as a comparative absence of regulation) does not necessarily equate to agency. Teachers granted autonomy may simply fail to achieve agency as they, for example, habitually reproduce past patterns of behaviour, or as they lack cognitive and relational resources. Conversely, agency may be shaped and enhanced by policy that specifies goals and processes, enhancing the capability of teachers to manoeuvre between repertoires, make decisions and frame future actions.

An example of this is provided by recent development work conducted in Scotland within a university/local authority partnership (Drew & Priestley, 2014). Here teachers worked with university researchers over the course of a full school year to develop the curriculum, drawing upon various cognitive resources. These included the goals of Curriculum for Excellence – the capabilities and attributes specified under the headings of the Four Capacities (Scottish Executive, 2004) – laid down in the policy framework, as well as a clearly defined process for school-based curriculum development through collaborative professional enquiry facilitated by university-based researchers (Priestley & Minty, 2012; Reeves & Drew, 2013). At the early stages of the project many participating teachers reported low confidence, confusion about curricular aims, tensions between conflicting messages in their work and a general sense of disempowerment. It is significant that involvement in the project led, in the majority of cases, to the subsequent achievement of agency by these teachers, suggesting how curricular specification might play a powerful role in enabling teacher agency. It is important to note here that these teachers were not simply implementing policy – this was not a case of teachers being manipulated into becoming agents of change. Nor were they being offered carte blanche to do whatever they wished. Instead, the affordances offered by the specification of goals and processes enabled them to become genuinely agentic as they actively developed and adapted the curriculum to meet both curricular goals and local needs.

In summary, therefore, the ecological approach to teacher agency offers considerable potential in enabling those who frame policies to more fully understand the implications of those policies for those who enact practice. It allows us to rigorously consider how the ecologies of teaching affect teacher decision making and teacher actions. And it potentially enables teachers to become more reflexive about their professional working practices, as they take on responsibility for the long-term development of the students they work with. In achieving these goals, the concept of teacher agency in general, and the ecological approach in particular, potentially offers a means for arresting and even reversing 25 years of misguided regulation of the work of teachers.

Acknowledgment

Many of the insights in this chapter were generated during an empirical research project, Teacher Agency and Curriculum Change. The authorship of the paper reflects the team conducting this research. The project was funded by the UK Economic and Social Research Council (project reference RES-000-22-4208).

References

Ball, S. J. (2003). The teacher's soul and the terrors of performativity. *Journal of Education Policy*, 18, 215–228.

Belo, N. A. H., van Driel, J. H., van Veen, K. and Verloop, N. (2014). Beyond the dichotomy of teacher- versus student-focused education: A survey study on physics teachers' beliefs about the goals and pedagogy of physics education. *Teaching and Teacher Education*, 39, 89–101.

Biesta, G. J. J. (2004). Education, accountability and the ethical demand: Can the democratic potential of accountability be regained? *Educational Theory*, 54, 233–250.

Biesta, G. J. J. (2009). Good education in an age of measurement: On the need to reconnect with the question of purpose in education. *Educational Assessment, Evaluation and Accountability*, 21, 33–46.

Biesta, G. J. J. (in press). How does a competent teacher become a good teacher? On judgement, wisdom and virtuosity in teaching and teacher education. In R. Heilbronn and L. Foreman-Peck (eds), *Philosophical Perspectives on the Future of Teacher Education*. Oxford: Wiley Blackwell.

Biesta, G. J. J. and Tedder, M. (2006). *How Is Agency Possible? Towards an Ecological Understanding of Agency-as-achievement. Working paper 5*. Exeter: The Learning Lives project.

Biesta, G. J. J. and Tedder, M. (2007). Agency and learning in the lifecourse: Towards an ecological perspective. *Studies in the Education of Adults*, 39, 132–149.

Brown, S. and McIntyre, D. (1992). *Making Sense of Teaching*. Buckingham: Open University Press.

Coburn, C. E. and Russell, J. L. (2008). District policy and teachers' social networks. *Educational Evaluation and Policy Analysis*, 30, 203–235.

Cowie, M., Taylor, D. and Croxford, L. (2007). 'Tough, intelligent accountability' in Scottish secondary schools and the role of Standard Tables and Charts (STACS): A critical appraisal. *Scottish Educational Review*, 39, 29–50.

Daly, A. J., Moolenaar, N. M., Bolivar, J. M. and Burke, P. (2010). Relationships in reform: The role of teachers' social networks. *Journal of Educational Administration*, 48, 359–391.

Donaldson, G. (2010). *Teaching Scotland's Future: Report of a review of teacher education in Scotland*. Edinburgh: Scottish Government.

Drew, V. and Priestley, M. (2014). *School-based Curriculum Development Through Collaborative Professional Enquiry*. A paper presented at the European Conference for Educational Research, 3 September 2014, Porto.

Emirbayer, M. and Mische, A. (1998). What is agency? *The American Journal of Sociology*, 103, 962–1023.

Fullan, M. (2003). *Change Forces with a Vengeance*. London: RoutledgeFalmer.

Gleeson, D. and Gunter, H. (2001). The performing school and the modernisation of teachers. In D. Gleeson and C. Husbands (eds), *The Performing School: Managing, Teaching and Learning in a Performance Culture*. London: RoutledgeFalmer, pp. 139–158.

Goodson, I. F. (2003). *Professional Knowledge, Professional Lives*. Maidenhead: Open University Press.

Hargreaves, A. (1998). The emotional politics of teaching and teacher development: With implications for educational leadership. *International Journal of Leadership in Education*, 1, 315–336.

Helsby, G. (1999). *Changing Teachers' Work*. Buckingham: Open University Press.

Keddie, A., Mills, M. and Pendergast, D. (2011). Fabricating and identity in neo-liberal times: Performing schooling as 'number one'. *Oxford Review of Education*, 37, 75–92.

Ketelaar, E., Beijaard, D., Boshuizen, H. P. A. and Den Brok, P. J. (2012). Teachers' positioning towards an educational innovation in the light of ownership, sense-making and agency. *Teaching and Teacher Education*, 28, 273–282.

Kuiper, W., Nieveen, N. and Berkvens, J. (2013). Curriculum regulation and freedom in the Netherlands – A puzzling paradox. In W. Kuiper and J. Berkvens (eds), *Balancing Curriculum Regulation and Freedom across Europe, CIDREE Yearbook 2013*. Enschede, the Netherlands: SLO, pp. 139–162.

Ladwig, J. (2010). Beyond academic outcomes. *Review of Research in Education*, 34, 113–141.

Lasky, S. (2005). A sociocultural approach to understanding teacher identity, agency and professional vulnerability in a context of secondary school reform. *Teaching and Teacher Education*, 21, 899–916.

Leander, K. M. and Osborne, M. D. (2008). Complex positioning: Teachers as agents of curricular and pedagogical reform. *Journal of Curriculum Studies*, 40, 23–46.

Leat, D. (2014). Curriculum regulation in England: Giving with one hand and taking away with the other. *European Journal of Curriculum Studies*, 1, 69–74.

Leat, D., Livingston, K. and Priestley, M. (2013). Curriculum deregulation in England and Scotland – different directions of travel? In W. Kuiper and J. Berkvens (eds), *Balancing Curriculum Regulation and Freedom across Europe, CIDREE Yearbook 2013*. Enschede, the Netherlands: SLO, pp. 229–248.

McKinsey & Co. (2007). *McKinsey Report: How the World's Best Performing School Systems Come out on Top*. Retrieved from http://mckinseyonsociety.com/downloads/reports/Education/Worlds_School_Systems_Final.pdf.

Nieveen, N. (2011). Teachers' professional development in curriculum design in the Netherlands. A paper presented at the European Conference for Educational Research, 14 September 2011, Berlin.

OECD (2005). *Teachers Matter: Attracting, Developing and Retaining Effective Teachers*. Paris: OECD.

Osborn, M., Croll, P., Broadfoot, P., Pollard, A., McNess, E. and Triggs, P. (1997). Policy into practice and practice into policy: Creative mediation in the primary classroom. In G. Helsby and G. McCulloch (eds), *Teachers and the National Curriculum*. London: Cassell, pp. 52–65.

Perryman, J. (2012). Inspection and the fabrication of professional and performative processes. In B. Jeffrey and G. Troman (eds), *Performativity across UK Education: Ethnographic Cases of its Effects, Agency and Reconstructions*. Painswick: E&E Publishing, pp. 41–66.

Priestley, M. (2011a). Whatever happened to curriculum theory? Critical realism and curriculum change. *Pedagogy, Culture and Society*, 19, 221–238.

Priestley, M. (2011b). Schools, teachers and curriculum change: A balancing act? *Journal of Educational Change*, 12, 1–23.

Priestley, M. and Biesta, G. J. J. (eds) (2013) *Reinventing the Curriculum: New Trends in Curriculum Policy and Practice*. London: Bloomsbury Academic.

Priestley, M., Biesta, G. J. J. and Robinson, S. (2013). Teachers as agents of change: Teacher agency and emerging models of curriculum. In M. Priestley and G. J. J. Biesta (eds), *Reinventing the Curriculum: New Trends in Curriculum Policy and Practice*. London: Bloomsbury Academic, pp. 187–206.

Priestley, M., Biesta, G. J. J. and Robinson, S. (in press). *Teacher Agency: An Ecological Approach*. London: Bloomsbury Academic.

Priestley, M., Edwards, R., Priestley, A. and Miller, K. (2012). Teacher agency in curriculum making: Agents of change and spaces for manoeuvre. *Curriculum Inquiry*, 43, 191–214.

Priestley, M. and Minty, S. (2012). *Developing Curriculum for Excellence: Summary of Findings from Research Undertaken in a Scottish Local Authority*. Stirling: University of Stirling.

Priestley, M. and Sinnema, C. (2014). Downgraded curriculum? An analysis of knowledge in new curricula in Scotland and New Zealand. *Curriculum Journal, Special Edition: Creating Curricula: Aims, Knowledge, and Control*, 25, 50–75.

Pyhältö, K., Pietarinen, J. and Soini, T. (2014). Comprehensive school teachers' professional agency in large-scale educational change. *Journal of Educational Change*, 15, 303–325.

Pyhältö, K., Soini, T. and Pietarinen, J. (2012). Do comprehensive school teachers perceive themselves as active professional agents in school reforms? *Journal of Educational Change*, 13, 95–116.

Reeves, J. (2008). Between a rock and a hard place? Curriculum for Excellence and the Quality Initiative in Scottish schools. *Scottish Educational Review*, 40, 6–16.

Reeves, J. and Drew, V. (2013). A productive relationship? Testing the connections between professional learning and practitioner research. *Scottish Educational Review*, 45, 36–49.

Sahlberg, P. (2010). Rethinking accountability in a knowledge society. *Journal of Educational Change*, 11, 45–61.

Salomon, G. (1992). The changing role of the teacher: From information transmitter to orchestrator of teaching. In F. K. Oser, A. Dick and J.-L. Patry (eds), *Effective and Responsible Teaching: The New Synthesis*. San Francisco: Jossey-Bass, pp. 37–49.

Scottish Executive (2004). *A Curriculum for Excellence: The Curriculum Review Group*. Edinburgh: Scottish Executive.

Sinnema, C. and Aitken, G. (2013). Trends in international curriculum development. In M. Priestley and G. J. J. Biesta (eds), *Reinventing the Curriculum: New Trends in Curriculum Policy and Practice*. London: Bloomsbury, pp. 141–164.

Stoll, L., Bolam, R., McMahon, A., Wallace, M. and Thomas, S. (2006). Professional learning communities: A review of the literature. *Journal of Educational Change*, 7, 221–258.

Vongalis-Macrow, A. (2007). I, Teacher: Re-territorialisation of teachers' multi-faceted agency in globalised education. *British Journal of Sociology of Education*, 28, 425–439.

Wilkins, C. (2011). Professionalism and the post-performative teacher: New teachers reflect on autonomy and accountability in the English school system. *Professional Development in Education*, 37, 389–409.

Part III

Changing the System

Collective Autonomy

> As social animals we are capable of cooperating more deeply than the existing social order envisions.
>
> Richard Sennett, *Together*[1]

In Part II, Andy Hargreaves warned about an excess of transparency as well as an excess of autonomy. Our notion of flip the system might easily be mistaken for an individual, 'free-for-all' professionalism that does not hold anyone accountable. But instead we believe in collective autonomy, as Hargreaves has defined it, 'the group at the local level acts with discretion and internal accountability while defining itself as part and parcel of the larger system'.

Of course such a version of autonomy requires system-wide cooperation between teachers. According to Richard Sennett, cooperation is an art and a skill which we seem to increasingly have lost – also at the policy level. As Sennett puts it, 'a formally fixed agenda inhibits evolution of a problem from within (Sennett, p. 237). Indeed, in Part I we saw what that looked like in education, and how punitive accountability has spread across the globe. In country after country, policy makers have tried to come up with standardized solutions, and failed. Evolution has to happen from within the profession, as different authors in Part II have pointed out.

Genuine cooperation is always deeply democratic, as Sennett makes us understand. 'In social and personal life we all come up against the limits [of our own] desire and will or *the experience of other people's needs which cannot be reconciled with our own*' (emphasis added). It is our view that there should not only be spaces linking professionals together within the collective profession – either at school or at a national level – but there should also be spaces where the collective profession is linked with the rest of society.

Part III explores what that might look like in practice. We start out at the systems level. Singapore has embarked on an ambitious change programme using a paradigm of collective autonomy. **Pak Tee Ng** describes how Singapore is building professional capital based on a system of decentralized centralization. Both Alderik Visser and Andy Hargreaves have already rightly reminded us of the dangers of a shallow focus on collaboration: 'we need more than mere "active participation" of teachers and possibly students.' Pak Tee Ng acknowledges this and comments on the future direction of Singapore's education system: 'It is in developing Decisional Capital that Singapore will find its breakthrough in educational reform.'

John Yeo then presents a powerful example of how that collaboration works in practice and results in better classroom practices.

Pasi Sahlberg discusses the exceptional educational success of Finland and claims it's largely due to the Finnish welfare state, as well as 30 years of deliberate education reform.

Another oft-cited example of educational change is Finland. As an American teacher, **Tim Walker** shares his unique experience. Through American eyes he contrasts his teaching in Finland and the United States. What Tim Walker describes about his work in Finland is an emphasis on social capital and decisional capital by teachers, in line with Sennett's thinking.

Taking that argument to the next level, **Kim Farris-Berg** and **Edward J. Dirkswager** argue for teacher-powered schools. Decisional capital resides with the teachers who have complete responsibility in how to run their school.

Teacher **Lori Nazareno** shows what it is actually like working in a teacher-led school: taking and having responsibility as a teacher for your own school in every aspect and in the end truly taking responsibility for the wellbeing and development of your own students.

But sometimes the educational system doesn't allow you to take that responsibility. What then? **Elisa Guerra** shares a powerful story in her vignette from Mexico. She became a teacher and started her own school based on the premise of shared responsibility.

Note

1 Sennett, R. (2012). *Together: The Rituals, Pleasures and Politics of Cooperation*. New Haven, CT: Yale University Press.

Chapter 11

Whole-Systems Approach

Professional Capital in Singapore

Pak Tee Ng

Introduction

In the groundbreaking book, *Professional Capital*, by Hargreaves and Fullan (2012), Singapore is used as an example at various points, to illustrate certain aspects of Professional Capital. This chapter follows on from that work by discussing more systematically how Singapore develops Professional Capital and the issues and challenges that it faces in the process.

Professional Capital

According to Hargreaves and Fullan (2012, p. 80), *professional* as a concept has two aspects. First, to *be professional* implies that one upholds high standards in conducting oneself at work. Second, to *be a professional* implies that others view one highly in relation to one's work standard, and this affects one's regard for oneself and the work that one does. *Capital* is an asset that needs to be invested, accumulated and circulated in order to yield growth. It is the value placed upon a person, group or entity that can be leveraged upon to achieve a desired goal (Hargreaves & Fullan, 2012, p. 1). Taking them together, Professional Capital is therefore a set of assets derived from the potential professional capacity in human resources in order to yield growth and improvement. *Professional Capital* is critical to successful education reform.

Professional Capital (PC) is a function of the interplay of Human Capital (HC) (personal skills and competencies), Social Capital (SC) (interpersonal or interorganizational relationships) and Decisional Capital (DC) (the ability to make discretionary judgments to suit local context) (Hargreaves & Fullan, 2012). Expressed formulaically, $PC = f(HC + SC + DC)$. Human Capital is about identifying and building economically valuable knowledge and skills of people through education and training. Social Capital is about tapping into the quality and quantity of relationships among people and/or organizations in order to access and maximize available human capital. Decisional Capital is about enabling individuals or groups to discern and act judiciously in circumstances that do not have fixed rules or concrete evidence to guide decision-making.

Developing Professional Capital involves developing all three components, which are highly interrelated. The development of one component facilitates and strengthens the development of the other two. Therefore, while this chapter discusses Human Capital, Social Capital and Decisional Capital systematically and in that order, it should be noted that in using a certain example to illustrate the development of one capital, the other two capitals are being developed as well. This chapter will discuss how Singapore implements system-wide policy reforms and initiatives to cultivate and promote the development of Human Capital, Social Capital and Decisional Capital among its educators in a concerted effort to build Professional Capital in the education system.

Human Capital

Human Capital is 'the economically valuable knowledge and skills that could be developed in people – especially through education and training' (Hargreaves & Fullan, 2012, p. 89). Developing Human Capital in the education system is about equipping each educator with the requisite knowledge and skills to undertake a role and responsibility, as well as possess the commitment to further develop this expertise.

Singapore is a very small country in Southeast Asia. It does not have any natural resources, except for its people. This made the development of Human Capital crucial. Prime Minister Lee Hsien Loong (Lee, 2013) said:

> In Singapore, we have focused on this [developing Human Capital] obsessively for a very long time. People are our only resource. We have made education, lifelong learning and talent development a national priority. We have built a good education system across the board – primary schools, secondary schools, institutes of technical education, polytechnics, [and] universities. We have got a professional Education Service, comprising well-trained, empowered teachers – good-quality people, properly paid, properly resourced, backed up with the authority and the ability to take initiatives and to do what they believe is best for their charges.

To develop Human Capital in the education system, teachers are recruited from the top one third of the graduating cohort in each year, and competitive remuneration is provided for them. All recruits undergo teacher training at the National Institute of Education (NIE). They receive a full monthly salary while studying at the NIE, and their training fees are fully borne by the Ministry of Education (MOE). Upon completion of their training, they are deployed to various schools in Singapore. Beginning teachers are immediately supported as soon as they embark on teaching. For example, the Structured Mentoring Programme (SMP), which is a two-year programme launched in 2006, provides systematic guidance and coaching for beginning teachers. Mentors for these beginning teachers are provided with training programmes to develop their mentoring knowledge and skills (Ng, 2012).

The MOE also provides generous resources for in-service training that is reflective of its commitment to teachers' continuous professional development. Each teacher is entitled to financial support for up to 100 hours of professional development courses of his or her choice. Under MOE's Teacher Growth Model (TGM), teachers have the flexibility to plan and pursue their professional development according to their professional needs and interests (MOE, 2012).

Part of the professional development aims to upgrade teachers academically. Launched in 2004, the Professional Development Continuum Model (PDCM) is a comprehensive framework that articulates a building-block approach to allow teachers to accumulate academic credits at the NIE. These credits can lead to formal certifications such as advanced diplomas, advanced post-graduate diplomas, and master's degrees. Teachers are supported through financial subsidies and a certain amount of time off from work in school (MOE, 2004; NIE, 2009).

Developing capable leadership is another part of Human Capital development. For example, selected vice principals and ministry officials (about 30–40 participants per cohort) undergo a six-month full-time programme at NIE, called the Leaders in Education Programme (LEP), which is specially designed to prepare them for school leadership (Ng, 2008a, 2013). Middle leaders at school attend a 17-week full-time Management and Leadership in Schools (MLS) programme at the NIE, which helps participants learn to lead teaching and learning in their subject areas and expand their roles beyond departments. During these programmes, the MOE even sponsors them for overseas study trips to expand their horizons.

Social Capital

Hargreaves and Fullan (2012) refer to Social Capital as 'how the quantity and quality of interactions and social relationships among people' can increase their knowledge and expand their network to access one another's human capital (p. 90). In *The Global Fourth Way*, Hargreaves, Shirley and Ng (2012, p. 84) describe how Singapore pursues a 'deliberate strategy to plant change and then cross-pollinate changes through networks and interactions. Indeed in Singapore, Social Capital is 'nationalistic'. Education Minister Heng Swee Keat (2013) pointed out:

> Good schools understand deeply the needs of their students, and constantly come up with good ideas to meet those needs. But that's not all. Truly good schools are those that bring the whole education system forward. Instead of competing with one another, they support the larger school system by generously sharing and collaborating with others. It is not

about having the best students. Instead, it is about helping every student in our system be his best.

In schools, the implementation of Professional Learning Communities (PLCs) brings teachers and school leaders together regularly to learn from one another through continuous professional dialogue and feedback. These PLCs are supported by a PLC framework and a Starter Kit provided by the MOE to all schools (TDD, 2010). At the national level, a school cluster system approach is implemented to encourage sharing of resources and best practices among schools. It localizes and contextualizes responses to needs, generating ideas and sharing resources at the grassroots (Sharpe & Gopinathan, 2002). Moreover, Singapore encourages a teachers-for-teachers approach where teachers from different schools who teach a common subject come together to strengthen their collaboration across schools. This is critical in keeping them growing professionally and driving pedagogical innovation in schools. Some examples of these teacher-for-teacher academies include the English Language Institute of Singapore (ELIS), the Physical Education and Sport Teacher Academy (PESTA), and the Singapore Teachers' Academy for the aRts (STAR).

The MOE also organizes an annual three-day learning festival called the ExCEL Fest (Excellence through Continuous Enterprise and Learning). During the festival, teachers all over the country share innovative practices in their schools and engage in collaborative conversations. With innovation and enterprise as its main thrust, the festival celebrates the spirit of inquiry and originality, thinking outside the box, resilience in the face of complexity, and sense of 'giving back' to the school community. This festival is open not only to teachers but also to members of the public (MOE, 2013). The ExCEL Fest is another example of how professional interaction and collaboration among educators are encouraged in Singapore. The social dynamics in the Singapore education system encourage the sharing of knowledge and innovative tools among schools for collective benefit.

Regular movement of professionals to different parts of the education system is another way of building Social Capital. This phenomenon is rather unique to Singapore. Teachers in the country are regularly posted into MOE as staff officers. Usually after two to three years of service as MOE officers, they are posted back to schools to assume higher-level appointments. This dynamic staff movement establishes a better understanding between policy-makers and practitioners in the education system. Teachers appreciate policies better and gain valuable knowledge regarding policy-making. Policy-makers benefit from the ground knowledge that teachers bring into policy-making.

Teachers are also seconded to NIE as teacher-trainers, while NIE academics regularly do their research in local schools. Such close networks increase social interaction, promote mutual understanding and develop theory and practice nexus. Teo Chee Hean (Teo, 2002), former Education Minister, commented:

> MOE will continue to second Education Officers to NIE as we believe that a period spent in NIE is good for the development of Education Officers and benefits the Education Service when they return. NIE also benefits from having experienced practitioners from schools teaching in their various programmes.

Through this dynamic movement of personnel between schools, MOE and NIE promote communication throughout the education system and break down the cultural barriers that often separate teachers, policy-makers and academics. This is how Social Capital is built into the Singapore education system: a vertical combination of a top-down and bottom-up approach while incorporating a 'lateral combination of networks and side-to-side interactions' (Hargreaves, Shirley & Ng, 2012, p. 87).

Decisional Capital

Emerging from a largely centralized system, Singapore is gradually implementing initiatives to decentralize its education system. As former Education Minister Tharman Shanmugaratnam (Tharman, 2005) elucidated:

> Quality in education will flow from schools and teachers taking ownership of the changes and experiments that they wish to implement, and from learners making their own choices. Ownership in schools is key as we go forward in education.

However, the approach is more accurately described as centralized decentralization (Ng, 2008b). Schools align themselves to broad strategic goals set by the MOE while exercising tactical empowerment in implementation to achieve these common goals. In such a situation, Decisional Capital becomes very important because it is the capital that enables school leaders and teachers to 'make wise judgments in circumstances where there is no fixed rule or piece of incontrovertible evidence to guide them' (Hargreaves & Fullan, 2012, pp. 93–94). In other words, Decisional Capital is important so that school leaders and teachers can make good discretionary judgments to tailor teaching and learning to suit their students' needs, while adhering to national goals.

Two examples here will show why Decisional Capital is important in Singapore. In the area of curriculum, teaching and learning, schools are encouraged to explore new areas of learning so that students may have a holistic education. However, there will be a critical point when teachers will need to make sound decisions to address conflicting demands in a tightly packed curriculum (Ng, 2008b, p. 259):

> On the one hand, we would like the students to have a holistic education. On the other hand, we need to achieve depth in the learning disciplines.

> The Science students ought to know something about the arts and the Arts students ought to know something about the sciences. Languages are important but so is an appreciation for music or sports. National Education is critical but so is Social and Emotional Learning. There are many good things to choose from but wise choices have to be made. It will be a tough and delicate balancing act.

In the area of Information and Communication Technology (ICT), Decisional Capital is crucial because Singapore has already moved beyond the stage of hardware or software provision. The challenge is for teachers to decide how ICT could be used profitably in the teaching and learning process to educate students who are 'digital natives'. Related issues of cyber-bullying and cyber-wellness now become new areas of challenge and teachers have not been adequately prepared for these. New rules will have to be made as Internet and social media become more and more prevalent in the lives of the young.

How does Singapore go about developing Decisional Capital? Firstly, as part of centralized decentralization, loose coupling between schools and MOE enhances the adaptability of schools to respond to developing situations, because this allows more degrees of freedom at the school level. Advancements in education require greater experimentation on the ground. Allowing a reasonable amount of 'chaos' to play out in schools paradoxically cultivates Decisional Capital because the dynamics of change draw out the expertise and collective intelligence of the professional teaching community (Ng, 2010). Secondly, critical reflection is encouraged among teachers and school leaders (Ng & Tan, 2009). Beyond practical needs in routine situations, critical reflection promotes insights into complex and uncertain situations, so that new knowledge may be generated for better decision-making. Such reflection is emphasized in development programmes for teacher and school leaders (see for example Ng, 2008a, 2013).

Developing Decisional Capital is challenging. Most administrators prefer neatness to untidiness. Most practitioners are more focused on immediate and technical concerns. But Decisional Capital is important at this stage of development in Singapore's education reforms. Decisional Capital is the basis on which the MOE will increasingly gain confidence in giving autonomy to schools, and practitioners will increasingly gain confidence to make tough decisions on the ground in the best interest of their students.

Conclusion

Hargreaves and Fullan observed that successful education systems build on Professional Capital to develop the teaching profession, considering its vital role in 'social justice and global prosperity' (Hargreaves & Fullan, 2012, p. 185). The effects of a strong and sound teaching force reach far beyond the confines of schools:

> Professional capital is about enacting more equal, high attaining, more healthy countries in just about every way that counts. This is why successful countries treat their teachers as nation builders, and how they come to yield high returns in prosperity, social cohesion, and social justice. In high-performing, socially just, and cohesive countries, teachers are not only dedicated, or even champions. Teachers are complete professionals. They are true pros who are well prepared, sufficiently paid, properly supported, continuously learning, collectively responsible, and shrewd in judgments after years of inquiry and practice.
>
> (p. 185).

Professional Capital is about creating a fraternity of teachers and school leaders who think and operate as a community of committed professionals. Singapore is currently regarded as one of the top education systems globally and this success can be explained by its continuous efforts to build on the professional capital of its teachers and school leaders. In many ways, Human Capital and Social Capital are much more developed and their presence and influence easier to discern in the Singapore education system. However, at this stage of Singapore's development, it is in developing Decisional Capital that Singapore will find its breakthrough in educational reform. Ng (2005) opines:

> It is no longer a matter of having more autonomy. It is now a matter of exercising that autonomy wisely and courageously.

To achieve courage with wisdom is of course easier said than done. Notwithstanding that, the teaching profession is a critical force for Singapore's nation building. Developing Professional Capital in the education system is an investment that Singapore will continue to take very seriously.

References

Hargreaves, A. and Fullan, M. (2012). *Professional Capital: Transforming Teaching in Every School.* New York: Teachers College Press.

Hargreaves, A., Shirley, D. and Ng, P. T. (2012). Singapore: Innovation, communication, and paradox. In A. Hargreaves and D. Shirley, *The Global Fourth Way: The Quest for Educational Excellence.* USA: Corwin, pp. 71–91.

Heng, S. K. (2013). Speech on 5 April by Mr Heng Swee Keat, Minister for Education, at MOE ExCELFest 2013 Awards Ceremony, at the Institute of Technical Education (ITE) College Central. Retrieved from http://www.moe.gov.sg/media/speeches/2013/04/05/speech-by-mr-heng-swee-keat-at-moe-excel-fest-2013-awards-ceremony.php.

Lee, H. L. (2013). Speech on 28 June by Prime Minister Lee Hsien Loong at the Opening of Unilever's Four Acres Singapore Campus. Retrieved from http://www.pmo.gov.sg/content/pmosite/mediacentre/speechesninterviews/primeminister/2013/June/speech-by-prime-minister-lee-hsien-loong-at-the-opening-of-unile.html#.U7pHj5SSx8E.

Ministry of Education (MOE) (2004). Professional Development Continuum Models for Teachers. NIE Press release, 13 August. Retrieved from http://www.moe.gov.sg/media/press/2004/pr20040813.htm.

Ministry of Education (MOE) (2012). New Model for Teachers' Professional Development Launched. Press release, 31 May. Retrieved from http://www.moe.gov.sg/media/press/2012/05/new-model-for-teachers-profess.php.

Ministry of Education (MOE) (2013). What is ExCEL Fest? Retrieved from http://www.excelfest.com/about-us/what-is-excel-fest-.

National Institute of Education (NIE) (2009). PDCM Master's Degree via the 4-3-3 Structure. Student handbook. Retrieved from http://www.nie.edu.sg/nie_cma/attachments/topic/035fd838fad0/PDCM_Handbook_for_applicants_August_09_Intake.pdf.

Ng, P. T. (2005). *The Learning School: Innovation and Enterprise.* Singapore: Prentice Hall.

Ng, P. T. (2008a). Developing forward-looking and innovative school leaders: The Singapore Leaders in Education Programme. *Journal of In-Service Education,* 34(2), 237–255.

Ng, P. T. (2008b). Going forward: Sketches in the drawing board. In E. T. J. Tan and P. T. Ng (eds), *Thinking Schools, Learning Nation: Contemporary Issues and Challenges.* Singapore: Prentice Hall, pp. 258–261.

Ng, P. T. (2010). Educational technology management approach: The case of Singapore's ICT Masterplan Three. *Human Systems Management,* 29(3), 177–187.

Ng, P. T. (2012). Mentoring and coaching educators in the Singapore education system. *International Journal of Mentoring and Coaching in Education,* 1(1), 24–35.

Ng, P. T. (2013). Developing Singapore school leaders to handle complexity in times of uncertainty. *Asia Pacific Education Review,* 14(1), 67–73.

Ng, P. T. and Tan, C. (2009). Community of practice for teachers: Sensemaking or critical reflective learning? *Reflective Practice,* 10(1), 37–44.

Sharpe, L. and Gopinathan, S. (2002). After effectiveness: New directions in the Singapore school system? *Journal of Education Policy,* 17(2), 151–166.

Teo, C. H. (2002). Speech on 26 January by Rear-Admiral Teo Chee Hean, Minister for Education and Second Minister for Defence, at the Official Opening of the NIE Complex at NIE Admin Building Foyer. Retrieved from http://www.moe.gov.sg/media/speeches/2002/sp28012002.htm.

Tharman, S. (2005). Speech on 22 September by Mr Tharman Shanmugaratnam, Minister for Education, at the MOE Work Plan Seminar 2005 at the Ngee Ann Polytechnic Convention Centre. Retrieved from http://www.moe.gov.sg/media/speeches/2005/sp20050922.htm.

Training and Development Division (TDD) (2010). *Schools as Professional Learning Communities.* Singapore: Training and Development Division, Ministry of Education.

Vignette 3

Changing Education in Action

Singapore: The Inquiring Teacher

John Yeo

Lesson Study is a platform for professional learning where teachers come together to jointly plan, observe, analyse, and refine actual classroom lessons, also known as research lessons. I have had the privilege of working with schools in helping them understand the purpose and structure of Lesson Study since 2009. In 2012, I was invited to observe a research lesson with a focus on inquiry-based learning with a group of teachers for a Singapore Secondary Two level. As I reflect upon the working dynamics of teachers' professional learning community, this particular incident has 'stuck' painfully with me, as it revealed some uneasy tensions, yet critical insights. While we acknowledge that schools of the twenty-first century should be a learning community where students as well as teachers learn together, this story captures a different 'eye', looking at some who are marginalised, especially in our crowded classrooms of today (Saito, Murase, Tsukui & Yeo, 2015).

The research lesson teacher was also the class's science teacher and held the position of a Senior Teacher in the school. In Singapore schools, Senior Teachers are 'good experienced teachers who serve as mentors and role models to younger teachers within their schools, sharing with them their teaching expertise and content knowledge' (Ministry of Education, 2001). When we met, she cordially welcomed me and handed me the lesson plan as well as a copy of the classroom seating arrangement. She then quietly suggested which groups I might observe more attentively, especially those with students who were generally more participative. In the same breath, she also suggested one that I should ignore for 'obvious reasons'. She pointedly highlighted a particular repeat student, let's just call him David. She said I should ignore him if he was 'acting up', and half-jokingly remarked, 'I will be happy if he doesn't distract the rest of the class and just sleeps quietly!' Naturally, my interest as a researcher was piqued, and my curiosity about David aroused.

The teacher expressed her surprise when David came to class that morning, as he was known to be frequently absent. During that shared space of group work, David looked passive and disengaged. Interestingly, the only time that the teacher spoke to him publicly was to tell him to sit properly, as a 'chair has four legs and not two legs', and he relented. However, within minutes, the boy shifted again and started rocking his chair, while the teacher no longer paid any attention to him. I quietly observed that throughout most of the lesson, his gaze was always fixated on the basketball court outside the window where he sat. Yet in the middle of the class, where students were engaged in group work, I noticed a peculiar chain of little actions. David was still rocking his chair, looking nonchalant about what was going on in his group, and interestingly, the groupmates also left him pretty much alone. While the groupmates were clearly stuck on a question and having a lively debate, I caught a fleeting moment where the boy actually stopped rocking his chair and inched closer to hear what they were talking about. I quickly zoomed my video camera to capture David's stance and paid attention to the twirling of his pen, which was very much a part of his normal behaviour. The twirling slowed down, and for a moment, I saw him putting the pen down on his table and caught his quick glance towards the others and to the worksheet. That said, within seconds he picked up his pen and resumed his rocking. It was obvious that none of his groupmates had noticed. Throughout those moments, and in fact right from the start, the groupmates had totally left David out of the discussion, with no forms of interaction between him and the others. It was as if he was invisible.

During the teachers' post-lesson reflection, as an invited knowledgeable other, I was privileged to share my observations and conclusions within this constructive discussion. After I shared my 'formal' ideas, I asked for an extension of a few more minutes to share a video clip. I asked the teachers to pay attention to the group work and examine David's actions closely. Quite spontaneously, some teachers sniggered while others passed comments about their own encounters with David. I asked the teachers to withold their judgement and just watch the segment of the video of the boy's reaction during the group discussion. After viewing, I asked the teachers if they observed anything peculiar, and an apprehensive silence hung in the air. Finally, a younger teacher hesitantly asked, 'Could it be that David seemed to have an idea on how to solve the problem while the rest of the members were still struggling?' Another teacher retorted and said, 'If he knew, why didn't he speak up?' and I saw some teachers nod in agreement. Tactfully, I asked the teachers if someone could give me a little background about David, and the form teacher repeated what the Senior Teacher had told me earlier, before the start of the class. The young teacher spoke up again and said, 'Actually, David's mum passed away when he was in Secondary One. At that time, I was still doing my practicum and I knew about his situation. I didn't follow up with him after my practicum and I haven't taught this boy since then.'

The rest of the story is really not so important, but that poignant silence served as a reminder to me as an educator. What coloured lens do I bring to my class and how do I view my students in terms of their learning? Is professional capital a way of investing in our students' overall well-being too, beyond the development of the intellect? How does the daily interaction between teachers and students as well as the peer interactions between students create that formative impact on who we are as individuals? Do we as teachers cultivate the humanity in our students, or are we solely focused on preparing our students for the tests?

Furthermore, how do we use platforms such as these professional learning communities to help teachers better develop the eyes to see students? Do we also develop the moral dimensions of teaching, and how might these be wrapped up in words and actions as we enter our classrooms?

John Yeo teaches the Master and Leadership programmes at the National Institute of Education (NIE), Nanyang Technological University, Singapore. As a Teaching Fellow with the Curriculum, Teaching and Learning academic group, he specialises in creative thinking, problem finding, curriculum design, teachers' professional learning, as well as authentic assessment. He has written and co-edited books such as *Mastering the Art of Authentic Assessment*, *Sustainable School Reform through Lesson Study for Learning Community* and others. Besides conducting in-service training for teachers, he also engages school and community leaders with dialogue on educational issues such as curriculum innovation and designing for 21st-century teaching and learning.

References

Ministry of Education (2001). *More Career Advancement Opportunities for Teachers*, September. Retrieved from Singapore Ministry of Education website: http://www.moe.gov.sg/media/press/2001/pr26092001.htm.

Saito, E., Murase, M., Tsukui, A. and Yeo, J. (2015). *Lesson Study for Learning Community: A Guide to Sustainable School Reform*. London: Routledge.

Chapter 12

Finnish Schools and the Global Education Reform Movement

Pasi Sahlberg

International indicators show that Finland has one of the most educated citizenries in the world, provides educational opportunities in an egalitarian manner, and makes efficient use of resources. But at the beginning of the 1990s, education in Finland was nothing special in international terms. The performance of Finnish students on international assessments was close to overall averages, except in reading, where Finnish students did better than most of their peers in other countries. The unexpected and jarring recession of that time period brought Finland to the edge of a financial breakdown. Bold and immediate measures were necessary to fix national fiscal imbalances and revive the foreign trade that disappeared with the collapse of the Soviet Union in 1990.

Finland is a unique educational system in that it has progressed from mediocrity to being a model educational system and 'strong performer' over the past three decades. Finland has been of interest to many because it has been able to build an educational system where most students learn well and where equitable education has translated into small variation in student performance between schools in different parts of country. But perhaps the most intriguing aspect of Finnish education is its unique, personalized way of perceiving good education: little competition between schools, moderate parental choice for schools, the absence of standardized tests, soft accountability, and conservative use of educational technology. In the world of educational change Finland is therefore an educational lone wolf that has traveled its own path while most other countries have joined the global education reform movement in their quest for better education.

The Finnish phenomenon in international education is primarily an offspring of the Programme for International Student Assessment (PISA) that was inaugurated in 2000. Until then, there had been more speculation than well-supported knowledge about where the most successful educational systems were, and prior to PISA, educators and policy-makers traveled to the UK, Germany, France, Sweden, the United States, and Australia, to mention just a few, in search of new ideas for school improvement and educational change. PISA changed the entire global educational landscape dramatically. The old education superpowers had to make room for Japan, South Korea, Canadian provinces of Alberta, Ontario and British Columbia, and Finland. After the next PISA cycles in 2003 and 2006 it was evident that two whole new areas of academic and practical inquiry had emerged. First to appear was the question of what makes some education systems perform better than others? This led to more in-depth investigations of Finland's schools and what made them perform so well in this new international test. Next came the question of what is wrong with those education systems that were thought to be successful, but whose performances have either stagnated to mediocre level or are declining. Many academics and policy analysts have researched these systems, trying to understand what is holding back the United States, England, Sweden, Germany, Norway, and some others from improving their education systems.

This second line of inquiry about global educational reforms dates back to the 1980s, when many Western countries noticed that their education systems would be unlikely to lead the way in the economic, technological, and social changes that were on the horizon. Because there were not enough good global data to compare how education systems performed, the inspiration for education reform often came from national policy reviews or new legislations. For example, *A Nation at Risk* (1983), a report published in the United States during the Ronald Reagan administration, and the Education Reform Act (ERA) of 1988 in England under Margaret Thatcher's government, represent well-known examples of influential efforts to enhance education. Both of these are important – not only for their respective countries but also for much of the rest of the world. Conservative public sector policies constituted a particular approach to educational change, which built on free-market-inspired competition and parental choice as the key principles of raising the quality of schools.

The reason for the popularity of market-based education policies was their common-sense logic: (1) competition among schools over enrollment improves student achievement; (2) schools need more autonomy in order to compete; (3) parents need freedom to choose schools for their children; and (4) the public needs information on student achievement based on common standards. This logic soon became the driving force in large-scale educational reforms in many countries. International development organizations, consultants, philanthropic institutions, and especially private corporations adopted market-based reform thinking. The United States, England, Chile, Australia, and New Zealand applied variations of this reform thinking. School competition and choice, standardization of teaching and learning in schools, standardized testing, accountability, data-driven policy-making, and privatization of public education soon spread to other countries, including countries in developing parts of the world.

Market-based education reforms became fashionable from the 1990s. They were especially influential in fragile transition and developing countries – Central and Eastern Europe, the former Soviet Union, and Latin America – where externally determined educational standards and national testing were adopted as the key drivers of educational change in circumstances that often lacked the capacity to steer foreign-designed reforms. Because there was no comparable international measure of how systems performed – in terms of quality and equity of the system – it was impossible to comment on how successful or harmful these new reform ideas actually were for education systems. It was PISA in 2000 that brought some light into this darkness.

The Global Education Reform Movement

The original idea for the Global Education Reform Movement, or GERM as it is also known, derives from Andy Hargreaves and his research on educational change (Hargreaves et al., 2001). We coined the term GERM in the second half of the 2000s after the results of the third PISA cycle became public. GERM is inspired by three distinct educational phenomena. The first was the breakthrough of constructivist approaches to learning that gradually shifted the focus of education reforms from the teacher to the student, and especially learning, in the late 1980s. The second was the growing public demand in the 1990s for guaranteed, effective learning for all pupils. Centrally mandated learning standards in tandem with aligned national standardized student assessments became the main attempts to improve the quality of educational performance in many parts of the world. The third phenomenon was the demand for decision-making authority to move from central offices to local governments in the 2000s. Decentralization of governance enhanced school autonomy and thereby also brought along stronger accountability for schools and teachers.

GERM has several manifestations, which vary from one education system to another. First, and perhaps the most common feature, is increased *competition* between schools for student enrollment. Almost all education systems have introduced alternative forms of schooling, to offer parents more *choice* regarding their children's schooling (OECD, 2013c). The voucher system in Chile in the 1980s, free schools in Sweden in the 1990s, charter schools in the United States in the 2000s, and secondary academies in England in the 2010s are examples of faith in competition as an engine of advancement. At the same time, the proportion of more advantaged students studying in private schools or independent schools has grown (OECD, 2013b). In Australia, for example, nearly every third primary and secondary school student studies in non-governmental schools (OECD, 2013). School league tables that rank schools based on their performance in national standardized assessments have further increased competition between schools. OECD data show that according to school principals across OECD countries more than three quarters of the students assessed by PISA attend schools that compete with at least one other school for enrollment (OECD, 2010). Finally, students especially in many Asian countries experience stronger pressure to perform better against their peers, due to the tough race to the best high schools and universities.

The second manifestation of GERM is the *standardization* of teaching and learning in schools. Shifting the focus from inputs to outcomes in education in the 1990s led to the popularity of standards-based education policies, especially in the English-speaking part of the world. These reforms initially aimed for a stronger emphasis on learning outcomes and school performance, instead of content, curriculum, instruction time, and structures of schooling. It has been the unquestioned belief among policy-makers and education reformers that the presence of high performance standards for schools, teachers, and students is a precondition of improved quality of teaching and better overall performance of schools. Standardization draws from an assumption that all students should be educated to the same learning targets, which has led to the prevalence of prescribed curricula and homogenization of curriculum policies worldwide.

Overly tight standardization narrows freedom and flexibility in schools and classrooms, which may be harmful to creativity and more personalized learning. It prevents teachers from experimenting, reduces the use of alternative pedagogical approaches, and limits risk-taking in schools and classrooms. Research on educational systems that have adopted policies emphasizing the steering of education through external standards on core subjects, suggests that teaching and learning are narrower and that teachers focus on 'proven methods' and 'guaranteed content' to best prepare their students for high-stakes tests (Au, 2009). The consequence is that the higher the stakes of these student tests, for both teachers and students, the lower the degree of freedom and risk-taking in classroom learning.

The third common feature of the global education reform movement is an *increasing importance of reading literacy, mathematics, and science* in schools, often at the expense of arts, music, physical education, and social studies. The dominance of these disciplines means that they also are elevated as prime targets for required improvement in national education reforms. According to the OECD and research on national education policies in a number of countries, national education policies are increasingly influenced by international student assessments, especially PISA (Ball, 2012; Breakspear, 2012; Wiseman, 2013).

Literacy and numeracy strategies that increased instructional time for the core subjects in England and in Ontario (Canada) are concrete consequences of the global education reform movement. The 'No Child Left Behind' legislation in the United States has forced most school districts in the country to shift teaching time from other subjects, especially from social studies, arts, and music, to teaching reading, mathematics, and science, so that schools are better prepared for tests that measure student performance and hold schools accountable in these subjects.

The fourth characteristic of GERM is *test-based accountability* – holding teachers and schools accountable for students' achievement through external standardized tests. School performance – especially raising students' measured achievement – is intimately tied up with the processes of evaluating, inspecting, and rewarding or punishing schools and teachers. Performance-based pay, data walls in teachers' lounges, and school rankings in newspapers are examples of new accountability mechanisms that often draw their data primarily from external standardized student tests and teacher evaluations. The problem with test-based accountability is not that students, teachers, and schools are held accountable per se, but rather the way accountability mechanisms affect teachers' work and students' studying in school. Whenever school accountability relies on poor-quality and low-cost standardized tests, as is the case in many places, accountability becomes what is left when responsibility is subtracted.

The fifth globally observable trend in educational reform is *school choice*. Parental choice is an idea that became commonly known as a consequence of Milton Friedman's economic theories in the 1950s. Friedman and many of his disciples and advisees – including president Ronald Reagan – state that parents must be given the freedom to choose their children's education and thereby to encourage healthy competition among schools so that they better serve families' diverse needs. Typically, school choice manifests itself through the emergence of private schools where parents pay tuition for their children's education. Today, there are scores of various types of alternative schools, other than fee-based private schools, to expand choice in education markets. Charter schools in the United States, free schools in Sweden, upper-secondary school academies in England, and religious schools in the Netherlands are examples of mechanisms to advance parental choice. School choice ideology maintains that parents should be able to use the public funds set aside for their children's education to choose the schools – public or private – that work best for them.

Finland vs. the GERM

Many have wondered what made Finnish schools so successful. The equitable education system is a result of systematic attention to social justice and early intervention to help those with special needs, and close interplay between education and other sectors – particularly health and social sectors – in Finnish society. Complimentary school lunches, comprehensive welfare services provided in all schools, and early support to those in need have been made available to all children in all Finnish schools – free of charge. Every child has, by law, a right to these welfare and support services in their school. Therefore, attempts to explain the success of the education system in Finland should be put in the wider context and seen as a part of the overall function of democratic civil society (Simola, 2015). Economists have been interested in finding out why Finland has been able to become the most competitive economy in the world, and educators are trying to figure out the secret of high educational performance of Finland. The quality of a nation – or its education system – is rarely a result of any single factor. The entire society needs to perform satisfactorily.

Education policies that have driven Finnish reforms since the 1970s, have been orthogonal to GERM. They have prioritized creating equal opportunities, raising quality, and increasing participation within all educational levels across Finnish society (Sahlberg, 2015). As a result, more than 99% of the age cohort successfully completes compulsory *comprehensive school*, about 95% continue their education in upper-secondary schools, and an additional 3% enroll in a voluntary 10th grade of *comprehensive school*. About 95% of Finns eventually receive the secondary education certificate that provides access to higher education.

Equity in education is an important feature in Nordic welfare states. It means more than just opening access to an equal education for all (or equality). Equity in education is a principle that aims at guaranteeing high-quality education for all in different places and circumstances regardless of children's family background, socio-economic status, domicile or individual conditions. In the Finnish context equity is about having a socially fair and inclusive education system that is based on equality of educational opportunities and fairness of allocating resources to education. As a result of the *comprehensive school* reform of the 1970s, education opportunities for good, quality learning have spread rather evenly across Finland (OECD, 2013). There was a visible achievement gap among young adults at the end of compulsory education in the early 1970s due to very different educational orientations associated with the old system. This knowledge gap strongly corresponded with the socio-economic divide within Finnish society at that time.

After abolishing early selection of children and streaming them according to academic ability in the mid-1980s, and thereby making learning expectations the same for all students, the achievement gap between low and high achievers began to decrease. Clear evidence of more equitable learning outcomes came from the *first* PISA survey in 2000. In that study, Finland had the smallest performance variations between schools in reading, mathematics, and science of all OECD nations (OECD, 2001, 2004, 2007, 2010, 2013a). A similar trend has continued in all PISA studies since then.

An essential element of the Finnish *comprehensive school* is systematic attention to those students who have special educational needs. Special education is an important part of education and care in Finland. It refers to designed educational and psychological services within the education sector for those with special needs. The basic idea is that with early recognition of learning difficulties and social and behavioral problems, appropriate professional support can be provided to individuals as early as possible.

A new special education system in Finland since 2011 is defined under the title of *Learning and Schooling Support* and all such students are increasingly integrated into regular classrooms. There are three categories of support to those pupils possessing special needs: (1) general support, (2) intensified support, and (3) special support. The first includes actions by the regular classroom teacher in terms of differentiation, as well as efforts by the school to cope with student diversity. The second category consists of remedial support from the teacher, co-teaching with the special-education teacher, and individual or small-group learning with a part-time special-education teacher. The third category includes a wide range of special-education services, from full-time general education to a placement in a special institution. All students in this category are assigned an Individual Learning Plan that takes into account the characteristics of each learner and thereby personalizes learning to meet each learner's abilities. As a consequence of this renewed special education system the number of those students categorized as special needs students will decrease.

Many believe that Finland's special-education system is one of those key factors that explain world-class results in achievement and equity of Finland's school system in recent international studies. My personal experience, based on working with and visiting hundreds of Finnish schools, is that most schools pay very particular attention to those children who need more help in becoming successful, compared to other students. Many teachers and administrators who have visited Finnish schools, among them experts and politicians from Chile, think the same way but are often stuck in the middle of *excellence vs. equity* quandaries, due to external demands and regulations in their own countries. Standardized testing that compares individuals to statistical averages, competition that leaves weaker students behind, and merit-based pay for teachers all jeopardize schools' efforts to enhance equity. None of these factors currently exists in the Finnish education system.

In the school year 2012–2013, almost one third of all students in *comprehensive school* took part in part-time or full-time special education within the old system. More than one fifth of *all students* were in part-time special education that focuses on curing minor dysfunctions in speaking, reading, writing, or learning difficulties in mathematics or foreign languages. Respectively, 8.5% of students were permanently transferred to a special-education group, class, or institution. The number of students in permanent special education has doubled in the last 10 years; at the same time, the number of special-education institutions has declined steadily since the early 1990s. Since 2011 only those students who receive intensified or special support in school are considered as special needs students. In the school year 2012–2013 in *comprehensive school* 12.7% of students were included in this new type of special education, 7.7% received special support, and 5% intensified support. In vocational upper-secondary education, approximately 14.3% of all students were in special education during the school year 2012–2013.

Unlike the Chilean school system, among many others today, the Finnish system has not been infected by market-based education reforms that typically emphasize competition between schools, high-stakes standardized student-testing policies, and privatizing public schools. The main reason is that the education community in Finland has remained unconvinced that competition and choice with more standardized testing than students evidently require would be good for schools. The ultimate success of a high-stakes testing policy is whether it positively affects student learning, not whether it increases student scores on a particular test. As a result, Finnish education today offers a compelling model because of its high-quality and equitable student learning. As Figure 12.1 shows, Finland, Canada, Estonia, Japan, the Netherlands, and South Korea have education systems that rate highly in quality and equity; they produce consistent learning results regardless of students' socioeconomic status.

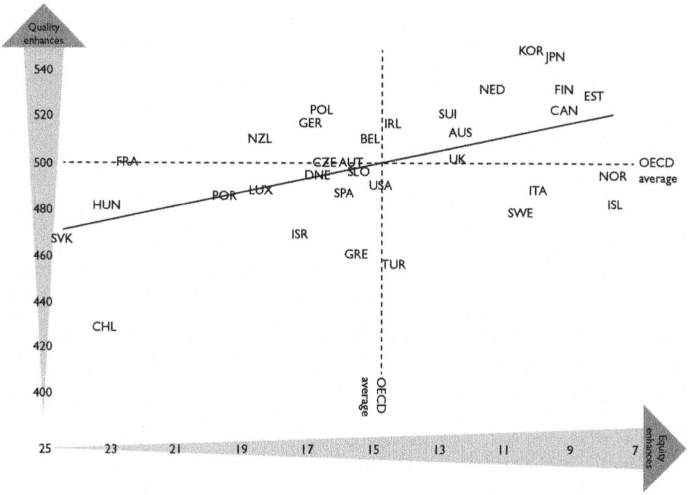

Figure 12.1 Equity and quality of education outcomes (mathematics) in OECD countries in 2012 (Sahlberg, 2015).

The high-performing education system in Finland is not a result of educational factors alone. Basic structures of the Finnish welfare state play a crucial role in providing all children and their families with equitable conditions for starting a successful educational path at the age of seven. Early childhood care, one year of free preschool for the entire age cohort of six-year-olds, comprehensive health services, and preventive measures to identify possible learning and development difficulties before children start schooling are accessible to all in Finland. In order to prevent children from being ranked according to their educational performance in schools, grade-based assessments are not normally used during the first five years of *comprehensive school*. An important principle in developing elementary education in Finland has been the removal of structural elements that cause student failure in schools.

GERM and Student Failure in School

Grade repetition in the old Finnish school system was not rare in elementary schools, and was an integral educational principle of the grammar school. In some cases, a student repeated the 3rd grade of elementary school in order to improve knowledge and skills required in the grammar school admission test at the end of the 4th grade. At the time of the introduction of the new nine-year comprehensive school, approximately 12% of students in each grammar school grade did not progress from their grade. Up to half of those graduating from upper-secondary grammar school repeated one or more grades at some point of their schooling (Välijärvi & Sahlberg, 2008). Furthermore, significant numbers of students dropped out of school before completion – often after not being able to progress from one grade to the next.

In the early days of Finnish basic school reform, grade repetition was seen as an inadequate and wrong strategy for fixing individual learning or social deficiencies. In the elementary school, grade repeaters who had difficulties in one or two subjects were often labeled as 'failing' students who also had behavioral and personality problems. This educational stigma normally had a dramatic negative impact on students and also lowered teachers' expectations regarding these students' abilities to learn. Grade repetition created a vicious circle that for many young people cast a negative shadow right into adulthood. Educational failure is linked to an individual's role in society and is characterized by unfavorable attitudes toward learning and further education. Grade repetition, in most cases, led to increased social inequality and lower equity, rather than helping students to overcome academic and social problems, as shown in Figure 12.2. In the Netherlands, France, Belgium, and Spain, according to the OECD, more than one quarter of students reported that they had repeated a grade at least once in primarily lower-secondary or upper-secondary school (OECD, 2010, 2011). Retention rates are much smaller in Nordic countries where less than 5% of students have repeated a grade at least once.

Comprehensive school quickly changed grade repetition policies and practices. The new comprehensive school did not completely remove the problem of repeating grades, but the number of students who repeated grades in the comprehensive school decreased significantly. Personalized learning and differentiation became basic principles in organizing schooling for students across society. The assumption that all students can achieve common educational goals if learning is organized according to each student's characteristics and needs became another foundation. Retention and ability grouping was clearly against these ideals. Different students have to learn to work and study together in the same class. Diversity of students' personalities, abilities, and orientations has to be taken into account in crafting learning environments and choosing pedagogical methods in schools. This turned out to be one of the most demanding professional challenges for teachers.

Even today, schools are searching for an optimal educational and economic solution for Finland's rapidly increasing diversity. It is true that Finland long remained ethnically homogeneous. However, since it joined the European Union in 1995, cultural and ethnic diversification has been faster than in other European Union countries, especially in larger cities' districts and schools, where first- and second-generation immigrants account for one quarter of the total population.

Minimizing grade repetition has been possible primarily because special education has become an integral part of each and every school in Finland. Every child has the right to personalized support provided early on by trained professionals as part of normal schooling. This special support is arranged in many different ways today. As described earlier, special education in Finland is increasingly organized within general mainstream schooling.

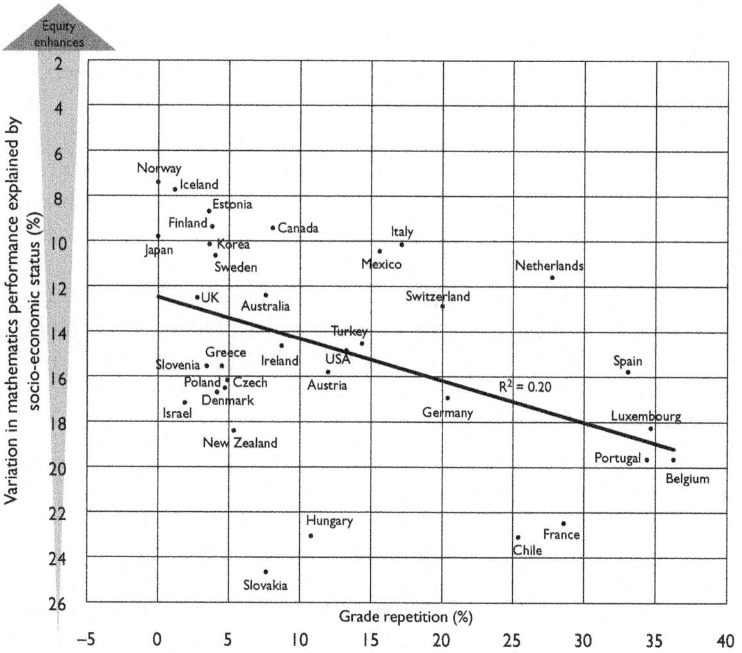

Figure 12.2 Grade repetition and equity in school education in OECD countries in 2012 (Sahlberg, 2015).

Upper-secondary schools – both general and vocational – operate using modular curriculum units rather than year-based grades. Thus, grade repetition in its conventional form has vanished from Finnish upper-secondary schools. This non-class structure has also abolished classes in which the same age-group of students moves from one lesson to another and from one grade to the next. In the early 1980s approximately 15% of students repeated a grade at least once. Today students build their own personalized learning schedules from a menu of courses offered in their school or by other education institutions. Studying in upper-secondary school is therefore flexible, and selected courses can be completed at a different pace depending on the students' abilities and life situations. Rather than repeating an entire grade, a student only repeats those courses that were not passed satisfactorily. Most students complete upper-secondary school in the prescribed time of three years, although some progress faster and some need more time than others.

Professionalism as a GERM Stopper

All teachers in Finnish primary, junior high, and high schools must hold a master's degree; preschool and kindergarten teachers must hold a bachelor's degree.

There are no alternative ways to receive a teacher's credential in Finland; the university degree constitutes a license to teach. Primary school teachers, who teach grades one to six, major in education, while upper-grade teachers concentrate their studies in a particular subject, e.g., mathematics, as well as didactics, consisting of pedagogical content knowledge specific to that subject.

Teacher education is based on a combination of research, practice, and reflection, meaning that it must be supported by scientific knowledge and focused on thinking processes and cognitive skills used in conducting research. In addition to studying educational theory, content, and subject-specific pedagogy, each prospective teacher for primary school and beyond completes a master's thesis on a topic relevant to educational practice. After completing secondary school and entering a teacher preparation program, successful completion of a master's degree in teaching generally takes five to seven and a half years, depending on the field of study.

A broad-based teacher education curriculum ensures that newly prepared Finnish teachers possess balanced knowledge and skills in both theory and practice. It also means they possess deep professional insight into education from several perspectives, including educational psychology and sociology, curriculum theories, student assessment, special needs education, and pedagogical content knowledge in selected subject areas. All eight universities that offer teacher education in Finland have their own strategies and curricula that are nationally coordinated to ensure coherence, but locally crafted in order to make the best use of the particular university's resources.

Subject teachers complete a master's degree in one major subject and one or two minor subjects. Students then apply to a university's Department of Teacher Education to study pedagogy for their focus subject. Subject-focused pedagogy and research are advanced in Finnish universities, and cooperative and problem-based learning, reflective practice, and computer-supported education are common. A higher-education evaluation system that rewards effective, innovative university teaching practice has served as an important driver of these developments.

Finland's commitment to *research-based teacher education* means that educational theories, research methodologies, and practice all play an important role in preparation programs. Teacher education curricula are designed to create a systematic pathway from the foundations of educational thinking to educational research methodologies and then on to more advanced fields of the educational sciences. Each student thereby builds an understanding of the systemic nature of educational practice. Finnish teachers also learn how to design, conduct, and present original research on practical or theoretical aspects of education.

Another important element of Finnish research-based teacher education is practical training in schools. Over the five-year program, candidates advance from basic teaching practice to advanced practice and then to final practice. During each of these phases, students observe lessons by experienced teachers, practice teaching observed by supervisory teachers, and deliver independent lessons to different groups of pupils while being evaluated by supervising teachers and Department of Teacher Education professors and lecturers. Practicum experiences comprise about 15 to 25% of teachers' overall preparation time.

Conclusion

PISA data provide interesting evidence to judge whether the premises of GERM are correct. There are three basic findings in PISA 2012 that are worth noting in order to see how the elements of GERM mentioned earlier are associated with the performance of education systems worldwide.

The first finding is that education systems that give schools autonomy over their own curricula and student assessments often perform better than schools that do not (OECD, 2013c). This contradicts the basic premise of GERM, which assumes that externally set teaching standards and aligned standardized testing are preconditions for success. PISA shows that success is often associated with balanced professional autonomy and a collaborative culture in schools. Evidence also shows that high-performing education systems engage their teachers in setting their own teaching and learning targets, crafting productive learning environments, and designing multiple forms of student assessments to best support learning and school improvement.

The second finding is that good average learning outcomes and system-wide equity are often interrelated (OECD, 2013b). Equity in education means that students' socio-economic status has little impact on how well they learn in school. Equity is high on the agenda in all successful school systems. A focus on equity gives high priority to universal early childhood programs, comprehensive health and special education services in schools, and a balanced curriculum that weighs arts, music, and sports, and academic studies equally. Fairness in resource allocation is important for equity, too. PISA 2012 (OECD, 2013b) shows that fair resourcing is related to the success of the entire school system: High student performance tends to be linked to more equitable resource allocation between advantaged and disadvantaged schools.

The third finding is that school choice and competition do not improve the performance of education systems (OECD, 2013c). In the OECD countries, school choice and competition between schools are related to greater levels of segregation in the education system. That, in turn, may have adverse consequences for equity in learning opportunities and outcomes. Indeed, successful education systems do better than those that have expanded school choice. All successful school systems have a strong commitment to maintain their public schools and local school control. The PISA 2012 data show that the prevalence of charter and free schools, and the related competition for students, has no discernible relationship to student learning.

The Finnish model of educational change is radically different from GERM's. A typical feature of teaching and learning in Finland is high confidence in teachers and principals regarding curriculum, assessment, organization of teaching, and evaluation of the work of the school. Another feature is the way schools encourage teachers and students to try new ideas and approaches – in other words, to make school a creative and inspiring place to teach and learn. What is important is that today's Finnish education policies are a result of three decades of systematic, mostly intentional development that has created a culture of diversity, trust, and respect within Finnish society in general and within the education system in particular.

References

Au, W. (2009). *Unequal by Design: High-stakes Testing and the Standardization of Inequality*. New York: Routledge.

Ball, S. (2012). *Global Education Inc.: New Policy Networks and the Neo-liberal Imaginary*. Abingdon (UK): Routledge.

Breakspear, S. (2012). *The Policy Impact of PISA: An Exploration of the Normative Effects of International Benchmarking in School System Performance*. OECD Education Working Papers, No. 71, OECD Publishing. Available at http://dx.doi.org/10.1787/5k9fdfqffr28-en.

Darling-Hammond, L. (2010). *The Flat World and Education*. New York: Teachers College Press.

Gardner, D.P., Larsen, Y.W. and Baker, W. (1983). A nation at risk: the imperative for educational reform. Washington, DC: US Government Printing Office.

Hargreaves, A., Earl, L., Moore, S. and Manning, S. (2001). *Learning to Change: Teaching Beyond Subjects and Standards*. San Francisco, CA: Jossey Bass.

Jensen, B., Weidmann, B. and Farmer, J. (2013). *The Myth of Markets in School Education*. Grattan Institute.

OECD (2001). *Knowledge and Skills for Life: First Results from PISA 2000*. Paris: Author.

OECD (2004). *Learning for Tomorrow's World: First Results from PISA 2003*. Paris: Author.

OECD (2007). *PISA 2006: Science Competencies for Tomorrow's World. Vol. I*. Paris: Author.

OECD (2010). *PISA 2009: Results: What Students Know and Can Do. Student Performance in Reading, Mathematics and Science. Vol. I*. Paris: Author.

OECD (2011). When students repeat grades or are transferred out of school: What does it mean for education systems? *PISA in Focus*, July 2011.

OECD (2013a). *PISA 2012 Results: What Students Know and Can Do: Resources, Policies and Practices. Vol. I*. Paris: Author.

OECD (2013b). *PISA 2012 Results: Excellence through Equity. Vol. II*. Paris: Author.

OECD (2013c). *PISA 2012 Results: What Makes Schools Successful? Resources, Policies and Practices. Vol. IV*. Paris: Author

Sahlberg, P. (2015). *Finnish Lessons 2.0: What Can the World Learn from Educational Change in Finland?* New York: Teachers College Press.

Simola, H. (2015). *The Finnish Education Mystery: Historical and Sociological Essays on Schooling in Finland*. London: Routledge.

Välijärvi, J., and Sahlberg, P. (2008). Should 'failing' students repeat a grade? A retrospective response from Finland. *Journal of Educational Change*, 9(4), 385–389.

Wiseman, A. (2013). Policy Responses to PISA in Comparative Perspective. In H.-D. Meyer and A. Benavot (eds), *PISA, Power, and Policy: The Emergence of Global Educational Governance*. Oxford: Symposium Books, pp. 303–322.

Vignette 4

Changing Education in Action

Finland: The Collaborating Teacher

Tim Walker

I was 21 and naïve. I had been offered a long-term job as a computer teacher at an urban elementary school outside of Boston, and I jumped at the opportunity – even though I knew nothing about teaching. I had just graduated from college without taking a single education course.

As a substitute teacher, I wanted to get my feet wet in a school setting, and see if I could make a career out of teaching. The principal assured me that the classroom teachers would join me for the lessons. And I liked this idea of collaborating with other teachers. As an untrained teacher, I could use all the help I could get. But I soon found out that things wouldn't go as I expected.

My colleagues weren't used to showing up to computer lessons. Although they were technically required to join the computer teacher for lessons, the previous teacher had given them a free pass. And I could see why most classroom teachers had preferred to skip out, and chisel away at their long to-do lists.

If I had been in their shoes, I probably would have done the same. They spent many hours teaching in their classrooms. Their students had to take standardized tests. They were formally evaluated.

Once I had joined the staff, the principal sent out a message to my colleagues, requiring that they accompany me for these bi-weekly 40-minute lessons. A few teachers embraced this new reality, and were eager to work with me to make computer lessons relevant to their students. But most teachers seemed too overwhelmed to do anything but catch their breath during lessons, watching me fumble along. Instead of supporting them, I felt like I was a leech, draining them of their strength as they were now required to join me in the computer lab.

During one lesson, a young first grade teacher shooed in her class and they joined me in the meeting area towards the front of the lab. She hung back towards the back of the classroom with her hands full of paper. Her face was sullen, and underneath her eyes were dark bags. With a look of shame, she sheepishly asked if she could work in the back while she watched me teach. How could I say no? And as I looked across the room, a realization smacked me in the face. Collaboration is virtually impossible when teachers are overwhelmed. The reason for this is quite simple.

Collaboration is all about the sharing of work. When teachers are stressed, it's easy to view collaborating as a luxurious add-on. And once teachers become convinced that they can't afford to work together, the sharing of work just doesn't happen. Overwhelmed teachers rarely leave their classrooms while they're at school. They even skip lunch. And at the end of each day, they're the ones who rush out of their schools, eyes set forward, hoping that they won't bump into a colleague, because they see this interaction as unproductive. In this environment, teaching starts to look like a rat race – where only the fittest survive. This is what I was observing as a computer teacher at a public elementary school in Massachusetts.

But I would later find out that this professional ecosystem wasn't exceptional. It seemed to be the norm in American schools. In a recent OECD study (TALIS, 2013), American lower secondary teachers report spending 27 hours per week just on classroom teaching, which is significantly higher than the average of 19 hours across TALIS countries. Additionally, these American teachers log more hours per week than their international peers (45 hours versus 38 hours).

Given the heavy workload, it's not surprising to learn that 50% or more of the surveyed American teachers report that they never teach jointly in the same classroom with a colleague or observe their colleagues teaching. On top of all of this, 42% of these US teachers state that they never engage in joint projects across classes or age groups. The OECD data suggests that this kind of collaborative activity can be linked to teachers' reported job satisfaction and their confidence in their own teaching abilities.

Four years after my stint as a computer teacher, I moved to Finland with my family. I had heard about the success of Finnish education, but this hadn't influenced our decision to move. My wife and I were looking for a less burdensome place to raise our children. Life in the Boston area was too fast for us, and we were having a hard time paying our bills. Within days of arriving in Helsinki, I was given the unexpected opportunity of a lifetime: the chance to teach fifth grade at a Finnish public school.

The teaching environment in Helsinki was nothing like I could have imagined. For years, my Finnish wife Johanna had tried convincing me that teachers in Finland took frequent 15-minute breaks between lessons. *Unbelievable*, I thought. She told me that they spent most of these breaks in the teachers' lounge, drinking coffee and conversing with each other. I rolled my eyes. Johanna even told me that they taught a lot fewer hours than American teachers. And according to her, a typical first grade teacher in Finland worked about half as much each week as I was working as a first grade teacher at a private school in the Boston area (25 hours versus 50 hours). This last bit was usually too much for me to hear, and I would scowl at her. But once I started teaching at a Finnish public school, I apologized to my wife for not believing her. She was absolutely right.

In Finland, I found a school structure that fostered rich collaboration among teachers. In nearly 50% of my lessons, I was paired with one or two of my colleagues. Teachers in my school were not just collaborating in the traditional sense, by planning and teaching lessons together – they were truly laboring together, sharing the burdens of teaching with each other. They were helping each other track down the resources they'd need for an upcoming lesson. They were discussing better ways to support needy students. They were analyzing the curriculum together. They were talking about how to improve recess for the kids. They were grading tests together. They were offering tech support to each other. To my surprise, this work often happened in between sips of coffee, during those 15-minute breaks throughout the day.

Strangely, the amount of required collaborative time at my Finnish school – about two hours each week – was similar to the required amount of collaborative time at my former public school in America. And yet, the degree of collaboration was strikingly different between the two schools. From my vantage point, American teachers were often too exhausted to benefit from mandated hours of collaboration. And outside of these times, they had difficulty justifying the idea of working together during their meager hours of free time. They reasoned that more could be done when working alone.

In the United States, a full-time teaching load is nearly 50% more than the typical full-time teaching load in Finland, which is just 18 hours in the classroom every week. More hours of teaching for American educators means that there are more hours of planning and bookkeeping. With this in mind, it's no wonder American teachers report such low levels of collaboration. They are squeezed for time.

But the heavy teaching load is not the only obstacle for American teachers. They lack a teaching schedule that provides them with built-in opportunities to work with their colleagues. In my second year of teaching in Finland, 70% of my scheduled lessons are co-taught. I am even teaching history alongside my principal! Furthermore, teachers in Finland have those frequent 15-minute breaks throughout the school day to collaborate with each other – often in the teachers' lounge.

Teaching in Finland has shown me what's possible in American schools and elsewhere. Collaboration among teachers can be fostered, but it will require bold steps. Teachers need many opportunities to work together, and a lighter teaching load to maximize the time that they spend together.

Tim Walker is an American teacher who has taught in Finland for several years. He has written for *The Atlantic*, *Education Week*, and other publications. Also, he keeps a blog about Finnish education, parenting, and culture at TaughtByFinland.com.

Reference

TALIS (2013). New insights from Talis 2013: Teaching and learning in primary and upper secondary education. http://www.keepeek.com/Digital-Asset-Management/oecd/education/new-insights-from-talis-2013_9789264226319-en#page1.

Chapter 13

Teacher-Powered Schools

Rising Above Education's Blame Culture

Kim Farris-Berg and Edward J. Dirkswager

> Problems have not arisen by themselves, but are the product of circumstances. Only by 'modifying the circumstances' can one disperse the difficulties they create.
>
> Jean Monnet, *Memoirs*[1]

In the United States, accountability trickles down: federal leaders pressure states, states pressure local school districts, districts pressure principals, and principals pressure teachers. Establishing layer upon layer of downward accountability, we've set up an expectation for compliance. All players are supposed to meet mandates set from the top to improve outcomes. Yet these expectations most often lead to a culture characterized by lack of ownership and by finger pointing (from all directions) when the requirements don't lead to adequate student performance. The incentives are not in place for everyone to work together to meet students' actual needs.

Teacher and former Minnesota state legislator Julie Sabo recently expressed her disillusionment with this situation to a local school district administrator who had just given her an excellent evaluation. 'You have evaluated me on how well I did what you told me to do,' Sabo said. 'You *should* be evaluating me on how well I did what the students needed to improve their learning.' She subsequently quit that position and describes herself on Twitter as a trainer and coach interested in new ways to imagine education through empowering teachers. She remains a teacher, but due to the current nature of the profession, she is no longer practicing with students in a school.

Sabo also objected to states' and districts' adoption of policies and practices that seek to 'get tough' with teachers, making them accountable for the outcomes of decisions they are not welcome to make. Teachers' sentiment, documented all over traditional and social media, is that too many state leaders and school district administrators across the United States are now saying, 'Use this curriculum, this instructional practice, these assessments, and this discipline policy. We'll choose the methods without knowing your individual students' needs and backgrounds, but teachers, your students' outcomes are your responsibility and will count toward your personal evaluation.'

Sabo is not alone. Mandated accountability and evaluation policies, imposed by policy makers in an effort to determine effectiveness, have fueled an increase in teachers' resistance to top-down reforms. Teachers report having little influence on policy and also say that, even in their own workplaces, they frequently feel their experience and knowledge is not recognized and put to effective use. A spring 2014 report from the Gallup organization found that, of 12 professions, teachers are least likely to agree with the statements 'My opinion seems to matter at work' and 'My supervisor creates an open and trusting environment' (MetLife, 2012).

Richard Ingersoll, Professor of Education and Sociology at the University of Pennsylvania, has conducted rigorous investigations of longitudinal data from the National Center for Education Statistics. In 2007 he found that teaching has far higher annual turnover than many higher-status occupations – e.g., lawyers, engineers, architects, professors, and pharmacists (Ingersoll, 2007).

That's not surprising. While the teaching workforce has been highly educated for the past 50 years, teaching is still set up as an industrial-era job lacking most of the hallmarks of a profession. In medicine, law, engineering, and other fields, practitioners have a great deal of influence over training, licensure, standards of practice, and accountability measures. They also enjoy a great deal of autonomy to apply their professional expertise to specific cases and situations.

In a 2007 *Educational Leadership* article entitled 'Short on Power, Long on Responsibility,' Ingersoll predicted the impact of failing to bring these opportunities into teaching.

> Top-down reforms draw attention to an important set of needs – for accountability on the part of those doing the work. But these kinds of reforms sometimes overlook another equally important set of needs – for autonomy and the good will of those doing the work. Too much organizational control may deny teachers the very power and flexibility they need to do the job, effectively undermine their motivation, and squander a valuable human resource – the high degree of commitment of those who enter the teaching occupation. Having little say in the terms, processes, and outcomes of their work, teachers may doubt they are doing worthwhile work – the very reason many of them came into the occupation in the first place – which may contribute to the high rates of turnover. Consequently, accountability reforms may not only fail to solve the problems they seek to address, but actually end up making things worse.
>
> (Ingersoll, 2007)

Less than a decade later, we are at an impasse. Teachers and unions are resisting being held accountable for results of outsiders' decision making, and many teachers believe it is their moral responsibility to work around some of those decisions for the sake of their students' success. Meanwhile federal, state, and district leaders continue to roll out mandates that attempt to improve effectiveness by controlling teachers' behaviors and choices.

What else could result from this but the blame culture that's been documented throughout the earlier chapters in this book? Almost inevitably in a top-down decision-making climate those on the top begin blaming the recipients of their mandates for being the cause of poor performance. The recipients, in the end the teachers but sometimes also district leaders and others, in turn blame those providing the mandates for making decisions that won't work for their students. Teachers say: 'Your mandates won't work! We need to protect ourselves from being the scapegoats of these ineffective policies!' Meanwhile top-down decision makers say: 'Well, these policies would have worked if you had only implemented them better and abandoned protections!' Students grow up and graduate while the adults around them engage in incessant finger pointing.

Fortunately, as many begin to recognize this, a new dialogue is emerging: how can we move past blame culture and work together to improve student learning?

Quality-improvement experts assert a design principle coined by Paul Batalden, M.D.: 'Every system is perfectly designed to get the results it gets.' Applied here it means this: if we want a system that incents various players to work together for better student learning, then we need to be willing to boldly open up the opportunity for a shift in the existing dynamics around autonomy and accountability.

Teacher-Powered Schools Align Accountability with Collective Autonomy

A growing number of educators and policy makers are already boldly exploring teacher-powered schools as a means to change. Teacher-powered schools combine any expectations for teachers' accountability with collective autonomy to make the decisions influencing school success.

In these schools, teacher teams are able to make the dramatic changes in school that they determine are needed to improve student learning, increasing their passion for their job. They are willing to accept accountability in the areas where they are able to secure autonomy to choose – even invent – their school's approach to learning and management.

Areas of autonomy can include the following:

- selecting colleagues
- selecting leaders
- determining tenure policy (if any)
- dismissing colleagues or recommending colleagues for transfer

- evaluating colleagues
- setting staff patterns (such as distribution of teachers and aides)
- allocating the budget (including salaries and benefits if desired)
- determining the learning program
- setting the schedule
- choosing their means of professional development
- setting school-level policies (such as discipline and homework policy)
- determining whether to take, when to take, and how much to count local school district or charter authorizer assessments
- making formal arrangements with local school district or charter authorizer to allow multiple measures in determining school success (not only a mean proficiency score).

Today there are more than 60 teacher-powered schools operating across the United States, from California to Minnesota and Colorado to Massachusetts, serving students from preschool to age 21. Some operate within school districts, and others operate as charter schools. Some have union-affiliated teachers, while others do not. There are teacher-powered schools in 13 states, in urban, suburban, and rural settings. A few have been running successfully since the early 1970s.

In *Trusting Teachers with School Success: What Happens When Teachers Call the Shots*, Kim Farris-Berg, Edward J. Dirkswager, and Amy Junge (2012) reported the findings of their in-depth investigation of teachers' decision making in 11 teacher-powered schools. They found that these teacher teams create school cultures with characteristics that emulate those of high-performing organizations.

For example, teams identify students' needs and design schools to directly meet those needs. School leaders, who are selected by teachers, work to support teacher teams' decisions – not the other way around. This can have critical impact at the district and state levels. As schools demonstrate success, they can influence district and state leaders to rethink their decision making and structures in support of teachers' work.

Public Support for Change through Teacher-Powered Schools

Support for teacher-powered schools as a means to change is astounding. A new United States opinion survey commissioned by Education Evolving, a Minnesota-based education policy design and advocacy group, and conducted by Widmeyer Communications, a Finn Partners Company, found that 85 percent of the general public think teacher-powered schools are a good idea, while a majority of teachers want to work in one (Education Evolving, 2014).

Specifically, more than 90 percent of the general public think teachers should have a 'great deal' or at least 'some' authority to tailor instruction to individual students, and that teachers should have a great deal or some authority over curriculum and choices of technology. The public also expresses overwhelming support for giving teachers the authority to select their colleagues and even control their school's budget (80 percent and 72 percent, respectively).

In addition, the public puts a great deal of trust in teachers to carry out these responsibilities effectively; 81 percent of those surveyed trust teachers 'some' or a 'great deal' to properly use this authority to make 'schools run better.'

Surprisingly, the public is even more enthusiastic about teacher-powered schools than teachers are, likely because teachers report a large amount of skepticism regarding the potential for transformation of their field. Still, an overwhelming 78 percent of teachers say teacher-powered schools are a good idea, and one in five teachers say they are ready to implement teacher-powered schools today.

Teachers Working with Communities to Lead Transformation

Teacher-powered schools call upon their state leaders, local school district leaders, charter authorizers, unions, and professional associations of teachers to help create the conditions in which teacher-powered schools can thrive. Where these leaders respond positively, teacher-powered schools develop and come to serve as a community-driven solution to improving student learning.

The means by which teachers secure collective autonomy to make the decisions influencing school success vary greatly based on the unique characteristics of each community, including state and local political climate, teachers' personal preferences, and union, district, and charter authorizers' openness to trying new things. In other words, there is no 'one best way' for teachers to arrange for their autonomy, although it is important to recognize that some arrangements are more susceptible than others to changes in leadership or management style.

The National Inventory of Teacher-Powered Schools, accessible at www.teacherpowered.org, details the different ways in which communities empower teachers with autonomy to collectively run their schools.

Teachers' willingness to push their communities to support the movement toward teacher-powered schools comes from a strong feeling that their students' needs are not being met by the approaches required by others. It also, but most often secondarily, comes from teachers' own need to be recognized as professionals who have the knowledge and experience required to meet their students' needs well.

These teachers believe in their ability to help students achieve better outcomes when they are able to work with colleagues and their communities to design and run schools. Teacher-powered schools allow teachers to exercise collective professional autonomy – defined as the balance and interaction between humans' dual needs for interdependence and control.

Neuroscientists, clinical psychologists, and others have conducted an enormous amount of research about what it takes for individuals to be pleased with themselves, as well as what it takes for them to remain productive and motivated. In his book *Drive: The Surprising Truth About What Motivates Us*, Daniel Pink (2009) sums the findings up well. He asserts that high performance in any organization requires a mix of group and individual control over task (what we do), time (when we do it), team (who we do it with), and technique (how we do it). This kind of autonomy, along with mastery (becoming better at something that matters) and purpose (making a contribution to a greater cause) in almost all circumstances produces better results than attempts at extrinsic motivation, such as the carrot-and-stick incentives of micromanagement and higher pay.

Writing specifically about current trends in education policy, Michael Fullan, Professor Emeritus at the Ontario Institute for Studies in Education, University of Toronto, echoes Pink:

> You don't develop a profession or an organization by focusing on sticks and carrots aimed at individuals. All high-performing entities develop the group to focus collectively and relentlessly on quality work linked to high expectations and standards. If you don't base policies and strategies on purposeful group impact you inevitably end up with low yield results along with gross distractions . . . This micromanagement madness creates a massive bureaucracy that has zero chance of working, which is precisely the track record of its impact in other political systems that have tried it.
>
> (Fullan, 2014)

Teacher-Powered Schools Creating Cultures Associated with High Performance

Setting up teacher-powered schools across a country will not by itself transform the country's public schooling. There will be mistakes, and even flops. As any nation considers whether to scale teacher-powered schools as a viable model of school governance, decision makers should be interested in the quality of the decisions teachers make both for themselves and for their students. It is, after all, how the teams of teachers opt to use their collective autonomy that has the potential to be transformative.

Farris-Berg, Dirkswager, and Junge (2012) argue in *Trusting Teachers with School Success* that the best way to evaluate the quality of decisions is to determine the extent to which teacher-powered school teams exhibit behaviors and choices that are indicative of the cultural characteristics associated with high-performing organizations. The researchers gleaned nine such characteristics from their review of the literature examining cultures of high-performing organizations in private and, to a lesser extent, public sectors. Then, using teacher surveys and site visits of 11 schools, they learned that teacher-powered school teams not only cultivate these characteristics, but their most prominent practices flow from them.

Teacher-powered schools create cultures where the teachers:

1. **Accept ownership.** Teacher-powered schools welcome autonomy and responsibility for making decisions. In the areas where they secure autonomy to make the decisions, they are willing to accept accountability for outcomes.

   Jill Mulhausen from Phoenix High School (9–12) in Kennewick School District in Washington reported, 'We do not have the ability to blame the system, the students, or the parents. We made the decisions. There isn't a bureaucracy handling them. So we'll accept accountability.'
2. **Innovate.** Teachers with collective autonomy take risks to try to create new things, challenge old processes, and continuously adapt. Most are constantly on the lookout for what's not working well and most will willingly put in extra effort to find new ways of doing things. They are not satisfied with the status quo when the responsibility for students' outcomes falls on them.

   They often group students by skill and not by age, for example, and most are committed to experiential learning. Five of the 11 teacher groups put middle- and high-school students in the position to direct their own project-based learning both inside and outside of the school building, in consultation with teachers.

   Nora Houseman from San Francisco Community School (K–8) in California's San Francisco Unified School District reported, '[As a teacher-powered school] we know we can't be mediocre. We need to be exceptional. If we're not then there is no meaning; no connection between our autonomy and students' [outcomes]. [Plus our outcomes] have a direct impact on me. My job and being able to work the way we work here depends on us doing well.'
3. **Share purpose.** Teacher-powered school teams create their schools' shared purpose, consisting of their mission, vision, values, and goals. In the 11 schools, teachers' shared purpose was always to nurture students as individuals. They don't view purpose statements as just words, but make them the basis of their collective decision making and expected behaviors. The teachers say this is the reason why they all buy in and remain committed to the work they are doing.

   As Redding, California teacher Alysia Krafel from Chrysalis Charter School (K–8) put it, 'A school purpose can so easily become just words that someone else wrote. In cultures where people don't have authority to make decisions, why would anyone bother remembering what the basic mission and goals are?'

   '[The shared purpose] was developed by [founding] representatives of our school community, and when there is a hard choice, it is where we go for guidance. When we hire new staff, we are looking for folks who can live these principles. It is now part of our culture and it is spread by living up to the ideals on a daily basis,' stated Kevin Brewster from Reiche Community School (K–5) in Maine's Portland Public Schools.

4. **Collaborate.** Teachers with collective autonomy participate in collaboration and leadership for the good of the whole school, not just a classroom. Their cultures are characterized by consultation, listening, being open to different opinions, working together, and mutual respect. There is a collective willingness to invest the time and effort it takes to develop a collaborative community.

   Stephanie Davis from TAGOS Leadership Academy (7–12), a school chartered by the School District of Janesville in Wisconsin, described teachers' collaborative work like this: 'Here we actually collaborate. [In the conventional school], where I worked before, there was little to no collaboration. There you're only responsible for your own class. A little for what's happening in your department. Not for the school. Here it's all teamwork. We're accountable for the whole thing, so we work together . . . It makes us feel like, "This is my school." It's mine. I'm committed to it. It's not just a place where I work.'

5. **Lead effectively.** Many teacher-powered school teams want to focus on learning and not administration, so they select principals and lead teachers to handle these duties. The selected leaders are seen as accountable to, and in service to, the group of teachers that is responsible and accountable for school success. Leaders' accountability isn't to outsiders. Collective teacher autonomy puts in motion an entirely different structure of accountability.

   A Connecticut teacher from High School in the Community (9–12) in New Haven Public Schools said, 'Because we elect our leaders, we have a strong vote of confidence in their work, and because [we require] those leaders to include us in all decision-making and troubleshooting, we have a significant understanding of what makes this ship run. I'm proud to be a part of this team.'

6. **Function as learners.** The school cultures created by teacher-powered school teams are characterized by a sense of common challenge and discovery, rather than a culture in which experts impart information.

   Teachers said that collective autonomy greatly increases their willingness to take on a learner role. Some had been involved with improvement efforts where teachers had input, but no real authority. Without authority, they said, it wasn't worth the time investment required to learn new things and innovate. It was almost impossible to implement and sustain any changes.

   James McGovern from Mission Hill K–8 School, a Boston Pilot School, said, 'We're all learners here. That's because of [the autonomy]. At my previous school there was no culture of learning among the staff. It wasn't the people. It was the structures preventing any real change. We had a progressive principal, but we couldn't move ahead. People didn't want to create something that would just be pulled back.'

7. **Avoid insularity.** Teachers learn from students, parents, youth culture, students' future employers and educational institutions, unions, districts, and technology trends. They also learn from other teachers who design and run teacher-powered schools. Some teams constantly pay attention to whether their learning, disciplinary, and after-school programs are supporting students' individual and cultural needs.
8. **Engage and motivate one another and their students.** Most teacher-powered schools put students in a position to be active, ongoing learners. They also address social and discipline problems as a part of students' learning, bringing in more social workers and giving students real responsibilities for co-creating and co-enforcing community norms. Many of these teachers measure students' engagement as a function of the teaching and learning methods they choose, and make adjustments as they learn more about what works and what doesn't for individuals (who, teachers note, need support to find their own sources of motivation).

   Karen Locke, a Minnesota teacher at EdVisions Off Campus (7–12), an online charter school, said, 'We're always learning how to teach in new ways. We are so challenged to try new things that will keep students interested . . . We have to be innovating all the time.'

   Nora Whalen of St. Paul, Minnesota's Avalon Charter School (7–12) said, 'Students come to Avalon credit deficient, skills deficient, and depressed. We have to relight the fire within them and sometimes that takes a long time, longer than what the traditional system is willing to take. Due to this, our graduation rates have taken a hit – we don't care about these numbers. What we care about is who these students are as they walk across the graduation stage, not when they do.'
9. **Assess performance.** Teacher-powered schools set and measure progress toward both teacher and student performance goals and act upon results to improve performance.

   To evaluate teacher performance, most use 360-degree or peer-to-peer teacher evaluation and make ongoing coaching and mentoring between colleagues the norm in order to ensure continuous improvement. Some teacher-powered schools in both charter and district settings – the ones with the highest levels of autonomy in each setting – have decided that all teachers in their schools will have just one-year, at-will contracts for work. Responsible and accountable for school success, these teachers want colleagues to continuously put forth their best effort and they want a means to remove colleagues who do not. Responsible and accountable for their school finances, they also know they must reserve the right to lay off even their well-performing colleagues when the budget is tight (although they work hard to find creative alternatives).

Union leaders have agreed to sign these waivers because teachers with autonomy arrangements have control over professional issues – something unions have sought for their members for decades. In these arrangements, teachers' employers don't make the decisions; teachers do. So, union leaders don't see as much need to represent these teachers' professional interests to their employers. Union leaders can shift their role to supporting teachers in their new working arrangements, including advocating for their continued autonomy.

Stephanie Davis said, 'We're always informally evaluating one another. This is not something that is inappropriate or that makes me nervous. It's out of love for the school. We all want the school to be the best and to fix weaknesses. We all feel safe to discuss our concerns.' San Francisco Community School teacher Jessica Fishman said, 'Coaching and mentoring creates accountability on another level – more than what comes from conventional evaluation.'

Teacher-powered schools also focus on and measure students' individual learning growth in academic, cognitive, and non-cognitive areas of achievement. As a result, teacher teams often choose and invent tools and processes that assess student learning beyond traditional means. For example, many teacher-powered schools use The Hope Survey to assess students' engagement in learning as an outcome of their own perceptions of their autonomy, sense of belonging, and goal orientation. Teachers use the findings to adjust their own practice to help improve students' outcomes in these areas (Newell & Van Ryzin, 2009).

Jenerra Williams of Mission Hill K–8 said, 'Of course there is a level of proficiency we want to see children achieve. That level is not just based on a score but also on who the child is and where they are developmentally . . . When things are not working with children, we bring that specific child or group of children to the forefront of our conversations with teachers who are working with the same age group. We have team meetings with the intention of gathering insight, ideas, and action plans to help the student move forward. We also talk specifically with the child about their take on it. What isn't working? Why? What could you do differently? What do you think you need? What can we (the teachers) do differently?'

While teacher-powered school teams describe many rewards, they also report challenges. First, this is pioneering work. The infrastructure of support is in early stages of development, with the Center for Teaching Quality (CTQ) recently publishing a practical guide called *Steps to Creating a Teacher-Powered School* at www.teachingquality.org/teacherpowered.

Even with CTQ's resources, these teachers work long hours and with great intensity, especially as they get their schools through the design and start-up stages. These teachers say they've never worked so hard, but most are also grateful to be so fulfilled and satisfied in their work. They do not regret their decision to pursue collective autonomy, for their own sake and for the opportunities they are able to offer their students. Most teacher-powered schools studied report that their turnover is low.

Most of the remaining challenges that teachers described had a common thread. That is, teachers who call the shots constantly have to justify why their unconventional ways of working and the unconventional learning models they create do not fit into conventional structures and expectations. For example, teacher-powered schools need professional development for collaborative decision making for their entire team, but are sometimes required by their school districts to have one of them attend school leader training designed for schools with top-down leadership structures. Some teacher-powered schools must report attendance according to a district course-and-class schedule, when their school schedule and coursework is entirely different.

Teacher-powered school teams want to spend their time on improving the cultures they are creating in their schools. They wonder if those who provide oversight and support could adapt their management approaches to be more open to differences.

Even with these challenges, teacher-powered school teams are successfully creating high-performing cultures. None of the teams set out with a checklist of characteristics associated with high performance. It just turns out that the design and management decisions they made, rooted in their collective knowledge, experiences, and ideas about school and student success, happened to emulate the characteristics present in high-performing cultures. These promising results help us to gauge the outcomes we could expect if more teachers were to design and run schools.

Teacher-Powered Schools Bringing Fresh Insights to Policy Questions

John E. Brandl, a former Minnesota state legislator and Dean of the Hubert H. Humphrey Institute for Public Affairs at the University of Minnesota, wrote in his book *Common Good*, 'Finding out what works is not enough. Policymaking must reside not in priority setting, information gathering, or budget allocation, but in designing arrangements such that the people assigned to carry out public responsibilities are inclined to do whatever it takes to accomplish them (Brandl, 2006).

The outcomes reported by Farris-Berg, Dirkswager, and Junge indicate that teacher-powered schools are, in practice, the kind of arrangement Brandl had in mind. The schools cast doubt on federal and state leaders' 'get tough with teachers' public school improvement strategy that consists of telling teachers what to do and how to do it by tying teachers' evaluations to mean proficiency scores, standardizing curricula, tightening licensure requirements, requiring adherence to pacing guides, and more. Teacher-powered schools implore these same leaders to consider trying collective teacher autonomy as a second major strategy at improvement.

Like most reasonable people, under current arrangements, teachers have sought to avoid accepting accountability for outcomes of decisions imposed from the outside. Yet the actions of teachers working in a teacher-powered school arrangement indicate that teachers are very willing to accept accountability for the outcomes of their own decisions.

The arrangement enhances teachers' commitment to improving their profession, improves their self-determination, and directs their collective focus where it is needed most – on individual students' learning. Teachers have also shown that in teacher-powered schools they resolve many of today's hot-button education issues, such as how to handle tenure and evaluation, themselves. There is far less need for politicians to take on heated battles and for states, cities, and districts to take on so much micromanagement.

Teacher-powered schools are not a panacea for today's education problems. As more and more teacher-powered schools come to exist, teachers will need to seize opportunities to define and improve their craft. Policy makers and education leaders will need to work with teachers to identify and remove barriers to creating high-performing cultures. Union and district leaders could choose to evolve their roles. Teacher training institutions could support teachers' migration to managing whole schools with autonomy and accountability. These ideas are just a start. Teacher-powered schools will evolve. Much more work will need to be done.

Yet the growing interest in these schools – and the solutions and alternatives they provide – shows we need to seriously explore how teacher-powered schools can be a part of our strategy to find solutions.

Let's open the door for teachers to power us forward in defining the most promising paths for public school improvement.

Note

1 Monnet, J. (1978). *Memoirs*. Garden City, NY: Doubleday.

References

Brandl, J. E. (ed.) (2006). *Common Good: Ideas from the Humphrey*. Minneapolis, MN: Hubert H. Humphrey Institute of Public Affairs.

Education Evolving (2014). Teacher-powered schools: Generating lasting impact through common sense innovation. www.teacherpowered.org.

Farris-Berg, K., Dirkswager, E. J. and Junge, A. (2012). *Trusting Teachers with School Success: What Happens When Teachers Call the Shots*. Maryland: Rowman & Littlefield Education. http://www.amazon.com/Trusting-Teachers-School-Success-Happens/dp/1610485106/.

Fullan, M. (2014). Carrots and sticks are wrong way to motivate teachers. *Globe and Mail*, 13 May. http://www.theglobeandmail.com/news/national/education/no-single-teacher-can-help-students-so-put-the-sticks-and-carrots-away/article18612504/.

Ingersoll, R. M. (2007). Short on power, long on responsibility. *Educational Leadership*, 65(1), 20–25. http://www.ascd.org/publications/educational-leadership/sept07/vol65/num01/Short-on-Power,-Long-on-Responsibility.aspx.

MetLife (2012). *The MetLife Survey of the American Teacher: Challenges for School Leadership.* www.metlife.com/assets/cao/foundation/Metlife-Teacher-Survey-2012.pdf.

Newell, R. J. and Van Ryzin, M. J. (2009). *Assessing What Really Matters in Schools: Creating Hope for the Future.* Maryland: Rowman & Littlefield Education.

Pink, D. H. (2009). *Drive: The Surprising Truth About What Motivates Us.* New York: Riverhead Books. http://www.danpink.com/books/drive/.

Chapter 14

From Top-Down to Inside-Out

Working in a Teacher-Powered School

Lori Nazareno

Let's travel back in time about 100 years. What was happening then? What was life like? What did schools look like?

Women were not allowed to vote, the radio was becoming a major communication tool, and cars were just beginning to change people's lives. Only 14% of homes had bathtubs, 8% had phones, and 95% of births happened at home. Two of every ten Americans could read and write, 6% had graduated from high school, and schools and classrooms looked very much like the schools and classrooms of today. In fact, so little has changed, that a teacher from 100 years ago would be quite comfortable were they to walk into today's classrooms.

Reinventing schools and the way that they operate is no small undertaking. But then reimagining the ways in which we communicate, travel, and live our day-to-day lives wasn't small either. If we considered how we traveled and communicated 100 years ago, and then expected that we would still operate as we did in those ways, one would think us insane. Yet, every day students and teachers return to schools that perpetuate the insanity of remaining stuck in a century-old paradigm.

Fortunately, there are pioneers who have built and tested new ways for schools to operate. One different way to redesign schools is to create teacher-powered schools where teachers have the autonomy to make authentic decisions about whole-school success. I am one of those pioneers.

In 2009 my colleagues and I launched the Mathematics and Science Leadership Academy (MSLA) in Denver, Colorado, a teacher-powered school. It was designed to serve and meet the needs of some of our city's most under-served students, most of whom were second-language learners and living in poverty. These students need, and deserve, a school that will prepare them for the future, not the past. These students need a school and classrooms that look and operate in dramatically different ways than the schools of a century ago. And they need a school that will address their needs as individual human beings, not simply their test scores. These students deserve a school where they see the significant adults in their lives modeling the skills and abilities that they will need to find success in the

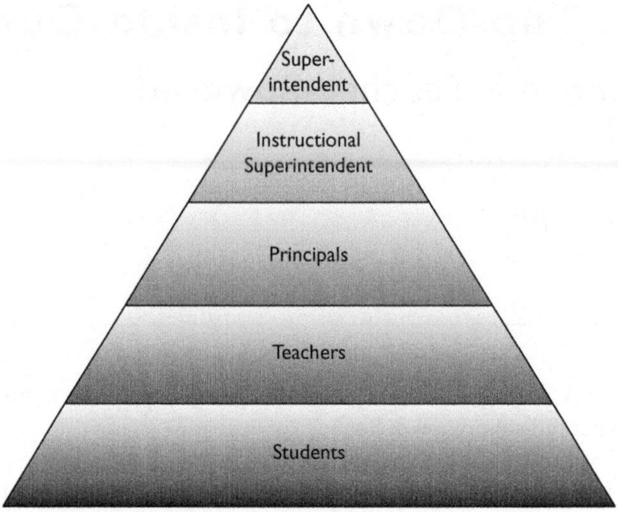

Figure 14.1 Top-down management in education.

future: collaboration, creativity, problem solving, and autonomy to make challenging decisions.

From Top-Down to Inside-Out

Historically, schools and districts in the United States have been structured to operate, and be managed, from the top down. This structure has its roots in the industrial age and is strikingly similar to the management structures seen in factories where a manager oversees assembly-line workers, and each assembly-line worker is responsible for adding something to the product as it moves along the line. Once the product has gone through each station, it gets spit out at the end as a finished product.

If we consider how this management structure has been superimposed on schools, we will see that there is a superintendent who supervises instructional superintendents, who supervise principals, who supervise teachers. This top-down structure perpetuates itself right down to the 'bottom' of the system and plays itself out by teachers then 'supervising' students in classrooms. The students are then treated like 'products' that are moving along the conveyor belt of education. At each station new knowledge and information is supposed to be dumped into their minds until they get spit out at the end of the line as a 'finished' product.

The industrial-age assembly-line structure works well if you want to ensure that the end products are all exactly the same, which, of course, means that there is no room for variation, individuality, or creativity. If we consider how this structure of our education system impacts students, who are people and not products, the costs are enormous.

We took a different approach at MSLA.

Students at the Center

During the design process for our school we put students at the center, rather than treating them like products on an assembly line. Before we even began thinking about what to teach, how to teach it, or who to hire, we delved deeply into who the students would be and what they would need to be successful. We also considered how to create a school that honored the individual strengths and abilities of both teachers and students. With students at the center, we designed the school from the inside out, rather than from the top down.

MSLA was designed to meet the specific needs of the students it serves. Seated in southwest Denver, Colorado, 70% of the students are English language learners, 95% are Latino, and 95% qualify for free or reduced-price lunch. Research suggests that these students need specific structures and supports in order to support their learning. These include:

- exposure to real-world activities to build background knowledge
- intentional development of oral language
- specific focus on the development of academic language.

Rather than try to create a one-size-fits-all school, we chose to design a school to meet the specific needs of the students who would attend. For far too long traditional models did not address students' specific challenges, nor did they capitalize on the inherent strengths of both the students and community. As a result, when designing MSLA there was an intentional effort to design a school to capitalize on the strengths of students to address their challenges.

During the design of the school it became quite apparent that some aspect of the school would have to be able to attract the most accomplished teachers, those who want to lead without leaving.

Figure 14.2 is a graphic representation of how students drove the design process and the pertinent questions that needed to be answered. In short, the leadership model of the school had its foundation in what would best serve students while also being able to attract the most accomplished teachers. Our school was designed from the inside out, with students in the middle.

Teaching from the Center

The concept of shifting from top down to inside out also applies to our beliefs about, and how we treat, students and teachers. Those schools that ascribe to an improvement model that relies on reward and punishment that come from the 'top' or outside is ignoring what is currently accepted about what motivates

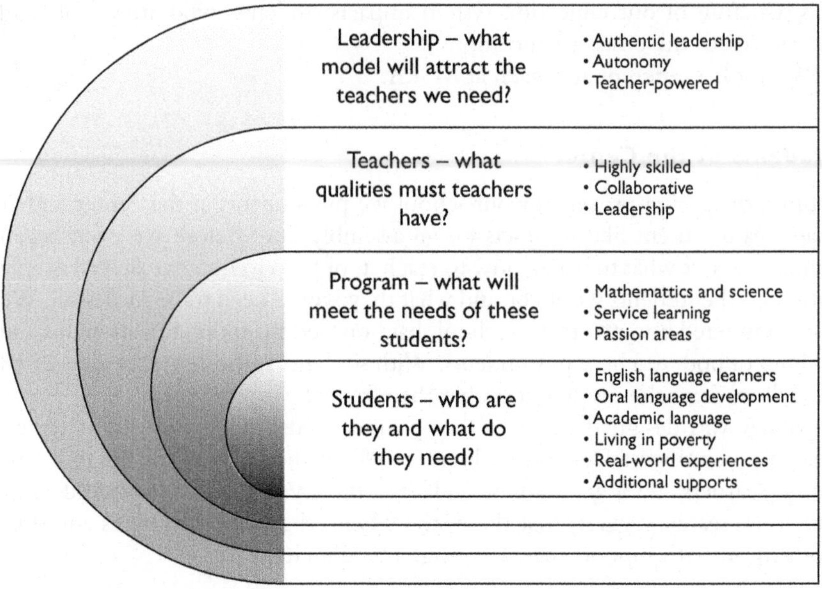

Figure 14.2 Designing schools from the inside out.

people to do great work. This is especially true if the work is highly complex and relies on knowledge work. While the promise of rewards and the threat of punishment may work well with some low-level tasks, they have repeatedly been proven to be ineffective in situations where intensive knowledge work is required. The top-down pressure to improve academic achievement not only does not work, it actually causes performance to decrease. And this applies to both students and teachers.

The approach that actually improves motivation and performance in knowledge work is one that takes an inside-out approach. Providing opportunities for students and teachers to have the autonomy, and to engage in the things about which they are passionate, works to improve motivation and performance. And this is what we do at MSLA.

Autonomy

Knowledge work done at high levels requires autonomy. Teachers at MSLA have the autonomy within their classroom to make adjustments to instruction based on the individual needs of each student, as long as it aligns with the overall mission and vision of the school. Margaret Wheatley in her book *Leadership and the New Science* said, 'The work of a team or organization needs to start with a clear sense of what they are trying to accomplish and how they want to behave together. Once this clarity is established, people will use it as their lens to interpret information, surprises and experiences. They will be able to figure out what and how to do their work.' She also said, 'We know that the best way to create ownership is to have those responsible for implementation develop the plan for themselves . . . it simply doesn't work to ask people to sign on when they haven't been involved in the planning process.'

Without autonomy, teachers act as workers on an assembly line who are simply carrying out someone else's plans. Teachers must have the opportunity to use their own intellectual capacity to solve the very complex challenge of student learning if they are to 'own' the results. When teachers do have this sort of autonomy, they are deeply committed to the outcome and the impact on student learning because they have invested themselves in the process of teaching and learning.

While teachers should have a great deal of autonomy, they should also have a deep-seated awareness of the overall mission and vision of the school and for what students should know and be able to do. In other words, teachers should have a balance between order and freedom, as Meg Wheatley explains. When teachers understand the overall goals of the school, they can then utilize their autonomy to help support all students in realizing the mission and vision.

In order to create this balance of freedom and structure, every year the teachers at MSLA engage in a weeklong retreat where they learn about the mission and vision of the school, its origins, and how that mission and vision play out in word and deed. Once staff members are well versed in what the school is about, where they are trying to go, and how they plan to get there, they then are provided the autonomy to do their part to get the students and school there. Given a clear mission and vision for the students and school, the staff then have the freedom to make their own contributions to success.

Passion

Teachers at MSLA are passionate about connecting with students and supporting their growth as individuals. And while they do care how their students do on standardized tests, this is not what they are passionate about, nor what they got into teaching for. The program at MSLA has built-in opportunities for students and teachers to connect with each other and with the things about which they are passionate.

Every week teachers and students get to participate in what we call passion areas. These are activities that are not usually part of a school that lives in a high-stakes testing culture. There are things like juggling, fishing, yoga, robots, Lego, magic, photography, and more. The activities are identified by both teachers and students based on what they are interested in and teachers are able to do. Students select the passion area in which they are interested, then once a week for an hour or two, students go to the teacher who is teaching the passion area in which they are interested. These activities allow for different teachers and students to get to know each other. And they get to connect around a common interest – something that calls from their heart.

From One Leader to Everyone a Leader

People often wonder how teacher-powered schools operate 'without' a leader. And this is one of the most striking misconceptions about teacher-powered schools. Rather than having 'no' leader, teacher-powered schools create an environment where *everyone* is a leader.

Traditional models of schooling, especially those in a high-stakes testing culture, are almost always structured so that there is only one identified leader. This, again, comes from the industrial era and model of schooling. The common thinking behind this is that with one leader, there is one vision, and one person who can be held responsible for performance. The problem, again, is that this model is not effective for knowledge work.

MSLA is a teacher-powered school whose tagline is, 'Where everyone is a learner, teacher, and leader.' While the intent is easily understood, execution of this idea can be challenging. Traditional concepts of leadership rely on the notion that one person is 'in charge' and everyone else follows. More and more evidence is emerging that indicates a significantly different type of leadership is needed and more effective, especially in schools. This new form of leadership aligns with the notion of everyone being a leader and focuses on capitalizing on the unique strengths and assets that each individual brings to a task or organization. MSLA is structured to do exactly that.

Leading from the Circle

At MSLA we developed a leadership structure that is circular in nature, rather than the traditional top-down triangular structure that exists in most schools.

We treat all responsibilities and decisions as existing as part of the overall circle of responsibilities within the school. The responsibilities have been divided up to create decision-making teams. Each team has a charge that outlines the scope of their work along with their responsibilities. And each member of the staff is on at least one of these teams. Teachers are placed on a team based on their individual interests and strengths. This team structure places some form of leadership in everyone's hands rather than all of the decision-making power residing in the hands of the manager or principal. Figure 14.3 illustrates the team structure at MSLA.

Creating the Teams

Originally, the school staff created some of the different teams based on the areas in which teachers had the most expertise and the most interest in having decision-making responsibility. The staff also had to consider all of the additional responsibilities that needed attending to in order to operate a school. Because there were responsibilities that teachers were, and weren't, interested in, the creation of two Lead Teacher positions was necessary. One of these

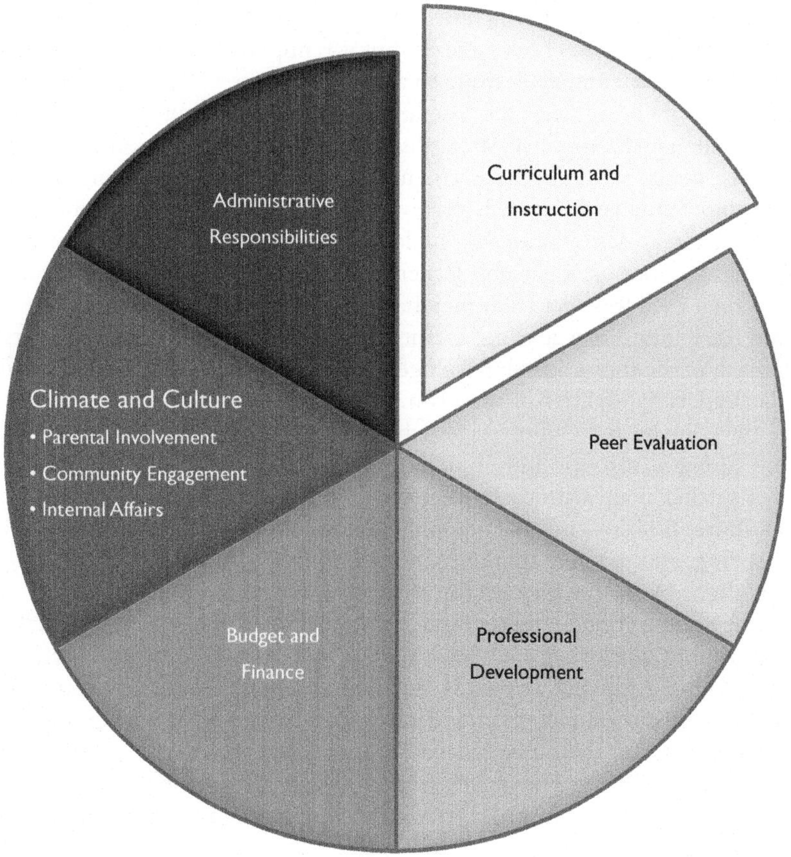

Figure 14.3 Possible team structure in a teacher-powered school.

positions has the responsibility to oversee all of the operational issues and one to oversee all of the academic issues. These Lead Teachers do not *make* all of the decisions, but rather make sure that the responsible parties make the decisions.

Each team has a clearly stated charge that defines the scope of their work and the ways in which decisions are to be made.

Every two to three years the staff reviews the number and content of the teams and makes adjustments based on student needs and teacher expertise. These teams are still responsible for complying with district policy but have the leeway to make decisions as long as they do not go counter to district policy.

Building the Teams

Once the types of teams are identified, then the task of figuring out who goes on what team begins. There is a significant level of intentionality that goes into the process of identifying which teachers go on what team. Teachers need to have an opportunity to choose a team, but it is important to balance the different strengths that individuals bring to a task.

Each staff member takes the Strengths-Finder Assessment,[1] a tool to identify an individual's top five strengths. To identify each person's leadership strengths, their five strengths are then compared against the Strengths-Based Leadership framework,[2] which places each of the strengths into one of the following categories: relationship building, executing, strategic thinking, and influencing. Once each person's leadership strengths are known, this information is then used to select team members.

We have found that it is important that each team has at least one person with each of the four leadership strengths. This is to ensure that there is balance in the leadership abilities of the team. For example, it might be tempting to have the Climate and Culture team wholly comprised of people with the leadership strength of relationship building. While a team like this would be terrific at getting along with each other and thinking of ways to improve climate and culture, if it does not include individuals with the strengths of executing, influencing, and strategic thinking, they might not actually get anything done that is aligned with the goals of the school.

Team composition is therefore a combination of self-selection and Lead Teacher input. Each staff member takes the Strengths-Finder Assessment, and the individual's top five strengths are then compared against the Strengths-Based Leadership framework to identify each person's leadership strengths. This information is then used to select team members.

Teachers can change teams each year, although at least one member remains from the previous year in order to ensure continuity and to carry the institutional memory for the team.

Coordinating the Teams

One representative from each team will also be a member of the School Leadership team, which serves in a role similar to a board of directors. Members of the School Leadership team are responsible for ensuring that the work of the teams is in alignment with the mission, vision, and values of the school. This team also has the authority to approve or send plans back to a team for revision, but not the authority to change a plan or decision.

From Accountability to Responsibility

Where there is a lack of responsibility, it is necessary for there to be measures of accountability. In other words, when one is not responsible for something, then some external process needs to be in place to hold one accountable. In teacher-powered schools, like MSLA, teachers are replacing accountability with responsibility. Rather than being held accountable for carrying out someone else's plan, teachers are being responsible for creating and executing their own plans and the subsequent results. This includes taking responsibility for student outcomes, teaching quality, and whole-school success.

Responsibility for Student Outcomes

When teachers have the autonomy to be able to make decisions about what is taught and how it is taught, they are eager to take responsibility for the impact on student learning. When they make decisions, they want to know if something works, or not. Teachers are eager to find out how their intellectual work has impacted student learning. And if it did not yield the results that they had hoped for, teachers are anxious to try something new in order to find a way to reach each student and support learning.

At MSLA one of the teams that supports teachers in knowing the impact of their instruction is the Data team. This team collects and analyzes school, grade-level, and individual student data to determine how students and the school are progressing in terms of meeting student learning targets. This team then coordinates with the PD, or Professional Development, team and the Peer Evaluation team to ensure that teachers are engaging in learning opportunities to improve their practice and that they are receiving timely feedback on their teaching practice in order to continuously improve. This data and feedback comes from peers, who work collaboratively to support student learning, not from a superior who is there to punish and reward. While the process might look similar, the purpose and intention behind it make all of the difference in the world.

And while student assessment data is important, it is *not* considered the most important measure of success. At MSLA, like at other teacher-powered schools, we consider a broad range of measures to determine student and school success, not just test scores. Some of the most important aspects of child development could never be determined by a standardized assessment.

At MSLA, we consider student participation in service learning and passion areas, student surveys, behavior, re-enrollment, and engagement in order to determine student success. And these things are more important than student test scores.

Responsibility for Teaching Quality

In traditional school structures, the principal is the primary person responsible for overseeing, managing, and evaluating teaching quality. This is because they are the 'manager' of the school. In teacher-powered schools where there either is no principal, or the principal no longer is the 'manager,' the responsibility for teaching quality is in the hands of the collective group of teachers. One of the ways in which teaching quality is continuously improved and evaluated is through the peer observation and evaluation process.

At MSLA, all teachers, including the Lead Teachers, engage in this peer observation and evaluation process. The teaching staff is divided into teams of three. The Lead Teachers create these teams by utilizing input from each teacher and what they know about the teacher. Each teacher identifies three teachers with whom they would like to work, and the Lead Teachers consider what they know about the strengths and challenges of each teacher on the staff. Every effort is made to include at least one person whom the teacher has identified and one person who has strengths in the area of challenge. For instance, if the Lead Teachers know that someone needs help in differentiating instruction, they will put someone who is strong with differentiation on their team. When possible, a National Board Certified Teacher (NBCT) is on each team as well. NBCTs are teachers who meet high and rigorous standards for what accomplished teachers should know and be able to do, including being deeply reflective about their practice and the impact that it has on student learning. As a result, we believe that NBCTs are best equipped to support teachers in being reflective practitioners and in reaching those high and rigorous standards.

Once the teams are established, they then engage in cycles of peer observation and feedback every four to six weeks. Prior to the observations, each team meets to discuss the successes and challenges that they have been having with their students. This meeting occurs during the staff meeting prior to the week of observations. Each teacher identifies an area they would like their team to observe and provide feedback for. The area chosen is selected from the rubric on which each teacher will be evaluated. At MSLA, the evaluation rubric is the same one that is used district-wide for Denver Public Schools (http://leap.dpsk12.org).

During the week when observations occur, two substitute teachers are hired for two consecutive days. Teachers on each team sign up to have the substitutes cover their classes during their observation times. For instance, if teachers A, B, and C are on the same team, teachers A and B will sign up to observe teacher C at 10 am; teachers B and C will sign up to observe teacher A at 11 am and teachers A and C will sign up to observe teacher B at 1 pm. Teachers then observe each other, looking for evidence that is identified on the rubric. This evidence includes not only teacher behaviors, but also student behaviors and work samples.

The teacher teams then meet after the observation to provide feedback and engage in coaching conversations. This meeting occurs during the staff meeting the week after observations. All of the information and evidence that is collected during this peer observation and feedback process is then shared with the Lead Teachers, who consider it when doing teacher evaluations.

The Lead Teachers also observe all of the teachers multiple times during the year. They engage in their own observation and feedback conversations with teachers and consider the information from the peer observation teams when doing final evaluation ratings.

In a school culture where everyone is seen as a leader and all are responsible for school success, every teacher becomes responsible for teaching quality. This includes the teaching quality of our peers, as well as us. When there is no outside 'manager' who holds us 'accountable,' we all become 'responsible' for improving and evaluating teaching quality.

Responsibility for School Success

When teachers in teacher-powered schools take responsibility for student outcomes and teaching quality, it stands to follow that they also take responsibility for whole-school success. The definition of a teacher-powered school is: a school where teachers have the autonomy to make decisions that impact whole-school success. And when teachers have this type of autonomy, they also accept responsibility for whole-school success. In fact, teachers reject the notion that they should take responsibility for success when they do not have the autonomy to make these types of decisions.

As mentioned previously, however, teachers' definitions of whole-school success go well beyond standardized test measures. While those test measures are considered, they are not the only measures used to define and determine success.

At MSLA, other measures include parent surveys, staff surveys, student surveys, student participation in service learning and passion areas, and student engagement.

While it is important for teachers and staff at a school to feel as though the school is a success, it is even more important for students and their parents to feel as though the teachers and school are meeting their needs. Because of this belief, the staff at MSLA takes seriously the information that is provided by parent and student surveys. From these surveys we can determine whether students and parents feel as though the staff cares about them and their learning, whether they feel as though students can get support when they need it, and whether or not they are learning. The degree to which students and parents feel cared for, welcome, supported, and able to learn determines self-efficacy, which is related to student learning outcomes. The staff also cares deeply about who the students are as people and citizens, not just about their standardized test scores.

Teachers at MSLA and other teacher-powered schools consider this broader definition of school success important, and are more than willing to take responsibility for those things that directly impact those outcomes. At MSLA, it is more important for teachers to be responsible for the outcomes and to their students and families, than it is to be held accountable to those outside their school community.

Conclusion

In the end, rethinking and redesigning school structures from the industrial era in order to fit with the knowledge era in which we live, will require 'flipping' a

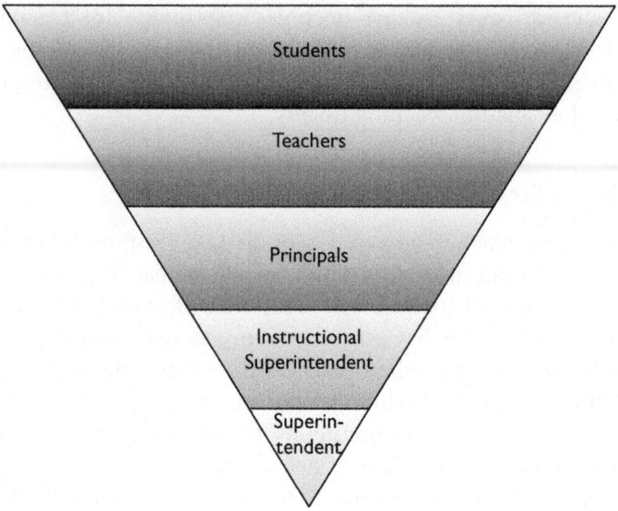

Figure 14.4 Flip the System.

system that has administrators in charge of decision making and accountability, and instead putting students and teachers at the top of that structure. In order to create the knowledge workers of today and for tomorrow, teachers and students must practice being knowledge workers. If students and teachers continue to be treated, and operate, as industrial workers, we will continue to create industry-prepared workers. Let's 'flip the system' in order to get new outcomes for the new world in which we are living!

Notes

1 Rath, T. (2007). *Strengths Finder 2.0.* New York: Gallup Press.
2 Rath, T. and Conchie, B. (2008). *Strengths-Based Leadership: Great Leaders, Teams, and Why People Follow.* New York: Gallup Press.

Reference

Wheatley, M. J. (1992). *Leadership and the New Science: Learning about Organization from an Orderly Universe.* San Francisco: Berrett-Koehler Publishers.

Vignette 5

Changing Education in Action

Mexico: The Embracing Teacher

Elisa Guerra

I became a teacher by accident.

Don't get me wrong. It's not that I don't love teaching. It's just that I had a different plan for myself. I hadn't even considered a career in education back then. It seemed . . . well, dull.

Maybe it was because of the way I was taught. Oh, I loved to learn. And I was always a good student. But school felt more like the necessary constraint all children had to go through to comply with a secret order – one that only grown-ups could grasp – and the burden we had to carry until adulthood.

There were many things I was interested in that I never got to learn at school. And then there were many things I was sure I could do without, but had to rattle endlessly towards perfection. School decided what I was to learn, when I was to learn that, and how I got to learn it. I had no say in that. And maybe neither had my teachers.

There were of course very good teachers, interesting classes and fun things to do. But they were, at least where I came from, scarce and hard to find, like little fireflies shining in a sea of darkness.

How could I even think about becoming a teacher? A ringmaster of a pathetic circus where children are painfully trained and – if well behaved – applauded by their encircling society?

Then I became a mother.

Founding a school was no piece of cake. But even more difficult than that was to live with the thought of the school system slowly chewing away my son's individuality and natural love of learning.

I borrowed money from my father, sold my car, rented a small space and opened a preschool with 17 children, including my own. I had no experience and no training. I hired a couple of teachers and began to teach myself as well. It was so much harder than I had anticipated. I was exhausted and broke, but happy. I came to respect and admire the teaching profession. It was truly hard work.

I studied at home to get my teaching degree and eventually got a Master's as well. The school – and our kids – began to thrive. I had found my element.

From the very beginning, our school, Colegio Valle de Filadelfia, searched to embrace diversity, promote collaboration and provide rich opportunities for learning. We focused heavily on arts, music, global awareness, physical excellence and challenging academics. We soon opened elementary classes and some years later also received secondary school students.

From the time I taught my kids at home, I had become fascinated with the brain and learning. Over the years, the model for our school evolved and was eventually franchised. Now there are five schools operating in different cities of Mexico. Two international schools will open in 2015, in Costa Rica and Brazil.

If we wanted our school to be a vibrant and challenging place for our students, it also had to prove the same for our teachers. The first thing we needed to recognize was that teachers are professionals, and as such they should be trusted to make their own judgments and allowed freedom to explore how they can best engage their students. If we wanted to improve the way children were educated, we needed to acknowledge teachers as agents of change.

I was a new teacher as well, and whatever lack of experience we had was compensated with tons of enthusiasm. But the road was not smooth. On top of the usual challenges of teaching, being a small private school came with its own set of hardships. We needed paying students in order to survive. Resources were always limited. Good teachers were hard to find and keep.

In time, a team of like-minded individuals was formed. Many of our first teachers are still with us, and they provide a sort of solid ground and warmth for the newcomers. I regard our teachers as highly self-motivated and perseverant people. 'By exhibiting agency, teachers can address and overcome many challenges' (Keogh, Garvis, Pendergast & Diamond, 2012).

Our schools are still young and we keep striving for excellence in learning and teaching. One of the many methods we have used to help us grow as a professional community has been what we call *shared experience protocols*. We devised this model for collaboration upon mixing and shaking ideas from other teaching groups (Allen, 1998) as well as our own. Basically, we use some time during our monthly meetings to share experiences, analyze problems, evaluate outcomes and make proposals in an organized fashion. The protocol sets the pace of interaction and helps us to stay focused.

I said before that I became a teacher by accident. But that might not be completely accurate. It is true that I was not expecting my life to take the path of education. But once I found myself there, it was my decision to stay. The discovery of a passion for teaching was the accident. To embrace the teaching profession was a choice.

Elisa Guerra is a social studies teacher and founder of Colegio Valle de Filadelfia in Aguascalientes, Mexico. She holds a Master of Education with a specialty in teaching and learning processes from Instituto Tecnológico y de Estudios Superiores de Monterrey. She is also a teacher trainer and an author of a series of textbooks for preschoolers with Pearson Education, focusing on early reading instruction and global culture awareness. She was among the Top 50 finalists for the 2015 Global Teacher Prize. Her blog is elisaguerra.net and her Twitter handle is @ElisaGuerraCruz.

References

Allen, D. (ed.) (1998). *Assessing Student Learning: From Grading to Understanding*. New York: Teachers College Press.

Keogh, J., Garvis, S., Pendergast, D. and Diamond, P. (2012). Self-determination: Using Agency, Efficacy and Resilience (AER) to counter novice teachers' experiences of intensification. *Australian Journal of Teacher Education*, 37(8), article 4. Available at: http://ro.ecu.edu.au/ajte/vol37/iss8/4.

Part IV

A Question of Mindset

Supporting and Activating Teachers

In Part III we focused on collective autonomy. This part focuses on the need to increase the capacity of teachers to act and to shape their own environments. The challenge that schools and whole systems are facing is twofold. First is how to not hamper those teachers who already are actively agents of change. Second is to increase the capacity of teachers to act for those who are not already doing so: those teachers who have the potential to act, but lack either the skills or the means to do so.

Instead of a machine-like process, Gert Biesta describes 'education [as] a process of communication, encounter, and interpretation'. Instead of a factory, we should liken the school more to a workshop in the Middle Ages: a workshop-like environment invites experimentation and 'experimentation invites the dialogic conversation, the open-ended discussion with others about hypotheses, procedures and results' (Sennett, 2012, p. 115). This is the discretionary space that is needed to act and at the same time allow the capacity to act to grow. Teaching is often likened to an art and a craft. Making that craft your own is deeply rooted in cooperation and collaboration. Education is about social relations, which can't be managed on a data board or imposed on a school community. 'Social relations are experiences in the gut' and a workshop-like environment allows for these experiences to happen (Sennett, 2012).

This final section focuses on how such a workshop environment can be put into practice on the school, board and national level. This calls for non-positional teacher leadership and different teacher roles. Traditionally, teacher leadership has been problematic in that it strengthened hierarchic systems and pulled teachers out of the classroom. But recent research on non-positional teacher leadership shows promise (Frost, 2014; Snoek, 2014). The case for flipping the system is at the same time a case for teacher leadership. **Barnett Berry**, **Noah Zeichner** and **Rachel Evans** argue that a new wave of hybrid teacher leaders is increasingly taking matters into their own hands: '*Teacherpreneurs* [who] teach students regularly, but also create and spread their own ideas while developing and using skills as boundary spanners.'

We get an almost literal look at the classroom and school as a workshop from

Arjan van der Meij, a physics teacher and teacher leader from the Netherlands who reflects on how peer review and *maker education* changed his practice.

How to increase the capacity of teachers to act on a national level is shown by **Ann Lieberman**, **Carol Campbell** and **Anna Yashkina**. In the Teacher Learning and Leadership Program (TLLP), teachers in Ontario can call on a well-endowed fund to innovate within their own personal setting. The result is educational change through professional development for and by teachers.

Swedish teacher and researcher **Eva Hartell** shows how by engaging teachers in professional learning communities around the well-researched practice of embedded formative assessment, you build a culture of inquiry, experimentation and focus on the learning process of both students and teachers.

Lesson material is an often overlooked aspect of educational change. But collaborative designing and sharing lesson material can also serve to engage in shared practice. In Russia, with an increasing top-down management system, publisher **Artiom Soloveychik** is using a shared resource model to create the space for teachers to interact and reflect on their pedagogical practice.

Tom Bennett calls for a 'polite revolution' by teachers in research and education. Instead of teachers passively doing what they're told by outsiders under the banner of 'evidence-based' education, teachers should actively engage with research, questioning not only the research itself, but also how research can help increase our practice and therefore turn teaching more into a profession. In line with flipping the system, he created researchED, which is turning into a global movement, a global workshop on education and research if you will.

One place where such a support system based on discretionary space seems to be missing is Korea. Primary teacher **Hyejin Bak** reflects upon the lack of support for her ambitions, and her decision to follow a PhD, which is taking her into unfamiliar territory both personally and also in a Korean context.

Schools never operate in a vacuum, and it is probably a necessity to engage the wider community surrounding the school. That is exactly what **Helen Janc Malone** and **Reuben Jacobson** are arguing for: empowering teachers through community partnerships.

Finally **Matt Esterman** shows how teachers can take professional development into their own hands through online engagement and an unconference model called EdCamp, which is being put into practice worldwide.

References

Frost, D. (2014). *Transforming Education through Teacher Leadership*. Cambridge: Leadership for Learning, p. 154.

Sennett, R. (2012). *Together: The Rituals, Pleasures, and Politics of Cooperation*. New Haven, CT: Yale University Press.

Snoek, M. (2014). *Developing Teacher Leadership and Its Impact in Schools*. Amsterdam: Hogeschool van Amsterdam, p. 246.

Chapter 15

Teacher Leadership

A Reinvented Teaching Profession

Barnett Berry, Noah Zeichner and Rachel Evans

Introduction

Education reformers and policy leaders, such as those at the recent International Summits on the Teaching Profession, often call for teacher leadership.[1] However, the concept of teacher leadership has not been well defined, and as a result, what it means for teachers to lead from the classroom varies widely.[2] Mark Smylie, a prominent researcher in the field of educational leadership, pointed out that while teachers have been 'looked to with increasing regularity as agents of school and classroom change,' the stark reality is that their roles are often defined by administrators – and their leadership is only recognized when supervisors either 'anoint' or 'appoint' them.[3]

However, based on empirical evidence as well as our own experiences, we believe strongly that if schools are to succeed in meeting all students' needs, then teachers' roles must shift dramatically so they can lead with their own ideas in spreading more effective pedagogical and policy-reform expertise. We make our case by first clarifying differing conceptions of teacher leadership – and the kind demanded for a reinvented profession. Then we outline why teacher leadership is so important. Next we examine how some nations have created conditions that encourage classroom practitioners to collaborate and to lead reforms (rather than merely being targets of them). Finally, we offer strategies for ramping up the spread of teacher leadership across the globe, drawing on insights from our work with the Center for Teaching Quality (CTQ) Collaboratory, a virtual community of educators.

Our analysis is grounded in our perspectives as American educators. One of us (Barnett) entered teaching decades ago, only to leave the classroom after a few years to undertake a career conducting research into and advocating for the profession. He founded CTQ and its virtual community of teacher leaders from across the world. The other two of us (Noah and Rachel) both teach and lead, without leaving the classroom – in the Seattle Public Schools – and are part of an effort to leverage teacher leadership to spread global education in our district. (Noah and Rachel are also leaders of CTQ-Global, a subset of the CTQ Collaboratory, which we describe herein.)

Defining Teacher Leadership

Over a decade ago Jennifer York-Barr and Karen Duke put together a comprehensive review of teacher leadership, a new field of inquiry at the time of this review's publication. They describe a great deal about the dimensions and characteristics of teacher leadership, but point out that although the literature is 'relatively rich' in regard to classroom experts' potential to lead, it is light on the 'evidence of such effects.'[4] Nevertheless, York-Barr and Duke thoughtfully outline how teacher leadership has evolved over time, pointing to three distinct waves, and in doing so, bringing greater clarity to the concept.

In *Wave 1*, teachers served in formal roles as grade-level chairs, department heads, or union representatives and took on managerial roles designed to 'further the efficiency of school operations.'[5] This means that teacher leadership could be mostly about the work that administrators did not want to perform.

In *Wave 2*, teachers took on instructional roles, helping to implement the prescribed schools curriculum, leading staff development workshops, and mentoring new recruits or showing them the ropes as *buddies*. These teacher leader roles have become a bit more commonplace today, especially with the formalization of induction programs for new recruits. But as other researchers have made clear, few school districts implement these programs with much fidelity. For example, although more new recruits have access to induction programs, few programs have the qualities (that is, mentoring by trained veterans, a reduced teaching load, and so on) known to improve the retention of teachers in the classroom.[6]

And in *Wave 3*, teachers began to lead what are now called professional learning communities (PLCs) in an effort to support collaboration and continuous learning among themselves. But as Andy Hargreaves has noted, 'many professional learning communities can be horrifically stilted caricatures of what they are really supposed to be.'[7] As researcher Joan Talbert has pointed out, most PLCs, while well intended, obsess over data and spreadsheets of student test scores and ignore 'the social nature of learning' among teachers. In part, PLCs have tamped down teacher leadership because administrators do not understand or know how to cultivate professionalism inside their school, and teachers often do not, as a collective, know what high-functioning PLCs look like.

We believe it is time for *Wave 4* of teacher leadership, whereby those who teach can also incubate and execute their own ideas. For us, teacher leadership for a reinvented teaching profession must be about classroom practitioners having the time and space to lead, and being rewarded for leading not only in their schools, but also across their respective education jurisdictions and nations. In Wave 4, teachers will serve in a variety of formal and informal roles, defined most prominently on the basis of their knowledge of students and communities. They will be producers of solutions rather than just implementers of someone else's.

As York-Barr and Duke pointed out, the school norms of isolation, individualism, and egalitarianism have historically undermined teacher leadership.[8] We believe that in Wave 4, teachers, some with positional power, but many without it, will lead the de-isolation of their profession, and drive the collective expertise of their colleagues in the best interests of students.

We have developed the concept of *teacherpreneurs* – a quintessential example of Wave 4 teacher leadership. Teacherpreneurs teach students regularly, but also create and spread their own ideas while developing and using skills as boundary spanners; they are change agents who communicate across different and often competing groups and establish links among them. According to British policy expert Paul Williams, difficult problems require boundary spanners who have interorganizational experience, transdisciplinary knowledge, and strong cognitive capabilities[9] – and we believe strong public schools face complex challenges that would be best solved with the leadership of those who teach students.

Teacher leadership, as a result, is not just about managing edicts from above or implementing a curriculum with fidelity, or mentoring a new recruit. It is about leading professional learning systems, serving in joint appointments with higher education and community-based organizations, conducting and publishing research, designing, scoring, and reporting on student assessments, creating partnerships with afterschool programs and social service agencies, and potentially so much more.

The evidence for teacher leadership is palpable.

Making the Case for Teacher Leadership

First, scholars have found that effective school leadership – that which leads to improved student learning – is more than just a list of behaviors enacted by an administrator or two. While reforms often position the principal as *the* instructional leader, recent analyses suggest that 'increasing teachers' involvement in the difficult task of making good decisions and introducing improved practices must be at the heart of school leadership.'[10] Effective school leadership is not about command and control from administrators. Instead, motivating students' high performance involves a complex, collective effort of leadership at many levels to establish trust among educators, parents, and students.[11] Schools that exhibit 'high trust' tend to involve teachers in collective decision making and are also more likely to spread reform initiatives.[12]

Second, researchers have found that students achieve more in mathematics and reading in schools with higher levels of teacher collaboration.[13] And economists, using sophisticated statistical methods and large databases, have concluded that students score higher on achievement tests when their teachers have opportunities to work with colleagues over a longer period of time and share their expertise with one another.[14] A recent Organisation for Economic Co-operation and Development (OECD) report, following on from its review of policies in top-performing nations, concluded that the most effective form of school leadership may very well be 'self-sustained teacher collaboration.'[15] Teachers in the United States have put an exclamation point on these empirical findings: More than 90% report that their colleagues contribute to their teaching effectiveness.[16]

Third, recent international studies have found strong links between teacher leadership and self-efficacy and improving teaching performance. For example, new evidence from Ontario's Teacher Learning and Leadership Program (TLLP) reveals that as teachers 'initiate, innovate, implement and share a wide range of projects with their school and peers outside their school,' they develop a variety of leadership skills and abilities.[17] Teachers reported skill development in communicating evidence of best practices and 'how to support each other's strengths.' In addition, while 85% of the teachers noted that their influence was evident inside of their schools, almost one third claimed their action research findings had reached colleagues across the district.[18]

Fourth, many countries face growing economic instability and poverty, necessitating new school designs. School buildings that once opened from 7 a.m. to 3 p.m. for 180 days a year will need to become year-round, 24/7 community centers. Even the best school principals and assistant principals do not have all the knowhow and/or bandwidth to address the learning needs of growing numbers of diverse students, many living amidst devastating economic conditions that can inhibit cognitive development.[19] To help these students succeed, many teachers will have to assume more diversified roles directly connected to the comprehensive services that families will need.

Finally, a recent survey found that 23% of America's teachers are 'extremely' or 'very interested' in filling hybrid roles as teachers *and* leaders. These findings are compelling, especially since the vast majority of teachers – 84% – are 'not very' or 'not at all' interested in becoming principals.[20] The same survey found principals' job approval ratings have dropped precipitously – from 76% reporting being 'very satisfied' in 2004–2005 to 59% in 2012. Major challenges facing principals include managing resources, meeting diverse learners' needs, and engaging parents and community. Little action has been generated around proposals for 'reinventing' the principalship; instead, the job has 'simply become not doable.'[21]

As David Frost has noted:

> Teachers really can lead innovation; teachers really can build professional knowledge; teachers really can develop the capacity for leadership, and teachers really can influence their colleagues and the nature of professional practice in their schools. However, what is abundantly clear is that teachers are only likely to do these things if they are provided with appropriate support.[22]

In fact, across the globe we find sound examples of some of those conditions that clear the way for teachers to both teach and lead.

Creating the Conditions for Teachers to Lead

Approximately 60 million teachers teach in very different contexts worldwide – making international comparisons of their status as leaders in their respective societies problematic. Fundamentally, if teachers are to lead, they must have both the agency as well as the recognition by their respective societies to do so. A recent survey spanning 21 countries reveals major differences in how the public perceives teachers. The 2013 *Global Teacher Status Index* points out that Finns have the most trust in teachers, while Israelis have the least. Chinese and South Korean parents are most likely to want their children to become teachers, with Chinese respondents being more likely to equate the status of teachers to those of doctors. In the US, Brazil, France, and Turkey, however, people think teachers are most similar to librarians.[23]

Top-performing nations like Finland and Singapore have built their success on teacher development and leadership – specifically by intentionally creating policies and programs so that classroom practitioners can learn from each other and spread their expertise in teaching.[24] Both countries invest heavily in pre-service preparation in order for teachers to have knowledge and skill to lead and share their insights with colleagues, administrators, and policy leaders. And in each of these two top-performing nations, the attrition rate of teachers is less than 3% annually – primarily because powerful policies are in place to support teaching as a career. Teachers only teach students approximately 17 hours a week. During the rest of the workweek, they collaborate on lesson preparation, visit one another's classrooms to study teaching, and engage in professional discussions with colleagues in (or beyond) their schools.

In fact, the recent 2014 Teaching and Learning International Survey (TALIS) – including data from 100,000 randomly selected teachers in 6,500 schools and 34 nations – hones in on some very important differences in the conditions under which teachers lead. We focus on six major findings from TALIS that help us better understand teacher leadership in an international context, with America as an instructive counterexample to top-performing nations like Finland and Singapore as well as others.

First, American teachers have the longest school day and spend the most time in front of students. US teachers work more hours per week than their global counterparts (45 hours versus an average of 38 in other nations) and spend more of that time teaching (27 versus the 19-hour TALIS average). This means US teachers have much less time for planning, collaboration, and professional development – and fewer opportunities to develop and use leadership skills. A recent analysis found that the US actually spends less on teachers' salaries per student by expecting its classroom practitioners to spend more time directly in front of students. On the other hand, Finland (and other top performers like Japan, Estonia, Poland, and Korea) all make financial investments 'to ensure that teachers have time outside of teaching to continuously improve their craft.'[25]

Second, American teachers less frequently observe and collaborate with one another to improve instruction. For example, 50% of American teachers never observe other teachers; only 5% in Korea and 20% in Singapore report the same. Compared to average teachers elsewhere, American teachers are twice as likely to lack opportunities to work with teaching colleagues across different student age groups and classes. And only 10% of US teachers reported receiving feedback from assigned mentors – compared to 38% in Singapore. Overall, teachers across the globe who engage in collaborative learning have higher job satisfaction and confidence in their abilities.

Third, while American teachers' planning and collaboration time is scarce, they must devote nearly three times as much time to general administrative tasks as do Finnish teachers, and they spend six times as long on extracurricular activities. US teachers are two and a half times more likely than peers in other nations to be required to spend time on 'unspecified tasks.'

Fourth, American teachers, compared to their counterparts, give their professional development lower ratings. The average American teacher reports spending a similar number of days engaged in professional development as his or her international peers. However, American teachers are uniformly less satisfied with content and delivery of their on-the-job learning opportunities. And no wonder – they are less likely than teachers elsewhere to report that professional development offers helpful feedback on their teaching practices, methods for working with special needs students, or strategies for assessing student progress. But they are by no means alone: between one fifth and almost one half of teachers in several nations (Denmark, Iceland, Italy, Spain, and Sweden) report that they have *never* received feedback in their current school.

Fifth, American teachers are less likely to be evaluated by expert peers. On average, teachers in other countries are twice as likely to be evaluated by peers as US teachers. American policymakers have made enormous investments in teacher evaluation of late, emphasizing rigor. However, in the US, most observations are conducted by administrators who may not be skilled teachers themselves or may not have much background knowledge in the subject or grade level they must assess. As a recent study has revealed, in the US, principals are 'hard-pressed for time to be instructional leaders.'[26]

Finally, even though American teachers report they are 'largely satisfied' with teaching, only one in three believes their work is valued by society and, by extension, the nation's policymakers.[27] Importantly, those countries where teachers feel valued tend to perform better on international measures of student achievement.

Informing Policymakers on What They Need to Know about Teacher Leadership

Policymakers considering the prospect of teachers leading in bold ways should know two things from the outset. First, the vast majority of classroom practitioners *can* lead – if they have the time and space to do so. Second, many teachers *already* are leading, but their efforts are tamped down by bureaucratic structures and administrators who do not know how to utilize them.

We (Noah and Rachel) know many teachers in our school district (Seattle) who have strengths and skills in curriculum development, instructional technology, assessment, or other areas of teaching and learning that could stretch their influence well beyond their classrooms. But tapping teachers' knowhow in this way is the exception. And when our US teaching colleagues *do* have the chance to lead, opportunities are often narrow, and can be idiosyncratic. They are not systemic. Sure, sometimes teachers are assigned to textbook adoption or curriculum alignment committees or are appointed as mentors for new recruits to teaching. But these roles are rarely designed by teachers themselves. And while serving important functions, these opportunities do not encourage teachers to find innovative solutions to the complex problems we face.

Teacher leadership is not just about creating a few more formal leadership roles for a few classroom practitioners. It's critical for administrators to leverage the strengths of all teachers while creating the space for *shared* leadership. And we have learned a great deal about the specifics from our own teacher leadership journeys in Seattle as well as our interactions with teaching colleagues in other locales, particularly in Toronto, Shanghai, and Singapore.

For us, much of our own learning about teacher leadership as US classroom practitioners has been experiential and episodic. And while both Noah and Rachel found ways to lead early in their teaching careers, the roles gave them little, if any, recognition for spreading their own ideas. Most, if not all, of their leadership activities were in addition to full-time teaching. For Noah:

> In my first few years of teaching, I served in several leadership roles in my school. I chaired a department, served on my school's Instructional Council, sat on a few different committees, and for three years, I served as our school's educational technologist. In these early years of my career, I received little support for how to teach *and* lead effectively. I learned by trial and error.

For Rachel, there was the issue of having to pay for her own leadership development:

> I came into teaching as a person with strong leadership skills, but it was years before I could effectively lead. I sought out every opportunity to learn how to teach my content effectively, twice paying out of pocket to attend conferences across the country. What I found fascinating and incomprehensible was that in my first few years of teaching, I did not observe any of my colleagues in action. There just wasn't a plan for that kind of professional development.

Many teachers, like Noah and Rachel, learn to lead through serendipity. Noah learned the importance of learning to lead by listening.

> One of my most pivotal experiences as a teacher trying to lead was during my second year of teaching. As co-chair of the family engagement committee, I coordinated mandatory home visits that teachers would carry out at the beginning of the next school year. As with many mandated initiatives, there was significant resistance among teachers and staff at our school. Some felt uncomfortable entering students' homes. Others did not have time to conduct the interviews the week before school. I presented the plan at staff meetings and worked with other committee members to match students with teacher mentors. I had many conversations with colleagues who were opposed to the home visits. While I believed that they were valuable and could strengthen our school's relationships with families, I quickly learned that I would not be able to impose my views on my colleagues. Instead, to effectively coordinate the home visits, I had to listen to the concerns of others. I had to find creative ways to help people feel more comfortable and to see value in the work.

Rachel is clear about how teachers learn to lead:

> In thinking about teacher leadership and reflecting on my own experiences, I have come to the conclusion that there is an order of operations. Before a teacher can lead in education, he or she must first be a content knowledge expert. This grounding is a prerequisite to having the confidence necessary to stand up and lead your peers. Then, teachers must have the time to collaborate with each other. This means more than just watching each other teach. It also means for teachers to talk about the methods they use, to research and share best practices and then try them out, and then discuss the results, and take action. If policymakers could help us create these opportunities, I am certain we in the United States would witness a significant drop in teacher attrition. We would see the average number of years of teaching experience climb, and our data would reflect higher student achievement. The added benefit of making time for teacher collaboration is that you are also preparing teachers to lead. You have to remember that I did not see any of my colleagues teach for my first three years – and to this day can count on two hands how many times I've seen colleagues teach, something that I find difficult to understand.

Teachers in top-performing jurisdictions learn to lead as they take part in ongoing reviews of one another's teaching practice. Teaching is very public, and all teachers, not just a few, are expected to lead instructional improvement by providing their peers with valuable feedback.

In Shanghai and Singapore, teachers are prepared in externships and are expected to develop inquiry skills in their pre-service preparation programs, which readies them to take on action research as practicing teachers. Marc Tucker has claimed that in these nations, the training of teachers in research techniques is not only a 'mark of professionalism,' but also a strategy to ensure that classroom practitioners systematically share lessons and use evidence to improve their teaching practices.[28]

Evaluation and compensation policies can be designed to drive teacher leadership. For example, Singapore's teacher evaluation system places a premium on teachers' development of the ability to 'address long-term fundamental issues . . . influencing the school's relation to the external world' as well as 'highlight and resolve issues that affect teacher effectiveness. Teacher evaluation in Singapore, with support from the Ministry of Education and union, is designed to encourage both public collaboration and professional participation, essential ingredients for building trust between schools and communities.'[29]

In the first five years of a teacher's career, Shanghai's government pays for him or her to complete 360 hours of required training. An additional 180 government-funded hours are available for interested teachers. Teachers are able to increase their salaries not based on student test scores but on whether they meet and exceed benchmarks tied to good teaching practices.

In Singapore, teachers are in front of students only about 12–17 hours a week – and when they aren't teaching, they often form their own research groups to solve problems of practice. They deconstruct one another's lessons. They publish their findings.

In addition, in Singapore, teachers are offered 100 hours of government-funded professional development each year. After 12 years, a teacher may be eligible for a sabbatical (possibly overseas) to study teaching. While much of Singapore's approach to teacher leadership has been driven by the Ministry of Education, the teaching union has played a major role in shaping professional learning communities. Like most teacher unions worldwide, the Singapore Teachers' Union focuses on salaries and working conditions but also invests considerably in its members' mastery of the latest developments in teaching pedagogy and methods.

Contrastingly, in the United States, very few teachers regularly observe one another. Teacher evaluation has become more data oriented in recent years, to be sure, but it typically offers few opportunities for teachers to give one another feedback (a process CTQ has labeled 'reciprocal mentoring').

In America, professional development is something that happens outside of the classroom, which is in stark contrast to what Rachel witnessed in a study visit to Shanghai, as part of her leadership efforts with CTQ and the Global Cities Education Network of the Asia Society. In the US, teachers might gather in rooms at the district office for sessions on the Common Core State Standards, travel to cities around the country to conferences about curriculum, or experience training from consultants in our schools regarding different grading or behavior management systems. This kind of professional development is not without merit, but it is detached from the classroom. Rachel describes it more fully:

> With our professional development, rarely do we engage in *how* we are teaching our students – the methods and teaching strategies we employ – and whether those pedagogical approaches are working. Instead, we focus on the *what*: the standards that we teach, how our curriculum is organized, and student data and outcomes. Again, all of this is important work and ideally, we would be able to do it all. However, that is impossible given the limited amount of time that we have.
>
> In Shanghai, when the Chinese teachers speak of 'professional development,' they immediately begin to talk about the various ways that they collaborate with one another and the system of peer-to-peer observation and mentorship that they value.
>
> In the United States, on the other hand, teachers immediately think of the external trainings in which they participate. The reason for this, in my opinion, is that when American teachers come together during the day to collaborate, they do not have time to talk about *how* they are teaching, they only have time to talk about *what* they are teaching. This is a big difference between our two systems.

Noah and Rachel's descriptions point to how teacher leadership in the United States is still in its nascent stages of development.

Occasionally one hears of schools that practice distributed leadership. Yet the practice of this distribution usually assumes a principal or other 'school leader' (not a teacher) is the source of authority, who then delegates or shares authority to make specific (usually isolated) decisions or offloads myriad instructional and administrative tasks. This is a very different kind of leadership than that which we see in top-performing nations where educators are expected to drive one another's professional learning and performance – and where they have the time, opportunity, and support to do so. The kind of leadership we are describing is much more akin to what Kim Farris-Berg labels 'collective autonomy,' where teachers *and* administrators are trusted by policymakers 'to embrace accountability and innovate' and those who teach students have the 'opportunity to choose – even invent – the learning methods and job structures they think will best improve learning in their schools.'[30]

After all, in the US, and unfortunately many other nations, evaluation and compensation policies, school conditions, and pre-service preparation programs have not been designed to encourage the spread of teacher expertise. In a vicious cycle, administrators struggle to imagine what teacher leadership can look like or how it can be supported within schools, districts, states, or the nation at large.

CTQ recently surveyed administrators from more than 30 American school districts and nonprofits, primarily those that had recently won federally funded grants (under the auspices of the US Department of Education's 'Teacher Incentive Fund' or Investing in Innovation or i3 Fund) to advance teacher leadership through new career pathways and performance pay. A vast majority of interviewees could not envision teachers leading in roles other than instructional coaches or perhaps as peer evaluators.

These organizations supported more than 500 teacher leaders, but only a handful of the administrators managing the grants had identified strategies to sustain the leadership roles after the federal dollars dissipated. Most of the interviewees struggled to 'imagine' a teacher in a hybrid role, assuming that teachers could lead only if they were released fully from the classroom or took on extra responsibilities after their typical teaching day. We believe that these administrators struggled with implementing the grant programs, in large part, because teachers themselves did not have much opportunity to design and implement the initiatives. Ironically, the federally funded initiatives were intended to support teacher leadership, but those who teach were not able to lead them.

Spreading Teacher Leadership Across the Globe

While no conventional inventories document examples of teacher leadership across the globe, we know of many diverse efforts to cultivate leadership from the classroom. For example, the Inter-American Teacher Education Network (ITEN), an initiative of the Organization of American States, networks education leaders who are interested in sharing knowledge, experiences, and good practices in the teaching profession.[31] The International Teacher Leadership (ITL) initiative, launched in 2008, works with classroom practitioners in 14 countries, and has modeled how all teachers can lead, even without formal designations.[32] ITEN provides an online space for interaction for all the teachers of the Americas, while ITL supports teaching colleagues in conducting action research and acting locally on their evidence.

Our own organization has evolved into an incubator of teacher leaders advancing a 21st-century teaching profession. Since 2003, we have supported growing numbers of teacher leaders in our vibrant online community, now known as the CTQ Collaboratory. As of early fall 2014, the Collaboratory includes more than 7,000 members. More than a third are engaged regularly in online conversations, and growing numbers (often in CTQ-paid roles) are instructional leaders, assessment experts, virtual community organizers, policy researchers, and published writers. About 8% of Collaboratory members teach and lead outside the United States.

For the last four years CTQ has supported cohorts of teacherpreneurs who still teach students regularly (usually about 12–15 hours a week), but have a chance to incubate and spread their own ideas. Noah had been one of them, researching teacher evaluation policy, developing CTQ-Global for international teacher leaders to connect in the Collaboratory, and advancing ways for his district to embed global competencies so he and his colleagues could better prepare their students as leaders. Noah describes more fully:

> As teachers, we are accustomed to closing our doors and teaching in isolation from our colleagues, parents, and community members. But as teacher leaders, it is important for us to make known our successes in the classroom and ideas that we have for improving our education system. Typically, there are not many ways to 'go public' from within schools. And if the news media do show up or the teachers' union publishes a story, it is usually *about* teachers rather than the teachers telling the story themselves.
>
> For the past five years, I have worked with the Center for Teaching Quality to find avenues for communicating my ideas in very public ways. I have coauthored reports with other teacher leaders, written articles for education journals, published many blog posts, and spoken before teachers and policymakers in my district and beyond.

The virtual community of the CTQ Collaboratory allows teachers to connect in deep and authentic ways, primarily because teachers themselves are leading the work. Rachel points out that:

> CTQ offers teachers a community. We can log in and join our colleagues from around the world in the Collaboratory to engage in discussion around myriad topics relevant to our profession. It's all teacher led. Specially prepared teachers are virtual community organizers who host the conversations, promoting inquiry and solutions-based thinking, writing, and action. There are also teacher-led webinars for discussing policy and research, with researchers and policymakers as guests. You learn a lot.
>
> Sadly, in this country, teachers' voices are likely most prominent as sound bytes captured during sidewalk interviews after union contract negotiations. And teachers are rarely at the table when policy decisions that impact the classroom are made. CTQ is out to change that with opportunities for teachers to share their perspectives, grounded in classroom expertise and what they've learned about policy and research. 'Going public' not only benefits the individual teachers and their communities, but also helps to change the public's perception of teachers.

Fueled by the CTQ Collaboratory, Noah's and Rachel's visible leadership is beginning to make a difference in their school district. During the 2014–2015 school year, Noah and Rachel have been two of four teacher leaders working in hybrid roles funded by Seattle Public Schools to advance global education in their district. They are facilitating a team of 15 teacher leaders who represent ten different schools. This shift from CTQ funding to district funding is significant because it is evidence that the school district values and is willing to fund the work of teacher leadership – not just with dollars, but with release time.

And teachers are ready for it. A recent poll found that nearly one in four teachers in America report being very or extremely interested in serving hybrid roles that combine teaching with leadership responsibilities. We suspect there is just as much interest in other countries where teaching is not yet fully professionalized.

Drawing on lessons from top-performing nations and the experiences we have in building a network of classroom leaders, we offer the following recommendations for spreading teacher leadership across the globe. CTQ has already created a modest opportunity for an international team of teachers to examine their professional learning systems in six cities – Denver, Lexington (KY), Seattle, Shanghai, Singapore, and Toronto.[33] Now it is time to take these ideas to scale. We conclude with three recommendations.

#1: Document What Teacher Leadership Looks Like

We previously noted that researchers have described a great deal about the dimensions and characteristics of teacher leadership, but they point out that while the literature is very descriptive of what teachers do, it has been light on the impact of those practitioners who lead from the classroom.

We have cited some of the growing research on teacher leadership. But what administrators and policymakers need more than empirical evidence are clear examples of what teacher leaders do and how their expertise spreads to their teaching colleagues in ways that benefit students.

We do not believe there is too small a supply of teacher leaders; we believe there is insufficient demand for what they can offer. Now is the time for teacher leaders to tell their stories – and not to be shy about the impact of their leadership. Coupled with research, a compelling narrative can inspire and inform new policies and programs to spread teacher leadership. Granted, there are numerous organizations that are beginning to support teachers in telling their stories. However, what is needed is a way to aggregate those stories to advance the concept of teacher leadership, spreading the technical know-how of how the work gets done and the political will necessary to reinvent the profession.

#2: Make Public the Conditions that Advance Teacher Leadership

Many teachers work in top-down, bureaucratic school systems. Leadership from the classroom will flourish only if the right conditions are in place, particularly *robust processes of collaborative inquiry* connected to processes of planning and decision-making.

We have learned from top-performing nations and our experiences that effective teacher leadership springs from schools with cultures that emphasize continuous improvement, administrators who embrace teachers as leaders and know how to utilize them, work structures that promote the spread of teaching expertise, and authority relationships that encourage upward, downward, and lateral influence. Time to lead is essential, as are opportunities for teachers to learn to lead. Externally mandated, one-size-fits-all staff development must be jettisoned in favor of professional learning systems fueled by the action research efforts of teachers themselves. In addition, a new generation of school leadership programs must be launched by universities, school districts, and nonprofits, that jointly prepare principals and teachers to lead together.

In any case, teachers themselves – and their unions – must identify 'bottom line' conditions for teacher leadership, measure those conditions in ways that bring forth rich description of them, and help decision makers in schools, district offices, nonprofits, government agencies, and ministries of education to understand what the conditions mean for the spread of teaching expertise.

#3: Establish a Network of Networks

There is no shortage of teacher networks. We have come across teacher networks that are far ranging in purpose and structure. In the United States we know of networks that ask teachers to sign on to a pre-determined policy agenda, as well as those that allow the sharing of better lessons. There are distinctive international examples, such as the one created by David Frost of the UK, so that teachers can 'shoulder the responsibility to change their own practice, raise the standard of normal practice in their schools and build professional knowledge together in their networks.'[34] While we need to know more about the ones that do exist, what is more important is to begin building a network of networks that serves as a hub for authentic teacher leadership opportunities. The reasons are three-fold: to share pedagogical expertise across context and cultures, to build momentum and synergy, and to make more visible the value that each individual network provides. A network of networks would connect teachers, with a variety of strengths and interests, to lead, creating their own agendas and inspiring others to expand the possibilities of teaching and learning reforms from the classroom. Just as the teachers' union in Singapore has played a significant role in advancing teacher leadership there, unions and associations elsewhere can play a significant role in networking the networks.

But we believe these synergies will begin from the grassroots, as growing numbers of teachers become more adept at leading and seek new ways to drive their own professional destinies. We have learned of the power and potential of the Internet and social media to bring teachers closer together. In the CTQ Collaboratory, we have witnessed how – with specialized preparation and support – teachers can put their pedagogical skills to effective use as virtual community organizers in leading the transformation of their profession. We see great promise in virtual communities of educators. As shifts to a global economy reinforce our interdependence, it is time to learn all we can from our colleagues in other contexts.

We do not see our three-pronged strategy as the only path to the kind of teacher leadership needed for 21st-century teaching and learning. But we do know that much of what needs to be done to connect, ready, and mobilize teachers *is already being done*. In the 1990s, Richard Elmore made the compelling case that many potentially productive reform policies and practices, like the ones represented by the brand of teacher leadership we described herein, often wither, because reformers fail to 'develop organizational structures that intensify and focus' the new reforms supported by too few 'intentional processes for [the] reproduction of successes.'[35] Policymakers need to have better images and strategies of how to get it done and sound evidence of where it is getting done and why. And teachers need more opportunities to learn from each and build synergies from within and across their respective networks. The reinvention of the teaching profession – and the educational experiences that will prepare students for a world that is more connected than ever – cannot be fully realized by changes in one school, one district, or even one country. Public schools everywhere face a future of rapid change, intensifying complexity, and growing uncertainty. It is time for us to connect, learn, and lead together.

Notes

1 Asia Society (2012). Teaching and leadership for the 21st century: The 2012 International Summit on the Teaching Profession. Retrieved from http://asiasociety.org/files/2012teachingsummit.pdf.
2 York-Barr, J. and Duke, K. (2004). What do we know about teacher leadership? Findings from two decades of scholarship. *Review of Educational Research*, 74(3), 255–316.
3 Smylie, M. A. and Denny, J. W. (1990). Teacher leadership: Tensions and ambiguities in organizational perspectives. *Education Administration Quarterly*, 26(3), 235–259.
4 York-Barr and Duke, ibid.
5 Ibid.
6 Ingersoll, R. M. and Strong, M. (2011). The impact of induction and mentoring programs for beginning teachers: A critical review of the research. *Review of Educational Research*, 81, 201–233.
7 Dewitt, P. (2012). Professional development with Andy Hargreaves. [Blog post, 24 May]. Retrieved from http://blogs.edweek.org/edweek/finding_common_ground/2012/05/professional_development_with_andy_hargreaves.html.
8 York-Barr and Duke, ibid.
9 Williams, P. (2002). The competent boundary spanner. *Public Administration*, 80(1), 103–124.
10 Louis, K. S., Dretzke, B. and Wahlstrom, K. (2010). How does leadership affect student achievement? Results from a national US survey. *School Effectiveness and School Improvement*, 21(3), 315–336.
11 Bryk, A. S. and Schneider, B. (2002). *Trust in Schools: A Core Resource for Improvement*. New York: Russell Sage Foundation.
12 Louis et al., ibid.
13 Goddard, Y. L., Goddard, R. D. and Tschannen-Moran, M. (2007). A theoretical and empirical investigation of teacher collaboration for school improvement and student achievement in public elementary schools. *Teachers College Record*, 109(4), 877–896.
14 Jackson, C. K. and Bruegmann, E. (2009). Teaching students and teaching each other: The importance of peer learning for teachers (no. w15202). National Bureau of Economic Research. Retrieved from http://www.nber.org/papers/w15202.

15 OECD (2011). Building a high quality teaching profession: Lessons from around the world. Background Report for the International Summit on the Teaching Profession. Paris: OECD.
16 MetLife Corporation (2010). The MetLife Survey of the American Teacher: Collaborating for student success. Retrieved from http://files.eric.ed.gov/fulltext/ED509650.pdf.
17 Lieberman, A. and Campbell, C. (forthcoming). The Teacher Learning and Leadership Program: Powerful and promising. Paper to be presented at the 2015 annual meeting of the American Educational Research Association, Chicago, IL.
18 Campbell, C., Lieberman, A. and Yashkina, A. (2014). The Teacher Learning and Leadership Program: Research report. Stanford University: SCOPE. Retrieved from https://edpolicy.stanford.edu/sites/default/files/publications/teacher-learning-leadership-program-research-report.pdf.
19 Tough, P. (2012, August 15). What does Obama really believe in? *The New York Times Magazine*. Retrieved from http://www.nytimes.com/2012/08/19/magazine/obama-poverty.html.
20 MetLife Corporation (2013). The MetLife Survey of the American Teacher: Challenges for school leadership. Retrieved from http://www.eric.ed.gov/PDFS/ED530021.pdf.
21 School Leadership for the 21st Century Initiative, Task Force on the Principalship (October 2000). Leadership for student learning: Reinventing the principalship. Retrieved from http://www.iel.org/programs/21st/reports/principal.pdf.
22 Frost, D. (2011) Supporting teacher leadership in 15 countries: The International Teacher Leadership Project, Phase 1 – A Report. Cambridge: Leadership for Learning, University of Cambridge Faculty of Education.
23 Dolton, P. and Marcenaro-Gutierrez, O. (2013). The Varkey GEMS Foundation 2013 global teacher status index. Retrieved from https://www.varkeygemsfoundation.org/sites/default/files/documents/2013GlobalTeacherStatusIndex.pdf.
24 Darling-Hammond, L. (2014). To close the achievement gap, we need to close the teaching gap. *Huffington Post*, 30 June. Retrieved from http://www.huffingtonpost.com/linda-darlinghammond/to-close-the-achievement_b_5542614.html.
25 National Center on Education and the Economy (2014). Statistic of the month: Teachers' salaries, class size and teaching time. Retrieved from http://www.ncee.org/2014/10/statistic-of-the-month-teachers-salaries-class-size-and-teaching-time/.
26 Maxwell, L. (2014). Principals pressed for time to lead instructional change. *Education Week*, 25 March. Retrieved from http://www.edweek.org/ew/articles/2014/03/26/26principals_ep.h33.html.
27 OECD (2014). Results from TALIS 2013: Country note, United States of America. Retrieved from http://www.oecd.org/unitedstates/TALIS-2013-country-note-US.pdf.
28 Tucker, M. (2014). Teachers as researchers: Another mark of professionalism. *Education Week*, 27 August. Retrieved from http://blogs.edweek.org/edweek/top_performers/2014/08/teachers_as_researchers_another_mark_of_professionalism.html.
29 Sclafani, S. (2008). *Rethinking Human Capital in Education: Singapore as a Model for Teacher Development*. Washington, DC: Aspen Institute, pp. 20, 21.
30 Farris-Berg, K. (2013). Can we trust teachers to successfully manage whole schools? *Larry Cuban on School Reform and Classroom Practice*. Retrieved from http://larrycuban.wordpress.com/2013/02/04/can-we-trust-teachers-to-successfully-manage-whole-schools-kim-farris-berg-part-1/.
31 Organization of American States, Inter-American Teacher Education Network (2014). What is ITEN? Retrieved from http://www.oas.org/en/iten/about.asp#sthash.D7cJQZ2q.dpuf.

32 International Teacher Leadership Initiative (2014). Teacher leadership: A non-positional approach. Retrieved from http://www.teacherleadership.org.uk/the-itl-initiative.html.
33 Center for Teaching Quality (2014). A global network of teachers and their professional learning systems. Retrieved from http://www.teachingquality.org/content/global-network-teachers-and-their-professional-learning-systems.
34 See David Frost on Blogging about teachers leading change. Retrieved from http://www.lflteacherleadership.org/home/about-david-frost/.
35 Elmore. R. (1996). Getting to scale with good educational practice. *Harvard Education Review*, 66(1). Retrieved from http://ed-share.educ.msu.edu/scan/TE/danagnos/te9206B.PDF.

Chapter 16

On Peer Review and Maker Education

Interview with Arjan van der Meij

René Kneyber

Every first Monday evening of every month a group of teachers get together for their monthly Pasting and Cutting sessions in The Hague in Holland. They heat up their soldering irons, wire up the 3D printer and arm their laser cutter to get busy with what they like best, making stuff: from experimentations with neopixels, to printing a 3D selfie, to getting a 220V-shock in an attempt to rebuild a bread-baking machine in order to brew home-made Fruittella. Their love for making things has bled into their classrooms, in the shape of FabClasses, where kids, in the spirit of the books Invent to Learn *and* The Art of Tinkering, *learn how to invent, to fabricate, and thereby to learn. But not only has this school, The Poplar, been the breeding ground of the Dutch Maker Education Movement, it has also become the starting point of Learning Power, a nationwide reform project that attempts to put teachers in the lead. In the following interview, science teacher Arjan van der Meij describes the difference Learning Power has made to his teaching life: 'This was the first reform where I felt taken seriously, as a professional.'*

The Learning Power Initiative

As a school we've had a rough period. We have had a change in leadership, at a time when we were certainly at our low point. The Inspectorate had given us a rating of *weak*, and in response we had started visiting each other's classes, armed with checklists, to try to improve on the situation. Around that time, I heard about this new initiative called Learning Power *(Leerkracht)*, where teachers were encouraged to visit each other's classes, to prepare lessons together and do 15-minute meetings called board sessions. So I went to our new school leader and told him I wanted to give this thing a go.

The initiative was started by Jaap Versfelt, a former McKinsey[1] partner who quit his job because he had had some troubling experiences with Dutch schools. His major worry was that schools weren't focused on improving their practice, that there was no reflection on pedagogical practice, and that teachers were not learning from their best colleagues. He wanted to change this culture, and in this regard he felt he could bring expertise from McKinsey to good use for education. He ran into some issues getting his plans funded, because the Ministry of Education doesn't support civilian initiatives. But he found help, mostly from the unions that helped him in setting up a pilot for his program.

I don't want to sound old, but I've seen a lot of reforms in my years as a teacher. Most of them were variations on the same theme; that is, all with a top-down approach. But this was something different right from the outset. Jaap Versfelt walked in and said: 'I know nothing about education, but I do know how to change a culture.' And that was so important to me: here was someone who took me seriously as a professional, but also understood that teachers didn't have all the answers.

So on the one hand, one might say that the program is very strict. If you want to change a school culture wherein you don't usually prepare classes together, or visit lessons, or improve on your practice every day, it requires a steady rhythm during a long period of time to change that culture. That's why you have to visit classes, prepare lessons and do a board session every week, without exception.

On the other hand, what you do within that structure is not laid out at all; within that rhythm of visiting and preparing lessons, it is entirely up to the teachers to decide in their weekly 15-minute board sessions what their goals are, and how they want to achieve them. Some groups might want to work on the relationships with their students, some might want to work on behavior, others might want to work on raising achievement, but it is all up to them. Then you decide which actions you're going to take to reach those goals. So as a teacher you feel you have a lot of ownership – these are your goals, not something that was cooked up by someone else – but you also feel the companionship of your colleagues, you really feel you're working on the goals together. That's why most teams continue working like this, even after the first eight weeks of introduction to the program. It's definitely a grassroots approach.

After the initial pilot with four participating schools, Jaap Versfelt and the other members of the Learning Power Foundation ramped it up to 16 schools, and currently 200 schools are in on the project. By 2020, he'll want to have reached more than 5,000 schools. It might even be possible, because the program is so inspiring that schools are spreading the word to other schools: it is turning into an out-of-control snowball! As a school we have clearly benefited from the entire project, and last year we got an award for being an excellent school. A pretty tight U-turn from being a weak school to begin with!

The Pedagogy of Maker Education

When I turned 35 I was given a magazine called *MAKE* by a colleague and a good friend of mine, filled with ideas and 'how tos', and I got hooked. As soon as I could, I bought a whole bunch of back issues. Some other colleagues and I decided our school would be a perfect place for our Maker experiments: there are computers, tools, machines, all other sorts of stuff. That has evolved into our Monday night Pasting and Cutting sessions.

While we were making things until deep in the night in our school, we sort of figured we ought to do this with our students as well. To make something is a wonderful process: it's invigorating, inspiring and infuriating at the same time, or in quick succession. We felt students would be missing out if they hadn't experienced it. So Per-Ivar Kloen, a biology teacher from our school, piloted a first group of students, as much an experiment for him as it was for the kids. And at the same time, it seemed, all across the globe teachers were starting to experiment with Maker Education, especially in the USA.

Our highlight until now was definitely the FabClass. Per-Ivar applied for a Dutch innovation fund called the Education Pioneers and got a small donation to start a group for kids to invent and construct their own designs. It was fantastic: all the kids were working on their own project. Like: creating a 3D board for Settlers of Catan, a remote-controlled airplane, a kite that takes pictures with a Raspberry Pi, a platformer computer game, a screen you can only see with special glasses, a foldable drum kit and, most notorious, an air rocket launch installation.

We started all of this because we felt it was fun, but after a few years of experience I have started to become convinced that this Maker Education is actually beneficial to children. Making things is, of course, nothing new to schools, as we have let children produce things before. But what is so special about Maker Education is that students actually *invent* things. After a while they start to have the *courage* to invent. It is a special kind of process and a special kind of skill to actually transform your idea into a functioning thing. Now this is of course important in economic terms, as we do want to have a creative workforce for the future. But it is also important for every student as a human being, to be able to give their ideas a space in the world, which can be a struggle. In many respects it is also the emancipation of the tinkering, Lego-addicted geek, like me. Funnily enough, when I left the school a few moments ago, there were still ten kids working in our Maker Space, and when I ask the most hardcore what they want to become, they tell me they want to become like me when they grow up.

Maker Education Reform

It is my dream to have a Maker Space in every school, but I'm against that happening through a top-down approach. It would be easy for our government to just order every school to have a Maker Space. And I've heard people say there should be a 3D printer in every classroom. But if that happened, and it was enforced, then it would just stand there collecting dust, a testament to how little teachers have to say about their own practice.

I would like to see it happen the other way around. Being a Maker Educator is not easy, it requires a certain type of skill. These kids will have ideas, but you won't have a clue how they are to complete it – that's all in the game of invention! On the other hand, you do need to have some experience in making things, you need to know how to work a soldering iron, how to work with electronics. Yet, it's all not as hard as it used to be: with a 3D printer, a laser cutter and a computer, the road to creating what you have come up with is a lot easier than it used to be. So I believe in Slow Reform, with a grassroots approach. There are so many things to learn for some teachers to be able to do this properly, and we should definitely go at it slowly. A good starting point would be if we turned every first Monday of the month into Maker Monday: all across the country Maker Spaces would open their doors from around 6 pm and teachers would be allowed to jump in for free. From the enthusiasm that would generate, we could start building networks all across the country, even internationally, expanding one step at a time.

Note

1 McKinsey & Company is a global management-consulting firm.

Chapter 17

Teacher Learning and Leadership Program

Professional Development For and By Teachers

Ann Lieberman, Carol Campbell and Anna Yashkina

> Tell me and I forget, teach me and I may remember, involve me and I learn.
>
> Benjamin Franklin

Introduction

For seven years (2007–14) in Ontario there has been an exciting and innovative program that has definitely flipped the responsibilities of providing professional development from learning from outside experts, to learning being led by insiders – the teachers. How did this come about? What can we learn from this long-term program? What is there about providing the conditions for learning, rather than telling people what to do, that demands our attention?

The Background and Development of the Teacher Learning and Leadership Program (TLLP)

In 2004, a new Minister of Education announced that 'teachers are professionals' and he was going to find a way to support them. A Working Table on Teacher Development was formed, made up of people from the Ministry of Education, the Ontario Teachers' Federation (OTF), affiliate teacher unions, and other provincial stakeholders. The Working Table developed a partnership between the Ministry (government) and OTF (union) to create a program that was acceptable to both the Ministry and the OTF. This is in itself a major step in connecting enabling and supportive policies with those who practice – the teachers. The Teacher Learning and Leadership Program (TLLP) was born and welcomed its first cohort in 2007.

The Context of Ontario

Ontario has the largest population in Canada. There are 33.6 million people in Canada. Ontario has 39% of the population and is home to the majority of new immigrants arriving in Canada. Ninety-five percent of the students attend public schools. There are 126,000 teachers in Ontario, each belonging to one of four teachers' unions affiliated with OTF. Their agreements were critical to the development of TLLP!

TLLP

The big idea behind TLLP was that teachers would write a proposal in which *they* would organize professional development. TLLP involves three goals developed by OTF and the Ministry to: support experienced teachers to undertake self-directed advanced professional development; develop teachers' leadership skills for sharing their professional learning and exemplary practices; and facilitate knowledge exchange for spread and sustainability of effective and innovative practices. TLLP aimed for a shared governance system. This means the procedures under which the program operates, the mechanisms (application forms, reporting, timing and templates used) were all developed in equal measure by the Ministry and the OTF. Importantly, TLLP is seen as one step on a continuum of teacher education and professional learning in Ontario.

Each year, experienced classroom teachers can apply individually or in a team to conduct a TLLP project over the course of one year. Teachers applying to TLLP have to describe what they plan to do, how they will do it, and how much it will cost. It has to be related in some way to provincial goals. It is suggested that TLLP projects do their work with one other person or a team. Selection of the projects is done in a two-phased approach. Teachers submit their proposals to their school board. The proposals are then adjudicated by a joint board–teacher union committee. Next, proposals selected by the board–teacher union committee are forwarded to a provincial TLLP committee with joint membership from the Ministry and teacher unions for final selection.

TLLP asks of teachers three questions: What did you learn? What did you learn about leadership? How will you share what you learned with others? This will be included in a final report after the year is over.

Every year there are two conferences. The first is entitled Leadership Skills for Classroom Teachers. Once teachers have received a letter saying that their proposal has been accepted, they are invited to these conferences, where workshops supporting them are available: How do you approach your teachers in your own school and other schools? How do you deal with your budget? How can you make conflict productive? And more. Teachers begin to realize that they are not only expected to create a year-long professional development project, but that they will be supported in the process. Every teacher also must write a final report describing what they have done during their year, what they learned and how they are sharing the learning with others. Teachers must also post resources and share in an online professional community for the TLLP. At the end of the year, teachers are invited to a Sharing the Learning Summit, where they set up displays of what they have done, who they have done it with and the materials and learning that has accrued during the year.

Here people not only share their learning, but see what others have done, as they are now in a community of learners (and leaders). By this time a number of teachers have become consultants throughout their province and some have gotten new jobs as a result of their work in TLLP.

Learning from Research

From 2012 to 2013 (Campbell, Lieberman & Yashkina, 2013a, 2013b), and from 2013 to 2014 (Campbell et al., 2014a, 2014b), we have done research on the TLLP to document the impact of the program on teachers' professional learning, their leadership and practices, other adults affected, and on student engagement and learning. We have also documented how this learning is being shared beyond the TLLP team and have tried to find out the longer-term impacts of participating in TLLP.

During cohorts 1–6, there have been 466 projects (approximately 78 projects per year). Seventy five percent of the projects have a TLLP core team of two to four people. The average funding is $14,412 (CDN). The most common focus for projects has been on differentiated instruction, technology, literacy and professional learning communities. As time has gone on, technology has become increasingly prevalent.

Examining Final Reports

At the end of the year, team leaders submit Final Reports on their project goals and successes, professional learning, project sharing, challenges and projected learning and impact beyond the TLLP funding. We examined all Final Reports, and conducted further in-depth analyses of a sample of 20% of these. Here we report on findings from analyses of 33 projects from the most recent cohorts (cohorts 5 and 6). In our sample, we ensured representation across geographical regions, French and English school boards, elementary and secondary panels, project team and budget sizes as well as project themes.

Project Goals

Most of the insight on professional learning goals, activities and impact came from our analyses of the Final Reports. Top project goals included approaches to improving knowledge and understanding (about 79%), as well as developing strategies (67%) and skills (48%). These goals were mostly focused on improving teaching and learning – such as learning a new approach and developing strategies for its implementation, or developing a brand new program or approach. Many projects involved developing collaborations within and across schools and divisions, such as supporting transitions from elementary to secondary schools. For some TLLP projects the goal was to establish community relationships, which meant reaching out and developing knowledge and connections beyond the school; for example, connecting to Aboriginal communities, engaging parents and developing school/community projects.

Professional Learning

This flipping of traditional ideas is evident in the TLLP's approach to professional learning. Teachers first come up with the professional development idea, then they research it themselves, rather than having information presented to them by experts.

It is interesting to note that when teachers are in charge of their own learning, they initially choose to learn with others by establishing a variety of collaborative arrangements (85%), and then look to the literature to educate themselves on research that might prove helpful to them (55%). For example, TLLP members develop professional collaboration to learn together by analyzing student data, reflecting on practice, creating resources, discussing strategies and sometimes teaching together. One project leader described the benefits of this:

> Another successful aspect of this TLLP has been the opportunity it provides teachers to collaborate and share ideas. In a busy school setting, there is often limited time for teachers to get together to discuss best practices.

Collaborations often extended beyond the school in a number of projects. TLLP participants in about a quarter of the projects engaged in professional networking either in field trips/meetings or online in blogs, webcasts, etc.

Engaging in action research, attending workshops and conferences, networking, and working with a specialist are the other activities mentioned in the reports.

Teacher Learning Benefits

The top identified benefit (as reported in 94% of the sampled Final Reports) was gaining new knowledge and improved understanding. This was usually about some specific strategies, such as problem-based learning, or teaching practices in general. Teachers in 76% of reports also stated that they acted on this new knowledge by changing their instructional and assessment practices. One of the project leaders describes the team's efforts to improve teaching practice:

> The team of teachers on this project learned to work together to reflect on current teaching practices, research new strategies and to put research into practice. Teaching is a profession that changes over time. As a group of teachers, we were able to support each other as we continued to re-evaluate our own instructional strategies and to make small changes to our practices to improve student learning.

In addition, teachers reported enhancement in their professional confidence and sense of self-efficacy:

> Our comfort level with the practice has increased dramatically and is incorporated into the day to day functioning of the classroom.
>
> During this project, the teachers involved learned to work effectively as a group to support each other as we learned to develop new instructional strategies in our own classroom . . .

TLLP participants also reported improvements in other areas such as research, presentation, technology and collaboration. Improvements in project management and leadership skills (e.g., budgeting, time management, human resources, conflict resolution, leading adult learning, planning and managing PD events) were also mentioned in over half of the reports.

To summarize, the professional learning that teachers acquire as a result of the TLLP project is multifaceted – teachers do not only grow as educators but also as learners, project managers and experts or leaders in their fields.

Teacher Leadership

The element of learning about teacher leadership in the TLLP is particularly striking in the results. We decided to encourage some teachers to actually write specifically about what they learned by writing a short narrative description in a vignette form. We provided some prompts for them, to help bound the stories and dig deeper into their leadership process. The prompts were:

> What did you do?
> Who did you do it with?
> What happened as a result?
> How are you sharing your knowledge?

The ensuing vignettes provided some interesting results in two particular areas, as can be seen below.

What Did You Learn about Leadership?

Nineteen teachers ended up writing a vignette. They ranged from 3 to 23 pages long. What we were able to see was how, for many, leadership knowledge and strategies grew during the process of implementing their projects. They talked about their project management skills (budgeting, time management, use of human resources and how they dealt with conflict situations). They also described how they had learned to work with other adults, as they planned with others, created events for others, and learned how to distribute the leadership of their teams.

Working with Colleagues

Fifteen of the 19 teachers who wrote vignettes worked with another person or a team. Four worked alone. All those who worked with someone else (or a team) wrote that an important lesson had been in gaining an ability to work with others and to encourage them to contribute (as well as learn). Learning *how* to do this turned out to be an important part of the work. In fact the themes they wrote about were: learning to collaborate, building relationships, sharing leadership, learning to use technology as part of leadership learning, going public with their teaching, and the challenges of both teaching and leading at the same time.

Although often one person had written the proposal, when the project actually started, teachers found themselves confronted with how to begin, keep people engaged and continue to move forward despite difficulties in the way. Sharing ideas, listening to others' ideas, constantly shaping the project in a group image, began to take precedence.

> Some of the greatest teacher and student learning that came from our TLLP collaboration was unexpected. We learned to pool our resources and created a program that combines all of our best learning as teachers.
>
> The collaboration has helped instill a level of confidence within our department that was not present before this chapter.

Half of the teachers wrote about how they had to learn to let go of the controls, even though it had been *their* idea and *their* proposal. Along with this, teachers learned to talk to people beyond their team and build networks. Some learned how to participate in professional dialogue about their project and how it was contributing to both teacher and student learning. They were learning how to both teach other teachers and also learn from them.

> As a team leader I learned a great deal about leadership and working with other adults. I learned the value of collaborative goal setting and planning and the importance of ensuring that all team members feel like valued contributors.
>
> In the area of mentorship, we formed contacts with other teachers interested in using iPads for special needs instruction and shared knowledge gained from the project.

Learning to share with others and encouraging them to help shape the project and its ideas was an important part of working with others.

Knowledge Exchange, Sharing Professional Learning and Spreading Practices

A priority goal of TLLP is to support teachers in developing and sharing their professional learning 'by, with and for teachers.' TLLP flips system improvement from top down to a collaborative professional approach.

Extending the Reach and Spread of Practices: The Provincial Knowledge Exchange (PKE)

To support further sustaining and spreading of practices from TLLP projects, the Provincial Knowledge Exchange (PKE) has recently been introduced to enable school districts to identify TLLP projects they wish to sustain and to provide funding for the teachers involved to support professional learning in other schools, including travel and time to support schools in other districts. We conducted a case study of one PKE which began as a TLLP project in one elementary school to implement a Balanced Math program. Through the TLLP and PKE, this project extended to 15 schools in 2013–14, and continues to expand. The approach to developing professional learning and spreading practices includes release time for teachers to participate in three-part series (2.5 days) of professional development, including collaborative professional learning, visits to classrooms, modeling of new practices, opportunities to plan for and implement practices in teachers' own classrooms, joint work on student assessment and lesson plans and provision of a supporting resource binder and shared Wiki space including samples of lessons, assessment resources, tip sheets and student work. The PKE operates on the basis of collaborative learning, where the PKE team teach and show teachers about the Balanced Math program, and provide practical resources for use, teacher participants observe the resources in use (through demonstration classrooms and modeled by the PKE team), and there are opportunities for teachers to co-plan and co-learn for their own use of the Balanced Math strategies. Teachers are also supported to apply Balanced Math and share their learning within and across the schools. Teachers act as leaders and facilitators with resources developed for co-creating and sharing professional knowledge.

Sharing Professional Learning

From our analyses of Final Reports for TLLP projects in cohorts 5 and 6, the majority of TLLP teachers were sharing their professional learning within their own school (85%) and across other schools in their school district (55%). A third (33%) of TLLP teacher leaders were sharing their learning further across a larger educational community in Ontario, and in some cases, nationally and/or internationally.

The majority of methods of sharing used by TLLP teachers focused on professional learning, development and collaboration; for example, through school- and district-wide professional development sessions (55%), staff meetings (45%) and established or newly developed learning communities (42%). Some TLLP members also engaged in modeling their practices (by opening their classes for other teachers and administration, demonstrating lessons during workshops or school visits), while others engaged in developing professional relationships and provided one-on-one mentoring to interested teachers from their own or other schools. Seeing other teachers implementing new practices in classroom added legitimacy to the project and sparked interest in those who observed. One TLLP teacher leader commented on the value of classroom observations:

> Although sharing this learning can be difficult outside of the teachers involved, interest from other teachers was generated through witnessing student engagement and creativity. Often teachers would inquire about the style of teaching because they could see that the students were passionate, involved and on task.

Several projects also attempted sharing their knowledge with the local community by organizing various community events, distributing newsletters and engaging a local TV station and newspaper.

Alongside professional sharing locally, another major area of sharing learning and knowledge exchange involved a larger professional community (beyond the school or district), including at national and even international levels. Online media, conferences and publications were used to reach those audiences. Increasingly, the majority of TLLP teacher leaders are using online media for professional networking, learning, collaborating and sharing purposes. Examples of online media use include posting information and resources on school/district and other educational organization websites, developing project-dedicated websites, engaging in discussions on online forums, tweeting, blogging and creating project-related groups on social networks:

> I have received an overwhelming amount of positive feedback by those who have been present for the Tap Into Teen Minds workshops and those who visit the blog. I have received e-mail and 'tweets' from other educators in North America and around the globe who are using the resources and strategies I have shared online to create their own iPad paperless classrooms with much success . . .

An online community specifically for participants engaging in and with TLLP, the Mentoring Moments NING, was visited 32,504 times between September 2013 and October 2014, for example.

Benefits of Sharing Learning

The vast majority of TLLP projects considered their main audience to be other teachers (85%), hence the focus on teachers' collaborative professional learning plus development of resources for use by teachers. In 45% of the projects, TLLP teacher leaders reported sharing with district administration, in many cases with the hope to spread the word about their innovation across the district. A minority of projects reached out to community partners and parents. We believe that supporting and encouraging TLLP participants to think about a wider audience can be beneficial for developing TLLP teachers' leadership and practices as well as for influencing and sharing learning and practices locally and beyond to flip the system towards teacher-led educational improvement.

The benefits of teachers leading the development of professional learning, sharing learning more widely and spreading practices are important. Our analysis of the sample of Final Reports identified several benefits of sharing learning from the TLLP project with a wider group of people. The main benefit is improved knowledge and understanding, which was reported in almost all Final Reports (94%). Almost a third of the Final Reports (30%) stated that educators (outside of the TLLP team) who received new learning were inspired to make a change in their practice; for example:

> This was a great day! I learned a lot and feel confident that I can start to implement this into my own classroom.

Yet another third (30%) of the projects claimed that this change in practice had already happened. For example, one TLLP team set to integrate a problem-based learning approach to teaching mathematics; they created a website where they shared resources, developed materials and reflections on their progress. Other benefits of shared learning were increased self-efficacy (e.g., teachers feeling more comfortable about the issue they were dealing with, a particular innovation or their teaching in general), and development of a stronger school community (as a result of sharing of learning/raising awareness among school community members).

Ultimately, as a member of OTF commented, TLLP flips the system by opening up teachers' voices, practices and classroom doors to lead innovation:

> when you talk of knowledge mobilization and this kind of catching fire of ideas and trying things out . . . part of what I think works against innovation is when people are afraid to take the risks. In ways, the TLLP says, 'Not only are we encouraging you to take the risks, but we're going to give you money to do it, and we're going to encourage you to talk to other teachers about it.' I mean, that is really not what was largely going

on in our system for a long, long, long, long time; if you were taking risks, you were closing your door and not telling anybody about it. It's really that attitude of, 'Get out of my way and let me teach; I'm closing my door so that nobody can actually see what I really am doing. But, oh, by the way – my students are doing fantastically well because I'm doing all these unusual things with them.' What the TLLP does is, it says, 'We're opening the doors, we're saying it's OK for you to do the stuff that's not just on the curriculum and not just on what is the prescribed way of teaching, and we're rewarding you for sharing it with other people.' So that's pretty amazing.

Developing Professional Resources to Spread Practices

An important method for teachers leading sharing of learning and mobilizing knowledge is through the development of resources and materials that can be used by other teachers, schools, districts and wider-community members. The majority of TLLP projects involved the development of practical materials that can be used in classrooms, such as sample lessons, lesson plans, assessment tasks and teaching strategies. These usable resources supported the spread of practices. Other professional resources developed included kits with recommended resources, development of a program or a framework for use in schools, research and literature review reports and videos of teachers demonstrating practices and students talking about the effects of those practices.

Teachers Learning, Leading and Sharing their Knowledge

After seven years of providing opportunities for project funding, TLLP is changing the culture of professional development in Ontario. The policies put forth by the Ministry of Education and the practices supported by OTF are providing a powerful example of the power of trusting, supporting and making possible professional development led by teachers, for teachers. What the evidence shows is that 'insiders' can learn both new ways of working with their students, and ways to lead their colleagues. They also share what they are learning with others. TLLP provides us with a rethinking of the existing professional development paradigm, which goes for compliance rather than collaboration, disparaging teacher unions rather than building shared solutions, and thinks of professional development being delivered from the 'outside' without participation and partnership from the 'inside,' imposing research on teachers without the practice that roots new knowledge in the everyday work of teaching and learning.

The evidence for supporting teachers to organize professional development has been enthusiastically encouraged by both the Ministry of Education and OTF. It is a huge and important shift of power and evidence and has clearly flipped the system!

References

Campbell, C., Lieberman, A. and Yashkina, A. (2013a). *The Teacher Learning and Leadership Program: A Research Report*. Toronto: Ontario Teachers' Federation.

Campbell, C., Lieberman, A. and Yashkina, A. (2013b). *The Teacher Learning and Leadership Program: Executive Summary*. Toronto: Ontario Teachers' Federation.

Campbell, C., Lieberman, A. and Yashkina, A. with Carrier, N., Malik, S. and Sohn, J. (2014a). *The Teacher Learning and Leadership Program: Research Report 2013–14*. Toronto: Ontario Teachers' Federation.

Campbell, C., Lieberman, A. and Yashkina, A. with Carrier, N., Malik, S. and Sohn, J. (2014b). *The Teacher Learning and Leadership Program: Executive Summary: Research Report 2013–14*. Toronto: Ontario Teachers' Federation.

Vignette 6

Changing Education in Action

Sweden: The Cared-For Teacher

Eva Hartell

Schooling and education is a hot topic in Sweden, a country with a long tradition of trusting teachers' capacity to provide affordance for pupils' learning. The Swedish school system allows plenty of leeway for teachers to interpret and enact the national syllabus in their classroom and to teach in a way that best provides for pupils in their own context, provided that their students make progress according to the regulations that govern compulsory schooling. During the last couple of years, there has been much discussion regarding education, focusing increasingly on international ranking results, finding someone to blame, trust in teachers decreasing through the suggestion of external examinations instead of teacher-based assessment, a growing market for schooling, etc. In my experience, I fear there is a real risk that teachers' professionalism is shrinking, and that the radically intensified discussion is distancing itself from what matters the most for student achievement: the core business of teaching and learning in classrooms.

For the last 20 years, the trend in Swedish schools has been toward decentralization. From state-run schools to municipality and free schools, this has both increased and decreased teachers' professional capacity to design student learning. To the best of my knowledge, over the last couple of years there has been an increase in reports concerning decreased achievements among pupils, as measured by national tests and international ratings – this has particularly drawn attention to these problems. Many stakeholders provide their own solutions to the alleged problems that benefit their agendas. In 2005, the municipality where I work was ranked lowest out of all municipalities, on a rating provided by one of the major teacher unions in Sweden. This turned out to be a wake-up call for politicians, who demanded that the local school office provide answers, and an analysis with strategies was launched. For me as a teacher it was also a wake-up call. The local school authorities actually seemed to care about my work in the classroom: although I realized that they did not have a clue about what was going on, they nevertheless wanted to know. Different support programs for teachers and principals were introduced, based on individual pupils' results, the overarching aims for these interventions being to provide additional opportunities for each pupil to prosper socially and academically.

Alongside this, however, both school management and teachers were, and still are, flooded with offers of different concepts, methods, and ideas from stakeholders, often promising fast results for increased student achievement. It can be quite challenging to orient oneself among such offers and resist the temptation to try them all, especially with the increased pressure of parent choice and school competition.

Affordance and Assessment for Learning

I will tell you about one of these initiatives, which involved providing affordance for teachers to embed formative assessment into their own teaching practice. Affordance is the ability of an environment, or an object, to allow an individual to perform an action. The following example is a story about one particular school, Tungelsta skola, and their ambition to embed formative assessment sustainably into the everyday life of classroom teaching. The goal of the project is 'to get teachers started' with using formative assessment techniques for eliciting evidence of learning and to then adapt it into their teaching to better meet learners' needs. In my role as a municipality supervisor/school developer I have had the opportunity to follow this municipality-run compulsory school, which has nearly 900 pupils from age six to 16 and about 50 teachers. The reason they chose to focus on formative assessment is the following statement by Dylan Wiliam: 'if you are serious about raising student achievement then you have to be focusing on AfL [Assessment for Learning], and if you are not focusing on AfL you are probably not serious about raising student achievement' (Wiliam, 2009, p. 34).

In my opinion, formative assessment is an integral part of teaching, ensuring pupils' growth as important. Playing with these words, we find 'assessment' originates from the Latin *assidere*, meaning to sit by, and when you translate the term 'pupil' back and forth from English to Swedish, some interesting things happen. First, you get *student* or *elev* (where *elev* originates from the French word *élever*, meaning to raise, uplift, or exalt), but pupil can also be translated to mean a part of the eye, in other words, the medical term 'pupil'. This may refer to the apple of one's eye, or *ögonsten* in Swedish, or even a sweetheart. So to me, working with assessments is like sitting beside my students, or 'sweethearts', to elicit evidence of their learning, and then putting that evidence into action in the classroom to better meet their needs.

Some of this student performance monitoring was already being conducted on a regular basis, but most often it occurred at the end of a unit with a time span of six or seven weeks, and was often in the form of a written test or a hand-in report. Failing students would be provided with further information to read and tasks to fulfil on their own to make up for their failure; the student-retesting schedule was fully loaded, and teachers (and students) felt stressed. This became a vicious circle, primarily for the students who continually failed, but also for the teachers whose workloads never ceased to increase.

Prior findings on formative assessment show that it is not as frequently implemented in classroom practice as the findings suggest, and implementation remains difficult. We looked at the work of Clarke and Hollingsworth (2002), Timperley (2011), Moss and Brookhart (2009) as well as Guskey (2002) to try to understand professional development (PD) and implementation efforts in general, and formative assessment specifically. They all recommend moving slowly, even during the actual implementation, regardless of how much patience is required before you see the results after an intervention. Implementing these key strategies in a sustainable fashion requires a long-term perspective and a common thread throughout the organization. Wiliam (2011) and Guskey (2002) emphasize the importance of a lifelong learning perspective in the teaching profession and problematize the prior ineffectiveness of many professional development programmes for teachers. Even though prior research suggests different models for PD, it is important to keep in mind that teachers' learning and professional development is difficult to reproduce (Black et al., 2004; Guskey, 2002; Timperley, 2011; Wiliam, 2013). According to Wiliam, this is because teachers are experts in what they are doing. To be able to change their behaviour, Guskey (2002) argues that teachers must see the results of students' achievements in order to be convinced of the intervention's utility. These results are not necessarily only academic achievements, but may also include attendance or participations in lessons.

Many teachers know that formative assessment is a beneficial way of working. However, knowing what to do is not necessarily the same thing as doing what they know they ought to do. Instead, the real challenge is to make teachers *actually* do what they know they are supposed to do. Therefore, according to Wiliam (2011), intervention with the purpose of embedding formative assessment must focus on changing teachers' behaviour instead of just telling them what to do, which traditional PD often focuses on. For this to occur, affordance for teachers is necessary. Moss and Brookhart (2009) suggested that school management's provision for the support structure for this is vital for embedding formative assessment.

Method and Discussion of Results

Despite well-stated ambitions from teachers up to members of the school board, and a number of interventions including seminars and lectures, we noticed that this was not encouragement enough to effect change in the mind-set about monitoring students' knowledge in real time. Even though many teachers (and principals) were familiar with the concept of formative assessment, not much had happened in the classrooms. Something needed to be done, but the question was what? A small delegation, including representatives of teachers and the school board, the principal and myself, made a visit to one school that was acknowledged to have implemented formative assessment successfully. We were convinced by this school not to reinvent the wheel, but to acquire an already proven professional development material: the *Embedding Formative Assessment* packs by Leahy and Wiliam (Leahy & Wiliam, 2010).[1] As the packs were written in English, I urged that they be translated into Swedish in order for the project to work. This model, which we now follow, provides a structure that includes two years of scheduled meetings, including collegial learning that both prompts and supports teachers to implement the key strategies for formative assessment into their classroom teaching, building on teachers' professional growth and strength, rather than the weaknesses of the individual teacher. Teachers work in groups (teacher learning communities) of 10 to 12, with one leader whose most important job is to sustain a supportive atmosphere in the group and not to be the expert. The 18 workshops, scheduled once a month, follow the same agenda but with different themes that are all connected to the key strategies for formative assessment. This includes collegial observations, wherein a colleague observes a fellow teacher practising one chosen technique in the classroom. Working with this model does not require an outside expert: the argument is that the teachers are already the experts and support each other in taking risks and learning from their mistakes.

We called the project TLC (Teacher Learning Communities), which also stems from my interpretation (as a translator) of the essence of how to implement formative assessment: with tender loving care.

The municipality's school board supports the project and acquired the material for the school with the goal that all schools would eventually join. Acknowledging the role of the school principal, the board is letting each school principal decide when (and if) their school begins the programme. When they decide to start, the school principal must schedule monthly TLC meetings in the school calendar for at least two years, which has proved very challenging.

It is tempting to say that we have already seen results from this first year of TLC, based on the actual increase of achievement reported in grades and national test results. However, everyone knows that changing student achievement takes time. One year of TLC alone cannot take credit for those improvements. However, we have identified some things that TLC can take credit for, as reported by both school managers and teachers. They are all consistent in saying that students are more engaged and active agents as a result of this implementation.

There has been a decrease in behavioural issues during lessons due to TLC, as students have become more active in their learning, and a decrease in skipping lessons has been identified, although this latter is considered a result of more long-term efforts, as every child is unique and the concerns surrounding them are very challenging.

Another interesting issue that we have discovered is that teachers who were weak in their classroom leadership became stronger in their leadership through the TLC model. According to the school manager, the TLC model provides these teachers with something to lean on. This is something that we are very interested in investigating, and it further contributes to the current discussion regarding student behaviour in Swedish schools. It is important to keep in mind that every school and every teacher have different areas of improvement that are based on their unique contexts. The way this school progressed might work at another school, but it is not automatically the case.

Time and a lot of work is required of all people involved, and the school principal must provide prerequisites for the TLC programme, allowing and demanding that teachers implement formative assessment in their everyday teaching. At Tungelsta skola, this was done in many ways, such as scheduling TLC meetings and putting these into the school calendar, and ensuring that all participants actually attend the meetings. It is also necessary to safeguard the intervention and teachers' workload by keeping other interventions away. However, more importantly, the school management must support, encourage, and expect teachers to take risks and learn from their mistakes and others' mistakes, and acknowledge the challenges of the profession through the perspective of life-long learning for teachers. The TLC programme provides a structure, including support from the school's management, which is significant according to Moss and Brookhart (2009). The combination of a structure that frames the interventions and yet provides freedom for teachers to adjust their learning to their classroom needs is a very compelling one, and unusual compared to other interventions I have come across.

The will and desire to see results exists everywhere and at all levels, and many parties will always come up with strategies to achieve these results. However, from my experience as a teacher, school developer, PhD student, and tax payer, I would recommend a critical approach to any offer of school improvement or teacher development programmes, from whatever level of the educational system, from teachers to members of the board of education.

School principals stand at the root of the reported success of this particular project. Within the municipality there are other schools using the TLC programme, but where principals are not serious about focusing on AfL, TLC is not as successful as it has been at Tungelsta skola, where the determined principal has provided affordance for teachers, and both demanded and encouraged them to take risks and make explicit change. Nevertheless, there are many challenges remaining. So far, the project has focused on getting the teachers started; the biggest challenge at the moment is getting pupils even more involved as active agents in their own learning.

The problem is that the concept of formative assessment is extremely popular in Sweden now and is a buzzword in school development. It is so popular, in fact, that it is on the verge of becoming both flawed and trite. The previously reported success of formative assessment (e.g., Black & Wiliam, 1998) took place in a classroom where teachers and pupils were actively involved in the process of learning, but as it becomes more popular, there is a danger of it being 'pushed through', without teachers or school leaders feeling an actual involvement.

Tungelsta skola looks forward to entering year two of TLC. Year two of the programme focuses on shifting the teaching and learning perspective to the student's perspective. So far, TLC has been successful in building teachers' capacities for formative assessments. A critical review is necessary to understand what has happened and in what way, which in turn can be used by others. I look forward to this review and especially to contributing to the discussion regarding the future in Swedish schools.

Eva Hartell is a teacher in the municipality of Haninge, and currently a PhD student at KTH Royal Institute of Technology in Stockholm.

Note

1 http://www.ssatuk.co.uk/ssat/support/teaching-and-learning/embedding-formative-assessment/.

References

Black, P., Harrison, C., Lee, C., Marshall, B. and Wiliam, D. (2004). Working inside the black box: Assessment for learning in the classroom. *Phi Delta Kappan*, 86(1), 8–21. Retrieved from http://www.questia.com/PM.qst?a=o&se=gglsc&d=5007120502.

Black, P. and Wiliam, D. (1998). Assessment and classroom learning. *Assessment in Education: Principles, Policy & Practice*, 5(1), 7–74. doi:10.1080/0969595980050102.

Clarke, D. and Hollingsworth, H. (2002). Elaborating a model of teacher professional growth. *Teaching and Teacher Education*, 18, 947–967.

Guskey, T. (2002). Professional development and teacher change. *Teachers and Teaching*, 8(3), 381–391. doi:10.1080/135406002100000512.

Leahy, S. and Wiliam, D. (2010). *Embedding Formative Assessment: A Professional Development Pack for Schools*. London, UK: Specialist Schools and Academies Trust.

Moss, C. M. and Brookhart, S. M. (2009). *Advancing Formative Assessment in Every Classroom: A Guide for Instructional Leaders*. Alexandria, VA: Association for Supervision and Curriculum Development (ASCD).

Timperley, H. (2011). *Realizing the Power of Professional Learning*. Chippenham: Open University Press.

Wiliam, D. (2009). *Assessment for Learning: Why, What and How? An Inaugural Professorial Lecture by Dylan Wiliam*. London: Institute of Education, University of London.

Wiliam, D. (2011). *Embedded Formative Assessment*. Bloomington, IN: Solution Tree Press.

Wiliam, D. (2013). *Principled Curriculum Design, Redesigning Schooling – 3* (ed. by P. Chambers). London: SSAT (The School Network) Ltd.

Vignette 7

Changing Education in Action

Russia: The Informed Teacher

Artiom Soloveychik interviewed by Jelmer Evers

> Everyone thinks that the essence of pedagogy is in psychology, but it's not. The essence of pedagogy is in ethics.
>
> Simon Soloveychik

So why do you like teaching and teachers?

I was a poor student and wasn't able to attend university after I finished school. I was drafted into the navy. Afterwards I went to university to study psychology and linguistics, mainly Noam Chomsky. Through a roundabout way I ended up in the US and made a living as a storyteller. I actually became quite famous. Subsequently I was asked to teach a storytelling course at Lesley College in Cambridge, a teacher training college.

I hesitated to become involved in education. I didn't want to be in a school ever again. What changed, though? I guess because I wasn't a successful student myself, I wanted to stand up for the students who fall behind. A child is never late or behind: you can learn so much in one year, which is why the influence of teachers is so huge. I want to change how teachers think. That's why I became involved in educational publishing.

Can you tell us a little bit about the background of *First of September*? Why did it start? How did it start?

I came from a family with an educational background. In fact my father was a famous educator and journalist. He wrote the influential work *Pedagogika dlya vseh (Parenting for Everyone)*; most Russians know his work.[1] He was also an activist for humanist education. He co-founded a magazine on humanist pedagogy during the communist era – *Novoe vremya (New Time)* – but it had to close down when the government realized that it could be dangerous. This was in 1986, four years before the Wall came down. It was situated in Moscow and he brought together the most open-minded teachers in the country. They were talking about free pedagogy, a pedagogy of collaboration, while the Russian educational system was (and is) very authoritarian.

In 1992 my father restarted his educational newspaper and named it *First of September*. He wanted to raise the issue of why kids go to school. What is the purpose of education? He was still on a mission. From the start he didn't want to make it too scholarly. There was a huge gap between classroom practice and educational research. The paper was named after the beginning of the school year, when there are still so many possibilities. Everything is still open. He said: 'The paper should be a new beginning!' He wanted to change classroom practice, have a real impact. There was a general newspaper, *First of September*, and subject-specific supplements focusing on pedagogy and content.

Sadly, in the first year the paper went bankrupt due to mailing issues. In 1993 my father asked me to help out. I came in and reorganized the paper. I increased the price of the supplements. This turned out to be a huge success. After the fall of the Soviet Union there weren't any good textbooks, so there was a huge demand for classroom materials and ideas.

In the spirit of my father's ideas, we wanted teachers to think for themselves, design their own instruction and focus on the students. Our slogan is: 'You are the best teacher, you have the best students.' Not many people agreed at first. But slowly and steadily demand and the newspaper grew. It all went well until June 2014, when we had to shut down the general newspaper. Luckily the monthly supplements go on.

Can you tell us about those other activities?

We have monthly subject-specific supplements, which come with a CD filled with teaching materials. We also have a digital subscription method. Besides this we run an online database of 25,000 lesson plans, accessible through a subscription. Teachers pay US$20 to access the database for its upkeep and at the same time they contribute to the database. It is a form of crowd-sourced development of educational resources. It is a huge success. It increases the professional development and self-efficacy of teachers and improves classroom pedagogy, focusing on interaction between teachers and students.

Other projects include the School of the Digital Age, which is a professional development program on Blended Learning. Teachers pay a flat fee and have access to a database of courses, which are also partly made by the participants themselves, increasing the database. We also are the biggest distance-education provider for teachers: we serve 18,000 teachers online, and 12,000 still by mail.

In 2002 we started the Pedagogy Conference Marathon: 24 days of focusing on education. Around 18,000 teachers from 64 out of 80 regions travel to Moscow each year. I think it is one of the biggest educational conferences in the world. It's like a circus. Each day we focus on different subjects. Teachers pay to attend, but they are also lecturers. Teachers have to register and choose beforehand. With scanning devices we have complete statistics on teachers' needs. This data is also used for social research and is the basis for decisions made by publishers and the government. It is based on the idea that teachers know what they need.

So do you consider *First of September* a success?

After the fall of communism, we had a big impact on how teachers thought about education. Teachers' views shifted gradually from authoritarian to more child-centered forms of pedagogy. Why and how was being discussed amongst teachers. In the nineties, teachers discovered that there were other ways of teaching. Teachers also became more skillful, better specialists. We built up many networks and relationships, always focusing on teacher agency. Our conference is called Day of Teachers of Physics, for example, not Day of the Subject of Physics.

But the climate in Russia has been changing since early 2000. The government introduced standardized testing in 2002. Bureaucracy has flourished since then and schools are under pressure to get results. The principals especially are under a lot of pressure. There is less and less space for them to maneuver. That is reflected in classroom practice: a more authoritarian form of teaching is on the rise.

Recently the government closed down our general education newspaper, which was a proponent of teacher and student voice. We could have continued to publish the paper, but that meant compromising on our message and that we didn't want to do. But we continue to publish the supplements and conduct our other business. The basic work continues. And that basic work is the core of our movement. It is about tackling narrowing standards. My father was against standards. You need to have higher standards. You will always have small goals and a small life if you just have government standards. Everything becomes small. Our supplements are essentially about the same thing: freedom of standards. Making your own choices. Focusing on the subject, pedagogy and the choices a teacher has there, in the classroom; that gives freedom.

Artiom Soloveychik is the editor-in-chief of the hugely popular teacher newspaper and educational publishing company *First of September*. The general newspaper had to close recently, but the subject-specific magazines and other educational projects remain a huge success. It is instrumental in giving teachers a voice and allowing them to collaborate on and share more progressive child-centered forms of education. *First of September* has 1.1 million subscribers. Its website has 7 million unique visitors each month and is the go-to source for professional development and discourse on education.

Note

1 Wikipedia: '. . . how to raise the heart, intelligence and spirit of a free man, and underlined the faults of conventional approaches to parenting. According to Soloveychik, parenting is the science about the art of bringing up children, the main idea of which is that parents by all means should increase a child's dignity. http://en.wikipedia.org/wiki/Simon_Soloveychik.

Chapter 18

The Polite Revolution in Research and Education

Tom Bennett

Context: When Is a Profession Not a Profession?

The past few decades have not been an easy time to be a teacher in the UK. Correction: it has not been an easy time to be a professional teacher in the UK, if by professional we mean a member of a corpus unified by a code of practice, a body of core wisdom and knowledge, and the autonomy to make meaningful decisions within its locus. In common with many other nations, UK education has seen the increasing burden of high-stakes accountability, micro-management and an increasingly target-driven culture. While no one could object to any of these pressures being present in a publicly funded institution, the over emphasis of a top-down hierarchy based on saturation levels of prescriptivism has produced a burden that alienates many from the profession.

If you are a teacher in the UK, you can expect to be told what syllabus to teach; the school can tell you which texts and units are to be studied. Additionally, central government can, through the institutional leverage of its notionally independent inspection quango[1] Ofsted, instruct a teacher in which methodologies of teaching are preferred. This last dimension of interference is by far the most radical and punitive. Until very recently, Ofsted has graded teachers on their individual lessons, when visiting and inspecting schools; the results of these inspections can decide if a school is allowed to continue to exist, or if senior staff retain their positions. In such an environment, appeasing the inspecting body becomes paramount, to the exclusion of all else. If the inspectors have a preferred teaching style, then that must be presented at all costs, and codified into the structure of everyday practice, regardless of how appropriate it is. Such decisions used to rest in the hands of classroom teachers, but no more.

Other factors play a part in stripping the autonomy of teachers: for decades, UK schools have been judged comparatively with their neighbouring schools in league tables, based on, until recently, a metric of five A*–C passes in the GCSE exams, including English and maths. Again, because of the high stakes of winning or losing at this metric, schools have focused on this elusive pass rate to the detriment of other areas, resulting in, for example, an over emphasis on interventions with borderline pupils, or on core subjects to the detriment of non core.

Such an environment of quantifiable accountability has eroded the emphasis on any aspect of education and teaching that is not immediately quantifiable. Simple metrics that mimic economic models of progress have been allowed to displace other, less fiscal measures of what we mean by success, or flourishing.

Why Research Has Been a Problem

In this context, teachers have suffered under any number of lashes, and one of the most common justifications for this process of deprofessionalisation has been research. When I entered teaching in 2004, I entered a profession that was in the grip of high levels of prescribed orthodoxy, and at every turn, these policies were supported – their proposers claimed – by evidence, by research. In one school I was told that my lessons would never be better than satisfactory (which in the English system actually means a sneering *unsatisfactory*) unless I clustered my tables into groups, which was apparently supported by all the research. I attended teacher training classes where I was solemnly inducted into the secret rites of Brain Gym – a series of physical exercises which allegedly improved cognition, including a direction to drink water to prevent the brain dehydrating – Neuro Linguistic Programming (Bandler and Grinder's[2] 'science of success' that claimed, among other things, to confer the user with the ability to discern lies from truth, influence the weak minded and lead behaviour silently) and many other researched axioms of the profession. And I accepted them, without question. Why wouldn't I? Why wouldn't I assume that trainers, mentors, institutions responsible for teacher training were on absolutely solid ground? Who was I to dispute their research?

Except that the evidence of my own senses didn't cohere with the theory. Brain Gym seemed to have no impact. Group work seemed to be the worst way of working at times. NLP struck me as New Age voodoo, but I persevered with them all, blaming myself for their failure to ignite my classes, and the learning of my children. But again, who was I to dispute the research? What contribution could my teaching practice make to the discussion which preceded me by decades and involved the great superstructures of the teaching establishments, the universities, the training colleges, the faculties of education?

40 Days in the Desert

After several years, an epiphany. I took a sabbatical at Corpus Christi College Cambridge where I spent a term on a Teacher Fellowship, during which I spent time outside of the classroom to research, among other things, the origins of the research that permeated the profession. The personal impact was enormous.

For a start, I discovered very quickly indeed that a great deal of educational research was simply poorly disguised advocacy, dressed in the gown of authority. Part of this was simply intellectual dishonesty on the parts of the authors, many of whom seemed to lack the integrity of purpose or ability to understand what an evidenced piece of research would look like. Many papers simply embarked with their conclusions decided from the outset, and looked for evidence to substantiate it (or not – some simply presented irrelevant data sets of the merely tangential, and then drew absurd conclusions from it). Some of the research barely referred to existent research in its own field. Some of it did, but in a highly selective fashion. Some of it seemed more suited to the fiction section of the library. Some of it was poorly written.

But one could say this of any field. What separated this research from poor research in other areas and fields was an effect that is perhaps uniquely concomitant to the social sciences, as opposed to the natural sciences. In the latter, empirical science has developed an established, uncontroversial series of methodologies that demand the participant operate within established parameters necessary to qualify as valid research. It's far from perfect, nor does it claim to be perfect, but its efficacy is evident every time one turns on a mobile phone or boards a plane. The social sciences, however, frequently fail to meet the standard of verification or replicability that we find in chemistry or physics, due, in the main, to the inherent problems of comparable controls in human agents. Issues of unpredictability, high causal density and a host of ethical issues, make studying the human a very different practice to studying the inert and relatively malleable subject of brute matter.

A blunt example will serve as an outline of where these magisterials diverge: were I to make a chemical claim that water will boil at 100 degrees centigrade, that claim can be assessed by a simple test – heating it to that temperature and observing the outcome. I can then check that my claim is sound by changing other variables such as position, height, air pressure, and so on, to see if they have any impact on my claim (and we find that some of them do). Verification can be fine tuned in this way. The process can be easily repeated by other parties, and their data can be compared to mine.

In the social sciences, this doesn't follow. If I make (again, a very blunt example, for demonstration purposes) the claim that 'a threat of gunfire will make people flee', then I encounter enormous difficulties. For a start, while many will do so, many will not; soldiers, for example. Deaf people. The suicidal. The very brave or indeed stupid. There are so many factors, that we struggle to determine which ones are relevant or not. Or to scale it down: if we try to make a claim about how a friend will react to, for example, a surprise party, we encounter similar problems. Their reaction will depend on so many variables – how they are feeling, their day up until that point, whether or not their partner has left them – that are unforeseeable and unpredictable except in principle alone. There are simply too many variables to contend with. While social sciences may enjoy some success correlating inputs and outcomes in large samples, the closer one gets to the atom of that sample, the less valid the propositional probability. Psychology, sociology, economics, education, all become matters of probability over a distance, with caveats and exceptions marbling their every claim.

Which doesn't mean that social sciences are inherently useless or uninteresting. But it makes it vital to remember that the outcomes of social scientific research require far higher levels of caution and awareness of context and variables before conclusions are inexpertly or hastily drawn. Unfortunately, this level of caution is often absent from research in education; far worse is the level of recklessness displayed by those who choose to take the research and use it for their own ends, either as political ammunition, or as sensational content for a media process. And finally, even the inhabitants of the educational system have been guilty of abusing this process, often driven by a need (perceived or imagined) to import a magic bullet into their school systems. Administrators of all levels are frequently under high levels of pressure to display progress, and quickly. It is far easier, and quicker, to show evidence of action by the importation of a poorly evidenced intervention, than to take more meaningful, but less obvious action.

Which is where the dysfunctional relationship between research and education emerges, and how it is allowed to thrive. The situation of educational research is similar to that of medicine in the 15th century, when anyone could claim almost anything, and wonder cures, miracle pills, faith healing and snake oil were not only available, but mainstream. In this context, Brain Gym is considered as reasonable an intervention as after-school revision classes; Thinking Hats as credible as textbooks. When research can justify anything, anything is justifiable. Teachers' roles in this are non-existent. They serve only to serve the system, slaves to whatever policy, intervention or methodology is preferred by line management and educational panjandrums. If a teacher is told that all children must be assessed for learning styles, and that audit should result in revised lesson plans, then that must happen, despite whatever reservations and experiential misgivings they may have. Their opinion, their entire craft, is marginalised to the point of obsolescence. The teacher is no longer a professional, but a delivery system. In this atmosphere, their replacement – by untrained staff, by MOOCs, by anything – is not only possible, but inevitable.

The Polite Revolution: Building a New Temple

In early 2013 I began an organisation called researchED. I was a full-time teacher who had developed a sideline in educational blogging and writing. This afforded me something of a modest media profile, and I frequently wrote for national teaching papers such as the *TES*, and appeared as an occasional vox populi as far as that went on radio and television. Through engagement with social media I had built up a healthy (or perhaps unhealthy) audience, and it was that which was to act as the catalyst for the next stage of this narrative.

One of my books I had published was called *Teacher Proof*, and it dealt with some of the faux scientific theories that pervaded education. I tackled Brain Gym and NLP, but also looked at Learning Styles, Multiple Intelligences, Bloom's Taxonomy, Group Work, Digital Natives, and a number of other currently fashionable orthodoxies that have as much to do with the strongly held values of their proponents than with any form of evidence base. One of my axioms was that while it was perfectly acceptable to hold a belief that, for example, children possessed learning modalities, it was necessary for the evidence for such a claim to be publicly available for scrutiny in order for others to decide if this was a matter of intuition, or faith, before it was adopted elsewhere. I have no issue with faith; but faith disguised as fact is a toxic vehicle for understanding. It also acts as a shackle to the professional judgement of the teacher practitioner, for example when teachers are expected to blindly accept a policy or intervention despite a lack of evidence to support it beyond the enthusiasm of its sponsor.

I was challenged, almost as a dare, by two key correspondents – Ben Goldacre, the doctor and writer, whose work precedes mine in this field immeasurably, and Sam Freedman, now the Director of Research at the UK Teach First organisation, and then an adviser to the UK Minister for Education – to hold a conference on educational research. At first it struck me as odd to contemplate it; after all, I had disputed its pillars so frequently. But I perceived an opportunity here – for teachers to become conversant with the difficulties and often inadequacies of what so many of them had assumed was settled wisdom, but also for more careful, cautious and potentially useful research to reach the classroom, by a process of face-to-face encounters between the producers of evidence and the artisans of its fruits: teachers. researchED was born.

I casually mentioned on Twitter that I was building this conference, and asked if anyone wanted to contribute; I had barely considered the consequences of this. By 2 am that night I was fielding hundreds of offers and queries. By the next morning I had over 300 messages offering help, support, venues, attendees, ticket enquiries, offers to speak . . . it was clear that a small fire had been lit, and now smouldered.

Four months later, we held the inaugural researchED conference at Dulwich College in South London. Five hundred paid attendees came out on a Saturday in their own time, mostly on their own purse, to listen, learn and discuss with each other what research actually said, and could do, for classrooms. Educationalists and academics from many of the UK's top institutions spoke for free, as did prominent teacher voices, representatives of intermediary institutions, teacher leaders, unions, charities. Over 200 people waited on a list for tickets. Before I held the event, a prominent member of one of the main British research institutions told me that we would never get teachers to come out in their own time to learn about teaching. Seven hundred people gave that the lie, and demonstrated, perhaps, one of the ways in which the relationship between teacher practitioners and the academics who informed their profession had become sour. One such member even told me that he couldn't see the point of discussing with teachers the research they were doing, because what could they add? The arrogance of some astonished me, although perhaps it shouldn't have.

After the event I was prepared to let it rest and return my focus to my real job; but the enthusiasm for the event failed to abate, and people almost insisted we hold another. Within a few months we had collaborated with schools in Birmingham and York to host regional researchEDs; smaller affairs, but all sold out. There was clearly an appetite. By February 2014 it was obvious that a second national event in London was not only feasible, but necessary, and in September of that year we held the second major conference, this time with 850 attendees and over 300 on the waiting list. We had representatives from both major political parties, even more academics, and a broader spectrum of speakers and theorists. Attendees came from as far as China to watch some of the most influential educational theorists and practitioners in Europe and beyond.

The success of the movement carried on like a boulder. researchED conferences are now in place for New York and Sydney in 2015, along with Glasgow, Scotland, Leeds, and two more in London. Perhaps more excitingly, researchED has played midwife to the Research Leads network, a burgeoning organisation that brings together teachers assigned to lead their school's engagement with educational research, in events based on networking and self-training. With the addition of our new website, we're starting to see an enormous involvement of teachers in their own destinies and professional development.

What Does This Mean?

It's still too early to properly understand the impact this has had on the profession, and it perhaps would not be an act of modesty to say that such an impact may well be local and transient. But from my partial perspective, it seems like something unusual and exciting has happened to the teaching profession. Tired of being governed into submission, weary of being expected to accept, digest and regurgitate the prescriptive orthodoxies of their structural superiors, teachers – some teachers – have mobilised in a virtual network aimed at their mutual collaboration and self-improvement. Rather than simply accept 'the evidence says' as the final word in a debate, some teachers have taken that phrase as a challenge to understand for themselves what research really says, and how valuable that observation is in their practice.

On one level, it's a movement that seeks to dispute the simple equation that information given from above is valid and valuable; scepticism is a necessary weapon in the contemporary teacher's arsenal. This is the aspect that I called being Teacher Proof – able to discern the cargo cult science from the efficacious. On another level, it's more than just being able to dispute and doubt, but also to actively seek evidence to inform and substantiate the types of intervention that teachers and schools perform in their practices.

This involves understanding a subtle distinction: teaching is not an evidence-based profession, nor, as Dylan Wiliam said at our September conference, should it ever be. Such an approach would doom practitioners to an existence where their every action had to be substantiated by a significant body of researched evidence. Anyone who works in education will vouch that this simply isn't possible. Nor, given the complexity of human action, would it be desirable.

But education should certainly be an evidence-augmented profession. Where possible, evidence must be the basis of decisions. Where it is absent, the role of craft is important. After all, no amount of randomised control trials can inform me how to speak to a child who is upset because their grandparent has passed away. A teacher's day is spent making decisions based as much on personal experience as anything else. This is the space for craft, and it is an important space – possibly even the most important.

Who would say that evidence should *not* be used in education, however? Such a claim is irrational. If evidence exists, it must be accounted for and, if necessary, disputed, modified or embraced. If there are limits to the evidence base, that must be understood. Where evidence is overwhelming, it should be adopted, or rejected on better grounds. Teaching is not, never will be, medicine. But it is itself, it is teaching. It isn't magic. If we have evidence, we should act on it.

And this is where professionalisation re-enters the conversation. Research, I claimed earlier, was used as an impediment to the professional identity of teachers. Given that the research communities aren't simply going to go away, the only sane alternative, the only alternative that saves us as teachers, is to become Teacher Proof, and to engage with it where necessary and where it possesses utility. If teachers consciously make themselves more research literate – sceptical or aware – then research ceases to be a trap, and instead becomes a springboard, a device for empowering the profession. Instead of a line manager, or head teacher or politician, blandly propping up their dogma with 'the research says', a muscular, mature profession can say 'does it really?'

For a teacher to be a true professional, they need to be aware of where intuition intersects with evidence, and where both end meaningfully. Craft is personal, intuitively understood, slow to accrue, difficult to rush; research is public, understood intellectually, often gained quickly (although understood at length). But one without the other is dangerous: craft without evidence can simply become a new orthodoxy, in the image of religion, defying evidence to the contrary. Research without craft is empty, overly abstract, and can become an exercise in pointlessness. If theory fails in practice, then the theorists need to ask why, not simply assume that practice is inadequate.

And this is where researchED, and similar movements, can revitalise and refresh the entire structure of teaching. A new model emerges, where teachers, rather than waiting for some imagined Moses to free themselves from the rack of Pharaoh, become Moses themselves. No more waiting for Superman. If the profession waits for a Messiah to make everything better, then not only will it wait until the stars freeze, but they don't deserve the name profession. It is time, I propose, that teachers cease to be helpless, and simply assume that they are more powerful than any other force in education.

Rather than wait to be directed to teacher training that may be turgid or irrelevant to the actual teacher needs, or more closely aligned with the bureaucratic requirements of a system that is driven by external proxy indicators of success, teachers can instead attend researchED events, for instance, and pick the professional development areas that interest them. Instead of accepting what they are told by vested interests pursuing unknown agendas, they can simply investigate for themselves what existent evidence bases say about these areas. Instead of experiencing evidence bases remotely, teacher practitioners can come and dispute for themselves the findings of research with the authors.

None of this would have been possible – or so fluidly possible – without the emergent power of social networks. Just as countries in the Middle East mobilised huge numbers of disparate, normally unconnected people into giant armies of unified purpose, so too have vehicles such as Twitter provided a medium where curiosity, rather than simply dissipating, can be focused from a lightbulb to a laser beam, and where frustration and powerlessness can become the fuel that feeds a transformational movement.

Through this model, teachers can a) personalise and b) control their own professional development; existent monoliths of orthodoxy that attempt to define and control the community of UK teachers can be sidelined and short circuited.

researchED is a grass-roots, wiki-style community of teachers who refuse to be passive recipients of a top-down educational elite who maintain their dominance by controlling access to who reads what research, and what good educational research means. We aspire to become research-literate instigators of research; educated filters and guardians of our own professionalism. We seek to be partners with educational establishments rather than consumers. Through conferences and face-to-face opportunities, to online communities of like-minded teachers and associates, our aim is to devolve power from the high priests of academia, to the classroom.

In essence, we're looking for a Reformation. A revolution, perhaps. A polite one. But a revolution, nonetheless.

Notes

1 Quasi Autonomous Non Governmental Organisation.

2 Grinder, J. and Bandler, R. (1979). *Frogs into Princes: Neuro Linguistic Programming*. Moab, UT: Real People Press, p. 194.

Vignette 8

Changing Education in Action

Korea: The Travelling Teacher

Hyejin Bak interviewed by Jelmer Evers

So how did you become a teacher?

I started teaching in 2006 when I was 22. My motivation wasn't idealistic. I had failed my university entrance exam and my family suggested I should get into education. I had wanted to study social sciences or international relations, but there was no one around when I was younger to talk to about what I should do, or to support me in my studies. My teachers didn't know much about it, and there was no internet, so I was all on my own when it came to making the decision to go into teaching. Teaching is a popular job, I reasoned; it brings job stability, and in times of economic crisis it is an especially good choice.

At first it was just a job, but soon after I started teaching and getting more experience I became aware of my responsibility towards my students. And the more interaction you have with your students, the more responsible you feel. I really enjoyed my teaching, but at the same time I wanted to expand my horizon.

I took a leave of absence to pursue a PhD in International Education in Seoul. After my master's degree, which I partly did in the United Kingdom, I felt a need to do more research. That's why I went on to pursue my old dream of going to university, but not only for myself: I wanted to be an example for my students. Show them that they should try new things. I still keep in touch with students I taught nine years ago, however.

It isn't common for a primary teacher to get a PhD and there isn't much of a challenge within teaching itself. Frankly, becoming a primary school teacher is too easy in Korea. About 95% of the teacher population comes straight out of teacher education, and they all have similar backgrounds. I think students need more diversity. It's a bit harder to become a secondary teacher. You can get a teaching degree after university.

Like I said, the path I'm taking is not a very common one, and it is especially unusual for female teachers to pursue a PhD, like I have. Getting a master's degree is a bit more common and is supported financially by the Department of Education, and studying abroad is also supported, although you only get half of your salary. Getting a PhD is not supported at all, however, and you have to save enough money to enter a graduate programme. In Korea, getting a PhD is something that an administrator might pursue, or someone who is already on an academic track.

Another obstacle I discovered is that my province is quite conservative and that Seoul was about the only place to study education in an international context. I want to be a lifelong learner, I want to be informed by educational trends worldwide and learn from other countries. And I wanted to do this at the best place possible, at the best university. That's why I took a leave of absence from my teaching job and left for Seoul.

Why exactly are you interested in international education?
I want to learn more about the global level of education. Teacher trainers don't know that much about the international context, it isn't really taught when you get a teaching degree. I've always been curious and I think we have much to learn from other countries. At the same time I want to be a role model for teachers. If I can do it, anyone can. Most Korean teachers don't engage in international networks because language is a big barrier. They feel that their English isn't good enough and that that alone is already a high enough hurdle to leap.

Are there any opportunities to apply what you learned when you get back?
I'm afraid to go back to my province. When I came back from the UK I was considered special. To fit in I pretended to be just like everyone else. My colleagues don't want to stand out that much, which is common in Korean culture. I wish it wasn't so difficult to express my own opinion to other teachers. But I'm female, young, I have a master's degree from the UK and now I'm getting a PhD. Whereas most teachers don't have any experience with other systems and cultures. When I go back, our regional office will probably consider me an English teacher, they don't know what to do with me. There aren't any opportunities besides traditional teacher roles. I will probably feel underused. It's really hard to build a network outside of your subject area.

Korea does have in-service training. That is a 60-hour training programme organized by the regional education office and there are semi-public training institutes. After three and five years there is mandatory retraining. You have quite a few options in which area you want to do this – more than 100. More options are done externally, with specialists from different fields. There are also professional learning communities around subjects. And more and more informal learning communities around special interests.

And is time an issue?
Yes, school work is very busy. There are lots of administrative things to do that concern both teaching and school-wide administration. I have to manage and administrate the budget for materials and I have to arrange everything for our native speaker who teaches English at our school. I don't really know why we have an administrative office. And after I'm done with teaching there isn't enough time to prepare. Usually I have to do that in the evening. Our head office asks

for a lot of documentation, and only now I can say that what they ask of us is almost impossible.

Is testing an issue in Korea?

In school we have mid- and end-term tests. They are open questions. Simple tests, formative. High school is very high pressure, preparing for SAT. But there is a pressure on primary schools as well, mainly from parents. And lots of private tutoring. Some kids just don't want to do it any more. And the gap between students who can afford tutoring and those who can't afford it is widening. This all leads to stress in our children.

What I would like and what I do as a teacher is to instil a growth mindset. We shouldn't push students to just memorize facts. That doesn't mean we shouldn't push them. We should challenge them to the best of their abilities. But also make it more playful. Make them enjoy learning.

So what would you do if you could change the system?

I would find ways to have teachers from diverse backgrounds in school. That would mean more creativity: at the moment, teachers are all the same and there isn't a lot of innovation. There is a conservative mindset: follow the rules, don't deviate from the standard. Public schools aim for the standard. Which is also related to culture, of course. But this means schools are very closed systems and I would really want to change that. Teachers need more experience in society. They need to learn how to network and meet more diverse people. Children deserve inspiring role models in school.

Hyejin Bak has been a primary school teacher in South Korea since 2006, and is currently studying as a doctoral student in the Lifelong Learning Department at the College of Education of Seoul National University. Her interests include the relationship between education and development, especially continuous learning and network of teachers. She has diverse experience in the education field, such as internship experience of fieldwork research about teacher fulfilment related to inclusive education for visually impaired students and volunteering for IT education and Korean culture class in Ghana. She has an MA degree in International Education and Development from the University of Sussex in the UK, and a Bachelor of Education degree from Chinju National University of Education in South Korea.

Chapter 19

Supporting and Empowering Teachers

The Role of School–Community Partnerships

Helen Janc Malone and Reuben Jacobson

Introduction

Teachers play many formal and informal roles: those of classroom instructors, data specialists, school leaders, mentors, after-school tutors, health-care providers, and more (Harrison & Killion, 2007; Henig, Malone & Reville, 2012). Classroom, school, and community realities dictate these roles regardless of whether teachers are trained for them. However, the current accountability movement within the United States tends to define the role of teachers within the instructional and curricular context, overlooking the informal roles teachers often carry, especially in high-needs schools. School–community partnership offers a strategy that has shown in practice to both sharpen teachers' roles within instructional practice and to empower teachers to guide and lead the development and implementation of results-focused partnerships (Chang & Lawyer, 2012).

The purpose of this chapter is to look at the role of partnerships in supporting and empowering teachers. Although partnerships alone are no panacea for removing teaching and learning barriers, they do offer a consideration on how to reimagine structures of support for teachers within the public education model and how teachers can be empowered through partnerships. Considerations expressed in this chapter are based on case-study data emerging from the field and a literature review on school–community partnerships.

Vignette: Los Angeles Education Partnership

Many education and community reforms within the U.S. are using formal or informal school–community partnerships as promising strategies, including: community schools, Promise Neighborhoods, Choice Neighborhoods, after-school programs, among others. These partnership strategies vary in many ways, including their structure, purpose, funding, and intensity. We begin with one example of a partnership strategy in Los Angeles, where teachers play a critical role as leaders of school–community partnerships that support some of the city's highest-need students.

Empowering teachers has always been the essential school improvement strategy for one community partner in Los Angeles. For over 25 years the Los Angeles Education Partnership (LAEP) has been working with high-needs schools to support teachers in multiple ways. They are not a 'provider' that enters the school as an external player and implements reforms *to* teachers. Rather, they are true partners and work *with* teachers to empower them to make their own reform. Core to their strategy is helping teachers work together through common planning time and conversations around a shared set of students. They work with the communities around the school and are knowledgeable about the cultural context.

When teachers working with LAEP had the opportunity to take ownership of their schools, they leapt at the opportunity. The U.S. public school districts seldom afford teachers autonomy over school governance issues. However, the Los Angeles Unified School District (LAUSD) has done just that. Its network of Pilot Schools affords teachers an opportunity to be innovative and create the schools teachers believe will best serve their students, where instructional excellence and equity go hand in hand. The Pilot Schools are designed by teachers to empower teachers through shared leadership of the school, professional learning communities (PLCs), and focus on inquiry-based teaching and interdisciplinary instruction. According to the district:

> The Pilot Schools are a network of public schools that have autonomy over budget, staffing, governance, curriculum and assessment, and the school calendar. These autonomies allow them to operate with greater flexibility in order to best meet their students' needs. Pilot Schools were created to be models of educational innovation and to serve as research and development sites for effective urban public schools.
>
> (LAUSD, 2014)[1]

LA teacher Jose Navarro helped apply for his school to become a Pilot School. He captured the opportunity for teachers to lead education reform efforts, saying:

> We're interested in who's going to be making decisions with the students in mind. Too long teachers have been out of the policy aspect of education. We've been receiving the orders. We'd like to be part of the conversation, make sure the right things are being done.
>
> (LAEP, 2014)

LAEP worked closely with teachers to create Pilot Schools that built on teachers' strengths and that saw the community as a core asset. In one case, teachers organized dozens of community meetings and spoke to hundreds of families to create support for their Pilot School proposal. They used the community schools approach to create the partnerships they needed to support students, teachers, families, and the community.

Community schools are (public) schools that work closely with community partners, often via an intermediary organization, in this case LAEP, and an on-site coordinator whose job it is to serve as a liaison linking students with an array of community services that support student learning and positive development (Dryfoos & Maguire, 2002). Navarro explains the appeal of the community school strategy from a teacher's perspective:

> Our job is to make these four walls magic. Everything has to happen within these four walls. But the reality is education starts way before they ever enter my room. So we need this collaborative environment. And not just on campus. It has to be within the community. And the community is growing. LAEP is, because of their resources, able to bring in people I could never get in contact with. And really creating a hub around each one of these students. But it all starts with the student in the middle. The teachers, the family, our community partners and growing out. But still that center is the student.
>
> (LAEP, 2014)

LAEP-supported teachers applying for LAUSD's Pilot Schools selected this model because it gives teachers freedom to work collaboratively, to personalize and customize learning, to focus on instruction while knowing that a variety of quality partners are utilizing their expertise to attend to other needs students might have (behavioral, medical, social, etc.). Further, teachers work with the community schools' coordinators to identify classroom-based needs that external partners can assist with (e.g., one Pilot School partnered with a community-based program, Reading Open Minds, and created a school-based book club to boost students' literacy).

For example, at the Social Justice Humanitas Academy (SJHA) Pilot School, community schools, Promise Neighborhoods, and other initiatives come together, and teachers are central figures in family and community engagement and play significant roles in the direction of the school. Teachers, the community school coordinator, and the principal meet every five weeks and review each student's academic and social–emotional backgrounds. They then work *together* to determine what they need to do to support the students' various needs.

The school–community partnership strategy empowers teachers to bring their students' academic and nonacademic needs to a team that includes the coordinator, and the coordinator gets the partners to meet those needs. As a lead partner, LAEP helps teachers, principals, and partners develop the skills to work together, rather than in isolation, to make the best possible decisions for children. According to Ellen Pais, the President and CEO of LAEP:

> If you were to go look at our Pilot Schools, for the most part, I think that teachers are very satisfied with the way the school functions and the opportunities they have to be professionals. And the opportunity they

> have to work with colleagues . . . and participate in problem solving at their school.
>
> (Personal communication, September 28, 2014)

As the SJHA community school coordinator wrote, Humanitas in this school featured 'teacher collaboration and leadership, inquiry-based teaching, interdisciplinary instruction, rigorous academics, and solutions-based learning' (Coalition for Community Schools, 2013). Now, other schools are reaching out to the educators and partners at these Pilot Schools to learn how they can utilize school–community partnerships to meet students' diverse needs.

The Pilot School example illustrates two notable considerations – the role of school–community partnerships and teacher empowerment. The two are complementary to each other. When schools invest in external partnerships, students and teachers gain access to services and tools that enable and promote teaching and learning in schools. Further, schools that are open to the community often provide teachers with flexibility to engage in collaboration, ongoing professional development, and shared leadership. The two elements are the central foci of this chapter.

Why Do Partnerships Matter? Because Caring For and Educating Students Is Not Just the Teachers' Job

The U.S. public education system continues to struggle with ways to close the achievement and opportunities gaps. The increasingly polarizing debate within the education reform space offers two competing narratives: a) that environmental and societal factors are only 'excuses' for poor instruction and that the achievement and opportunities gaps can be effectively alleviated by high-quality core academic instruction alone, or b) that inequity in the larger social context does enter classrooms and can be most effectively addressed via school–community partnerships. Beyond the rhetoric, practice tells us that we need to attend to both: to consider partnerships as a possible strategy to decrease barriers to learning and complement learning, and to empower teachers in the partnership process.

Human development researchers have long argued that youth are influenced and shaped by both their internal and external ecological environments, by micro, meso, and macro contexts (Bronfenbrenner, 1994; Center for Social and Emotional Education, 2010; Epstein, 1987). This means that teachers alone cannot possibly address all the needs of children. Parents, faith-based leaders, community partners, and others have important roles to play in partnering to support students' ecology of needs. Research shows that ecological environments interact, and when schools work to build partnerships with external stakeholders, they benefit both students and teachers (Blank & Shah, 2004; Bryk & Schneider, 2002; Henderson & Mapp, 2002). The ecological approach to youth development serves as the foundational base for school–community partnerships.

In the U.S., as is true in many parts of the world, often, where you live guides opportunities for learning and success. Middle- and upper-income families tend to have access to diverse preventative medical and social service, to year-round learning-enrichment opportunities for their children, and to supportive, stable developmental spaces. Many lower-income families, especially those living in areas of concentrated poverty, do not have such opportunities. Duncan and Murnane (2014) estimate that the difference in family investment in student learning between low-income and wealthier families adds up to $100,000 in individual-level investment over the course of K–12 education. Further, longitudinal research finds a 6,000-hour learning gap by elementary grades alone between lower- and upper-income students (Alexander, Entwisle & Olson, 2014).

These disparities influence teachers and schools. A national study by the Center for American Progress reports that 61% of teachers purchase food for their students and that nearly half work to connect families and students to appropriate social and welfare services, including helping to fill out governmental assistance forms and referrals (Chang & Lawyer, 2012). Yet, teachers often have minimal in-service training in attending to non-learning student needs (Ladson-Billings, 2001; MetLife, 2012; Rotherham & Mitchel, 2014). Teachers often have no formal leadership or decision-making role in helping to create learning environments that best support their students. Principals are in similar situations and have similar accountability pressures. Strategic external partnerships can play an important role for public schools in supporting educators and their students.

Table 19.1 The spectrum of school–community partnerships.

School-Based Partnerships			Place Based
Family/Interagency Collaboration	*Full-Service Schools*	*Full-Service Community Schools*	*Community Development*
• Coordinate service delivery • Promote student learning and development • Set specific and limited goals	• Deliver school-based service • Provide academic, health, and social services • Wrap social, family, and health services around educational goals	• Deliver coordinated, school-based set of services with community input • Promote community and parent engagement • Engage families as key players, partners	• Use the school as a social center • Provide a broad array of services • Seek to strengthen community infrastructure

Adapted from: Valli, L., Stefanski, A. and Jacobson, R. (2014). School–community partnerships: A typology for guiding systemic educational reform. *Policy Brief*, February. College Park, MD: Maryland Equity Project, College of Education, University of Maryland.

More research on school–community partnerships is needed, but there are some frameworks that illustrate key elements. The next section highlights ways schools and partners operationalize their relationship to support teachers.

How School–Community Partnerships Support Teachers

School–community partnerships exist on a continuum. Noam and Tillinger's (2004) work on intermediary space illustrates the partnership dynamics. They argue that school–community (out-of-school-time) partnerships are evolving. To be successful, they must remain responsive and fluid to best support young people, their families, and school needs. Most often, the relationship between schools and external partners is distant and disconnected, with each institution operating in its own organizational silo, leaving the burden of making the connection on young people and families. There are three types of partnerships, Noam and Tillinger argue, with varying levels of connection, that capture intentional partnerships that promote stronger school–community connections: a) functional partnerships, whereby schools and partners discover their overlapping interests, create joint goals and memoranda of understanding for the use of facilities, resources, and procedures; b) interconnected partnerships, where schools and partners develop an inclusive system focused on relationship and trust building; and c) transformational partnerships, where both partners undergo organizational and cultural change to work together to best support all stakeholders.

Valli, Stefanaski, and Jacobson's (2014) partnership typology further explores the connection between schools and external partners (see Table 19.1). They characterize different partnership types, from least to most comprehensive, as family/interagency collaboration, full-service schools, full-service community schools, and community development. The authors acknowledge that particular strategies may blend between one or more partnership types. Still, the typology provides a useful way to think about the level of comprehensiveness in the partnership. A significant difference between the types is whether partners are providing services *to* the school or *with* the school (which would include teachers).

Teachers have a role to play in each of these partnership types. In the family/interagency collaboration and full-service schools types, teachers may be consulted about which students need support. In the more comprehensive and participatory full-service community schools type, teachers are likely to play the aforementioned role but also to be empowered to work with partners and families to set the direction for the school, including the role of partners.

The noted frameworks illustrate the spectrum of school–community partnerships, and how partnerships help to support the process of teaching and learning.

In practice, there are many types of school–community partnerships, all of which support teachers to varying degrees. The following examples illustrate notable school–community partnerships:

- Communities In Schools (CIS) is currently being implemented in some 3,000 public schools across the U.S. as a dropout prevention program. Schools partner with external community-based organizations to offer an array of services and programs that enable and enrich students' learning inside the schools. To date, 99% of CIS students stayed in school, 96% of eligible students graduated from high school, and 84% met their academic performance goals. A national teacher evaluation study of CIS shows favorable outcomes for students and teachers. A majority of surveyed teachers (77%) felt that external partnerships provided students with conditions for learning. Nearly 70% of teachers reported that the students' attendance, readiness to learn, and engagement in the classroom increased as a result of CIS. Over 70% of teachers reported that due to CIS, they felt they are more effective instructors, that their jobs are less difficult than before, that they enjoy teaching more, and are better able to improve student achievement inside the classroom.[2]
- Elev8 Baltimore (Maryland), one site of a national community schools model, offers immunizations, health screenings, mental health preventative care, manages chronic conditions, runs a variety of athletic programs that promote fitness, and fosters a positive school climate focused on social relationships, mutual respect, and inclusiveness. These services have helped to promote well-being of all students and their families, strengthened school–family–community partnerships, and positively affected students' school attendance and academic performance. The program has enabled teachers to focus on instructional practice improvement and professional collaboration, knowing conditions for learning are attended to through community partnerships.[3]
- City Connects in greater Boston (Massachusetts) customizes preventions, interventions, and enrichment services for every child in their schools, working closely with teachers, families, and service professionals. Each City Connects school has a community liaison officer who coordinates learning and development services for students. Thus, all students have access to a variety of services to support their learning, from tutoring and homework assistance, to mental and physical health specialists, and social workers. A decade-long, rigorous, longitudinal evaluation of the initiative has found that student engagement with City Connects halved the effects of poverty, doubled the likelihood of high school graduation, and increased students' test scores by 17 percentile points in math and 13 percentile points in reading. According to the annual principal survey, 100% of teachers reported that they were able to fully support students in their classroom, due to the available services provided by City Connects, and 92% of teachers felt they could focus their attention on instruction and practice improvement.[4]
- ExpandEd Schools (New York), run by The After School Corporation (TASC), have expanded their school day in over a dozen New York City

schools in order to give teachers more flexibility and time for teaching, instructional improvement, planning, and ongoing development. The schools utilize community partners to support students' health and developmental needs, as well as to provide in-school support to teachers, such as tutoring, small-group instruction, and enrichment activities. The schedule flexibility helps teachers have more time to focus on practice improvement and collaboration.[5]

- Hillcrest Elementary School in San Francisco, a community school, has bridged the divide between teachers and partners, between school day and after school. The school created 'linked day' positions with partners, after-school staff who start during the school day so they can get to know teachers and their goals and bridge that content and personalization to students in after school. As Hillcrest Elementary School Coordinator Stefanie Eldred said, 'As much as this was about the kids, the teachers were the primary focus of our work when we started. We wanted to help teachers get what they needed to feel supported and to be able to focus on quality and innovative instruction' (Coalition for Community Schools, 2013).

What the above examples illustrate is that school–community partnerships could help to create conditions for learning by mediating external factors that influence learning while supporting and enriching learning opportunities. Partnerships also could enable teachers to focus on their primary roles as instructors, curricular specialists, school leaders, and coaches (Harrison & Killion, 2007), while also seeing direct benefits brought by external partners – healthier, engaged students, who are more regularly attending classes and participating actively in the learning process.

When schools build relationships with community partners, external stakeholders tend to become more familiar with the school, school staff, and could more effectively support teachers (Epstein et al., 2002; Leithwood & Jantzi, 2006). Principals, teachers, and external partners build mutual trust and a shared vision of what the school is and ought to be (Bryk & Schneider, 2002). The social capital built across the horizontal systems (e.g., schools, health agencies, libraries, community-based after-school programs, parks and recreation) strengthens trust and relationships among adults serving students and enables them to work collaboratively to solve problems (Bryk & Schneider, 2002; Villarruel et al., 2003). The responsibility for each student is shared – teachers know what students need, external partners work to provide support to meet the identified needs, and teachers focus their expertise to provide high-quality, personalized instruction (Friedlaender et al., 2014).

How School–Community Partnerships Empower Teachers

In the previous section we illustrated how school–community partnerships could enable teachers to focus on instruction and practice improvement. In this section we note how school–community partnerships could serve as a strategy for teacher empowerment.

Empowerment of teachers in a partnership process calls for an interaction of horizontal and vertical structures. The MetLife Teacher Survey (MetLife, 2012) reports that less than half of surveyed American teachers hold a leadership role in their schools. Teachers who do hold a leadership role tend to value principals who engage in distributed leadership and offer freedom and flexibility for teachers to have their voices heard, for their decisions on an array of issues to matter, and to have the power to make decisions that directly impact students (The Wallace Foundation, 2011).

School districts and school leaders both play a key role in facilitating opportunities, incentivizing relationships with diverse stakeholders, and enabling flexible organizational and managerial structures that could bring schools and communities together and empower teachers in the process. Three practices emerge in the school-improvement literature as supportive to teacher empowerment: positive school culture and climate, professional learning communities, and shared leadership.

Positive school culture and climate matters to the process of teaching and learning (Friedlaender et al., 2014). As the national Equity and Excellence Commission (2013) report stated, 'A collaborative school culture, where teachers are respected, their voices heard and their professional development needs met, is essential for success, particularly with children with the most learning needs. For teachers to succeed they must have the time, materials and school environment that foster learning and collaboration' (p. 24). Research on school–community partnerships indicates that when schools work collaboratively with external partners to support students' developmental and learning needs, students tend to do better in school and achieve academically (Henderson, 2011). Such positive environments also help teachers feel both supported and empowered as instructional leaders (Thapa & Guffey, 2013).

Professional learning communities (PLCs) offer another avenue for empowering teachers. PLCs could potentially encourage ongoing, facilitated professional learning, often cross-departmental and interdisciplinary (Bryan & Henry, 2012; DuFour & Eaker, 1998). PLCs take teachers out of their classroom isolation and into collaborative settings where they could jointly analyze student-level data, debate, develop, make decisions, and innovate new instructional strategies to improve practice (Anderson, 2013). To be effective, teachers tend to see more benefits when PLCs become inquiry-based, problem-solving entities with shared understanding of problems and a collective vision, goals, and accountability. PLCs could also be an effective vehicle to connect teachers with community stakeholders, where teachers could challenge the status quo alongside community members (Gerstl-Pepin & Aiken, 2009). For instance, a study by the Harvard Family Research Project (2010) has found that when teachers work together with after-school partners, they are better able to align instruction during and outside of the typical school day.

Research and practice tell us that teachers tend to feel empowered to recruit and work with partners when leadership is seen as shared among school staff and partners. Principals play a critical role in empowering teachers and bringing the wider community into the fold (The Wallace Foundation, 2011; Van Voorhis & Sheldon, 2004). According to The Wallace Foundation (2011), when principals share leadership with teachers and other staff and work collaboratively, they are deemed more effective by teachers than principals who adhere to the traditional, hierarchical structures of leadership and decision-making (Adams & Jean-Marie, 2011). This it not to say that principals do not have a formal authority to guide the work of a school, but rather that distributed leadership creates incentives for practice improvement across stakeholders, invites shared responsibility and innovative methods that challenge the status quo (see Finnigan & Stewart, 2009; Spillane, 2013; Wagner & Kegan, 2013). Further, when teachers feel empowered in schools, through both formal and informal roles, they tend to build and perceive their school culture as inclusive and collaborative and more open to school–family–community partnerships (Seashore Louise, Leithwood et al., 2010; Waters, Marzano & McNulty, 2008). In a review of partnership programs and best practices in school–family–community partnerships, the National Education Association (NEA) argued that teachers should share ownership for the direction of the school, be part of the decision-making structures on partnerships, and receive professional support on developing partnership skills (Henderson, 2011).

Each of the three strategies outlines conditions for school–community partnerships, whereby all stakeholders could have a seat and a voice at the proverbial 'table' and an opportunity to engage together in strategies that serve the needs of students in schools, to customize opportunities, assist individual needs, and personalize learning. Teachers in such environments have access to multiple collaboration networks, teacher to teacher, teacher to family, teacher to community partner, teacher to family and community, and so on. Teachers thus become empowered as learners, as professionals, as leaders in a school community, and as a central partner in the teaching and learning process.

As illustrated by LAEP (in the opening of this chapter), the community school strategy, one type of school–community partnership, makes shared leadership a central operational component.[6] The governance structure of typical community schools engages teachers, the principal, community partners, and students in matters of academic mission and alignment and practice improvement sharing (Melaville, Jacobson & Blank, 2011). Even though including teachers in these site councils is considered 'best practice,' New

York State, for example, codified the participation and support of teachers in a community schools strategy by requiring the teachers' union to sign off on all applications for their statewide community school grant program (New York State Department of Education, 2013). In Cincinnati, the community learning centers (another name for community schools) are governed by the Local School Decision Making Committee (LSDMC), which includes oversight and input pertaining to school bylaws, setting goals, and 'coordinating and overseeing the development of the school as a Community Learning Center' (Cincinnati Public Schools, 2014a). Members of the LSDMC may include up to three teachers, up to three parents, up to three community members, and up to three non-teaching staff (including the principal). The Board of Education established the LSDMC in a board policy (Cincinnati Public Schools, 2014b).

The shared leadership model illustrated by LAEP and other noted school–community strategies demonstrates that teachers should not only have a seat at the table, alongside external partners, but could be leaders in a comprehensive partnership strategy (Blank, Berg & Melaville, 2006).

Empowering Teachers and Closing the Opportunity Gap

The U.S. is rapidly changing. According to the new Census (2012) data, public schools are becoming majority minority (non-White) and increasingly lower income. As Prudence L. Carter and Kevin G. Welner (2013) note in their book *Closing the Opportunity Gap*, 'Schools do not exist as an independent social institution, somehow separate from larger society. Instead, our schools and students are steeped within the folds of formidable economic, political, cultural, and social contexts' (p. 218). Therefore, schools and communities are inherently intertwined, and teachers cannot be expected to meet all students' needs on their own. Fostering external partnerships and empowering teachers are two ingredients in a broader effort to promote educational excellence and equity (Carter & Welner, 2013).

As the role of the teacher is changing and focusing on personalizing learning, teachers need to see community partners as a way to support learning. The new demands of Common Core State Standards, 21st Century Skills,[7] and the need to prepare students to work in collaborative environments require teachers to think about external partners as assets in their teaching repertoire. Relying on the teacher to focus only on mathematics and English language arts will not suffice if we are to stay true to our broader aspirations for an American education.

Despite knowing that 'teachers can't do it alone,' that today's students face significant challenges to their preparedness and success, and that our students are growing up in an increasingly interconnected world, we lack research on how to best prepare teachers to participate in creating the partnerships they will require in a school setting. We need more research on how collaborations between teachers, schools, and community partners support students' needs and better learning opportunities. Further research is also needed on how school–community partnerships could foster teacher empowerment as leaders in strategic partnerships. Existing evidence is largely based on promising practices, qualitative and survey data. Rigorous evaluations of school–community efforts should be examined to offer insights on how to build, strengthen, and sustain partnerships that support and empower teachers.

In order to 'flip the system,' we should entertain the notion of more intentionally interconnecting vertical and horizontal structures of school management – expanding the voices of those in the front lines, teachers, families, community members and organizations, and young people. This chapter in particular focused attention on the interaction of schools and community partners as the primary vehicle for rethinking what it takes to create conditions for effective teaching and empowered teachers. As research and practice continues to pay attention to the role of community partners in education reform, districts, states, and national policies need to enable partnerships and teacher empowerment. This means that vertical systems would need to create incentives for collaboration, shared leadership, and partnerships that engage schools with families and communities. It also means that our teacher and administrator pre- and in-service programs ought to offer professional development on ways leaders for education can build lasting, meaningful partnerships with diverse stakeholders, that support teaching and learning. Such practices are happening across the country in pockets. Our collective next step is to scale promising practices that put students and teachers at the center of the education enterprise.

Disclosure: Both authors are affiliated with the Institute for Educational Leadership, which houses the Coalition for Community Schools.

Notes

1 To learn more, visit http://pilotschools.lausd.net.
2 To learn more, visit http://www.communitiesinschools.org/.
3 To learn more, visit http://www.elev8baltimore.org/.
4 To learn more, visit http://www.bc.edu/schools/lsoe/cityconnects/.
5 To learn more, visit http://www.expandedschools.org/.
6 See http://www.communityschools.org//resources/part_two_structure_and_function_.aspx.
7 21st Century Skills are defined as core academic subject-matter skills, life and career skills, learning and innovation skills, and information technology. See http://www.p21.org/about-us/p21-framework.

References and Further Reading

Adams, C. M. and Jean-Marie, G. (2011). A diffusion approach to the study of leadership reform. *Journal of Educational Administration*, 49(4), 354–377.

Alexander, K., Entwisle, D. and Olson, L. (2014). *The Long Shadow: Family Background, Disadvantaged Urban Youth, and the Transition to Adulthood*. New York: Russell Sage Foundation.

Anderson, S. E. (2013). The enduring challenge of achieving effective teaching on a larger scale. In H. J. Malone (ed.), *Leading Educational Change: Global Issues, Challenges, and Lessons on Whole-System Reform*. New York: Teachers College Press, pp. 42–46.

Blank, M. J., Berg, A. C. and Melaville, A. (2006). *Growing Community Schools: The Role of Cross-Boundary Leadership*. Washington, DC: Coalition for Community Schools.

Blank, M. J. and Shah, B. (2004). Educators and community sharing responsibility for student learning. *ASCD Info Brief*, January.

Bronfenbrenner, U. (1994). Ecological models of human development. In *International Encyclopedia of Education, Vol. 3.*, 2nd edn. Oxford: Elsevier, pp. 37–43. Retrieved from http://www.columbia.edu/cu/psychology/courses/3615/Readings/BronfenbrennerModelofDevelopment(short%20version).pdf.

Bryan, J. and Henry, L. (2012). A model for building school–family–community partnerships: Principals and process. *Journal of Counseling & Development*, 90, 408–420.

Bryk, A. and Schneider, B. (2002). *Trust in Schools: A Core Resource for Improvement*. New York: Russell Sage Foundation.

Carter, P. L. and Welner, K. G. (2013). Building opportunities to achieve. In P. L. Carter and K. G. Welner (eds), *Closing the Opportunity Gap: What America Must Do to Give Every Child an Even Chance*. New York: Oxford University Press, pp. 217–229.

Census Bureau (2012). *Current Population Survey (CPS), School Enrolment Supplement*. Washington, DC: U.S. Department of Commerce.

Center for Social and Emotional Education (2010). School climate research summary. *School Climate Brief*, 1(1), January, 1–16.

Chang, T. and Lawyer, C. (2012). *Lightening the Load: A Look at Four Ways that Community Schools Can Support Effective Teachers*. Washington, DC: Center for American Progress. Retrieved from http://cdn.americanprogress.org/wp-content/uploads/issues/2012/01/pdf/chang_wraparound.pdf.

Cincinnati Public Schools (2014a). Community involvement: Board policy 9142. Retrieved from https://community.cps-k12.org/sites/boardpolicies/9000%20COMMUNITY%20ENGAGEMENT/9142%20Policy%20Community%20Involvement%202-24-2014.pdf.

Cincinnati Public Schools (2014b). Local Schools Decision Making Committees. [Web page.] Retrieved from http://www.cps-k12.org/community/get-involved/lsdmcs.

Coalition for Community Schools (2013). Magic number: Community schools and the new federal promise neighborhoods funding. [Blog post, 21 August.] Retrieved from http://coalitionforcommunityschools.blogspot.com/2013/08/magic-numbers-community-schools-and-new.html.

Darling-Hammond, L. (2013). Inequality and school resources: What it will take to close the opportunity gap. In P. L. Carter and K. G. Welner (eds), *Closing the Opportunity Gap: What America Must Do to Give Every Child an Even Chance*. New York: Oxford University Press, pp. 77–97.

Dryfoos, J. and Maguire, S. (2002). *Inside Full-Service Community Schools*. Thousand Oaks, CA: Corwin Press.

DuFour, R. and Eaker, R. (1998). *Professional Learning Communities at Work: Best Practices for Enhancing Student Achievement*. Bloomington, IN: National Education Service.

Duncan, A. (2014). Dear colleague letter: Resource comparability. Washington, DC: Office of Civil Rights, U.S. Department of Education, October. Retrieved from http://www2.ed.gov/about/offices/list/ocr/letters/colleague-resourcecomp-201410.pdf.

Duncan, G. J. and Murnane, R. J. (2011). *Whither Opportunity? Rising Inequity, Schools, and Children's Life Chances.* New York: Russell Sage Foundation and Spencer Foundation.

Duncan, G. J. and Murnane, R. J. (2014). How we can strengthen schools serving low-income children. *Education Week*, August. Retrieved from http://www.edweek.org/ew/articles/2014/08/06/37murnane.h33.html?cmp=ENL-EU-NEWS2.

Epstein, J. L. (1987). Toward a theory of family–school connections: Teacher practices and parent involvement. In K. Hurrelmann, F. Kaufmann and F. Losel (eds), *Social Intervention: Potential and Constraints.* New York: DeGruyter, pp. 121–136.

Epstein, J. et al. (2002). *School, Family and Community Partnerships: Your Handbook for Action*, 2nd edn. Thousand Oaks, CA: Corwin Press.

Equity and Excellence Commission (2013). *For Each and Every Child: A Strategy for Education Equity and Excellence.* Washington, DC: U.S. Department of Education. Retrieved from http://www2.ed.gov/about/bdscomm/list/eec/equity-excellence-commission-report.pdf.

Finnigan, K. and Stewart, T. (2009). Leading change under pressure: An examination of principal leadership in low-performing schools. *Journal of School Leadership*, 19(5), 586–618.

Friedlaender, D., Burns, D., Lewis-Charp, H., Cook-Harvey, C. M. and Darling-Hammond, L. (2014). Student-centered schools: Closing the opportunity gap. *Stanford Center for Opportunity Policy in Education – Research Brief*, June. Retrieved from https://edpolicy.stanford.edu/sites/default/files/scope-pub-student-centered-research-brief.pdf.

Gerstl-Pepin, C. and Aiken, J. (2009). Democratic school leaders: Defining ethical leadership in a standardized context. *Journal of School Leadership*, 19(4), 406–444.

Goldhaber, D. and Brewer, D. (1999). Teacher licensing and student achievement. In M. Kanstoroom and C. E. Finn, Jr. (eds), *Better Teachers, Better Schools.* Washington, DC: Thomas B. Fordham Foundation, pp. 83–102.

Harrison, C. and Killion, J. (2007). Ten roles for teacher leaders. *Educational Leadership*, 65(1), January, 74–77.

Harvard Family Research Project (2010). Partnerships for learning: Promising practices in integrating school and out-of-school time program supports. Retrieved from http://www.hfrp.org/publications-resources/browse-our-publications/partnerships-for-learning-promising-practices-in-integrating-school-and-out-of-school-time-program-supports.

Henderson, A. (2011). *Family–School–Community Partnerships 2.0: Collaborative Strategies to Advance Student Learning.* Washington, DC: National Education Association.

Henderson, A. T. and Mapp, K. L. (2002). *A New Wave of Evidence: The Impact of School, Family, and Community Connections on Student Achievement.* Austin, TX: National Center for Family & Community Connections with Schools, Southwest Educational Development Laboratory.

Henig, J., Malone, H. J. and Reville, P. (2012). Addressing the disadvantages of poverty: Why ignore the most important challenge of the post-standards era? In J. Mehta, R. J. Schwartz and F. M. Hess (eds), *The Futures of School Reform.* Cambridge, MA: Harvard Education Press, pp. 119–149.

Ladson-Billings, G. (2001). *Crossing over to Canaan: The Journey of New Teachers in Diverse Classrooms.* San Francisco: Jossey-Bass.

Leithwood, K. and Jantzi, D. (2006). Transformational school leadership for large-scale reform: Effects on students, teachers, and their classroom practices. *School Effectiveness and School Improvement*, 17(2), 201–227.

Little, P. (2013). School–community learning partnerships: Essential to expanded learning success. *Expanding Minds and Opportunities: The Power of Afterschool and Summer Learning for Student Success*. Retrieved from http://www.expandinglearning.org/expandingminds/article/school–community-learning-partnerships-essential-expanded-learning-success.

Los Angeles Education Partnership (LAEP) (2014). *New school*. [Video file.] Retrieved from http://www.laep.org/news/videos/.

Los Angeles Unified School District (LAUSD (2014). LAUSD Pilot Schools. Retrieved from http://pilotschools.lausd.net/apps/pages/index.jsp?uREC_ID=190037&type=d&pREC_ID=393572.

Melaville, A., Jacobson, R. and Blank, M. B. (2011). *Scaling Up School and Community Partnerships: The Community Schools Strategy*. Washington, DC: The Coalition for Community Schools.

MetLife (2012). *The MetLife Survey of the American Teacher: Challenges for School Leadership*. New York: Author. Retrieved from http://files.eric.ed.gov/fulltext/ED542202.pdf.

Miller, P., Wills, N. and Scanlan, M. (2013). Educational leadership on the social frontier: Developing Promise Neighborhoods in urban and tribal settings. *Educational Administration Quarterly*, 49(4), 543–575. doi:10.1177/0013161X12471531.

New York State Department of Education (2013). 2013 community schools grant initiative. Retrieved from http://www.p12.nysed.gov/funding/2013-community- schools-grant-initiative/community-schools-grant-initiative-2013-application.pdf.

Noam, G. G. and Tillinger, J. R. (2004). After-school as intermediary space: Theory and typology of partnerships. In G. G. Noam (ed.), *New Directions for Youth Development: After-School Worlds: Creating a New Social Space for Development and Learning*. Thousand Oaks, CA: Jossey-Bass, pp. 75–114.

Rotherham, A. J. and Mitchel, A. L. (2014). *Genuine Progress, Greater Challenges: A Decade of Teacher Effectiveness Reforms*. Washington, DC: Bellwether Education Partners. Retrieved from http://bellwethereducation.org/sites/default/files/JOYCE_Teacher%20Effectiveness_web.pdf.

Seashore Louis, K., Leithwood, K. et al. (2010). *Learning from Leadership: Investigating the Links to Improved Student Learning*. Final Report to The Wallace Foundation. Minneapolis, MN: University of Minnesota.

Spillane, J. P. (2013). Diagnosing and designing for schoolhouse practice: Educational administration and instructional improvement. In H. J. Malone (ed.), *Leading Educational Change: Global Issues, Challenges, and Lessons on Whole-System Reform*. New York: Teachers College Press, pp. 37–41.

Thapa, A. and Guffey, S. (2013). A review of school climate research. *Review of Educational Research*, 83(3), 357–385.

The Wallace Foundation (2011). *Research Findings to Support Effective Educational Policies: A Guide to Policymakers*, 2nd edn. New York: Author.

Valli, L., Stefanski, A. and Jacobson, R. (2014). Typologizing school–community partnerships: A framework for analysis and action. *Urban Education*, 8 September, pp. 1–29.

Van Voorhis, F. and Sheldon, S. (2004). Principals' roles in the development of US programs of school, family and community partnerships. *International Journal of Educational Research*, 41(1), 55–70.

Villarruel, F. A., Perkins, D. F., Borden, L. M. and Keith, J. G. (2003). Community youth development: Partnership creating a positive world. In F. A. Villarruel, D. F. Perkins, L. M. Borden and J. G. Keith (eds), *Community Youth Development: Programs, Policies, and Practices*. Thousand Oaks, CA: Sage Publications, pp. 1–24.

Wagner, T. and Kegan, R. (2013). Conclusion: Bringing the outward and inward focus together. In M. Grogan (ed.), *The Jossey-Bass Reader on Educational Leadership*, 3rd edn. San Francisco: Jossey-Bass, pp. 220–254.

Waters, T., Marzano, R. J. and McNulty, B. (2008). *Balanced Leadership: What 30 Years of Research Tells Us About the Effect of Leadership on Student Achievement*. Denver, CO: Mid-Continent Research for Education and Learning.

Vignette 9

Changing Education in Action

Australia: The Connected Teacher

Matt Esterman

Being Connected Means We Aren't Just Down Under Any More!

To be honest, I think I've always had a voice. Whether it was because I was lucky enough to be born into a supportive family in a great country with wonderful opportunities, or whether it was through debating and public speaking (to be more literal), I have never felt truly disenfranchised or disaffected beyond the usual Western cynicism with politics.

This is much different when I start talking about myself as a teacher. As a teacher, I sometimes have to fit a mould whilst also breaking it open. I have to be the professional who ticks administrative boxes and also inspires and engages my students beyond a basic transmission of content. As a young teacher, I often felt that seniority was often mistaken for authority and that innovation could only come from the top down.

Two things have changed this thinking for me. One is Twitter (and related technologies) and the other is TeachMeet. Both have helped me establish and cultivate an amazing professional learning network, and both have, I hope, made me a better teacher with a bigger voice. Also, both have allowed me to connect with people beyond the gates of my school, beyond national borders and – perhaps more importantly – beyond the world of education.

Twitter is one of those funny technologies that is now being used for purposes probably unintended by the creators. Far from it being a hub of educational discourse when I first found out about Twitter, it was (and still is) being accused of allowing many random people to talk about their favourite cupcakes. I admit that many, many tweets are probably about non-educational materials – even some of my own tweets are about food or politics or other not-quite-edu-ideas – the reason I now use Twitter is to remain connected with educators and non-educators who are interested in sharing ideas about our craft and how to do it better.

A telling sign of the usefulness of Twitter is that key institutions such as the Australian Institute for Teaching and School Leadership (ATISL), which is currently chaired by Professor John Hattie, are highly active on Twitter and other social media, connecting teachers and the wider community with the policies, practices and vision of the education community on a national and international scale. State and Federal education ministers and departments use it, unions and system leaders use it, even some leading thinkers such as Yong Zhao, Stephen

Heppell and Will Richardson regularly engage in the use of social media to connect.

However, it's not enough – to paraphrase Will Richardson – to merely connect. We need to leverage those connections to make sure that we are sustaining a thriving community of practice and dialogue. We need to make sure that if we find a great resource, we share it. If we hear about a great idea at a conference, we tweet about it. If we see great examples of practice, we celebrate them. If we want to know an answer, we ask our Personal Learning Network (PLN) and we'll get the answer we want and many that challenge our thinking in different ways.

In a similar vein, TeachMeets have proven to be an exciting and engaging model of professional learning for teachers. Starting in Scotland in 2006, beginning in Sydney in 2011,[1] and now spread throughout Australia and other countries in various forms (EdCamps[2] are a close cousin of TeachMeets[3]), the idea of teacher-driven professional learning is becoming part of the discourse. This is essential in a future where teachers will be increasingly accountable for their growth, whilst at the same time shrinking budgets prevent more and more teachers from gaining access to high-impact professional learning experiences.

A TeachMeet is an event hosted by an educator, where people who gather are not just participants but also presenters. Usually – though each TeachMeet is different – presentations will go on for two to seven minutes, in order to keep the event fast paced. There may be a theme, such as creativity, so that the presentations have a common thread. Much of the learning happens in the breaks, where participants can network with the presenters and each other. Often TeachMeets will result in a TeachEat at a local pub or restaurant to keep the conversation going.

The beauty of TeachMeets is that they can be in person or virtual; they can be short (about an hour) to long (about a day); they can be held in pubs or classrooms or libraries. In Sydney, we've held them at the Australian Technology Park, the State Library of NSW, the PowerHouse Museum, the Sydney Theatre Company's Wharf Theatre, and even Taronga Zoo. The focus is about bringing teachers together to share lots of ideas and have lots of conversations so that they can build stronger relationships and networks in order to organically evolve as educators and as a profession.

TeachMeets have helped many people find their voices and this is especially true for me. I find it an absolute privilege to have met outstanding teachers from all sectors and all contexts, brought together in a common vision that we can and must do the best for our students. Whether a Minster of Education or a first-year graduate, we all have a voice that can have an impact on the lives of others. I am indebted to those in my professional network who, whether they know it or not, make me a better educator every day and allow me to explore my own voice.

Matt Esterman is a History teacher and eLearning Coordinator at St Scholastica's College, Glebe Point, in Sydney, Australia. He holds a BADipEd,

Master of Learning Science and Technology, Master of Arts (Modern History) and is currently enrolled in the Master of Research programme at Macquarie University, looking at user voice in the design process for new learning spaces and school buildings. He is an active participant in TeachMeets, ICTENSW, ACEL and Twitter conversations such as #histedchat (a regular chat for History teachers). His blog is www.mesterman.wordpress.com and his Twitter handle is @ mesterman.

Notes

1 http://www.smh.com.au/national/education/lesson-in-numbers-teachmeet-aims-for-a-world-record-20120301-1u60o.html.
2 http://www.edutopia.org/blog/why-edcamp-kristen-swanson.
3 http://edublogs.org/2010/10/01/edublogs-weekly-review-edcamps-and-teach-meets-a-new-kind-of-professional-development/.

Conclusion

Flipping the Education System

Jelmer Evers and René Kneyber

> The way out is through the door. Why is it that no one will use this method?
>
> Confucius

In this book we have moved from a critique of neoliberalism and its managerial perspective on professionalism to a more democratic, even *educational*, professionalism.

In these final words we want to voice some final advice on how to 'flip the system' using six guidelines for future action: trust, honour, finding purpose, collaboration, support and time. Depending on the differences between all systems, this might be advice linked to the government level, to the union level, to the level of school leadership or the professional level, or even to students and parents. Yet, just before we do so, we want to highlight a point we've made before – that is, that we can liken the process of 'flipping the system' to a process of emancipation. We could of course understand emancipation in a more modern sense – as a process of demystification whereby the teachers who are to be emancipated wait for someone to emancipate them, a situation aptly described by Jacques Rancière as 'The Emancipator and His Monkey' (Rancière, 1991). Rancière proposes a different approach to emancipation. He doesn't see emancipation as a possible end point of a social trajectory, brought about by the successful intervention of others, but rather, as he points out in *Nights of Labor*, it is a process of 'self-emancipation' which is 'self-affirmation as a joint-sharer in a common world' (1981, p. 49). At the heart of this 'new idea of emancipation' lies the notion of 'equality of intelligences as the common prerequisite of both intelligibility and community, as a presupposition which everyone must strive to validate on their own account' (ibid., p. 51). As Biesta (2014) reflects:

> [Rancière] argues that we must start from equality – 'asserting equality, assuming equality as a given, working out from equality, trying to work out how productive it can be' – in order to maximize 'all possible liberty and equality' . . . The one who doesn't start from here but instead starts out from distrust, and 'who assumes inequality and proposes to reduce

> it' can only succeed in setting up 'a hierarchy of inequalities . . . and will produce inequality ad infinitum'.
>
> (Ibid., pp. 51, 52)

So as a teacher, it's not enough to 'wait' until someone gives you your autonomy, and it is not enough to persuade your 'neoliberal oppressor' to lift you from your minority status. The only thing that will make a difference is to act under the presupposition of being equal and to see how far it takes you.

With that said, we want to move from this teacher perspective to a more general perspective. As we've mentioned before: trust and giving autonomy to teachers are hardly contentious notions. Yet 'trusting teachers' is too often understood as 'trusting that teachers will do as they are told', and autonomy is either falsely understood as 'anything goes' freedom for teachers, or teacher autonomy is so limited that it can hardly be called autonomy. So here we want to voice some advice on focal points for educational policy. If we truly want to reposition teachers at the heart of education, what should we do?

1. Trust

> Trust should be guarded to the end: 'without trust we cannot stand'.
>
> Onora O'Neill[1]

Testing, accountability, rankings, they are all the product of distrust and the cause of further distrust. Teachers mistrust their school leaders and their governments, governments mistrust teachers and their unions. And even if mistrust is not that apparent, there is certainly a culture of suspicion.

But without trust, an educational – or one could argue *any* – system will not be able to function, as Hargreaves has rightfully pointed out in his article. We daresay it is not so much trust in teachers or students, but *trust in the government* that is pivotal to a successful educational system, and it is something governments should actually pursue. A DfE might pursue questions such as 'how do we get teachers to employ evidence-based practices?', or 'how do we score higher on PISA tests?', but what should be on the policy agenda is 'how do we gain trust?' and 'how do we raise confidence in (public) education?' It is something the Department of Education in Ontario, for example, has understood remarkably well. Apart from wanting to raise achievement, one of their other pillars has been to *raise public confidence*. During their investigations they found that many parents wanted class sizes to be lower, and even though 'evidence' is limited (see, for example, Hattie, 2008) and it is an extremely expensive intervention, they still felt it was important to limit class size to 21 pupils, because parents *voiced their concern* on the matter.

It is a perfect example of what Giddens (1994) might refer to as generative politics. A *space* that links the state to reflexive mobilization in the society at large. Generative politics work through providing the actual material conditions and organizational frameworks that enable people to take collective charge. These spaces should not have an agenda that is developed 'top down', but should be organic, they should *enhance* active trust, they should enhance professional autonomy to those groups affected by the outcomes, and they should lead to a decentralization of political power (Sachs, 2003, p. 145).

So in order for trust to rise, there should be spaces where teachers, students, the state, teacher educators, politicians and so on actually meet. Not having these spaces, for example in the situation of a managerial approach to professionalism, 'hinders rather than facilitates dialogue among them. It does not allow the development and facilitation of networks' (ibid., p. 146). It is precisely here where the idea of 'professional capital' takes its meaningful place in a flipped system, not just to enhance student learning, but also in order to generate trust and confidence within the system.

2. Honour

> Pride is something you can have, but honour you must receive.
>
> Thijs Jansen, Gabriël van den Brink and Jos Kole

For teachers, there is something more at stake in engendering trust. And if they want to earn trust, they will have to start addressing the issue of professional honour. Having pride as a professional is not enough, but professionals should deliberately strive for honour, by raising and upholding a high professional standard for each other, in order for the profession as a whole to be taken seriously by the rest of society. A structure this might assume is that of the General Teacher Council in Scotland, wherein teachers record their professional learning, and which has parallels with how other professions, such as lawyers and accountants, make sure that members of their profession keep developing.

Another way to increase professional honour could be to strengthen horizontal accountability: teachers assess other teachers, and schools assess other schools. The benefit of this is twofold: first, by using horizontal accountability the need for vertical accountability is lessened, and it allows for the use of standards that come from within the profession. Secondly, professional assessing of colleagues from within the school and in other schools allows great opportunities for inspiration, motivation and professional learning.

A third important part of increasing professional honour is through strengthening teacher preparation. Teacher preparation should never be a training, but should be an actual education, where teachers are inserted in a profession. So teacher preparation should be about more than learning practical teaching skills: it should also be about focusing on learning to reflect on educational purposes, on how to structure and influence the work environment either at a school level or a national level.

A final part of improving professional honour would be, although we tend to be hesitant in terms of systemic context, to create a strong professional organization that reflects on matters that involve teachers. It could also provide a useful space for policy makers and teachers to meet, albeit that a strong union would have to support its efforts.

3. Finding Purpose

> If you stand for nothing, you will fall for everything.
>
> Unknown

We have mentioned before that because there was a pedagogical void in the first place, because teachers did not have a coherent and rigorous perspective on what they wanted to achieve and how they were meant to achieve it, the 'door was left open' for something so completely alien to education as neoliberalism, with all its economic intent and managerial lingo, to invade education so totally. The first thing that should happen, therefore, is teachers reconnecting with the purposes of education, as Gert Biesta has argued in the second part of this book, and to give this new reconnection fitting words with which to convey through a fresh language a new established feeling of purpose. We of course do not want to prescribe what this *pedagogy* should look like, or what this language should entail, as each country should strive to establish a new language based on its own broader culture. But as Biesta's three-dimensional model of 'good' education effectively demonstrates, even the simplest model can provide effective arguments against one-dimensional reforms.

On the other hand, we do want to explicitly warn that teachers should not allow themselves to be divided over how to teach. Teachers have to acknowledge that there is no pedagogical creed, no canonical way of teaching and learning. The teaching profession has weakened itself by being divided over issues like direct instruction versus self-directed learning. The so-called 'math wars' in both the United States and the Netherlands exemplify this. Teaching and learning isn't that clear cut. Teaching requires a constant and rigorous look at a context of the child in time and place and at yourself as a teacher. What should always be the case, however, is that professional discourse is intense and rigorous to such an extent, i.e. its voice should ring so loud, that it reduces the 'political voice' to a smaller, yet equal level.

4. Collaboration

> By three methods we may learn wisdom: first, by reflection, which is noblest; second, by imitation, which is easiest; and third by experience, which is the bitterest.
>
> Confucius

Whether it be to spread professional capital, or to inspire and motivate teachers, there is wide consensus between the contributors to this book that collaboration is pivotal to successful teaching. We believe that it is important that teachers collaborate as widely as possible, within schools, between teachers and schools, between teachers and researchers on a regional and a national level. This collegial collaboration should never take the form of contrived collegiality, but should always be development focused, with unpredictable outcomes (for example see Datnow, 2011). The most revolutionary approach to utilizing the strength of collaboration is the teacher-powered school that Lori Nazareno and Kim Farris-Berg and Ed Dirkswager propose. By removing formal management from the school and replacing it solely with non-positional or distributed leadership, non-contrived collegiality can start taking full root at a school level. Indeed, creating strong relational networks seems paramount to increasing teacher agency.

But we also believe in a network of a new sort. One area of major concern, as mentioned by Stephen Ball in Part I, and also in the research he has published, is that 'more and more states are losing the ability to control their education systems – something we can refer to as *denationalization*.' Through networks of international organizations, corporations, NGOs and philanthropist organizations, policies are no longer bound by national borders. At the same time there is an increasing discomfort amongst teachers against the standardized accountability reforms. If these reforms are boundless, universal and global, so should the alternative be that this book proposes. Therefore the teaching profession should strive for a global awareness that there is a universal tenet despite our cultural differences. To achieve this, the easiest road would be for teachers to connect through social media such as Twitter and Facebook, as is happening already. But as we have made a plea for 'spaces', there should also be physical places in terms of time and physical space, where teachers from around the world meet to discuss the issues they are dealing with on a national level.

5. Support

> To lead people, walk behind them.
>
> Lao Tzu

Talk to any teacher and they will have small and great ideas on how to improve their practice; some will not extend further than increasing the well-being of the children in their classroom, but other ideas might be grander, such as the notion of Maker Education as presented by Arjan van der Meij in Part IV of this book. Some will be content with improving their own practice, for their own specific situation, but sometimes ideas will flourish and will want to move outside of the classroom.

Who should support these grassroots initiatives? It is without question that they are in need of support, lest what grows withers and shrinks away, leaving a disillusioned teacher behind. But it's also a case in point for a flipped system:

do we support teachers – with great ideas – or do we force them to execute the ideas of others? In Part II, Howard Stevenson and Alison Gilliland made a passionate plea for unions to take up the opportunity to support initiatives of teachers who have started moving bottom up, but in Part IV Ann Lieberman, Carol Campbell and Anna Yashkina have shown through the Ontario example of TLLP that a collaboration between the ministry and unions is equally capable of supporting teachers with great ideas through an innovation fund. Another course of action could be that a school or a board will provide support for teachers with great ideas. It is, however, crucial that teachers are not only supported, but that they are also supported in engaging and building a network of teachers, or researchers, around them.

6. Time

> When teachers are surviving, they are not focused on student learning.
>
> Kai-Ming Cheng

When we view teachers as professionals, rather than as labourers, we say 'no' to teachers with a toolkit of prescribed methods and content, with little to no pre-service training, and very little to prepare, reflect and collaborate, who spend a lot of their working hours in front of the classroom. If we believe that teachers should have time to collaborate, build trust, assess their peers, innovate and construct a new language of education, we are also saying 'yes' to less time in front of a class. If we do not, it is not a real 'yes', it is simply asking too much.

John Bangs and David Frost made a similar point in this book when they noted that teachers' job satisfaction is a fundamental component of good education, to the extent that they propose that 'all policies should be evaluated to see whether they enhance teacher self-efficacy and job satisfaction.' We believe that systems that grant teachers time to develop, to collaborate, to influence policy, to support one another, are of the utmost importance. An interesting approach to this could be to generate new teacher positions, the key idea being that you do not take ambitious teachers out of the classroom but let them combine being a teacher with another role. Such a hybrid role could be that of 'teacher/policy maker', where teachers still spend time in front of the classroom but also are spending time at the policy-making level, or the 'teacher/scholar', or the 'teacher/adviser', all constructed through a similar approach. But even for those who want or have to work full time in a school, spending more than 19 hours in front of a class per week seriously hampers the capacity to place teachers in the lead.

In Conclusion

This book is by no means an end point: we want to view it as a 'beginning' in the Arendtian sense. What we hope is that through the notion of 'flipping the system', we have offered a new and fresh take on the development of the teaching profession, and have laid down its potential benefits, providing sketches of a road map that can help teachers, school leaders and policy makers to improve on their system.

We know, of course, that change in education is complicated, messy and slow and does not happen overnight. Therefore we would like, in conclusion, to recollect the words of Hillel the Elder, the very same words that we used to end the preface of this book:

> If I am not for myself, who will be for me?
> But if I am only for myself, who am I?
> If not now, when?

Note

1 http://downloads.bbc.co.uk/rmhttp/radio4/transcripts/20020403_reith.pdf.

References

Biesta, G. J. J. (2014). *The Beautiful Risk of Education*. Boulder, CO: Paradigm Publishers.

Datnow, A. (2011). Collaboration and contrived collegiality: Revisiting Hargreaves in the age of accountability. *Journal of Educational Change*, 12(2), 147–158.

Giddens, A. (1994). *Beyond Left and Right: The Future of Radical Politics*. Oxford: Polity Press.

Hattie, J. (2008). *Visible Learning: A Synthesis of Over 800 Meta-Analyses Relating to Achievement*. New York: Routledge.

Rancière, J. (1981). *The Nights of Labor*. Philadelphia: Temple University Press.

Rancière, J. (1991). *The Ignorant Schoolmaster: Five Lessons in Intellectual Emancipation*. Redwood City: Stanford University Press.

Sachs, J. (2003). *The Activist Teaching Profession*. Berkshire/New York: Open University Press.

Contributors

Audrey Amrein-Beardsley is currently an Associate Professor in Mary Lou Fulton Teachers College. Dr Amrein-Beardsley's research interests include educational policy, educational measurement, research and evaluation methods, and more specifically, high-stakes tests and value-added methodologies and systems. She is author of approximately 50 peer- and editorially reviewed journal articles and most recently an academic book published in 2014 titled *Rethinking Value-Added Models in Education: Critical Perspectives on Tests and Assessment-Based Accountability*. Given her scholarly contributions in these areas, from 2011 to 2014 she was named as one of the top edu-scholars in the United States, honoured for being a university-based academic who is contributing most substantially to public debates about the US educational system.

John Bangs, a former teacher in special education in the Tower Hamlets area of East London, has been Chair of the OECD's Trade Union Advisory Committee for Education, Training and Employment since 2010. He is currently Special Consultant to the General Secretary of Education International. Between 1990 and 1993, he held the position of Principal Officer, Special Education and National Curriculum, in the National Union of Teachers, England and Wales, and from 1993 to 2010 was the NUT's Head of Education, Equal Opportunities and Professional Development. John is the author of numerous articles on teacher policy in the *Times Educational Supplement* and other papers and magazines.

Tom Bennett is a school teacher and the director of researchED, a grass-roots, teacher-led organization that brings the academic and teaching communities together in an attempt to raise the quality of communication and interaction between both. A former Teacher Fellow of Corpus Christi, Cambridge University, he is the author of four books on teaching, including *Teacher Proof*, an investigation into the darker side of the education research machine. A regular in print, television and radio, he also acts as the *Times Educational Supplement*'s behaviour adviser, and trains extensively in this area.

Barnett Berry is founder and CEO of the Center for Teaching Quality (CTQ), based in Carrboro, North Carolina. At the core of Barnett's work is a simple and powerful conviction: US public schools will not realize their promise without drawing on the many excellent teachers we have right now. A former inner-city high school teacher, Barnett has worked as a social scientist at the RAND Corporation, served as a senior executive with the South Carolina Department of Education, and directed an education policy centre while he was a professor at the University of South Carolina. In the mid-1990s, he worked with the National Commission on Teaching & America's Future (NCTAF), in developing its seminal report, 'What Matters Most', which led to his founding of CTQ. Barnett has authored more than 100 peer-reviewed journal articles and book chapters and published many other academic reports and articles for the popular education press. His first book, *TEACHING 2030*, penned with 12 classroom experts, paints a powerful portrait of what the profession can and must look like, now and in the future. *Teacherpreneurs: Innovative Teachers Who Lead but Don't Leave*, his second book, details the contours of a bold brand of teacher leadership needed for US public schools. He blogs at Advancing the Teaching Profession, addressing today's most pressing education issues.

Gert Biesta (www.gertbiesta.com) is Professor of Education (Theory and Policy) and Director of Research at the Department of Education, Brunel University London. He is also visiting professor (Art Education) at ArtEZ Institute of the Arts, the Netherlands, and an associate member of the Education Council of the Netherlands, the advisory body on education of the Dutch government and parliament. His work focuses on the theory of education and the theory and philosophy of educational and social research. In addition he conducts empirical research in such areas as democratic education, teacher professionalism, adult education and vocational education. His latest book, *The Beautiful Risk of Education* (Paradigm Publishers, 2014), won the 2014 Outstanding Book Award of the American Educational Research Association (Division B).

Art Broekman is a geography teacher at the Rudolf Steiner College in Rotterdam. He has a special interest in teaching, education and development. He conducted a three-month thesis field research on teacher motivation and incentives in Indonesia in 2010. In 2011 he obtained an MA degree in Human Geography. He specializes in international development, education in developing countries and GIS.

Carol Campbell is Associate Professor of Leadership and Educational Change at the Ontario Institute for Studies in Education (OISE), University of Toronto, and Director of the Knowledge Network for Applied Education Research (KNAER). She is an appointed Education Adviser to the Premier and the

Minister of Education in Ontario, Canada. Carol is known for her commitment to combining evidence from professional knowledge and research to develop professional capacity for educational improvement. Her previous roles include: Executive Director of the Stanford Center for Opportunity Policy in Education (SCOPE) at Stanford University, USA; serving in the Ontario Ministry of Education as a Senior Executive Officer for The Literacy and Numeracy Secretariat and being appointed the Ministry's first Chief Research Officer; and academic and policy roles in the UK, including as a member of faculty at the Institute of Education, University of London, and a Policy Adviser for the government in England, including the development of a framework for teachers' professional recognition and development as part of the London Challenge.

Edward J. Dirkswager is a retired health care business executive and consultant with a long-term involvement in designing organizations to motivate those involved to produce high-quality, exemplary results and superior service. He is editor of *Teachers as Owners: A Key to Revitalizing Public Education* (R&L Education, 2002), a practical guide for people interested in starting or encouraging the start-up of schools with teacher autonomy. He is former chair of the board of the National Cooperative Bank in Washington, DC.

Rachel Evans is a teacherpreneur and National Board Certified Teacher at Denny International Middle School in Seattle, Washington, where she teaches eighth-grade Language Arts and Literature. She received her Master's in education from the University of Washington in 2009 and holds endorsements in English Language Arts and Social Studies. Since 2010, Rachel has been an active member of the district's International Schools Leadership Team, working collaboratively with colleagues to shape international education for Seattle Public Schools. She is a Virtual Community Organizer with the Center for Teaching Quality Collaboratory.

Jelmer Evers is a history teacher in a secondary school and is involved in classroom innovation. Jelmer gives advice, workshops and guest lectures on new forms of pedagogy and is involved in designing a new innovative teacher training college. He writes columns and articles for educational magazines and has edited *Het Alternatief*. He was nominated for Teacher of the Year 2012 and named one of the Netherlands' 23 'New Radicals' by national magazine *Vrij Nederland* in 2013. He was nominated for the Global Teacher Prize in 2014.

Kim Farris-Berg is an independent education strategist advancing game changing ideas in education policy and practice. She is lead author of the book *Trusting Teachers with School Success: What Happens When Teachers Call the Shots* (R&L Education, 2012). She also co-authored *Steps To Creating a Teacher-Powered School* with Lori Nazareno and the Center for Teaching Quality (2014).

For further information, visit www.teacherpowered.org and http://www.teachingquality.org/teacherpowered.

David Frost is a member of the Leadership for Learning group at the University of Cambridge Faculty of Education. He is one of the co-founders of the LfL Network, which is committed to developing democratic forms of leadership and learning. His ongoing research focuses on teacher leadership. Through partnerships with schools and local authorities he has developed strategies for supporting teachers as agents of change who play key roles in the creation and transfer of professional knowledge. He is currently the Programme Director for the HertsCam Network. Over a period of more than twenty years David has coordinated networks which support teachers as leaders of change and innovation. These have acted as test-beds for his ideas on teacher leadership and, since 2008, he has led the International Teacher Leadership initiative which has partner programmes in fifteen countries around the world. He is co-author of 'Teacher self-efficacy, voice and leadership: towards a policy framework for Education International' and editor of the recent book, *Transforming Education Through Teacher Leadership* (LfL, 2014).

Alison Gilliland, a former primary school teacher, has been working for the last ten years in teacher professional development for the Irish National Teachers' Organisation (INTO). The INTO is the main teacher union for primary teachers in Ireland and has over 40,000 members. Alison leads the design and delivery of individual teacher and whole-school CPD for INTO members.

Andy Hargreaves is the Thomas More Brennan Chair in the Lynch School of Education and Professor in the Carroll School of Management at Boston College. Before that, he was co-founder and co-Director of the International Centre for Educational Change at the Ontario Institute for Studies in Education. Andy serves as adviser in education to the Premier of Ontario, is President Elect of the International Congress for School Effectiveness and Improvement, and is ranked by Education Week as the #6 scholar with most influence on US education policy debate. Several of Andy's books have received Outstanding Writing Awards including the $100,000 Grawemeyer Award in Education for 2015 for Professional Capital, with Michael Fullan. Andy holds an Honorary Doctorate from the University of Uppsala in Sweden and is a Fellow of the Royal Society of Arts in the UK. Andy consults with organizations and governments all over the world. His most recent book, *Uplifting Leadership* (with Alan Boyle and Alma Harris), is published by Wiley Business, 2014.

Reuben Jacobson serves as the Senior Associate for Research and Strategy for the Coalition for Community Schools. In that capacity he develops and implements the Coalition's research agenda, conducts and analyses research on community schools, communicates research findings to the field, and works with the Coalition staff on overall strategy including policy and building local capacity. Prior to joining IEL Reuben worked at the American Institutes for Research (AIR) in Washington, DC as a research analyst in education. In addition, he spent two tremendously challenging and wonderful years teaching fifth- and sixth-grade students in DC Public Schools as a DC Teaching Fellow. Most recently, Reuben worked on a study of teacher incentives at the University of Maryland – College Park. He is an alumnus of IEL's Education Policy Fellowship Programme and the Education Pioneers Fellowship. Reuben has a BA from the University of Wisconsin, a Master's degree in Education Policy from the George Washington University, a Master of Arts in Teaching degree from American University, and is currently pursuing his PhD in Education Policy at the University of Maryland – College Park.

Helen Janc Malone is the Director of Institutional Advancement and the Director of the National Education Policy Fellowship Program at the Washington-based Institute for Educational Leadership. Her areas of expertise include: education policy and leadership, expanded learning, systems-level change in the national and global contexts. She is the Chair of the American Educational Research Association Out-of-School Time Special Interest Group, a Board Director for the PDK International Chapter of Harvard University, and serves on the editorial boards of two journals, *Afterschool Matters* and the *Journal of Expanded Learning Opportunities*, in addition to her posts as a peer reviewer for several academic journals focused on educational change, youth development, and school–community partnerships. Her recent select publications include: *Leading Educational Change: Global Issues, Challenges, and Lessons on Whole-System Reform* (Teachers College Press, 2013), 'The Search Stage' (*Journal of School Counseling*, 2013), *The Futures of School Reform* (Harvard Education Press, 2012, co-authored chapter), *New Directions for Youth Development: Expanded Learning Time and Opportunities* (Jossey-Bass, 2011), *Year-Round Learning: Connecting School, Afterschool, and Summer Contexts to Support Learning* (Harvard Family Research Project, 2011, co-author). She has co-founded two special interest groups within the American Educational Research Association. Dr Malone has given distinguished lectures domestically and abroad and has appeared in mass media, including PBS, C-SPAN, Huffington Post, and has run two Education Week blogs. Dr Malone holds a B.S. in political science from Towson University, M.A. in higher education policy and leadership from University of Maryland, College Park, and an Ed.M. and Ed.D. in education policy, leadership, and instructional practice from Harvard University.

René Kneyber is a mathematics teacher in a secondary school. He has written popular books on classroom authority and discipline and has edited multiple high-profile books, including the Dutch book *Het Alternatief* and the Dutch translation of *Embedding Formative Assessment* by Dylan Wiliam. In 2015 he became a member of the Dutch Education Council on royal commendation.

Ann Lieberman is currently a senior scholar at Stanford University. Her major areas of research are teacher knowledge, learning and leadership. She is internationally known for her work on finding a way to get teacher knowledge to go with research knowledge. She has written or edited eighteen books, scores of articles and chapters, all focused on the teacher, leadership and school reform. She has been at the forefront of arguing for policies that enable teacher learning and leadership that recognizes the complexities of teaching.

Lori Nazareno is currently Teacher-in-Residence: School (Re)Design at the Center for Teaching Quality. She was a Co-Lead Teacher and science teacher at Mathematics and Science Leadership Academy, Denver Public Schools. She has co-authored a free, step-by-step guide to starting a teacher-powered school.

Pak Tee Ng is Associate Dean, Leadership Learning and the Head of Policy and Leadership Studies Academic Group at the National Institute of Education (NIE), Nanyang Technological University (NTU), Singapore. He is currently the Executive Editor of *Educational Research for Policy and Practice*, the flagship journal of the Asia-Pacific Educational Research Association. He is also an Associate Editor/Editorial Board Member of several international refereed journals. He has authored several books and numerous journal articles, book chapters and conference papers.

Mark Priestley is currently Professor of Education and Director of the Curriculum and Pedagogy Research Cluster in the School of Education at the University of Stirling. His research interests relate to the school curriculum (especially curriculum change) and the professional work of teachers. Mark started his career in education as a teacher of History, working in a number of secondary schools in England and New Zealand. He is at present a member of the British Educational Research Association (BERA) Council and serves on the Scottish Educational Research Association (SERA) Executive Committee.

Sarah Robinson is an Associate Professor at the Centre for Teaching Development and Digital Media, Faculty of Arts at Aarhus University in Denmark. Sarah is an Educational Anthropologist who has researched policy in practice and teacher agency. She is currently researching Entrepreneurship Education in Higher Education and the role of the university in society.

Pasi Sahlberg is a Finnish educator, author and scholar. He has worked as schoolteacher, teacher educator, researcher and policy-adviser in Finland and has studied education systems and reforms around the world. His best-selling book *Finnish Lessons 2.0: What Can the World Learn from Educational Change in Finland?* won the 2013 Grawemeyer Award. He is currently a visiting Professor of Practice at Harvard University's Graduate School of Education.

Howard Stevenson is Director of Research, and Professor of Educational Leadership and Policy Studies, at the School of Education University of Nottingham. He has researched school sector labour relations issues for over twenty years and has undertaken several funded research projects in this area. He is the author (with Bob Carter and Rowena Passy) of *Industrial Relations in Education: Transforming the School Workforce* (Routledge, 2010).

Dick van der Wateren has a PhD in Earth Sciences and more than twenty years of research experience in the North and South Polar regions, Southern Africa and Europe. He has been a high school science and geography teacher for nearly twenty years. Over the last ten years he has been involved in programmes for gifted and talented students, digital learning projects, maker education, teacher training and student counselling and coaching. He publishes and blogs about the link between education science and teaching, creativity in the classroom, discovery learning, student autonomy, testing and accountability.

Alderik Visser is a historian, educational scientist and author. Formerly employed at the universities of Berne (CH), Utrecht (NL) and Leyden (NL), he presently works as a teacher-researcher at the Wolfert van Borselen bilingual school in Rotterdam, the Netherlands, where he teaches History, Philosophy and IB Theory of Knowledge.

Anna Yashkina is an Instructor and Researcher working with the Department of Leadership, Higher and Adult Education at the Ontario Institute for Studies in Education (OISE), University of Toronto. Her professional interests include educational leadership, teacher learning and development, and school improvement. Anna can be contacted at anna.yashkina@utoronto.ca.

Noah Zeichner is a National Board-certified social studies teacher in Seattle, Washington. From 2011 to 2014, he served as a Center for Teaching Quality (CTQ) teacherpreneur, teaching part time while supporting CTQ's global teacher leadership initiatives and coordinating a student-led festival called World Water Week. Noah co-facilitates the annual Global Leadership Summer Institute for Teachers and organized the inaugural Washington State Global Issues Network Conference. He received the World Affairs Council of Seattle's 2013–14 World Educator Award and was one of fifty international finalists for the 2014–15 Varkey GEMS Foundation Global Teacher Prize.

Index

Note: Page numbers in **bold** are for figures, those in *italics* are for tables.